BOOK NUMBER. **05-15**

This Book is the property of the
HALTON COUNTY BOARD OF EDUCATION
This book is on loan to you for the current
school year. Please print your name in the
appropriate space.
The Board expects you to use this book with
care and return it in good repair without
unnecessary pencil or ink marks.

Thank You

School Yr. Beginning	Name	Subject & Section
2005	Joe Douglas	
2005	Lucas Walasek	

ACTON HIGH SCHOOL

International Business

Canada and Global Trade

Authors

Mike Schultz

David Notman

Ruth Hernder

THOMSON

NELSON

Australia   Canada   Mexico   Singapore   Spain   United Kingdom   United States

THOMSON

✳

™

NELSON

International Business: Canada and Global Trade

by Mike Schultz, David Notman, Ruth Hernder

Director of Publishing
David Steele

Publisher
Carol Stokes

Executive Managing Editor, Production
Nicola Balfour

Executive Managing Editor, Development & Testing
Cheryl Turner

Program Manager
Leah-Ann Lymer

Project Managers
Caron MacMenamin
Geoffrey Dean

Developmental Editors
Maryrose O'Neill
Jennifer Howse
Martha Ayim
Jane McWhinney
Wendy Thomas

Senior Production Editor
Joanne Close

Copy Editor
Dianne Horton

Proofreader
Linda Szostak

Indexer
Noeline Bridge

Composition and Cover Design
Fizzz Design Inc.

Production Coordinator
Sharon Latta Paterson

Permissions/Photo Research
Christina Beamish
Susan Berger
Lisa Brant

Printer
Transcontinental Printing Inc.

National Library of Canada Cataloguing in Publication Data

Schultz, Mike, 1950-
    International business: Canada and global trade

Includes index.
ISBN 0-7725-2932-9

1. International business enterprises–Management.
I. Notman, David II. Hernder, Ruth III. Title.
HD62.4.S39 2002   658'.049
C2002-900504-3

The brand names and photographs that appear in this book do not represent endorsements, but rather are business-related examples relevant to the content of the text.

Contents

Introduction x

Chapter 1 *International Interdependence* 2

  1.1 **Evolution of Global Trade** 4

  1.2 **History of Canadian Trade** 9

       International Company Profile: Hudson's Bay Company 11

  1.3 **Canada's Economic Identity** 17

  1.4 **Advantages and Disadvantages of International Trade** 22

       International Business Career Profile: Executive Director,
       North American Fur Association 25

  1.5 **Barriers to International Trade** 28

  Canada's Trading Partners: Focus on Cuba 36

  Chapter Challenges 38

  International Business Portfolio 39

Chapter 2 *The Importance of International Business* 40

  2.1 **Aspects of International Business** 42

       International Business Career Profile: Canadian Government
       Trade Commissioner and International Business Educator 47

  2.2 **Why Do Companies Expand Internationally?** 50

  2.3 **Reasons for Recent Growth in International Business** 54

  2.4 **Advantages of Doing Business in Canada** 59

       International Company Profile: CCL Industries Inc. 62

  2.5 **Preparing for the International Workplace** 66

  Canada's Trading Partners: Focus on the United States of America 72

  Chapter Challenges 74

  International Business Portfolio 75

Chapter 3 *International Competitiveness, Productivity,
            and Quality* 76

  3.1 **Establishing a Global Presence** 78

  3.2 **Achieving Competitive Advantage** 82

  3.3 **The Meaning of Productivity** 86

  3.4 **Canada's Global Challenge** 90

       International Business Career Profile: Vice-President of
       International Sales, Spin Master Toys 91

3.5 **Quality Control and Continual Improvement** 99

International Company Profile: Rocky Mountain Bicycles 100

Canada's Trading Partners: Focus on Vietnam 104

Chapter Challenges 106

International Business Portfolio 107

Chapter 4 *Changes in Canada's Global Business* **108**

4.1 **What Is Change?** 110

4.2 **The Global Marketplace** 115

International Company Profile: SNC-Lavalin Group Inc. 123

4.3 **The Changing Workplace** 128

International Business Career Profile: Municipal Government
Consultant 134

4.4 **Staying Domestic or Going International?** 135

Canada's Trading Partners: Focus on Brazil 138

Chapter Challenges 140

International Business Portfolio 141

Chapter 5 *International Agreements, Organizations,
and Policies* **142**

5.1 **Positioning in the Global Economy** 144

International Company Profile: Robertson Inc. 147

5.2 **Corporate Globalization** 150

5.3 **International Trade Agreements** 157

International Business Career Profile: President, MALKAM
Cross-Cultural Training, Ottawa 164

5.4 **Organizations Influencing Global Trade** 168

Canada's Trading Partners: Focus on Belgium 174

Chapter Challenges 176

International Business Portfolio 177

Chapter 6 *International Business Opportunities
and Trends* **178**

6.1 **Understanding International Opportunities** 180

International Company Profile: Magna International 182

6.2 **Identifying International Opportunities and Trends** 189

6.3 **Mapping International Trends** 193

International Business Career Profile: Wonderful International
Digital Quest 201

Canada's Trading Partners: Focus on Ireland 210

Chapter Challenges 212

International Business Portfolio 213

Chapter 7 *Avoiding and Managing Common Mistakes and Problems* 214

7.1 **Common Pitfalls** 216

International Company Profile: E.D. Smith & Sons, Inc. 223

7.2 **Problems with Standards** 224

7.3 **Realistic Marketing** 228

International Business Career Profile: International Business
Consultant in Asia 232

7.4 **Infrastructure and Services** 235

Canada's Trading Partners: Focus on China 240

Chapter Challenges 242

International Business Portfolio 243

Chapter 8 *Culture and International Business* 244

8.1 **Customs and Culture** 246

8.2 **Culture and Consumer Needs and Wants** 252

International Company Profile: Sa-Cinn Native Enterprises Limited 256

8.3 **Culture and International Business Practices** 258

International Business Career Profile: Translator 264

8.4 **Disappearing Diversity** 265

Canada's Trading Partners: Focus on Russia 268

Chapter Challenges 270

International Business Portfolio 271

Chapter 9 *Political and Economic Factors Affecting International Business* 272

9.1 **The Political Process: Government's Role in International Trade** 274

International Organization Profile: Junior Team Canada 278

9.2 **Assessing Global Political Risks** 279

9.3 **Economic Factors Related to International Business** 284

9.4 **Managing International Financial Risks** 293

International Business Career Profile: Journalist 297

Canada's Trading Partners: Focus on North and South Korea 298

Chapter Challenges 300

International Business Portfolio 301

Chapter 10 *Global Business Ethics and Social Responsibility* 302

10.1 **Understanding Business Ethics and Social Responsibility** 304

International Company Profile: Ecotourism and G.A.P Adventures 308

10.2 **Ethical Issues Affecting the Conduct of International Business** 312

10.3 **Taking Action, Ethically** 321

International Career Preparation: Junior Achiever 328

Canada's Trading Partners: Focus on Mexico 330

Chapter Challenges 332

International Business Portfolio 333

Chapter 11 *International Marketing* 334

11.1 **International Marketing Strategies** 336

International Business Career Profile: CEO, Innovation Giftware Corporation 343

11.2 **Global Marketing** 345

11.3 **The International Marketing Mix** 354

International Company Profile: Cinnaroll Bakeries 356

Canada's Trading Partners: Focus on Spain 364

Chapter Challenges 366

International Business Portfolio 367

Chapter 12 *Logistics and Global Distribution* 368

12.1 **Logistics** 370

12.2 **Distribution and Modes of Transport** 377

12.3 **Export Planning** 385

International Business Career Profile: Logistics Practitioner, Canada WorldWide Services 388

International Company Profile: PBB Global Logistics 390

Canada's Trading Partners: Focus on Japan 392

Chapter Challenges 394

International Business Portfolio 395

Reviewers

Bill Baker
J.W. Baker Consulting
Markham, Ontario

Scott Boassaly
Sir Robert Borden High School
Nepean, Ontario

Ray Guy
Niagara College
Niagara-on-the-Lake, Ontario

Mark Kot
Hamilton Board of Education
Beamsville, Ontario

Vince De Luca
St. Catharines Collegiate Institute
St. Catharines, Ontario

Rocky Landon
Kingston, Ontario

Zenobia Omarali
Toronto District Board of Education
Toronto, Ontario

Laura Pinto
Waterloo, Ontario

John Pownall
York Region District School Board
Toronto, Ontario

Lila Read
Waterloo, Ontario

ACKNOWLEDGEMENTS

We are extremely grateful to the many educators and Canadian business people who provided current data, reviewed portions of the manuscript, and offered suggestions to help make the first edition of *International Business: Canada and Global Trade* as correct, accurate, user-friendly, and Canadian-focused as possible. Those educators who reviewed our manuscript are listed on a separate page, and we thank them most sincerely.

The authors would like to provide a special thanks to the editors and staff at Nelson and Irwin for their tireless support of this project: to Geoff Dean for his quiet competence; to Jane McWhinney and Wendy Thomas who shaped our work, to Caron MacMenamin, who co-ordinated this complex project, to Maryrose O'Neill, Martha Ayim, and Jennifer Howse who keep making us sound great, to Mike Czukar, who used his skill and patience to provide this resource to the teachers when they needed it, and to Leah-Ann Lymer, who supported us with her warmth, her reassurance, and, during the crazy times, her sanity.

It is also important to acknowledge the outstanding contribution that Dr. Robert Wilson has made to this and other Nelson projects. Dr. Wilson developed the ICE model of assessment, which focuses on using assessment to encourage student academic growth. His work has motivated many, including the authors of this text, to consider assessment as an integral part of the learning process. He is a mentor, a friend, and a brilliant educator.

Michael Schultz, David Notman, and Ruth Hernder
January, 2003

Dedications

To my wife, Elyse. This one's for you. MS

To the memory of my dear friend, Dave Dick. He taught me more about this subject (and about life) than he ever realized. He is missed. DN

To my family, Bruce, Jordan, Jessie, and Jamie. RH

Conclusion: *The International Business Plan* 396

Glossary 399

Index 410

Credits 419

INTRODUCTION

The Spirit of International Business

The twenty-first century will be marked by growing global interactions in all areas of human and business activity.

Economically, Canada will depend more than ever on business resulting from global trade.

International Business: Canada and Global Trade will help you to understand international business from Canada's perspective.

In the years ahead, you may find yourself studying, working, or travelling in another country. Perhaps you will work for an international company in Canada or abroad. This text will help you to gain a greater appreciation of the global forces and issues affecting you, your community, Canada, and other countries.

Within the covers of this book, you will find an engaging mix of entrepreneurship, economics, finance, marketing, and even geography and history. These disciplines come together within the common themes of international business.

International Business: Canada and Global Trade begins by giving you some historical background on how Canada became a major international trader. You will then learn about the importance of competitive advantage and how Canada is organized to trade around the world today, and how it is planning for the future.

You will investigate the factors that motivate companies to engage in international business. You will learn about common mistakes that companies have made when trying to enter international markets. You will gain an understanding of the kinds of political, economic, and social factors that affect a country's chances for attracting business.

You will also learn about the effects of culture on international business, and the ethics and social responsibility involved. Your study will end with an analysis of the marketing and logistics strategies required to brings goods and services to a foreign country.

Special Features

- Each chapter opens with a photo and a chapter summary. **Chapter Topics** lists the main sections of the chapter. **Prior Knowledge** helps you to think about what you already know. **Inquiries/Expectations** outlines the key questions you will be able to answer by the end of the chapter. **Important Terms** lists the business terms that you will learn.

- Each **International Company Profile** describes a Canadian company that does business with other countries. You will learn about the growth of the company and the challenges it faces.

- Each **International Business Career Profile** features a person following a particular career in international business. You will learn why the individual chose his or her career, and the education and background required.

- **Web Link** connects you to *www.internationalbusiness.nelson.com*, where you will find related Web links.

- **ICE Activities** appear after each main section within a chapter. They will help you to review and think about what you have just read. ICE stands for Ideas, Connections, and Extensions. The ideas lead to connections to the real world. The connections help you to interpret the world in a personal way.

- **Canada's Trading Partners** profiles a country with which Canada trades. You will learn about the country's trading relationships, and you will have an opportunity to do some Internet research.

- **Global Thought** provides quotations by various people about an issue or event related to international business.

- **Trade Talk** gives background information on a particular business issue or event.

- **Trade Tips** provides useful business advice and information.

- **Think About It** raises an idea or issue for you to consider.

- Each chapter concludes with **Chapter Challenges**, which are questions and activities categorized as **Knowledge/Understanding**, **Thinking/Inquiry**, **Communication**, and **Application**.

- The **International Business Portfolio** assignment at the end of each chapter will help you to build the skills required to complete either a Trade Manual or a Business Plan at the end of the course. Instructions for creating a Business Plan are found in the **Conclusion** on page 396.

- Difficult business terms and concepts are defined in the **Glossary** beginning on page 399.

- A comprehensive **Index** begins on page 410.

Chapter 1

International Interdependence

International trade has evolved from small groups of people bartering goods and services to all the countries of the world becoming economically interdependent. Every day, Canada exports natural resources, manufactured goods, and consulting expertise all over the world, and imports from many different countries the things we want and need. How is Canada's economy improved through global trade, and what is our role in this new international economy?

Chapter Topics

➤ 1.1 – Evolution of Global Trade 4

➤ 1.2 – History of Canadian Trade 9

➤ 1.3 – Canada's Economic Identity 17

➤ 1.4 – Advantages and Disadvantages of International Trade 22

➤ 1.5 – Barriers to International Trade 28

➤ *Canada's Trading Partners: Focus on* Cuba 36

➤ Chapter Challenges 38

Prior Knowledge

- Why do businesses in different countries trade with one another?
- How does international trade increase the interdependence among nations?
- What advantages do Canadian consumers gain from exporting goods to other countries?
- If you wanted to import goods to Canada, what barriers would you have to overcome?

Inquiries/Expectations

- How has international business activity affected the links between and interdependence among countries?
- What are some of the advantages and disadvantages for a nation as it increases its interdependence with other nations?
- What are some barriers to international business activity and how can countries lower those barriers?
- How has Canada established international business relationships with its major global partners over time?

Important Terms

- capital intensive
- commune
- currency exchange rate
- end-product imports/exports
- *Export and Import Permits Act*
- guilds
- interdependence
- *Investment Canada Act*
- labour intensive
- primary industries
- primary resources
- protectionism
- resource-based imports/exports
- self-sufficiency
- semi-manufactured items (products)
- *Special Economic Measures Act*
- tariff
- *United Nations Act*
- World Trade Organization (WTO)

1.1 Evolution of Global Trade

Self-Sufficiency

Self-sufficiency is the ability to provide for all of your basic needs, such as food, clothing, shelter, and water, without relying on anyone else. A country is self-sufficient when it provides everything its population needs to survive without having to trade with other countries. Canada's Aboriginal peoples were largely self-sufficient in that they hunted or gathered their own food, made their clothes from the skins of the animals they ate, and developed the skills necessary for making weapons, shelters, and tools. However, the Aboriginal peoples of Canada also had sophisticated trade networks in place before the arrival of Europeans. Historian Olive Dickason relates how the Huron people, in what is now Ontario, traded their agricultural products—corn, beans, squash, and tobacco—with the northern peoples in return for meat, hides, and furs. Archaeological evidence also shows that obsidian and copper, which were used in tools and weapons, were mined and traded among Aboriginal peoples on the North American continent for thousands of years. One obsidian quarry in British Columbia has been dated at 8000 B.C.E.

Figure 1.1 What basics of survival would one buffalo provide for a family in a self-sufficient society?

Relative self-sufficiency has been typical of every developing civilization across the globe, and is being achieved now in remote areas of the Amazon Basin and the New Guinea Highlands. As long as people were unaware of goods available in other, more technologically developed parts of the world, they used what was available or they would not have survived. As transportation developed, from horses to carts to ships, different cultures began to come into contact with one another. Each culture had something different to share with another, such as food, crafts, materials, and technology. Self-sufficiency, although still possible, seemed no longer desirable. In the best cases, as trade developed, providing food for your family became easier, there were more options for earning a living, and people began to live longer and healthier lives.

Groups within countries have often refused to give up their self-sufficiency. Amish and Old Order Mennonite groups attempt self-sufficiency in their communities to limit their contact with outsiders for religious reasons. During the 1960s, many groups rejected traditional cultural norms, such as military service or corporate jobs, and founded **communes**, self-sufficient communities based on the principles of communal property and shared responsibility for food production, education, child care, and so on.

Figure 1.2 Communes, such as this one from the 1970s, try to be self-sufficient communities.

Follow the link at
www.internationalbusiness.nelson.com
to find out more about trade among the
Aboriginal peoples of the Americas.

THINK ABOUT IT

What are some of the advantages of a completely self-sufficient society? What are some of the disadvantages?

Although many attempts at communal living were short-lived, there are still communities throughout the world making efforts at self-sufficiency. The word "commune" has proved too limited to describe all these groups, however. Communities that attempt to become somewhat self-sufficient are called *intentional communities*, which include ecovillages, residential land trusts, communes, student co-ops, and urban housing cooperatives. There are well over 500 intentional communities in the world today. Some examples are Pangaia, a Hawaiian society that believes in the benefits of raw food; Arcosanti, a town in the high desert of Arizona designed to be ecologically sound; and Los Horcones, a Mexican community based on the principle of total self-sufficiency. In Israel, Kibbutzim, or communal farms and factories, share all labour, profits, property, and child rearing.

Early Trade

Over 3000 years ago, camel caravans transported figs, scented oils, and rare woods across the deserts of North Africa to the area where Western civilization began, the Tigris-Euphrates region. They traded for olive oil, spices, and Babylonian artifacts. At the same time, China was trading silk and tea for spices from India and clothing from northern Europe. The Phoenicians were expert boat builders and sailed the Mediterranean Sea with ships full of gold and silver, fruit and wine, and ebony and ivory, trading with countries along the Mediterranean and Black Sea coasts. They established a trade centre at Carthage on the north coast of Africa. Greece later took over trade in the region, opening up the Mediterranean area to goods from India and Central Asia.

Figure 1.3 The Tigris-Euphrates region.

During the time of the Roman empire, goods flowed into and out of Rome across the then-known world. As they conquered lands, the Romans created provinces from Great Britain to Spain, from Egypt to Iraq. Some of the roads, bridges, and canals that were built by the Romans served as trade routes for centuries after the fall of the empire. In Roman times, merchants supplied Rome with wine, honey, and marble from Greece; jewels, marble artifacts, and timber from Asia Minor; silks and spices from China; dyes, textiles, and glass from Arabia; grain, ivory, papyrus, and wild animals from Egypt and North Africa; fruit, gold, and wine from Spain; amber, hides, and horses from Germany; pottery, wool, wine, and precious metals from Gaul; and tin, iron, and copper from Britain.

The First Trade Regulations

During the Roman empire, trade had been free for the most part, as governments did not impose restrictions on what could be traded. Few protectionist policies were in place. Merchants carried their goods along the sometimes dangerous land and sea trade routes that extended all the way from China and India to Europe. But with the decline of Rome around 500 C.E., the area that we know as Europe was overrun by conquering groups from Mongolia and northern and eastern Europe, who took what they wanted instead of trading for it. Communities were forced to become self-sufficient again, trading with other communities in local markets or fairs, but rarely venturing to foreign lands.

During the early part of the Middle Ages (476 C.E.–1000 C.E.), all of Europe was in upheaval. Communities formed around religious or political loyalties, often enforced by military might. Towns grew up around monasteries, cathedrals, and castles, and the local rulers collected taxes and tithes (tributes of merchandise and crops) to maintain their authority and their lifestyle, and to finance wars at home and in foreign lands.

Eventually, these feudal towns became part of larger holdings, and the concept of provinces, states, and nations began to emerge between 1000 C.E. and 1500 C.E. Economic activity began to concentrate in the larger towns. Merchant and craftspeople associations, called **guilds**, organized within the town, became as powerful as town governments, and, in some cases, replaced town governments entirely. These guilds controlled the manufacturing and sale of the products made by the people of the town. Metal work, jewellery, food, cloth, salt, and many other products were controlled by guilds. No goods could be imported into a town if they competed with local products. The guilds made foreign merchants or traders pay a fee if they wanted to trade in the town, and some outside merchants were shut out of the market entirely. Eventually the guilds became powerful enough to influence the trade policies of the entire country, placing import taxes on foreign goods that would compete with guild-made products.

Figure 1.4 The illustration above shows many types of occupations found in a medieval town. Can you identify some?

Trade and Exploration

During the fifteenth and sixteenth centuries, Portuguese, English, Spanish, French, and Dutch explorers and navigators set out across the Atlantic Ocean to find a westerly route to the rich spice markets of Asia. However, they found the land masses of North and South America blocking their route to the Far East. The European exploration and claims of land in North and South America were carried out because the rulers in the powerful empires of Europe wanted to expand their control over international trade.

TRADE TALK

Pepper has been the most important spice since Roman times. The cities of Alexandria, Genoa, and Venice owed their economic success to pepper. It was one of the earliest items traded in Asia and Europe. In 1101, victorious Genovese soldiers were each given two pounds of pepper as a gift for their successful Palestinian conquest. In the Middle Ages, Europeans often used pepper to pay rent, dowries, and taxes, and Shakespeare mentions pepper in his plays. The need for pepper inspired Spanish exploration and spice trade in the fifteenth century.

Figure 1.5 The search for spices, like pepper, led to the exploration of the globe.

The world, as Europeans knew it at the time, stretched from England east to China, and trade flourished among the nations that knew of one another. Rulers of nations and feudal lords fought wars over the rights to trading routes, especially those that carried spices, which were one of the most important trade commodities of the time. Spices preserved food and made it last longer and taste better. Healers used spices as medicines to cure various illnesses and conditions. In addition, spices provided pleasant scents for an unsanitary—and often unpleasant smelling—world. As public demand for spices increased, a large market opened up. Those countries and traders who could fill that demand could make huge profits.

Unfortunately for European spice merchants, the regions where spices grew were in India and China, and the merchants who travelled overland had to go through Turkey to get to those markets. By the sixteenth century, the reach of the Turkish empire had grown until it included Egypt and North Africa as well as countries in Europe, so the empire controlled much of the territory through which the traders would pass. The capital, Istanbul (formerly Constantinople), was a major trade centre between Europe and Asia, and Turkish ships patrolled the Mediterranean guarding the all-important sea routes.

Even if European traders could get through, transportation was a massive problem, the routes were full of dangers, and journeys took years to accomplish. Under such circumstances, European rulers and merchants began to look west, rather than east, in the hopes of reaching Asia and India. The economic benefits would be enormous for the country that could find the sea route to the wealth of the Far East. During the centuries of exploration and conquest, self-sufficiency took on a new meaning as the great empires of Europe each tried to acquire territory throughout the world where they could have exclusive rights to the resources of those lands and peoples.

For example, the Spanish empire that had started to expand in the fifteenth century eventually extended from what is today Alaska down through the western United States, Mexico, Central America, and into Chile; it included the Caribbean islands, Colombia, Venezuela, and Argentina. There were also Spanish-held territories in Africa and in the far-away Philippine Islands (which were named after King Philip II of Spain). Christopher Columbus claimed the Caribbean islands of the West Indies for Spain in 1492, and established a colony in the region shortly thereafter. The colonies provided Spain with fish and agricultural products, especially sugar. Administrators collected taxes, which were sent back to Spain. More wealth went to Spain in the form of the stolen riches of the Mayan and Incan empires, as well as the gold and silver produced by mines in North and South America. Spain introduced the slave trade into the Americas to provide labour for its vast sugar plantations and the silver mines that were becoming increasingly important to the Spanish economy. By the sixteenth century, silver from the Americas was being used in trade all over the world.

But the Spanish imperialists were not alone. Other European adventurers and explorers competed for control of the land that they claimed for their rulers, ignoring the Aboriginal peoples who were already in those places. There was a rush to find a sea route to the Far East. It was Portuguese navigator Bartolomeu Dias who, in 1488, was the first European to sail around the southernmost tip of Africa to the Far East. By the sixteenth and seventeenth centuries, the rulers of France, England, and the Netherlands were also set on claiming territory and riches around the world. The more gold and silver and trade goods an empire could acquire—by theft or trade—the wealthier it was, and the wealthier empires were the more powerful and could best defend themselves against the other empires that were after the same booty.

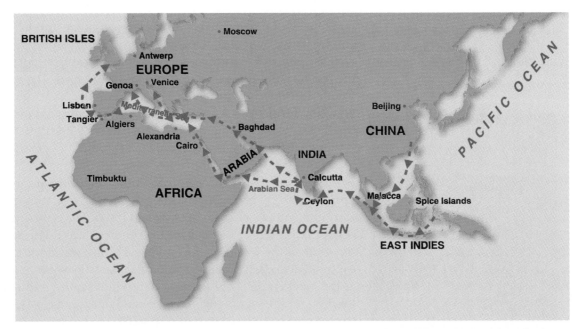

Figure 1.6 This route was originally used by Arab and Chinese traders. The eastern part was based on an ancient caravan route 6400 kilometres long, linking China (source of silk) with the eastern Mediterranean.

ICE Activities for 1.1

Ideas	Connections	Extensions
1. (a) What does the term self-sufficiency mean when used to describe a country or a community?	(b) Profile a self-sufficient community. Include an explanation of why the community chose to become self-sufficient.	(c) Describe briefly at least five changes that would take place in your life if Canada were to become self-sufficient. Think about changes that you would consider positive and others that you would consider negative.
2. (a) How did guilds control trade in their regions?	(b) Compare guilds with the labour unions of today.	(c) Write a journal for a day in the life of a person in the year 1250 C.E. Choose one of: an artisan, a knight, a farmer, a mother with small children, a feudal lord, or a merchant.
3. (a) Explain the connection between European exploration of North and South America and international trade.	(b) Research the relationship between the Dutch or Portuguese empires and the pursuit of increased international trade. Create a mind map or concept web to illustrate your findings.	(c) Using your findings from 3. (b), write a paragraph describing how European explorers violated the human rights of the Aboriginal peoples they encountered.

1.2 History of Canadian Trade

The European Connection

In 1497, just five years after Columbus landed in the Caribbean, John Cabot (Giovanni Cabotto), an Italian whose ships were financed by England's King Henry VII, landed on the shores of Newfoundland, off the east coast of North America. Cabot, too, was looking for spices (his father was a spice merchant) and believed that he had found a new route to the Orient. Cabot did not find spices, but he did find fish.

Even though he did not find spices, Cabot was not discouraged. He mapped the coast and returned to England, convincing spice merchants there to finance another voyage. Cabot set off with four ships this time and was never heard from again. In 1508, his son Sebastian also tried to find the route to the Orient. He, too, was disappointed by the rugged, cold North American continent. Canada, it seemed, had little to offer other than fish.

GLOBAL THOUGHT

The sea there is swarming with fish, which can be taken not only with the net, but in baskets let down with a stone... his companions say that they could bring so many fish that this kingdom would have no further need of Iceland, from which place there comes a very great quantity of stockfish [cod].

– Letter to the Duke of Milan from Raimondo Soncino, a London agent who reported on Cabot's voyage, December 18, 1497

The waters off Newfoundland had fish in great abundance. During the 1500s and early 1600s, hundreds of fishing boats came from Europe in the spring of the year to fish for cod in the waters off the east coast of Canada. The cod, which had a large market in Europe, was dried, salted, and taken back to markets in England, Spain, and Portugal at the end of the fishing season.

Other ships came out from Europe to trade with the Aboriginal peoples for furs. The Iroquois, Montagnais, and Algonquin peoples traded furs with Europeans on their ships before there were any permanent European settlements on land. Beaver skins were becoming very popular as a material in hats. Beaver fur was waterproof, durable, and could be shaped into many different styles. Beaver hats became a fashion rage that was to last for more than a century and that provided the stimulus for exploration and settlement in Canada. Although European explorers continued to try to find a westerly route through or around North America to the silks and spices of the Far East, it was becoming clear to the French, Dutch, and English imperialist rulers that there was also wealth to be gained by controlling the fur trade within the continent.

Figure 1.7 The *Nonsuch*, des Groseilliers' ship.

It was Samuel de Champlain, in the early 1600s, who established the first permanent settlements in this country. He had been sent out from France to colonize Acadia and then Quebec because the French king, aristocracy, and merchants recognized the potential riches that could be gained from the fur trade. It was that trade which provided the stimulus for settlement in the region of North America that would become Canada.

The French protected their monopoly on the fur trade to such a large extent that two French explorers and entrepreneurs, Pierre-Esprit Radisson and Médard Chouart, Sieur des Groseilliers, were prevented in 1660 from setting up their own company by their government. Radisson and des Groseilliers had reached as far as the Great Lakes, where they negotiated with Aboriginal groups in the area for their furs. The French Governor of Quebec would not issue the traders a licence and fined them for trading, so the two traders decided to approach the English.

Radisson and des Groseilliers captured the imagination of King Charles II of England with their project of a fur-trading expedition into Canada, because furs were in great demand in Europe. On June 3, 1668, Radisson and des Groseilliers set sail for Canada. Radisson's ship was damaged in a storm and had to return to England, but des Groseilliers arrived safely at James Bay and the party erected Charles Fort. During the spring of 1669, several hundred Aboriginal people came to the fort with their furs to trade. This success consolidated the group of investors. They applied to the King for a Royal Charter, granted on May 2, 1670, and formed The Governor and Company of Adventurers of England Trading into Hudson's Bay or, as it is now known, the Hudson's Bay Company (HBC).

Figure 1.8 Trading at an early Hudson's Bay Company trading store.

For almost a hundred years, until the English defeated the French and took control of Canada, French fur trading merchants competed with the English HBC for control of the lucrative fur trade. Both the French and the English companies were given exclusive trade rights, or charters, by their respective European governments, and the two sides fought for exclusive control.

International Company Profile

Hudson's Bay Company

Figure 1.9 The Hudson's Bay Company point blanket has been sold at Company fur trade posts and then retail stores since it was first manufactured and marketed in 1780. It is a symbol of continuity, despite HBC's changing focus and operations.

The Royal Charter granted to "The Company of Adventurers" gave the Company (later HBC) the rights to "sole trade and commerce" and control of all lands whose rivers and streams drain into Hudson Bay (over 3.9 million square kilometres of land). This area would come to be known as Rupert's Land, named after Prince Rupert, the Company's first governor. It represents over 40 percent of modern-day Canada.

HBC controlled the fur trade (and a great deal of the politics) in Canada. Numerous competitors challenged this control, but by means of treaties and mergers, HBC remained pre-eminent. The Company traded with the Cree for furs. The Cree did not trap furs themselves, but acted as the agents for other fur trappers as far west as the Rocky Mountains. HBC sent the furs to its head office in London, UK, and the head office sold the furs on the European market.

After Confederation in 1867, HBC turned over control of all of its land holdings to the government of Canada under the Deed of Surrender in 1870. After 1870, while the fur trade continued as the focus of several Company departments, new areas of business were developed. A wholesale department was started to sell goods to the new mining, farming,

and manufacturing businesses. In 1909, HBC established three separate departments: land sale, fur trade, and retail. By the mid-1920s, it had a large chain of retail stores and had opened flagship stores in six major western cities.

HBC gradually let go of its fur trading, land management, resource acquisition, and wholesaling divisions, and concentrated on the retail end of the business. In a highly publicized round of takeovers in 1978-79, HBC acquired controlling interests in two large Canadian retailers, Zellers and Simpson's, and later acquired numerous regional retail chains. Today, HBC is Canada's oldest corporation and largest department store retailer.

The Canadian marketplace, during the late 1990s and early 2000s, experienced a consolidation, with HBC acquiring many of its other department store competitors. New in the retail scene is the development of "power centres" and "big box stores," many of which have U.S. parent companies. HBC introduced Home Outfitters to compete with this type of development. Competition from e-commerce has also been met by the Company through its Web site. Canadian consumer shopping habits have changed dramatically.

HBC will always be considered one of the historic businesses of Canada, helping develop the nation along with its trade.

• •

1. What was the Hudson's Bay Company's relationship with Aboriginal peoples?

2. How has HBC remained competitive in the early 2000s? What else could HBC do to keep pace with Canadian consumer shopping habits?

Trade had an immediate effect on the Aboriginal populations. The Cree and their Assiniboine allies were the main suppliers for both French and English fur trading companies. These Aboriginal groups traded furs with the companies and then traded European goods with the northern hunting peoples. The Cree had developed a successful distribution network into western Canada. The hunting groups that became involved in trade began to produce surplus goods. The animals they trapped for fur were not being used just for survival; that is, for food, clothing, and shelter. The principle of self-sufficiency was replaced by the principles of trade: create a surplus, trade the surplus for goods that you cannot make yourself, sell some of those goods to others for their surplus, trade that surplus for goods, and so on. It was the beginning of **interdependence**, the reliance of two or more groups on the actions of one another to fulfill certain wants or needs.

Settlements were established to support the fur trade, and settlement attracted more immigration. As people from all over Europe began arriving, connections to the home countries were preserved through trade. The settlers relied on the trade with Europe to provide numerous manufactured goods that could not be made in Canada. Canada had not developed strong manufacturing industries, but sent its surplus of natural resources to Europe for processing and manufacturing. European companies relied on Canadian raw materials for their businesses, and Canadians anticipated the arrival of ships from Europe carrying manufactured goods. Our trade relationship with Europe, then, traces back to the beginnings of European settlement.

Early Trade between Canada and Europe

From Europe to Canada	From Canada to Europe
stylish clothing	fish
household furniture	fur
manufactured food	metals
precision tools	wheat
	wood

Figure 1.10 What is the difference between the goods sent to Canada and those sent to Europe?

The American Connection

Figure 1.11
Raw sugar cane.

The region of North America that became the United States was being explored and settled at the same time as the exploration and settlement of Canada was taking place. The differences, however, were significant. In Canada, the English and the French were the major competitors. In the United States, the Dutch and the English were competing. Dutch traders worked for the West India Company, a business formed by wealthy Dutch investors in Amsterdam to take advantage of the trade opportunities in the Caribbean and to break the Spanish trade monopoly in that area. The Dutch saw the possibilities of the fur trade as well, and set up a fur trading post in what is now New York City.

The most important difference between early Canadian and American trade was the influence of trade with the West Indies on the American economy. The end of Dutch rule in North America came in 1674, when the British and Dutch signed a peace treaty. However, the West Indian connections that had been made by the Dutch West India Company still existed. By 1720, American trade looked very different from Canadian trade in that Canadian traders focused on the

European connections, especially France and England, while the United States developed a much more diversified network of trading partners stretching well into South America.

The importance of sugar in the history of American trade cannot be overestimated. Sugar was so important it was called "white gold." American farmers provided food for the Caribbean markets. Ships loaded with corn, wheat, barley, oats, and livestock left the port of New York between November and January. The ships returned full of sugar between April and June.

Figure 1.12 The sugar processing flow by which sugar cane becomes processed sugar used in food and candies.

The sugar was processed in New York. Brown sugar was refined into white table sugar, which was then either made into candy or bagged for sale. The residue of the sugar refining process was molasses, which was distilled into rum. These finished products were then picked up by British or American ships and traded in Europe or taken back to the West Indies. British workers used West Indian products, such as the sugar for their tea, but not before it was processed in an American port. This trade was very profitable for the thousands of American businesses involved, from insurance companies to farmers, and from shipbuilders to traders and merchants. American trade became much more varied than Canadian trade. Especially after the American Revolution of 1775-83, the United States exported not only raw materials like cotton, but also processed goods like cotton yarn, fabric, and manufactured cotton clothing. Canada's trade was still dominated by raw materials, which were sent back to England to make manufactured goods.

The American Revolution and the War of 1812 put a strain on the relationship between Canada and the United States. During the revolution, English Loyalists either fled or were deported from the United States to Canada. After the revolution ended in 1783, the United States was irritated by the failure of the British to withdraw from American territory along the Great Lakes and by British maritime policies, which prevented American ships from trading in Europe and allowed the kidnapping of American sailors to serve on British ships. The United States declared war on Great Britain in 1812, but the war was fought mainly by the Canadians and Americans along the Ontario and Quebec borders. Several unsuccessful attempts were made by both the United States and Canada to invade the other's territory. Despite these political problems, many Canadian businesses were beginning to look south towards the United States for a trading partner, instead of east towards Britain.

During these years, Canada was still dependent on the fur trade. In 1779, a group of 16 merchants, united by their personal financial interests, formed a consortium, called the North West Company. It was Canadian-owned, not British, and it began to provide fierce competition for The Hudson's Bay Company, which had become a monopoly since the defeat of the French in Quebec in 1759. The North West Company also competed with the American Fur Company. This competition caused the American government to pass a law in 1816 making it illegal for Canadians to trade furs in the United States. This was one of the first **protectionist** efforts of the United States, and it effectively forced the two major Canadian fur trading companies to join forces. The competition was hurting both companies, because the American market was no longer available to either one.

In 1821, the Hudson's Bay Company and the North West Company merged under the name of the Hudson's Bay Company. The result was a fur trading company that covered vast regions of northern North America and that was the most powerful company on the continent.

By the 1840s, silk had replaced beaver as the material of choice for hats in Europe. This trend seriously affected the European demand for beaver pelts. In Canada, over-trapping had depleted the beaver stocks. Settlements were gradually encroaching on trapping grounds. The fur trade in Canada was never to regain its significance.

As the importance of trade between Canada and the United States increased, some Canadians began to fear a political alliance with the United States. Trade expanded naturally from north to south, because the Rocky Mountains prevented easy access to the West Coast. The major economic and industrial centres of both countries were located on the Eastern seaboard and in the central regions. It seemed logical, to some, that from an economic standpoint the United States and Canada should unite. Others believed in a united Canada. The ties to Britain were stronger, they said, than the ties to the United States. A united Canada would have access to all its own resources and would be able to develop many international trade opportunities. Canada became a nation in 1867, partially as a response to the desire to have access to all of Canada's natural resources as international trade goods and partially in response to the fear of unification with, or even domination by, the United States.

Figure 1.13 Building a cross-country railroad. What benefits do you think the CPR gave to Canadian business?

A group of Canadian and British business people began to argue for a railway across Canada, from the east to the west coast. They believed that the railway would improve the trade potential of Canada's vast natural resources, would help the newly independent country develop international export markets, and would encourage the creation of more provinces that would join Confederation. The Canadian Pacific Railway (CPR) track was completed to the west coast in 1885, and it provided the means to ship goods and people from coast to coast and brought British Columbia into Confederation.

Confederation and the CPR may have prevented union with the United States, but they did not stop the growth of commerce between the two countries. The United States would become Canada's largest and most important trading partner, and, even today, Canada and the United States continue to negotiate trade policies and issues.

The Pacific Rim Connection

The trade with Asia that motivated the early explorers to risk their lives and brought them to North America did not really resume its importance for Canada until the last half of the twentieth century. Japan led the way with a policy of modernization after the Second World War. When the war ended in 1945, Japan's industries were all but destroyed. With North American aid, factories were rebuilt to high standards, providing modern manufacturing facilities. Japanese culture stressed education and a strong work ethic, and Japan aggressively pursued international trade opportunities.

Japan entered North American markets in the early 1950s with inexpensive toys, novelties, and electronic equipment. For a decade, the phrase "Made in Japan" was synonymous with "cheap." Many Japanese companies, notably Nikon and Canon, tried to counter this image, but it was the Totsuko Company, later called Sony, that became the most famous Japanese company in the world, and all because of its pocket radio.

Japan's reputation for cameras, electronics, and automobiles grew steadily throughout the latter part of the twentieth century. Household brands such as Honda, Nintendo, Sanyo, Fuji, and Panasonic are all from Japan, and, in only a few short decades, have managed to become some of the most popular brands in the world. Japan has led the other Pacific Rim countries into international trade and is now a major trading partner with Canada.

Figure 1.14 Transistor radio, circa 1955.

TRADE TALK

The transistor was developed by three American physicists at Bell Telephone Laboratories in 1948. For this achievement, the three shared the 1956 Nobel Prize in physics. The transistor replaced the much larger vacuum tube, so electronic products could be much smaller and powered by batteries. The world's first transistor radio went on the market in the United States in December 1954, just in time for the Christmas season. The Japanese company Totsuko developed a transistor small enough to power a radio that could fit into a pocket. It sold for $45 in 1957 (equivalent to $400 in 2002). The demand was huge for Totsuko's new radios. When the Totsuko Company decided to export its radios, it had to give the product a name that North Americans could pronounce and that had an association with sound. In January 1958, the Totsuko Company was renamed Sony.

Mexico and the Americas

In 1993, Canada signed the North American Free Trade Agreement (NAFTA) and began the work of eliminating all tariff barriers among the United States, Canada, and Mexico by the year 2008. NAFTA was an initiative spearheaded by the United States, and although the United States has a much stronger trading relationship with Mexico already in place, Canada is benefiting as well. The large Mexican consumer market provides new opportunities for the sale of Canadian products, and Canadian branch plants can take advantage of lower Mexican labour costs to manufacture goods for shipment to the southern United States. Prior to the agreement, Canada did very little trade in Central and South America.

Trade between Mexico and Canada increased significantly after the agreement was signed. NAFTA's success caught the attention of other Central and South American countries. An effort to unite the economies of the Americas into a single free trade arrangement was initiated at the Summit of the Americas, held in December 1994 in Miami, Florida. The heads of state of the 34 democracies

TRADE TALK

The Republican party in the United States is distrustful of the more socialist countries in the southern hemisphere, notably Nicaragua and El Salvador, and has resisted attempts to create the FTAA. The Democrats, on the other hand, wish to proceed cautiously, with membership limited to the countries that can demonstrate "democratic freedoms."

Contentious issues also concern labour and trade, but both parties agree to exclude Cuba.

in the region agreed to construct a Free Trade Area of the Americas (FTAA) and to complete negotiations for the agreement by 2005. Canada has taken a leadership role in these negotiations, partly because of a successful bilateral trade agreement negotiated with Chile and partly because political differences between the American Democrats and Republicans make it difficult for the United States to assume the role.

It is difficult to predict the future of Canada's trade with Central and South America. Our largest trade partners are still, in order, the United States, Japan, and the United Kingdom. But trade shifts in unpredictable ways, as shown by Japan's post–Second World War emergence as a major trading power. At the very least, the proposed FTAA will offer Canadian businesses interesting opportunities.

ICE Activities for 1.2

Ideas	Connections	Extensions
1. (a) What was the impact of the fur trade on Canada?	(b) Make a list of all the roles people played in the fur trade (e.g., trapper, trader, processor, ship captain). Select one of the roles and profile it in depth.	(c) Is the fur trade still important in Canadian business? Explain.
2. (a) What were the differences between American and Canadian trade during the 1700s?	(b) Prepare a brief report on the history of American trade in one of the following areas: tobacco, cotton, or sugar.	(c) Discuss the reasons that the United States has had a much more varied processing/ manufacturing history than Canada.
3. (a) List some of the reasons why Canada traded with Europe during the eighteenth century.	(b) Compare a list of Canada's top 10 trading partners today with a list of Canada's top 10 trading partners 50 years ago. Explain any differences.	(c) How do you think Canadian international business and trade would be different today if Canada had remained a French colony instead of becoming an English colony in 1759?

1.3 Canada's Economic Identity

Changes in Canada's Economic Identity

THINK ABOUT IT

What are the advantages of keeping natural resources and the manufacturing plants that process those resources close together? For which industries would this be most important?

Historically, Canada has traded its **primary resources** to countries that then convert them into semi-manufactured goods or end products and resell them to their own populations or in the international marketplace. Often, Canada buys back its own resources that have been transformed abroad. Industries based on primary resources are **capital intensive**; that is, they require a large investment of money in machinery, but they are not **labour intensive**; they do not require a large number of skilled workers. It is economically feasible, therefore, to trade raw materials that can be extracted by semi-skilled workers using expensive machinery to countries that use cheap, skilled labour to convert the raw materials into finished products.

Many Canadians still feel that our economic identity as "hewers of wood, drawers of water" is the image of Canadian industry. Canada continues to export large amounts of raw materials; however, Canada's international trade has shifted in the last few decades. According to Statistics Canada, primary **resource-based** exports fell as a proportion of total merchandise exports, from 43 percent to 18 percent over the past 32 years, while **semi-manufactured** and **end-product exports** increased from 57 percent to 82 percent. These statistics certainly dispel the myth of Canada as a land of only trappers and loggers, farmers and fishers.

The extraction of natural resources from Canadian lands and waters is no longer an unskilled, low-technology task. All of Canada's primary resource-based industries are increasingly adopting advanced technology. This technology is forcing wage rates higher in the primary industry sector, in order to attract skilled and knowledgeable workers.

Canada's trade in services is also growing rapidly. The buying and selling of knowledge-intensive activities is a rapidly growing sector of the Canadian economy. Investments in research and development and quality education contribute to Canada's international leadership in many service areas.

Web Link

To find out more about Canada's industries, follow the link at www.internationalbusiness.nelson.com.

Figure 1.15 Canada has many primary resources. The primary industry sector increasingly uses advanced technology.

Canada's Major Industries

Primary Industries

Primary industries, also called extractive industries, take raw materials from nature, process them slightly, and sell them to other businesses that use them to make other products or to provide services. Wheat farming is an example of a major primary industry in Canada. The wheat is harvested from the fields, and the grain is separated from the stalk. The grain is then sold to a milling company for further processing. The miller is part of the manufacturing sector, not the primary industry sector. The major primary industries in Canada are agriculture, fishing and trapping, forestry and logging, and energy and mining.

	Primary Resource	Examples
Agriculture	Crops	hay, field crops, tree fruits or nuts, berries or grapes, vegetables, seed
	Livestock	cattle, pigs, sheep, horses, game animals, buffalo
	Poultry	hens, chickens, turkeys, chicks, game birds, exotic birds
	Animal products	milk or cream, eggs, wool, furs, meat
	Other agricultural products	greenhouse or nursery products, Christmas trees, mushrooms, sod, honey, maple syrup products
Fishing and Trapping	Groundfish	cod, haddock, halibut, pollock, turbot, catfish
	Finfish	herring, mackerel, tuna, salmon, smelt, eel
	Shellfish	lobsters, oysters, clams, mussels, scallops, shrimps, crabs
	Other marine life	marine plants, lumpfish roe
	Wildlife pelts	fox, beaver, lynx
	Ranch-raised pelts	mink, fox, sable, nutria, chinchilla
Forestry and Logging	Lumber	home construction, furniture
	Pulpwood	paper production
	Firewood	heat
Energy and Mining	Metals	gold, copper, zinc, nickel, iron ore, uranium, silver, platinum, cobalt, lead
	Non-metals	potash, diamonds, salt, asbestos, peat, sulphur
	Structural materials	cement, sand and gravel, stone, lime, clay
	Fossil fuels	crude petroleum, natural gas, coal
	Hydro-electric power	electricity, turbines

Figure 1.16 Canada's major primary industries.

Manufacturing

Manufacturing industries include both the processing and fabrication sectors. Grinding wheat into crude flour is an example of a manufacturing process. The flour needs more processing before it can be used. A company that refines and enriches the flour is fabricating a product that is considered a manufactured good. A manufactured good does not require further processing. Figure 1.17 identifies the areas in which Canadian manufacturers have an international reputation.

Industry	Examples	Canadian Product
Processed food	meat, fish, poultry, canned, preserved, or frozen fruits and vegetables, milk and other dairy products, cereal and flour, animal feeds, vegetable oils, biscuits and cookies, chocolate and other candy, tea and coffee, dried pasta	
Beverages	soft drinks, beer, wine, distilled spirits	
Rubber	tires, tubes, hoses, belts, other rubber products	
Plastic	pipes, foam, sheets, film, bags, other plastic products	
Leather	tanned hides, footwear, luggage, purses, coats and jackets	
Textiles	manufactured fibre, yarn, woven cloth, knitted fabric, natural fibres, felt, carpets, mats and rugs, canvas, textile dyeing and finishing, tire cord fabric, clothing, linens	
Wood	shingles and shakes, veneer, plywood, cabinets, doors, window frames, boxes, pallets, coffins, caskets, particle board, preserved wood	
Furniture and fixtures	household furniture, metal office furniture, other office furniture, bed springs and mattresses	
Paper	wood pulp, newsprint, paperboard, building board, boxes, paper bags, coated and treated paper, stationery	
Printing and publishing	business forms, platemaking, typesetting and book binding, book publishing, newspaper, magazine, and periodical publishing and printing	
Primary metals	ferro-alloys, steel foundries and other primary steel industries, steel pipes and tubes, iron foundries, aluminum, copper and other non-ferrous metal smelting	

(continued)

Industry	Examples	Canadian Product
Fabricated metals	boilers and heat exchangers, tanks, plates, doors and windows, prefabricated portable metal buildings, ornamental and architectural metal products, wire and wire rope, industrial fasteners, upholstery and coil springs, basic hardware	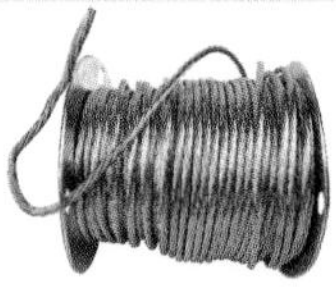
Machinery	agricultural implements, commercial refrigeration and air conditioning equipment, compressors, pumps and industrial fans, construction and mining machinery	
Transportation	aircraft and aircraft parts, automotive parts, automobiles, truck and bus bodies, commercial and non-commercial trailers, mobile homes, railroad rolling stock, shipbuilding, recreational vehicles	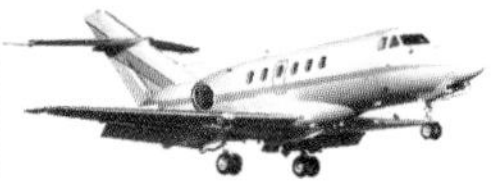
Electrical and electronics	small electrical appliances, major appliances, lighting fixtures, electric lamps and shades, radio and television receivers, telecommunications equipment, computing equipment, batteries	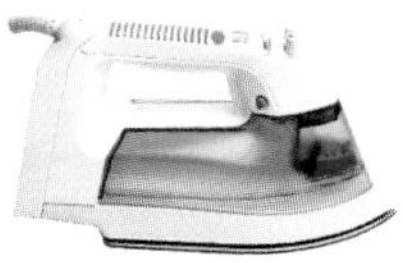
Non-metallic minerals	clay products, cement, concrete, glass products, abrasives, lime, asbestos products, gypsum products	
Petroleum and coal	asphalt, refined gasoline and oil, lubricating oil, grease, coal, natural gas	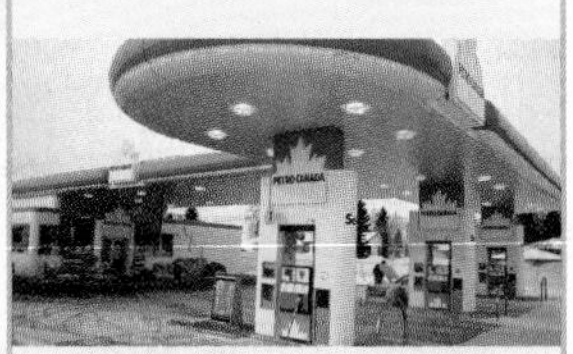
Chemicals	industrial chemicals, fertilizer materials, resins, pharmaceuticals and medicines, paint and varnishes, soap and cleaning compounds	
Other manufacturing	recording and controlling instruments, clocks and watches, ophthalmic goods, jewellery and precious metals, sporting goods, toys and games, brooms, buttons, floor tile, musical instruments and sound recordings	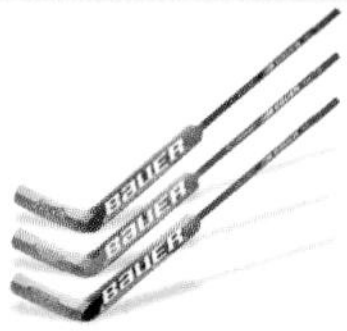

Figure 1.17 Canada's major manufactured products.

Global Thought

In the past, some analysts have argued that foreign corporations operating in Canada do most R&D at their head offices abroad, and therefore, only a few high-tech and high real-wage jobs are created in Canada. However, as far as trade in commercial services is concerned, such a claim does not find much support since 1985.

– S. Prakash

Services

Service industries do not sell tangible items (items a person can touch), although rental services will allow customers to use tangible items such as DVDs for a period of time. Services provide intangibles that people need or want, such as cleaning, accommodation, entertainment, or transportation. Services are also activities that are often performed by experts who can do what untrained people cannot do: pilots, mechanics, accountants, engineers, doctors, teachers, architects, builders, and chefs, for example. One of the fastest growing sectors of the service industry is in consulting services, where the client pays for advice. Canadian consultants are popular all over the world in many areas including communication, construction, and energy.

Service	Examples
Commercial services	communications, construction, insurance and other financial services, computer and information services, royalties and licence fees, management services, intellectual property services, non-financial commissions, equipment rentals, advertising and related services, research and development services, architectural, engineering, and other technical services, miscellaneous services to business, audio-visual services, and personal, cultural, and recreational services
Travel	business and personal travel
Transportation	transportation of persons and goods (freight) by air, water, and land
Government	domestic and international transactions arising from government, diplomatic, commercial, and military activities, education, healthcare, and social/community services

Figure 1.18 Canada's service industries.

ICE Activities for 1.3

Ideas	Connections	Extensions
1. (a) What are Canada's four major primary industries?	(b) Prepare a chart profiling one of the primary industries. Include the brand name or the name of a company that works with each of the types of products in your chart.	(c) What are the current statistics for Canada's primary industries as a percentage of our exports? Do you think the figure is likely to increase or decrease? Explain.
2. (a) What are 20 categories of Canadian manufacturing?	(b) Find examples of a Canadian manufacturer for each of the specific products listed in one of the manufacturing categories.	(c) Speculate as to why another country might want the specific products you looked at in 2. (b).
3. (a) What four service industries provide the bulk of trade in Canadian services?	(b) Prepare a brief report on a company that exports a Canadian service.	(c) Which type of Canadian service do you think has the potential to increase its exports? Explain why.

1.4 Advantages and Disadvantages of International Trade

Advantages of International Trade

The fundamental reason for international trade is to sell something that we don't need or have made for trade and to buy something we do need. That simple transaction leads to other benefits. Trade creates jobs, attracts investment, attracts new technology and materials, and offers Canadians a wider choice in products and services. This range of choice provides more competition in the marketplace, which encourages competitive pricing, technological advances, and improved services, including the education and training of Canadian employees.

Jobs provide salaries and wages to employees. Employees use their wages and salaries to pay taxes, save, or spend. When employees pay taxes, the government can provide services and create more jobs. When they save, the capital markets can lend money to others, who will either spend it on consumer goods and create demand or spend it opening or expanding a business, which will create more jobs. When employees spend their salaries and wages, they create demand, which creates new or expanded businesses. These new businesses create jobs and the cycle expands.

If something occurs to slow down this expansion, then the cycle starts to reverse. Higher interest rates, for example, will cause people to stop borrowing and save more, which decreases demand. Higher taxes will leave less income to spend, and demand will decrease. To keep the cycle expanding, business opportunities must increase. Participating in the global marketplace provides Canadian businesses with growth opportunities and, therefore, helps to expand the business cycle.

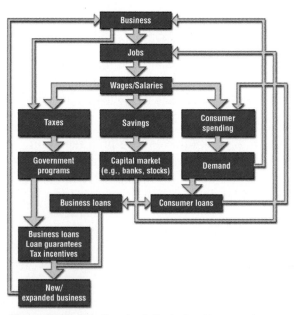

Figure 1.19 This flowchart illustrates the complex interconnections among businesses, employees, consumers, governments, the capital market, and the creation of new businesses.

Meeting Our Needs

The hobby of collecting sports cards recently went through a revival. They come in packages of four or five crisp, new cards, with a picture of a team member on the front of each card and the player's statistics on the back. Many people collect these cards. Often, a new package of cards contains cards that the collector already has. These duplicates become surplus cards, or cards the collector uses to trade with other card collectors. During trade negotiations, the traders look through one another's surplus pile and select cards they do not have. If collector A has six cards that collector B wants, then collector A is entitled to have six of collector B's surplus pile. If collector A does not want six of collector B's cards, then collector B either reduces his or her demand or makes a different deal. Trade is always balanced if it is fair.

International trade works in a similar way. Canadian farms grow more than Canadians eat. Canadian manufacturers make more products than Canadians use. Canadian service providers have the capacity to provide their services to people both inside Canada and outside Canada. Many businesses can create a surplus inventory of goods and services.

However, there are many goods and services that Canadians want or need that Canadian businesses do not provide. For example, the Canadian climate does not allow for our farmers to produce crops like pineapples and bananas. The countries that make the products and provide the services that we need or want may also need products that we can make and are willing to trade. Both trading partners, then, get something they need by trading something they do not need.

The Top 25 Product Categories Imported by Canadian Businesses

Motor vehicles	Plastic and synthetic resin
Electronic parts and components	Chemical products
Motor vehicle accessories, parts, and assemblies	Indicating, recording, and controlling instruments
Other machinery and equipment	Primary steel
Electronic computing and peripheral equipment	Non-conventional crude oil
Aircraft and aircraft parts	Agricultural implements
Motor vehicle engine and engine parts	Electrical industrial equipment
Motor vehicle stampings	Plastic products
Construction and mining machinery	Communication and electronic equipment
Industrial organic chemicals	Motor vehicle wiring assemblies
Materials handling equipment	Motor vehicle steering and suspension parts
Pharmaceutical and medicine	Television receivers
	Motor vehicle wheels and brakes

Figure 1.20 Canadian businesses import a wide range of products.

Job Creation

Unlike the bartering that used to go on between trading partners, now businesses receive money from selling their products or services to foreign businesses. Foreign businesses buy Canadian products and services, which leads to more jobs for Canadians. Exports are critical to the Canadian economy. One out of three Canadian jobs depends on exports. More than 40 percent of everything that Canadians produce is exported, and more than 50 percent of everything that Ontarians produce is exported. Every $1 billion in exports means 6000 jobs for Canadians.

When trade is balanced, businesses in both importing and exporting countries remain profitable and may even grow. This growth often results in more jobs for citizens of the countries. Employees use their wages and salaries to buy goods and services, some of which may be imported.

Attracting Investment

Investment follows trade. Many foreign companies, when demand for their products is proven through trade with Canada, will invest in an office, factory, or distribution warehouse in Canada to simplify their trade and to reduce costs. This capital investment creates other jobs in construction, sales, and office management. Canada also attracts international investors who trade Canadian securities, buy Canadian government bonds, speculate in Canadian real estate, or invest money in other Canadian financial products.

New Technology and Materials

The development of new technology promotes competitiveness and profitability. If a business can create a machine that works better, faster, or cheaper (or preferably all three), then that business will produce a more competitive product for both national and international markets. The search for new technology is a global search.

This newly developed technology is as much a product to be exported as the DVD player or industrial machinery that the technology helps to make. Some companies sell the rights to their patents to foreign companies, collecting an annual fee, royalty percentage, or a one-time payment. Other companies manufacture the high-tech machines and then sell them to foreign factories or send a technician to the buyer's factory to have the technology installed on site.

The biotechnology industry in Canada is exceptional, second only to the United States in the number of biotech companies. This industry invests heavily in research and development, hiring highly trained workers for this growing sector.

Diverse Products and Services

A century ago, Canadian parents put oranges in their children's Christmas stockings as a very rare and expensive treat. The invention of rapid, refrigerated transportation methods brought fresh oranges to Canadian grocery stores from Florida, California, Mexico, Spain, Morocco, and Israel, and made them as available as juice for breakfast. Foreign trade opens up the world as a market, delivering a wide range of foods, high fashions, and new inventions to the Canadian market.

Foreign travel, banking, consultation, and other services are also available to the Canadian consumer. Businesses must now consider that their competition for similar products and services is no longer just in the same city but anywhere in the world. Canadian consumers and businesses receive the benefits of this global competition, such as lower prices, better quality, and functional design.

Tina Jagros

Executive Director, North American Fur Association

Tina Jagros is a modern-day fur trader. As Executive Director for the North American Fur Association (NAFA), she promotes both wild and ranched Canadian fur around the world. NAFA represents Canadian and American fur farmers and trappers who market their product through the North American Fur Auctions.

NAFA does not sell fur garments; it brings together the manufacturers and designers who buy the product through auctions at Association events. One of Jagros's responsibilities is to arrange for the participation of many well-known designers and retailers in the NAFA shows and seminars. By including their garments in NAFA events, designers can demonstrate their fashion ideas.

The auctions NAFA organizes are a direct descendent of the original Company of Adventurers, which held the first auction in 1670. Originally established to market Canada's first real export, beaver pelts, Hudson's Bay Fur Sales became North American Fur Auctions in a 1989 corporate changeover. Jagros promotes Canada's fur trading tradition by organizing fashion shows, preparing consumer retail seminars, conducting product workshops, and advertising in international markets, including China, Russia, Korea, Japan, Eastern Europe, Western Europe, and North America.

Jagros educates consumers in other countries on the qualities of Canadian fur products. Travel is a big part of her job. Jagros's ability to speak several languages and her understanding of different cultural attitudes are assets.

While Canada may not be the largest producer of fur pelts in the world, it is a leader in high-quality pelts. This is a direct result of our climate and the expertise of our fur farmers and trappers. Canadians are international leaders in animal husbandry techniques and humane trapping standards.

One direct result of Jagros's work is that China has become a major market for Canadian fur products, buying as much as 50 percent of the Canadian mink crop. Through fashion events in many Chinese cities, Jagros has raised the profile of Canadian fur products and the NAFA brand with the Chinese media and consumer.

Jagros recently undertook a different challenge: selling Canadian fur products to Russia. While Russia has its own successful fur industry, the Canadian industry is larger. Canadian furs are also of a better quality than those produced in Russia today. Add to this the fact that Russia is a big consumer of fur products (50 million fur hats every year, for example). Jagros looks forward to developing good business in Russia.

In international business, nothing can be taken for granted. A successful career in international trade requires business expertise, experience, and preparation. Jagros's background in International Economics from the University of Toronto and her family background in the fur trade have given her the tools necessary to succeed in a major international organization.

The fur industry is an example of supply-and-demand economics; fur has once again become one of Canada's important exports. Almost 100 000 Canadians are involved in the fur trade today.

• •

1. Which two foreign markets has Tina Jagros helped to develop for Canadian furs? How did she accomplish this?

2. Some groups oppose the fur trade. Identify one of their concerns. How might Jagros respond to this concern?

International Business Career Profile

Disadvantages of International Trade

The global marketplace has made it very easy for Canadian businesses to purchase products from international suppliers and to sell products to international consumers. This is advantageous for the most part, but it can also create problems for both Canadians and foreign populations. The political, economic, and cultural impact of trade can create increased prosperity for some, but can lead to economic exploitation, loss of cultural identity, and even physical harm for others.

Support of Non-Democratic Systems

Coffee is a non-nutritional beverage made from relatively inedible beans. Growing coffee beans exclusively will not provide food for a country's people. The major land reform disputes in countries like Nicaragua and El Salvador centre on the fact that the landowners want the land to grow coffee beans for export, a very profitable cash crop. The farmers who grow the coffee, however, would like to use more of the land to grow food for their families. Because the farmers do not own their land, their wishes are ignored. When people who do not consider the general population's welfare are making the decisions about land use or surplus production for export, those decisions can cause great hardship.

Cultural Identity Issues

Culture is a major export of the United States. American films, music, television programs, magazines, and books are very popular worldwide. Each one of these exports promotes American values and displays American lifestyles. The "culture consumer" in another country is sometimes overwhelmed with American ideals. Products, as well, carry cultural messages. There is more in Coca-Cola than carbonated water, sugar, and flavouring. There are also the values of the culture that makes this product. Coca-Cola, McDonald's, Nike, and Microsoft all sell products that symbolize American values and reflect American corporate culture. French sparkling water, British fish and chips, Italian soccer shoes, and Canadian software manufacturers compete with these products not just for a share of the market, but also for a share of the mind.

Social Welfare Issues

Maintaining safety standards, minimum wages, workers' compensation, and health benefits cost Canadian businesses and Canadian taxpayers a great deal of money. Countries that do not maintain these high standards can make products less expensively. Canadian consumers can buy running shoes for less, but the shoes may have been made in factories with substandard safety conditions. Every year such factories cause death and injury to far too many workers. Supporting this type of trade by buying these products perpetuates the problem.

Figure 1.21 The fair trade symbol is used on certain products to let you know that you are supporting the advantages, and not the disadvantages, of global trade.

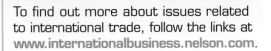

Web Link

To find out more about issues related to international trade, follow the links at www.internationalbusiness.nelson.com.

Environmental Issues

Canadian businesses have been encouraged by consumers, labour groups, and government to treat Canada's air, land, and water with care and respect. Pollution controls, recycling laws, and emission controls are just a few examples of environmental protection measures in place in this country. Many other countries do not have these rules. Some businesses find Canada's environmental protection laws too expensive and move their business to a less regulated country.

Political Issues

Wars and strife often occur because of natural resources. Thousands of people have been killed for control of oil; others for control of the diamond trade or farmland. Trade in precious commodities can cause a number of political alliances that do not contribute to the welfare of the people in the trading nation. Instead, trade contributes only to the profit of the companies and countries doing business there.

ICE Activities for 1.4

Ideas	Connections	Extensions
1. (a) List and briefly describe five benefits of trade.	(b) Select a Canadian exporter. How has trade benefited this firm? Be specific.	(c) Select a category from the list of the top 25 product categories imported by Canadian businesses in Figure 1.20. Discuss how your life would be altered if the products in this category were not imported.
2. (a) Outline five disadvantages to trade.	(b) Give a specific example of a cultural message carried by three different American-made products.	(c) Prepare a brief report on one of the following issues, where possible using specific examples of how international businesses are involved: war, famine, child labour, environmental issues, infrastructure development (roads, telecommunications).
3. (a) Explain how Canada's international trade has been affected by environmental issues.	(b) Research a recent environmental issue that has directly affected a Canadian business that sells its product internationally.	(c) Create an organizer to show three possible solutions to the problem you researched in 3. (b). Consider the pros and cons of each solution and decide which one would be most likely to succeed.

1.5 Barriers to International Trade

Tariffs

A **tariff** is a tax imposed by the local government on goods or services coming into a country (imports). Tariffs increase the price of the imported product or service in the local market. Governments use tariffs to protect local businesses from low-priced competitive products from other countries. For example, a man's dress shirt, made in Canada, may cost a retail menswear store $50. To make a profit, the menswear store doubles the price and sells the shirt for $100. But an Indonesian shirt manufacturer would only charge $40 for a similar quality shirt. The landed cost to the menswear store, after shipping and handling, is $45 per shirt. This shirt sells in the store for $90, saving the consumer $10. If the menswear store buys all its shirts from Indonesia, and other menswear stores search for non-Canadian sources, then Canadian shirt manufacturers will not be able to sell shirts at a competitive price, and many people who are employed in the shirt industry will lose their jobs. So Canada places a tariff of 22 percent on imported shirts in order to protect Canadian shirt manufacturers.

The addition of the tariff means that the shirt from Indonesia now costs the menswear store $53.80 ($40.00 + $8.80 [22% of $40.00] = $48.80, plus shipping and handling costs of $5.00 per shirt). The shirt would now cost the Canadian consumer about $108.00, making the Canadian shirt the better buy and supporting the Canadian shirt manufacturing industry.

Canada can encourage trade with specific countries by lowering our normal tariff rates on their exports. We can expect reciprocal treatment on goods Canada exports to those countries. This may eventually lead to greater tariff reductions, and possibly even to free trade agreements that reduce tariffs to zero. Canada has free trade agreements with the United States, Mexico, Chile, and Israel among others.

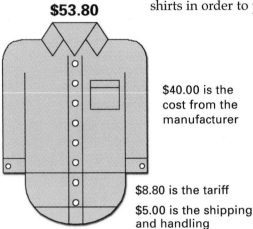

$53.80

$40.00 is the cost from the manufacturer

$8.80 is the tariff

$5.00 is the shipping and handling

Figure 1.22 A tariff increased the price of this imported shirt.

Currency Fluctuations

Every sovereign nation has its own currency. Canada's dollar is accepted as legal tender in all transactions in Canada, and Canadians know what their currency can buy. They know that $25 will purchase two movie tickets, and that $25 is a good hourly wage rate. Canadian consumers who borrow money to buy a car or take a trip know that they will pay interest on their loan. In other words, most Canadians know how to use Canadian dollars in Canada. But what if someone wishes to use Canadian dollars to buy products in another country?

The rate given by one country for another country's currency is called the **currency exchange rate**. International banks exchange with other international banks the large volumes of foreign currency they receive from international business transactions. The rates given during these trades set the current daily exchange rates for the two currencies. For example, if one bank exchanges 25 000 000 Canadian dollars for 11 243 799.38 British pounds, this means that the Canadian dollar is worth 0.449752 of a British pound and that each British pound is worth 2.22345 Canadian dollars. This rate is in effect until another major transaction takes place, possibly that same day.

The fluctuating value of currency on international markets can be a major barrier to trade. For example, assume that a Canadian business agreed to import $2 million worth of wine from France. If the exchange rate of the Euro shifts four cents between the time the product was ordered and the time it arrives, the wine shipment will now cost the dealer an extra $80 000 CAD. A loss like that may be the total profit for the entire order. Many businesses are wary of currency fluctuations and do not import for that reason.

As a country's currency is devalued in relation to another country's currency (as the Canadian dollar is currently lower in value compared to the American dollar, for example), the country with the devalued currency can sell more to the other country. American shoppers can save money by buying Canadian goods. This stimulates Canada's exports to the United States, but discourages Canadian businesses (and cross-border shoppers) from importing American goods and services.

Web Link

For current currency exchange rates, follow the links at www.internationalbusiness.nelson.com.

Investment Regulations

Canada's federal *Investment Canada Act* (ICA) "provide[s] for the review of significant investments in Canada by non-Canadians in order to ensure such benefit to Canada" (s. 2). Investors who are non-Canadians must comply with the provisions of the ICA, which requires them to file a notification when they commence a new business activity in Canada or each time they acquire control of an existing Canadian business. The acquisition or investment will be reviewed if both the investor and the vendor (other than a Canadian) are from a country that is not a **World Trade Organization** (WTO) member and if the value of the business being acquired in Canada is over $5 million. If the investor's or vendor's country is a WTO member (other than a Canadian), any direct investment in excess of $223 million (for the year 2003) is reviewable. Even for WTO investors, however, the $5 million limit applies if the Canadian business being acquired in the investment

THINK ABOUT IT

Why do you think the federal government is concerned about foreign investment in uranium, financial services, transportation, and culture in particular?

- produces uranium *and* owns an interest in a uranium property
- provides any financial service
- provides any transportation service
- is a cultural business involved in the publication, distribution, production, sale or exhibition of books, magazines, periodicals, newspapers, film, video recordings, audio or video music recordings, music in print, or radio communication in which the transmissions are intended for direct reception by the general public, any radio, television, and cable television broadcasting undertakings, and any satellite programming and broadcast network services

In other words, if the investment involves the acquisition of a company which produces uranium and owns an interest in a uranium property, or engages in financial services, transportation, or culture and is worth over $5 million, a review must take place.

Environmental Restrictions

Canada protects its environment with a number of regulations. A large portion of Canada's economy depends on its natural resources. Foreign insects and diseases could destroy entire industries and seriously harm the Canadian economy. For example, the mad-cow disease in Europe virtually destroyed the beef industry in Great Britain. Restrictions on imports are in place to protect Canadian crops and livestock, and fish and forests from contamination. Canadian law requires that all foods, plants, fish, animals, and their products brought into Canada must comply with Canadian standards. Inspectors from the Canadian Food Inspection Agency are in charge of the process at international arrival points.

To cut our personal emissions, reducing the amount we drive and driving a fuel-efficient vehicle are two of the most important steps we can take. Consider this: Switching from driving an average car to driving an average SUV for one year will waste more energy than leaving a refrigerator door open for six years or a television turned on for 28 years!

– David Suzuki

Canada is also a signatory to the Convention on International Trade in Endangered Species of Wild Fauna and Flora (CITES). This agreement prohibits trade on some 30 000 wild animal and plant species, from whales to parrots and from coral to cacti.

Products that do not meet Canadian environmental standards are not allowed to enter Canada. Certain toxins, hazardous chemicals, waste products, and vehicles without proper emission controls are examples of restricted goods.

Foreign Relations and Trade Sanctions

Canada uses trade sanctions to influence the policies or actions of other nations. (In a few countries, Canada also uses additional military, peacekeeping, or policing actions.) Canada attempts to stop human rights abuses, war, revolution, terrorism, smuggling, slavery, or piracy in other countries by imposing sanctions instead of using force. Sanctions can include placing limitations on official and diplomatic contacts and travel; seizing or freezing assets in Canada that belong to the offending nation's government, its leaders, or its people or businesses; and legally restricting trade between Canada and the target state. Often, Canada joins with other nations that share our views to implement the sanctions jointly (or multilaterally). The laws of Canada that can be used to impose trade and economic sanctions are the *Special Economic Measures Act* (SEMA), and the *Export and Import Permits Act*, as well as the *United Nations Act*. The Minister of Foreign Affairs and International Trade is responsible for these statutes.

The *United Nations Act* incorporates into Canadian law the decisions passed by the United Nations Security Council (UNSC). United Nations sanctions are imposed under Chapter VII (Article 41) of the United Nations Charter. A UNSC decision taken in relation to Article 41 imposes a legal obligation on Canada (as a UN member) to uphold the decision domestically by enacting regulations under the United Nations Act.

Even without a UNSC resolution, authority exists for Canada, under SEMA, to impose sanctions in relation to a foreign state either "for the purpose of implementing a decision, resolution or recommendation of an international organization of states or association of states, of which Canada is a member, that calls on its members to take economic measures against a foreign state" or "where the Governor-in-Council is of the opinion that a grave breach of international peace and security has occurred that has resulted or is likely to result in a serious international crisis."

The Export and Import Permits Act is used to impose trade sanctions on goods by means of three regulations: the *Area Control List* (ACL), the *Export Control List* (ECL), and the *Import Control List* (ICL). The Area Control List (ACL) is a list of restricted countries, and special permits are required for any Canadian businesses wishing to trade with countries on the ACL. The Export Control List is a list of restricted goods. The Canadian government prohibits the export of military goods and technology to countries whose governments have a persistent record of serious violations of the human rights of their citizens, for example. The Import Control List is a list of goods that are not permitted into Canada. Generally, the Import Control List is not used to impose sanctions on a foreign state. In exceptional circumstances, however, goods originating in a particular country have been added to the Import Control List to implement an intergovernmental arrangement or commitment between Canada and other countries.

Safety Regulations

The federal government of Canada makes laws primarily to protect Canadians. The government regulates and administers commerce and trade in specific goods under the following acts:

Food and Drugs Act	Canada Agricultural Products Act
Meat Inspection Act	Fish Inspection Act
Consumer Packaging and Labelling Act	Plant Protection Act
Health of Animals Act	Administrative Monetary Penalties Act
Seeds Act	Feeds Act
Fertilizers Act	Canadian Food Inspection Act
Plant Breeders' Rights Act	Customs Act
Hazardous Products Act	Weights and Measures Act

Each of these Acts affects both domestic companies and foreign imports. Canadian pyjama manufacturers, for example, must make a product that is flame retardant. All pyjamas imported into Canada must also be flame retardant. Imported food must be as safe as domestic food. Products brought into Canada for resale must conform to the same packaging and labelling requirements as goods produced in Canada. Each of these Acts sets up numerous regulations. These regulations could act as barriers to trade for foreign exporters who may need to make costly changes in their manufacturing procedures to conform to Canadian standards.

Immigration Policies

Since the first settlers arrived in New France in the early 1600s, Canada has been a nation that depended on immigrants to grow the country and its economy. The Canadian economy benefits from their skills and financial investments. Immigrants and refugees become consumers the moment they arrive and, as Canada's population is declining, they help maintain the size of the Canadian market. Since their tastes and culture are rooted in other countries, immigrants and refugees create a demand for imports and contribute to trade between Canada and their home countries. They also share their culture with Canadian communities, making Canada more culturally diverse.

Citizenship and Immigration Canada, a department of the federal government, establishes policies to regulate the admission of visitors, workers, students, immigrants, and refugees from other countries.

Visitors

Canada welcomes visitors. People coming to Canada for short stays, such as tourists, students, or foreign workers, always spends money, either on goods and services consumed, or on products they purchase to take home. According to the Canadian Tourism Commission, Canada's tourism industry generated $15.3 billion from foreign visitors in 1999. Foreign visitors made 19.4 million overnight trips to Canada in 1999.

Many international companies wish to transfer key managers and specialists to Canada for a period of time. They must apply for a work permit for the individual; if the work permit is granted, these individuals may later apply for Permanent Resident Status in Canada.

Web Link

For more information on Canada's tourism industry and for updates on immigration and refugee protection policies, follow the link at www.internationalbusiness.nelson.com.

Figure 1.23 Immigrants about to become Canadian citizens swear an oath of allegiance to the country.

Immigrants

People wishing to relocate from their home country to Canada must have a Canadian Immigrant Visa. (An immigrant who wishes to settle in Quebec must also apply for a Quebec Certificate of Selection.) Canadian permanent residents are allowed to live and work anywhere in Canada, they receive many of the benefits of Canadian citizenship, they are permitted to apply for Canadian citizenship after three years, and they may sponsor family members for Canadian Permanent Resident Status.

There are two ways to qualify for Canadian Permanent Resident Status: as an Independent Immigrant or as a member of the Family Class. Independent Immigrants are divided into two categories:

- Skilled Worker Category: Assessment relies on a point system, designed to indicate the likelihood of success in Canada. Points are calculated based on criteria including age, education, skills, occupation, language ability, certain demographic factors, and personal suitability.
- Business Category: Investors, entrepreneurs, and self-employed people are selected based on their abilities to make a contribution to the economy or, in certain cases, the cultural and artistic life of Canada.

To qualify as an immigrant under Family Class, an individual must be supported by a close family member (that is, spouse, parent, grandparent, adult child) who is a Canadian citizen or permanent resident already living in Canada and who promises to support the new arrival.

Refugees

Refugees are people who have fled their country to escape persecution or war. The persecution could be physical violence, harassment, wrongful arrest, or threats to their lives. They may be persecuted for reasons of race, religion, gender, nationality, political opinion, or membership in a particular social group. Refugees cannot rely on their own government to provide them with legal or physical protection. They have to try to find safety in other countries.

"Asylum" is somewhere one can go to find safety. To grant asylum means to offer protection in a safe country to people who are in danger in their own country. Individuals who flee to Canada have their refugee claims heard before they are granted refugee status. In 2001, approximately 11 000 refugees were granted asylum in Canada.

Sometimes refugees flee to countries where they are still not safe or where they cannot stay. Such refugees may be "resettled" in Canada, as permanent residents. In 2001, approximately 10 000 refugees in need of protection were selected to be resettled in Canada.

All refugees in Canada are allowed to participate fully in Canadian society, to seek work, and to go to school. All kinds of refugees come to Canada, both adults and children; in their home countries, they may have been in school or university, skilled workers, members of a profession, or farmers or labourers. They help make Canada the richly diverse country that it is.

Dealing with the Trade Barriers

Major political debates are still raging concerning trade. Should Canada be bringing down the barriers to trade, or should we be creating more barriers? Is freer trade good or bad for Canada? Opinions on this issue vary, but the statistical evidence is that Canada's economy has benefited from freer trade. There is certainly a movement at all levels of government to pursue a freer trade policy. Numerous trade missions, organized by federal, provincial, and even some municipal governments, have visited foreign countries in an attempt to develop more trade with them.

The federal government has indicated a willingness to establish the FTAA. Canada has strong ties to the United Kingdom and is using them to forge trade deals with the European Union at preferred tariff rates. The Asia-Pacific Economic Cooperation (APEC) was established in 1989 in response to the growing interdependence among Asia-Pacific economies. APEC has since become the primary regional vehicle for promoting open trade and economic cooperation with Canada and the other twenty member countries. And the World Trade Organization (WTO) is influencing and ruling on international trade policies and on some existing bilateral and multilateral agreements.

As for currency fluctuations, businesses can deal with the fluctuations in the value of the Canadian dollar by buying foreign currency. If a Canadian business committed to buying $2 million worth of French wine, then the trading partners can agree on a specific currency exchange rate, or the Canadian business can buy Euros on the day of the order to cover the outstanding invoice.

Canada's immigration policies are constantly being reviewed to allow more people to come to Canada. The Canadian government supports foreign tourism with numerous initiatives such as government support for Canadian hotels that advertise abroad. Environmental concerns are debated and the wishes of companies doing business outside Canada are considered. The Investment Canada Act replaced the more restrictive Foreign Investment Review Act and significantly loosened restrictions on foreign investment in Canada, allowing the establishment of almost any new business by foreign investors without government review. Canada's Trade Commissioner Service at our consulates and embassies abroad develop trade contacts and manage foreign relations with other nations. Canadian foreign policy is definitely pro-trade.

Figure 1.24 Trade missions are undertaken by various levels of government to encourage trade at the municipal, provincial, and federal levels.

ICE Activities for 1.5

Ideas	Connections	Extensions
1. (a) Describe briefly the seven barriers to trade.	(b) Select one of the barriers to trade and explain why a specific product cannot be traded because of this barrier.	(c) In your opinion, how does the barrier to trade you used for your example in 1. (b) affect the Canadian consumer? Does the barrier bring advantages or disadvantages to Canadians?
2. (a) What determines the currency exchange rate?	(b) Research any foreign country other than the United States or France to discover the cost in Canadian dollars of a room in a major hotel chain.	(c) Find a currency that has fluctuated significantly in the past five years in its exchange rate with the Canadian dollar. Explain the reasons for the fluctuations. How would this affect Canada's trade with this country?
3. (a) Explain how safety regulations protect Canadian consumers.	(b) Working with a partner, investigate current issues involving one of the Acts listed on page 31. Summarize the different points of view in one of these issues.	(c) Prepare arguments for one side of a debate on the statement "There are too many trade regulations in Canada."

Canada's Trading Partners: Focus on Cuba

After the Cuban revolution in 1959, Fidel Castro, the leader of the revolution, declared Cuba a communist country. All foreign-owned industries were nationalized, including the many businesses owned by citizens in the United States. Castro's government also worked to create a close trade relationship with Russia. Today, Cuba is one of the few remaining communist governments. The United States placed a trade embargo on Cuba, partly because Cuba had nationalized American companies and partly because the United States wanted to help overthrow the communist government that was less than 200 km off the Florida coast. The American government passed two laws in an attempt to prevent other countries, including Canada, from doing business in Cuba. The Toricelli Act requires all American firms to prevent any of their subsidiaries from trading with Cuba. The Helms-Burton Act permits American citizens to sue any foreign business that benefits from property that was expropriated, or nationalized, by Cuba.

A company wishing to trade with Cuba must deal directly with the communist bureaucracy that runs the country. Usually, international trade is trade between businesses in different countries rather than trade between the nations themselves. Each nation sets its own trade regulations; tax structures, such as duties and tariffs; and shipping regulations, but agents for individual firms perform the actual exchange of goods. The government would not be directly involved in making the deal. With Cuba, however, a Canadian business may not make a trade deal with a Cuban business but may make a deal with the Cuban government, and today many Canadian businesses do trade with Cuba. The problems in trading with a government are different from the problems in trading with an individual company. When doing business with a government, several different departments must approve each deal. This process can take several months to complete, and the government can reconsider at any time and cancel the order. Deals with individuals are much simpler and more dependable.

The collapse of Russian communism in the early 1990s destroyed the major trading relationship that Cuba had built with the Soviet Union. This forced Cuba to look for new trading partners and provided opportunities for Canadian businesses. Canadian companies such as Leisure Canada Inc. took advantage of the fact that there is no American competition and have provided a great deal of direct investment in Cuban ventures.

Looking to the Future

Will Cuba remain communist when Fidel Castro dies? It's anyone's guess. Cuba could develop as a free market economy and then the United States would enter the Cuban market. Leisure Canada anticipates rapid growth in the Cuban economy following the inevitable lifting of the American trade embargo. All Canadian companies trading with Cuba have risked a great deal and have overcome trade barriers unique to Cuba in order to have Cuba as a trading partner. It is to be hoped that Canadian companies that have built Cuban loyalties and established a market presence will be rewarded for their patience and perseverance.

Figure 1.25 "Cuba Libre" means "free Cuba."

A SNAPSHOT OF CUBA

Size Relative to Canada: Cuba is 110 860 sq. km, approximately twice the size of Nova Scotia at 55 284 sq. km.

World Region: Caribbean

Capital City: Havana

Language: Spanish

Currency: Cuban peso

Population: 11.1 million (1999 est.)

Time: Noon in Ottawa (EST) is noon in Havana.

Climate: Tropical moderated by trade winds. The dry season is from November to April and the rainy season is from May to October.

Type of Government: Communist. The state plays the primary role in the domestic economy and controls practically all foreign trade.

GDP per Capita: $2340 CAD (1998 est.)

Figure 1.26 Workers harvest sugar cane in a field.

Labour Force by Occupation: Services and government 30 percent, industry 22 percent, agriculture 20 percent, commerce 11 percent, construction 10 percent, transportation and communications 7 percent (June 1990)

Membership in World Organizations: International Chamber of Commerce (ICC), World Trade Organization (WTO)

Importing Partners and Products: Total value: $3.2 billion CAD (c.i.f., 1999 est.)
Partners: Spain 16 percent, Venezuela 15 percent, Mexico 7 percent (1999 est.)
Products: petroleum, food, machinery, chemicals.

Exporting Partners and Products: Total value: $1.4 billion CAD (1999 est.)
Partners: Russia 25 percent, Netherlands 23 percent, Canada 16 percent (1999 est.)
Products: sugar, nickel, tobacco, shellfish, medical products, citrus, coffee.

Travel Advisory: It's always a good idea to do some research before you travel. Following are some tips for travelling to Cuba.

- The U.S. dollar is the only accepted currency in Cuban stores and hotels.
- Petty theft is a problem, but violent crime is not.
- The Cuban phone system is very poor, so a cell phone or satellite phone capable of making international calls is essential.
- Cubans like to do business in Spanish, so hire a translator if you don't speak Spanish.

Business Etiquette:

- Be prepared for Cuban business people to be friendly and outgoing with a sense of humour.
- When dealing with the government, avoid wasting an official's time. Explain what you want and how the official can assist you. Be specific. Be prepared to talk business right away without much preamble.
- Exchange business cards at the beginning of meetings.

THINK ABOUT IT

What uncommon trade barriers do Canadian businesses have to overcome in order to trade with Cuba?
What are the opportunities for Canadian businesses in Cuba? Why are these opportunities different from those other nations provide for Canadian companies?
Why does the United States still not recognize Cuba?

Country Link

Follow the link at
www.internationalbusiness.nelson.com
to find out more about Canadian trade with Cuba.

Chapter Challenges

Knowledge/Understanding

1. Match each of the following terms to the correct definition or description below:
   (a) self-sufficiency
   (b) protectionism
   (c) interdependence
   (d) capital-intensive industry
   (e) labour-intensive industry
   (f) United Nations Act
   (g) primary industries
   (h) tariff

   (i) requiring a substantial investment of money in machinery
   (ii) incorporates into Canadian law the decisions made by the United Nations Security Council
   (iii) using tariffs and duties to impede imports of foreign goods to protect domestic producers
   (iv) agriculture, fishing and trapping, forestry and logging, energy and mining
   (v) the reliance of two or more groups on the actions of one another to fulfill needs
   (vi) a tax imposed on goods or services coming into a country
   (vii) requiring a large number of skilled workers
   (viii) the ability to provide for all of your needs without relying on anyone else

2. What contribution did trade make to the development of Canada?

3. What are tariffs and why are they used?

Thinking/Inquiry

1. Canadians have been called "hewers of wood, drawers of water." What does this phrase mean when it is applied to the Canadian economy? How valid is this comment for today's Canadian industries?

2. Protesters of WTO summits and FTAA organizational meetings argue that international trade can cause serious hardship, such as poverty, for developing countries. Prepare a response that considers both sides of the question.

3. Working in a small group, brainstorm the differences between British and Canadian trade interdependence in the eighteenth century and today. Then, still working as a group, discuss the reasons for the changes that have taken place.

Communication

1. Prepare a poster, multimedia slide show, or other visual presentation that demonstrates the significance of one of the following for the development of international trade in Canada: the fur trade, an early European explorer, Aboriginal traders, a Canadian primary industry, trade barriers.

2. Select a business in your community that imports, exports, or does both. Arrange an appointment to interview by phone or in person a spokesperson for this business. Be sure to inform the person that you will not take up any more than fifteen minutes of his or her time, and that you will be discussing the role of exporting and/or importing in this business. Your task is to discover the importance of trade to this business. The person being interviewed will appreciate that you are asking informed and intelligent questions.

3. Debate this statement: Canada should trade with Cuba. Use information from this chapter to support your argument.

Application

1. Prepare a large mind map or concept web to show how international trade has changed Canada economically and socially from its earliest days up to the present.

2. Using a format similar to the one used for the Snapshot of Cuba in the Canada's Trading Partner feature on page 37, develop a snapshot of a country to which you would be interested in exporting Canadian products or from which you would be interested in importing products.

3. For each of the following countries, research the main trade barrier that a Canadian business would face when dealing with that country: South Korea, Namibia, Paraguay, Myanmar, Belarus. Create a chart to show the specific trade barrier for each country and to explain the reasons for the barrier.

Doing Business with a Foreign Country: The International Business (IB) Portfolio

At the end of this course, you will apply your learning by creating an international trade manual. Your manual, which also acts as a summative assessment activity, will provide information for businesses that are considering a trade relationship in another country (an international business partner, or IBP). Near the end of the course, you will present your information either during a teacher-student interview, or to your class. In your presentation, you will educate your teacher or fellow students, who are acting as potential exporters or importers, about the opportunities and risks associated with doing business in your trading partner country. The method of presentation will be up to you.

As you work through this text, you will research your chosen country extensively to gather information about its economy, culture, government, history, and geography. In each chapter, you will work on an activity that focuses on one aspect of your country. Gather each completed assignment in a portfolio to use at the end of the course when you create your manual. The following sources of information will be useful for compiling your portfolio.

Use reference books such as encyclopedias, almanacs, and atlases to gather summary data about your IBP country.

- Embassies and consulates both in Canada and in your IBP country, chambers of commerce, tourist boards, and economic development centres are particularly valuable sources of information.
- Current newspaper articles from the news, business, and travel sections address the current business climate as well as cultural and political factors in Canada and your IBP country. Magazines may also provide in-depth information about specific countries, companies, or industries.

- Numerous Web sites provide both summary and detailed information. Country profiles and background information are available from government Web sites. Industry Canada, the Department of Foreign Affairs and International Trade, and the Forum for International Trade are only some of the Web sites that provide detailed information about companies, markets, and trends at home and abroad. Access these links from the Nelson Web site at **http://www.internationalbusiness.nelson.com**. An Internet search tip: using the phrase Doing business in (name of your country) at a search engine such as Google will also generate a wealth of information. Quotation marks around "Doing business in" will give you links that contain that entire phrase.
- Brochures, posters, catalogues, postcards, videos, or even Microsoft PowerPoint presentations from companies, airlines, travel bureaus, government agencies, and other organizations involved in international business can be valuable.
- Last but not least, talk to people. Interview individuals who have lived in, travelled to, or worked in your country of choice. Talk to business people currently involved in trade with your IBP country. Take special note of careers that interest you.

Activities

1. Select a country to research throughout this course keeping these points in mind:
   - The country must already be a trading partner with Canada.
   - The country must not be one of the 12 trading partners described in the text.
2. Determine how you will store your portfolio documents. Binders or expansion files are two possibilities. Locate your storage container and label it.
3. Write letters or e-mails to all relevant sources asking for information about your IBP country as early as possible.
4. Write one or two paragraphs describing the history of Canada's trade relations with your IBP country.

Chapter 2

The Importance of International Business

Engaging in international business allows companies to expand their search of new markets or products. Importers engage in international business to supply customers with goods and services that may not be available in their own country; exporters, to expand the reach of their business and gain sales volume; and manufacturers, to find the most economical way of producing their goods. Today, more and more Canadian students are acquiring the knowledge and skills required to succeed in international business.

Chapter Topics

➤ 2.1 – Aspects of International Business 42

➤ 2.2 – Why Do Companies Expand Internationally? 50

➤ 2.3 – Reasons for Recent Growth in International Business 54

➤ 2.4 – Advantages of Doing Business in Canada 59

➤ 2.5 – Preparing for the International Workplace 66

➤ *Canada's Trading Partners: Focus on the* United States of America 72

➤ Chapter Challenges 74

Prior Knowledge

- Which of the Canadian businesses that you deal with have an international trade link?
- Why would a Canadian business want to expand into international markets?
- Why would international businesses want to trade with, or invest in, Canadian businesses?
- What strategies could you use to prepare to work in international business?

Inquiries/Expectations

- How have Canadian companies and industries benefited from increasing global business activity in the past few decades?
- What are some of the factors that motivate companies to engage in international business?
- What proportion of Canada's gross domestic product and jobs are directly affected by its international business activity?
- What kinds of skills and competencies are required for employment in international business?
- How can the education and training opportunities that are available in other countries help students prepare for international careers?

Important Terms

business climate
export
foreign direct investment (FDI)
goods
import
international business
Organisation for Economic Cooperation and Development (OECD)

outsourcing
portfolio investment
private-sector investment
products
public-sector investment
raw materials
services

2.1 Aspects of International Business

International business is all the business activities needed by producers to create, ship, and sell goods and services to consumers. International business involves international trade, the importing and exporting of goods and services, licensing the use of assets in other countries, and foreign investment.

International Trade

The fundamental premise of all business, even in the new information age, is trade. And international trade is the basis of international business. International trade involves companies in one country fulfilling the needs and wants of another country by selling products to companies, organizations, or governments in that country (**exporting**). It also involves companies bringing in products and services to satisfy the needs and wants of their own consumers (**importing**). In other words, exporting is the process of enabling products grown or made domestically to travel to a foreign country, thereby broadening the market of the exporter and perhaps even creating a demand for products. Importing is the process of enabling goods to enter the domestic market.

Market opportunities not only exist in those countries and industries already developed by free market economies, but perhaps are even greater in countries that are just beginning to explore and establish free markets.

– *Entrepreneur* Magazine

The **products** that are imported or exported can be either goods or services. **Goods** consist of **raw materials** (natural materials that have not been processed, such as lumber, fish, and minerals), semi-manufactured goods (goods that have been partially manufactured, such as automotive parts or electronic components), or manufactured goods (merchandise such as cameras, clothes, or toys). **Services** are activities that individuals, groups, organizations, or companies perform to advise or assist other individuals, organizations, or companies. Governments, banks, insurance firms, telecommunications companies, consultants, tour operators, medical professionals, transport companies, water and electricity suppliers, translators, housekeepers, and dry cleaners all offer services of one kind or another.

Companies must carefully select the product they choose to import or export. For example, if imported grapevines are discovered to have earth on them, the vines can be rejected and returned. If it happens that an agricultural product is quarantined because of a virus, then it will be burned. Manufactured goods must meet the standards of the country to which they are shipped. For example, cars must follow the pollution guidelines of the host country. If a country has an outbreak of foot and mouth disease, then all countries dealing with it must strictly follow its safety measures. It is also essential to be aware of the taxes in the recipient country. If wine is shipped from Canada to Germany in a container ship, for example, the purchaser would have to pay the German taxes.

Importing

Canadian companies import products for various reasons. Canada may need products that are only available, or can be obtained more conveniently and economically, from foreign sources; Canada may import products that other countries specialize in or products that are of a better quality than those that can be purchased here. For example, Canada imports hand-crafted carpets from the Middle East (a particular specialty of that area) to make them available to Canadian consumers.

When a company wants to import a product, it needs to be sure that there is a demand for the product in Canada. No importer can be successful if the goods remain in a warehouse because no one wants to buy them. Next, the importer needs to contact foreign suppliers. Sometimes finding a supplier who can supply products when you want them can be a challenge. Once a supplier has been found, the purchase needs to be finalized. For example, the importing and exporting companies need to agree on who will pay for shipping, when the items will be delivered, and how payment will be made. Then, finally, the importer needs to check the order when it arrives to be sure that everything is included and that there is no damage.

When importing goods, it is also important for a company to know exactly what it can sell in Canada. If a company does insufficient research and the merchandise it imports is not of the quality expected in the Canadian market, importers may be saddled with the cost of the unsaleable merchandise. Researching specifications on equipment or visiting the factory will enable the purchaser to ask questions about the product to see whether it meets Canadian needs.

Canada's Exports and Imports, 1997 to 2001 ($ billions)

	Exports of Goods and Services					Imports of Goods and Services				
	1997	1998	1999	2000	2001	1997	1998	1999	2000	2001
World	347.1	375.5	417.0	477.9	467.6	330.3	359.3	385.0	425.3	412.9
United States	267.4	297.9	340.0	391.2	382.6	244.3	268.4	285.3	305.9	293.1
EU	25.0	27.1	28.0	31.7	30.9	32.8	34.8	38.0	43.7	45.4
Japan	13.5	11.0	11.0	11.9	10.8	9.9	11.0	12.4	13.6	12.5
ROW*	41.1	39.5	37.9	43.0	43.2	43.3	45.2	49.3	62.0	61.8
	Exports of Goods					Imports of Goods				
	1997	1998	1999	2000	2001	1997	1998	1999	2000	2001
World	303.4	326.2	365.2	422.6	412.5	277.7	303.4	326.8	363.3	351.0
United States	242.5	269.3	309.2	359.6	350.8	211.5	233.8	249.3	267.7	255.5
EU	17.9	19.0	19.3	22.1	21.8	24.2	25.2	28.4	33.4	35.1
Japan	11.9	9.6	9.6	10.3	9.3	8.7	9.7	10.6	11.7	10.6
ROW	31.0	28.2	27.2	30.6	30.6	33.3	34.7	38.5	50.5	49.9
	Exports of Services					Imports of Services				
	1997	1998	1999	2000	2001	1997	1998	1999	2000	2001
World	43.8	49.4	51.7	55.3	55.1	52.6	56.0	58.2	62.0	61.9
United States	24.9	28.5	30.8	31.7	31.8	32.9	34.6	36.0	38.3	37.7
EU	7.1	8.1	8.7	9.6	9.2	8.6	9.6	9.6	10.3	10.3
Japan	1.6	1.4	1.5	1.6	1.5	1.2	1.3	1.8	1.9	1.9
ROW	10.2	11.3	10.7	12.4	12.6	10.0	10.5	10.8	11.6	12.0

Figure 2.1 Statistics Canada tracks Canadian imports and exports of goods and services. What has been the trend in exports and imports since 1997? Why do you think Canada's imports and exports decreased during 2001?
* ROW: Rest of World
– *Statistics Canada*

Exporting

When a company exports its goods or services to another country, it must go through an exporting process. The exporter needs to find potential business or individual customers, meet the needs of those customers, agree on sales terms with the buyer, provide the products or services to that buyer, and complete the transaction. The exporter must also be prepared to overcome challenges such as establishing a company presence in the country to which it wants to export, developing sufficient production capacity to manufacture goods for export, coping with the high costs of doing business in other countries, and understanding the way that business is done in the target country.

Once a product has been sold for export, it is packed for shipping according to weight and volume. The faster a product is shipped, the more it costs. For example, if a farmer is shipping produce or perishable materials, then more care—and cost— will be required. Shipments to and from Canada are usually made in containers, which come in different lengths with prices ranging according to size.

Although many companies across Canada have found that exporting can play a key role in their growth and prosperity, exporters in Ontario account for almost half of the export revenue of Canada as a whole. And a few large manufacturing companies generate most of this revenue. The primary exports from Ontario are (in order): automotive products, machinery and equipment, industrial goods, forestry products, agricultural and fishing products, and consumer goods. According to Statistics Canada, in 2001, the United States was Ontario's largest export market at approximately 93 percent, with Europe (3.3 percent), Asia (1.6 percent), Latin America (0.6 percent), and Africa and the Middle East (0.4 percent) making up the balance.

Figure 2.2 In 2002, kick scooters were a big fad. The scooters were exported by J.D. Corporation in Taiwan and distributed to Canadian retail stores through the company's authorized distributors in this country.

GLOBAL THOUGHT

In Canada in 2001, there were 1300 companies that each exported more than $25 million worth of goods annually. They comprised a mere 4 percent of all exporters, but they accounted for more than 81 percent of Canada's exports in that year. By contrast, there were 21 000 companies that each exported less than $1 million worth of goods. These companies comprised 68 percent of all exporters, but they accounted for less than 2 percent of all exports.

– Bruce Little

Starting an Import or Export Business

The question, "When is a company ready to trade internationally?" is a major one for a company. It can be answered only after a company has investigated its management commitment, its competitive advantage, its cash flow, and its capacity to produce products that will sell in the target market. If management decides to commit to international expansion, it must be willing and able to provide strong financial and personnel support.

Just as with developing, marketing, and servicing in the domestic market, experience in marketing and servicing a product intended for export will be useful in creating a business plan for international involvement. When a company decides to import or export, it must create a viable plan. An investment of time and money is essential for success, and companies must choose their markets carefully. The planning will include gathering information and arranging for any necessary assistance. An understanding of the company's strengths and competitive advantage will focus its international strategy. The more markets a company enters, the more direct the company's involvement in those markets, and the more aggressive its expansion plan, the greater the cash flow it will need to support its strategies. Large, medium, and small businesses can all seize opportunities to trade internationally.

Web Link

Follow the link at www.internationalbusiness.nelson.com to get current information on Canadian imports and exports.

Trade Missions

Outgoing trade missions are visits by selected Canadian firms to a target foreign market. Incoming trade missions are visits to Canada by foreign buyers and investors, which are designed to increase the visitor's knowledge of Canada as a potential source of supply and a place to invest or arrange a joint venture. Trade missions are useful for several reasons. Mission organizers are usually familiar with the target market, and can help put a company interested in exporting in touch with officials of the target countries. They can also help participants gather useful information and insights from the other delegates. Mission organizers handle many of the logistical details associated with the trip, leaving participants free to concentrate on their business.

Team Canada is a government-sponsored trade mission that promotes Canada as a good place to do business. It is led by the Canadian prime minister who is joined by other federal ministers, provincial premiers, and territorial government leaders as well as representatives from government agencies and from Canadian businesses that are interested in importing or exporting goods or services. For example, in 2002, Export Development Canada (EDC) participated in the trade mission to Russia and Germany to build relationships and to provide advice to Canadian companies interested in these markets. A primary purpose of the mission for EDC was to enable the agency to maintain important contacts with the Russian government and with key Russian banks and industries on behalf of Canadian businesses.

TRADE TALK

Export Development Canada is a Canadian financial institution that is devoted exclusively to providing trade finance services to support Canadian exporters and investors in 200 markets, 130 of which are in developing markets.

Figure 2.3 Prime Minister Chrétien, the provincial premiers, and the territorial leaders in Moscow's Red Square during a 2002 Team Canada Inc trade mission to Russia.

Team Canada has helped over 2800 Canadian business people generate over $30 billion in new business through its missions to China (1994), India, Pakistan, Indonesia, and Malaysia (1996), South Korea, the Philippines, and Thailand (1999), Beijing, Shanghai, and Hong Kong (2001), and Russia and Germany (2002).

Trade Shows

Trade shows and trade fairs allow a potential purchaser to communicate with suppliers. Such fairs can provide potential or newly established exporters with an opportunity to promote their products and services, identify potential sales opportunities, develop valuable business contacts, and locate agents and distributors.

Trade shows often focus on one industry. For example, Canadian Trade Ex of Vancouver arranges trade shows for the forestry, mining, construction and industrial supply communities of Canada. The Saskatchewan Trade and Export Partnership arranges the Canadian Western Agribition, which is one of the largest livestock shows in the world, with nearly 2000 exhibitors, 15 different commercial beef cattle breeds, horses, bison, elk, llama, swine, dairy, sheep, and poultry competitions as well as displays of specialized livestock. The Packaging Association of Canada manages the annual PACex International exhibition of packaging and food processing machinery, equipment, services, and products.

Companies can find out about trade shows through the Internet, trade publication advertisements, and suppliers. Canadian companies attending trade shows should be aware that when they take product samples (Canadian farm equipment, for example) to foreign trade shows, they must declare to customs officials in that country the purpose of bringing in the sample. Documentation is then issued as proof that the equipment is Canadian so that the exhibitor-company will be allowed to bring the equipment back to Canada. Companies can call customs officials to find out whether certain goods may be taken into that country, what they can expect to pay, and what documentation or taxes would be required for entry of the goods.

Exporting Goods and Services

More companies are involved in importing and exporting goods than in other types of international business. These companies sell in foreign markets goods made in Canada or import into Canada goods made in other countries. Canadian companies export such goods as lumber, textiles, clothing, furs, aircraft, trains, minerals, and chemicals. As shown in Figure 1.20 on page 23, Canadian companies import a wide range of products including machinery, vehicles, and electronic components.

Canada is also becoming more and more active in exporting services. According to the Canadian government's 2002 *Third Annual Report on Canada's State of Trade*, the value of Canada's export in services has grown from $87.6 billion in 1997 to $110.2 billion in 2001. In buying services, the purchaser pays for the knowledge, creativity, or manual work of the provider. With today's facilities in electronic communications, Canadian companies can perform business functions for foreign firms without leaving Canada. For example, call centres across Canada (especially in New Brunswick and Ontario) take customer service calls on behalf of

International Business Career Profile

Canadian Government Trade Commissioner and International Business Educator

The most important aspects of international business, says Ray Guy, are personal relationship-building and cultural understanding. In his 30 years as a Canadian Government trade commissioner, he was posted to Canada's embassies and high commissions in such diverse countries as Pakistan, Hungary, the United Arab Emirates, Hong Kong, and the United States. He promoted exports of Canadian products and services, helped Canadian companies establish joint ventures, and encouraged direct foreign investment in Canada.

Guy recalls some of his career highlights. In Abu Dhabi, a personal relationship with the University of El Ain's chancellor led to Canadian universities helping develop a medical faculty at the university. With the help of EduCansult, Guy organized a medical seminar, bringing Canadian deans of medicine over to speak. Beating out competition from the United States, Britain, and Egypt, EduCansult then developed the curriculum and staffed the college.

Other memorable projects? Helping firms like RCA Canada win a contract to build an earth satellite station in Pakistan; introducing Bombardier LRC passenger trains to California; and redirecting major EduCansult business to Dubai.

In Guy's last assignment as senior trade commissioner in Detroit (through which 40 percent of Canada's exports travel), he helped introduce Canadian SMEs (small- and medium-sized enterprises) to the U.S. auto industry and directed "New Exporters to Border States," a practical introductory program for companies. He also worked with key U.S. Customs and Immigration officials to ensure smooth traffic flow across the Canada–U.S. border.

Now Guy teaches graduate courses in international business management at Niagara College, using a curriculum planned by the Forum for International Trade Training (FITT), which can lead ultimately to the prestigious designation Certified International Trade Professional (CITP). Recently, Guy received the Award of Excellence for this post-graduate program from the North American Small Business International Trade Educators (NASBITE).

With the college's International Division, Guy is gearing up to deliver the post-secondary program at the Shanghai Commercial School in China. Under his leadership, Niagara College has introduced an internship program for third-year students to work with companies involved in international business, in order to apply their learned skills in logistics, finance, importing and exporting, and international marketing and market research.

Guy points out that even though the United States is often treated as one market, there are many diverse markets within the country; contrast the north and south, or the eastern and western states. "Trading in Europe requires particular attention to languages and culture. In parts of Asia, packaging quality is essential because gift-giving is an important part of the culture. In Canada and the United States, business is focused on quality, price, delivery, and a speedy decision. In Asia, Latin America, and the Middle East, time is required to nurture personal relationships to develop trust before success can be achieved."

Why do Canadian companies enter international business? Guy feels it's because they find the challenge motivating and exciting, and success a greater thrill and enjoyment.

1. What does Ray Guy consider the essential ingredients in successful international business? Give an example of each ingredient.

2. Guy worked with officials at U.S. Customs and Immigration to ensure that Canada–U.S. border crossings were smooth. What strategies might Guy have suggested?

American corporations. And Canadian companies can import such services from companies in other countries. The export service is not restricted to the private sector. When a Japanese student takes a distance education course at Athabasca University in Alberta, for example, the university is exporting a public service.

Many businesses that operate in the international marketplace are a blend of the two main types of business; they sell both goods and services. For example, Cirque du Soleil, a Quebec-based company that has revolutionized the circus arts, was begun in 1984 by stilt-walker and fire-eater Guy Laliberté. The company's international headquarters and production centre are in Montreal, but it has offices in Amsterdam, Singapore, and Las Vegas. From its beginnings in street theatre and circus tents, Cirque du Soleil has grown into a company that performs all over North America, in Europe, and in Asia. It has eight different shows playing simultaneously on three continents. In 2001, it started New Ventures, a business unit with ambitious plans to take the company into a broader range of entertainment-related business activities: entertainment complexes in major world cities, interactive museums, "surreal" nightclubs, and interactive hotels, for example. Cirque's shows and entertainment are not goods, but can be considered performance services that it exports.

Figure 2.4 Cirque du Soleil exports its entertainment services around the world.

However, Cirque du Soleil has already ventured into other fields associated with its theatrical and circus arts shows—the sales of goods such as DVDs, videos and soundtracks, and souvenirs. Many souvenirs are manufactured for Cirque du Soleil in countries such as China and Taiwan and are exported to Canada, Europe, or the United States. Cirque du Soleil thereby becomes the importer of that merchandise. Through such involvement in the import and export of goods, Cirque du Soleil is clearly more than an entertainment or service business.

Foreign Investments

International business involves foreign investments as well as importing and exporting. These investments may be in partnership with other international institutions or companies, either in the public or the private sector. **Public-sector investments** involve putting money in state- or government-owned assets—for example, part-ownership of state-owned oil and gas entities or of telecommunication companies around the world. **Private-sector investments** can be held in a variety of publicly held companies (those with shares traded on a stock exchange) or privately owned companies, or through the creation of new companies of either type.

Foreign investments fall into two categories: **foreign direct investments (FDIs)** and **portfolio investments**. Foreign direct investment usually occurs when a company in one country wishes to expand into another country. This can be done through either establishing a subsidiary operation or setting up a joint venture. A Canadian company may wish to purchase a controlling interest in a foreign company to influence its direction or management. It may wish to invest in a company in another country to obtain further information, to decide whether to seek patents or possibly to purchase all or part of the company, to ensure a source of supply, or to acquire new technologies.

An international company can invest directly in land or property (in countries where foreign ownership is permitted), contribute to the construction of offices or manufacturing plants, or finance the development of a research facility, large infrastructures, or projects, such as airports, public transport, transportation systems, dams, industrial kilns, mines, or telephone and electricity systems.

The Walt Disney Company's building of Disneyland Paris is an example of direct foreign investment in the entertainment industry. EuroDisney, a publicly held French company in which the American Walt Disney Company holds a controlling share, manages Disneyland Paris. The Walt Disney Company, the parent company, benefits directly from the success of EuroDisney; it earns royalties on the revenues of the Paris theme park, and receives management fees from EuroDisney. Similarly, some of Cirque du Soleil's new financial partners have invested in building special facilities for the Cirque's shows. "Creativity is worth as much as money," says Guy Laliberté, "so if [an investor provides] the money, we'll bring the creativity and that should provide a perfect, balanced partnership."

In a portfolio investment, an investor buys a share of a foreign company but has no controlling interest and little say in how the company is run; the investor (a company or person(s)) simply wants to earn a share of the foreign company's profit. The investor may also buy bonds to obtain interest income or non-voting shares to get dividend income from the foreign firm. Canadian banks or other financial institutions may lend money to foreign companies. Portfolio investments are usually less risky than direct investments.

ICE Activities for 2.1

Ideas	Connections	Extensions
1. (a) Explain the terms "import" and "export."	(b) Give examples of the following: a goods import, a goods export, a service import, and a service export.	(c) Why is exporting an attractive option for both large and small businesses? Explain how the challenges in exporting might differ for a small and a large business.
2. (a) What is a trade mission? Explain how trade missions help Canadian businesses.	(b) Research a recent Team Canada trade mission and explain the purpose of that mission.	(c) Working in a small group, select a product you would like to export. Brainstorm why you might join a trade mission to that country and how some of the contacts you make would help you succeed in your export venture.
3. (a) Explain the differences between goods and services.	(b) Create a comparison chart showing the different challenges faced by a Canadian exporter of goods and an exporter of services.	(c) In your opinion, is the export of goods or of services more likely to benefit the Canadian economy?

2.2 Why Do Companies Expand Internationally?

Companies participate in international business for many reasons. They engage in international business to increase sales, to obtain resources or needed materials and goods, and to expand the territory for their sales and sources of supply. Many companies begin trading internationally as a way of expanding their markets and increasing profits after they have established themselves domestically.

Expanded Markets and Increased Sales

The combination of expanded markets and increased sales allows a company to increase its profits. Any business, whether it is a small operation or a large international corporation, has to make a profit. A successful business makes money; an unsuccessful business does not. While moving into international markets increases the risk factor, it can also increase the likelihood that businesses will make more sales and profits. For some companies, the increase in profit means that they can sponsor, and make donations to, causes that they believe in. For socially responsible international businesses, increased sales can mean a positive impact on the international community.

Figure 2.5 Sir Elton John performing at a special charity performance in December 2002 in London, England. The concert was held to benefit the Elton John AIDS Foundation and was presented by M·A·C Cosmetics and the M·A·C AIDS Fund.

M·A·C Cosmetics and Estée Lauder Companies Inc. are two businesses that have increased their sales and broadened their markets by establishing themselves internationally. Both companies originated as small local businesses in their own countries. Both companies were started by entrepreneurs who saw a market for their products and who were willing to take the risk of starting a business to satisfy consumer needs and wants in that market.

M·A·C (Makeup Art Cosmetics) was founded in Toronto in 1984 by makeup artist Frank Toskan and his business partner, Frank Angelo. Four years later, M·A·C expanded into an international market when the company opened its first American outlet in New York City, a theatre and fashion centre where it would have a definite market. Today, M·A·C's international locations include New York, Los Angeles, Paris, Sydney, the Philippines, and the United Arab Emirates. Through the years since the company started, M·A·C cosmetics have been worn by many internationally known actors, models, and singers, such as Madonna, k.d. lang, and Neve Campbell.

M·A·C's success has allowed the company to fulfill its goal of becoming a socially responsible international business. In October of 2002, the United Nations Development Programme (UNDP) presented a Special Recognition Award to John Demsey, the President of M·A·C Cosmetics, and to the M·A·C AIDS Fund for its "tremendous efforts in the fight against HIV / AIDS." According to UNDP, when M·A·C introduced its first VIVA Glam lipstick in

1994, the company "decided that every cent of the selling price of the [product] would go to fund the M·A·C AIDS Fund." As of date of the award, the company, "its employees, its retail partners, and its customers together [had] provided over $20 million USD. . . for the M·A·C AIDS Fund."

Some companies expand their markets and increase their sales by acquiring other companies. In 1994, Estée Lauder Companies Inc. acquired a 51 percent interest in M·A·C Cosmetics; in 1998 it bought the balance of the company. In her *Time* magazine article "Beauty Queen Estée Lauder," Grace Mirabella says that in 2000 Estée Lauder Companies Inc. controlled 45 percent of the cosmetics market in U.S. department stores, sold its products in 118 countries, and had $3.6 billion USD in sales. However, while Estée Lauder had clearly become successful internationally, it had not been known as a trend-setter. Through the acquisition of new, trendier companies such as M·A·C, Bobbi Brown Essentials, and Tommy Hilfiger fragrances, Estée Lauder Companies Inc. has moved into wider markets. As Mirabella (who was editor-in-chief of *Vogue* magazine for 17 years) says, "Lauder's company may not be able to set trends, but it is never going to be left behind by them."

Web Link

Follow the link at www.internationalbusiness.nelson.com to find out more about M·A·C Cosmetics and Estée Lauder companies.

Controlling Expenses

Controlling expenses is at the heart of every business decision, and companies often enter the global arena to minimize their costs. They examine carefully the resources they need—products, services, human resources, parts, components, capital, technologies, and information—to assess whether they are making the best buying decisions and whether less expensive sources are available. By searching beyond their own borders, companies hope to find more economical solutions to the production and manufacturing challenges they face. They may choose to take advantage of the lower labour costs in other countries, move manufacturing plants closer to natural resources, invest in new, more efficient technology, or profit from another country's innovations or tax structures.

For example, to reduce expenses in human resources and services, a company might hire computer programmers in Lithuania; they earn the equivalent of $340 per month and live an above-middle class lifestyle. To reduce expenses VR1, a video game company headquartered in Boulder, Colorado, and owned by a Japanese company, has producers and artists in Toronto and programmers in Russia. Its patented technologies and game designs are published around the world. **Outsourcing** (obtaining something by contracting it from another source) of human resources internationally often produces needed work less expensively. India's large 40-million workforce is a cost-effective contender, and some international companies outsource their computer programming and some labour-intensive manufacturing there.

GLOBAL THOUGHT

True support of human rights would not allow Western corporations to exploit cheap labour in developing nations or spur civil conflict for economic gain.

– *Warren Allmand*, President, Centre for Human Rights and Democratic Development

Diversification

A small national company or a large international company may choose to enter specific international markets in order to diversify its product line. Within the field of cosmetics, for example, Estée Lauder Companies has acquired companies with widely diverse market specialties. Each of its companies meets the cosmetic needs of different target markets: both genders; different skin types and colours; teenagers and older people seeking anti-aging skin care; actors, entertainers, and models; people living with diseases that disfigure their skin; and the trendy and the traditional in major cities all over the world.

In another form of diversification, companies have a foothold in a number of countries so that they do not depend entirely on the economy of any one country. Even though, as globalization spreads, certain trends seem to have a ripple effect in all countries, companies engaged in international business can protect their investments and their markets by dealing with companies in a variety of countries. A recession in one country will have a limited effect on sales or profits if other countries are doing well economically.

Competitiveness

Many companies expand globally for defensive reasons—to protect themselves from competitors or potential competitors, or to gain advantage over them. As global companies profit from less expensive sourcing and labour in foreign locations, they can sometimes undercut smaller local businesses.

In today's business environment, even a local small business with no aspirations beyond its domestic borders is competing with international businesses. Community hardware stores, for example, may have to face competition from huge international superstores such as Home Depot. Or a neighbourhood, locally owned video store may face competition from a larger international company such as Blockbuster Video, whose aim is to be "the global leader in rentable home entertainment by providing outstanding service, selection, convenience, and value." A local store may have a more limited selection because of its small size, but it may also be able to offer more personal service, a more specialized stock, or even lower prices. On the other hand, local stores may find it difficult to compete with the selection and price that multinational companies can offer, and, if their businesses are too threatened, they may find it expedient to seek wider markets or merge with a larger, possibly international, company.

Figure 2.6 The first Blockbuster store opened in 1985. Today, there are 52 million member accounts in North America, as well as several million accounts worldwide.

ICE Activities for 2.2

Ideas	Connections	Extensions
1. (a) List reasons why companies participate in international business transactions.	(b) Find an example of a domestic business that has faced competition from an international company. What effect have the two businesses had on each other?	(c) What do you think would be the outcome of continued competition between international and domestic companies? Explain your answer.
2. (a) Why was Estée Lauder Companies interested in acquiring M·A·C Cosmetics?	(b) Present an example of an acquisition and explain why the acquisition occurred.	(c) M·A·C Cosmetics is described as having a social conscience. Research other projects that M·A·C supports. Find ways in which other companies in your community demonstrate a social conscience. Do international companies have a responsibility to be socially conscious? Do customers have a corresponding responsibility to make socially conscious purchasing decisions? Explain your answers.
3. (a) List three possible ways that companies can save costs by operating in other countries.	(b) What are some of the potential effects of the cost-saving strategies in 3. (a)?	(c) A North American international company may reduce its labour costs by hiring workers in other countries. What are the implications of this move for workers in those countries? For workers in North America?

2.3 Reasons for Recent Growth in International Business

International business has grown rapidly because of recent developments in communications technology and transportation, increased business confidence, freer borders, and increased global competition.

Developments in Communication Technology

Increasing use of communications technology such as e-mail, conference calls, and videoconferencing is one of the main reasons international business has grown so rapidly in recent years. Businesses that keep up with the latest in innovative communications will maximize their opportunities. Estée Lauder, for example, now uses the Internet to offer personalized communication with its customers.

Customers visit a company's Web site because they are interested in that company's brand(s). The company in question can then build a database from these Web site visits and use it to market its products to those customers in a way that is most convenient for them. For example, Estée Lauder can let Clinique customers know about such things as lectures on dermatology in their area, offer them free samples to introduce them to a new product, or even remind them of their partner's upcoming birthday with some gift suggestions.

Follow the link at www.internationalbusiness.nelson.com to find out about recent developments in communication technology.

Figure 2.7 Estée Lauder launched her company in 1946.

Technology makes business communication easier, but it does have its limitations. Although business may be transacted 24 hours a day, employees and business travellers need to know the time zones for different countries when conducting business.

THINK ABOUT IT

If it is 2:00 P.M. in Paris, what is the time in Tobermory, Ontario?

For example, if you want to have a conference call with people in international offices, you should try to schedule it within business hours for each person who will take part in the call. If you send a fax or e-mail from Montreal at nine in the morning, the recipient in Hong Kong will likely not see it for at least another ten hours; however, it's still more efficient than scheduling phone calls outside of work hours, which is often the only way to reach someone in person on the other side of the world.

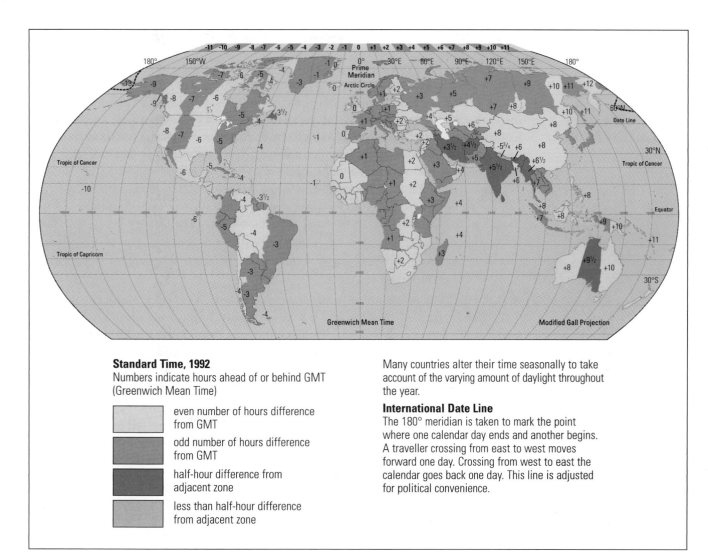

Standard Time, 1992
Numbers indicate hours ahead of or behind GMT
(Greenwich Mean Time)

even number of hours difference
from GMT

odd number of hours difference
from GMT

half-hour difference from
adjacent zone

less than half-hour difference
from adjacent zone

Many countries alter their time seasonally to take
account of the varying amount of daylight throughout
the year.

International Date Line
The 180° meridian is taken to mark the point
where one calendar day ends and another begins.
A traveller crossing from east to west moves
forward one day. Crossing from west to east the
calendar goes back one day. This line is adjusted
for political convenience.

Figure 2.8 Time zones of the world.

Time Zones

There are 24 time zones in the world. As seen on the map above, time is measured
in hours ahead of or behind the time in Greenwich, England. The International
Date Line marks the dividing point between days.

Before the introduction of the time zones, railway schedules were very
confusing, because at every stop there was a different local time. It was Canadian
Sir Sandford Fleming, the "Father of Standard Time," who, in 1878, recommended
the brilliant solution of creating "standard time" in each area and dividing the
world into standard time zones 15 degrees longitude apart, thereby solving
a worldwide problem.

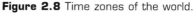

To find out more about time zones
in different countries visit the link at
www.internationalbusiness.nelson.com

Developments in Transportation

Faster means of transport have greatly increased international trade. Goods can now be carried around the world by airplane within a day. Crossing the Atlantic Ocean took three weeks by clipper ship in the 1800s; ten days by steamship by the early twentieth century; 24 hours by seaplane in the 1930s; and 3.5 hours by Concorde jet in the 1980s. In addition, the availability of perishable goods such as meat, fresh produce, and cut flowers has been greatly increased by the use of refrigerated trucks and refrigerated containers to go on ships, trains, and trucks.

Canada's transportation system includes five modes of transport: ship, rail, airplane, truck, and pipeline. For more information about how these modes affect Canadian imports and exports, see Chapter 12.

- Shipping by sea (or lake) is used for national and international deliveries. Maritime transport of bulk cargo and container shipping accounts for 80 percent by volume of total world trade.

- Rail is widely used within Canada, and also between Canada and the United States and Mexico. The Canadian rail system is one of the world's most efficient transportation systems, with penetration into the United States, intermodal facilities, and reduced transit times within the rail system.

Figure 2.9 Sea (or lake) and air are just two of Canada's modes of transport.

- Truck, tractor-trailer, and bus transportation are heavily used on the extensive highway systems throughout North America, with a huge amount of cross-border traffic. Truck trailers often move by rail for long distances, and loading and unloading intermodal facilities are increasing.

- Air is also used for national and international deliveries, mainly for business papers, rush parts and supplies, and small and light or valuable goods. Air cargo is gradually becoming more viable. Hamilton Ontario's International Airport is a busy cargo airport, and in early 2002, Mirabel International Airport just outside Montreal was dedicated entirely to air cargo planes.

- Pipelines across Canada and into the United States are a cost-effective way to transport natural gas and crude oil over great distances to Canadian and international markets.

Freer Borders

Business transactions across international borders have recently become smoother. Countries that have few barriers to moving goods, services, and resources across their borders become attractive to businesses in other countries. The lowering of customs duties and the reduction of other trade barriers can be negotiated through trade agreements among countries and groups of countries.

In 1995, the World Trade Organization (WTO) was formed to reduce restrictions to international trade. With almost 150 members today, the WTO facilitates agreements that have been negotiated and signed by many of the world's trading nations and ratified by their respective governments. The goal is to help producers of goods and services, exporters, and importers conduct their business internationally. The WTO also helps in the following areas: trade negotiations, trade disputes, monitoring of national trade policies, technical assistance and training for developing countries, and cooperation with other international organizations.

Business Confidence

International trade has become less risky, less costly, and less time-consuming. National and international institutions such as banks, postal services, and insurance companies, for example, have agreements that provide for better credit services, currency conversion arrangements, and insurance against damage and nonpayment. With reduction in business risk, companies can feel confident in searching worldwide for new ideas, products, manufacturing processes, and intellectual property to import them to the home country or to establish a presence in the other country.

Thanks to the increasing security of the Internet, wireless communication is easier and safer. Large courier companies that operate worldwide now also make deliveries predictable and timely. The ability to plan confidently allows companies to operate more efficiently, and more reliably.

Global Competition

Global competition has been increasing steadily because new products are being introduced quickly, and often successfully, around the world. If a company sets up a business in another country or begins to export to another country, it may be introducing a manufactured product or a service that is a novelty in that country, or improving on what is already available there. If that new item or service becomes a success, domestic competitors already established in a country, or other foreign companies, may want to capitalize on the new market. Domestic and international competition in the new product may heighten.

When Disneyland Paris opened in 1992 with an unprecedented investment of $3.5 billion, for example, it was the first trans-European theme park. It relied on attendance from the whole of Europe to succeed. In spite of some economic difficulties, Disneyland inspired other multinational entertainment companies to enter the European theme park market: Universal Studios opened a park in Spain; Warner Brothers in Germany; and LEGO in Denmark, the UK, the United States, and Germany. European theme-park attendance is now booming, and LEGO, which began the first small-scale Legoland in Denmark in 1968, has announced plans to open another 15 foreign theme parks by 2050. Disney is still the largest theme park operator in the world, but it now has many strong international competitors.

TRADE TALK

Toronto-based Forrec Ltd. is a world leader in theme park design. It has worked on 48 theme park, water park, entertainment centre, resort and casino projects (including Paramount Canada's Wonderland) in 20 countries on 5 continents during the past 30 years. Legoland Deutschland (2002) was the first for which they were fully responsible.

Forrec coordinated everything from concept, master plan, landscape architecture, designing rides, including the work of consultants in several countries, and Lego employees. There were seven Forrec employees on site. Up to 45 architecture, engineering and computer specialist colleagues in Toronto were drawn in during the 18 months of construction.

Fifty million Lego "bricks" went into the construction of the $240 million park. Legoland Deutschland searched for a firm that could handle everything and coordinate design and construction effectively. "Forrec was the only place we could find that, worldwide."
– Albert Warson

ICE Activities for 2.3

Ideas	Connections	Extensions
1. (a) How have recent improvements in transportation affected the way companies transact business internationally?	(b) Visit your local grocer. List 10 fruits, vegetables, or meats that have arrived from other countries. Where are these goods from? Outline the different means of transport by which they may have arrived in this store and estimate how long each portion of the trip took.	(c) Some people feel that the food we consume should come as much as possible from local sources. How would following such a suggestion affect your life? How might it affect others' lives? Discuss the possible reasons for this suggestion, and the pros and cons of international trade in foods.
2. (a) List ways in which the development of communication technology has changed the way companies do business internationally.	(b) Set up a hypothetical conference call between business partners in Ontario, Saskatchewan, Tokyo, and Amsterdam. What would be the best time of day (EST) to talk?	(c) According to recent studies, Canadians would increasingly prefer to buy from a Canadian, rather than a foreign, Web retailer. While the number of Internet purchases is growing, still only about 2 percent of retail is through e-commerce. Discuss how the trend towards e-commerce can affect the way companies do business internationally.
3. (a) Why has confidence in international business grown?	(b) Give an example (other than those given in this chapter) of an international business that has increased global competition by introducing an innovative product or service.	(c) Why do you think the World Trade Organization helps developing countries with technical assistance and training?

2.4 Advantages of Doing Business in Canada

There are many good reasons to do business in Canada and with Canada, both for domestic companies and for foreign companies. The Canadian government lists the following advantages to foreign direct investment in Canada:

- lower production and business costs
- excellent human resources
- a positive business climate
- almost seamless North American markets
- good infrastructure
- quality of life

Canada and the United States are next-door neighbours and major trading partners. We share many of the same values, and at least two-thirds of Canadians speak the same English language. Therefore, it is not surprising that we often compare our country to the United States.

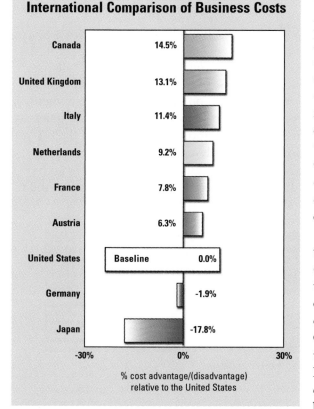

International Comparison of Business Costs

Country	% cost advantage/(disadvantage)
Canada	14.5%
United Kingdom	13.1%
Italy	11.4%
Netherlands	9.2%
France	7.8%
Austria	6.3%
United States	Baseline 0.0%
Germany	-1.9%
Japan	-17.8%

% cost advantage/(disadvantage) relative to the United States

Figure 2.10 2002 comparison of business costs in eight countries and their percentage cost advantage (or disadvantage) as compared to the United States, which is used as the baseline.
– KPMG

Lower Production and Business Costs

In January 2002, International Trade Minister Pierre Pettigrew stated: "Canada is the low-cost leader among industrial nations. As the overall lowest-cost country for conducting business, Canada offers distinct and compelling advantages to those global firms seeking the best location to establish or expand their operations." According to the study "Competitive Alternatives: Comparing Business Costs in North America, Europe and Japan" completed in January 2002, by management consulting firm KPMG, Canada is the most cost-effective industrial nation in which to do business.

The study results are achieved by measuring the combined impact of 27 cost components (e.g., land, telecommunications, utilities, wages) that are most likely to vary in different countries, on an after-tax basis. This report marked the third consecutive year that Canada held this ranking. Canadian business costs are 14.5 percent lower than in the United States (see Figure 2.10). Canadian labour costs were 20–40 percent lower than labour costs in the United States. For example, employee benefits in the United States cost on average 34 percent of an employee's total salary, while comparable Canadian benefits cost on average 26 percent. This difference represents a cost saving for employers choosing to move to Canada.

According to Location Canada's Web site, Canada also has the lowest phone rates and Internet access charges in the G8 countries.

Every company will be affected in some way by production input costs, which include the cost of construction, electricity, transportation, and telecommunications. Canada compares favourably to the United States: Canadian construction costs are 15 percent lower, electricity costs 24 percent less, and transportation costs are 13 percent lower.

Human Resources

Canada has a high-quality skilled labour force, thanks to its level of educational achievement and the high number of first-class business schools in the country. In fact, in January 2001, the UK *Financial Times* noted that eight Canadian business schools ranked among the top management schools in the world. According to the *World Competitiveness Yearbook*, in 2001, Canada had the highest percentage of individuals of any country with at least a college or university education. In addition, as a measure of the skilled workforce Canada provides, eighteen of the 40 top engineering schools in the NAFTA countries are in Canada.

Canadian labour turnover rates (the frequency with which a worker leaves one job for another) are half the American rates, resulting in greater stability for companies as well as lower overall costs. Canada is at the forefront in the use of communications technology. And the **Organisation for Economic Cooperation and Development (OECD)**, the Paris-based group of industrial democracies, has pointed out that Canada has the highest computer literacy rate in the G8. The Canadian government puts such a great value on technology skills that it offers "fast-track immigration" for immigrants with such skills. They and their spouses face fewer limitations when they apply to immigrate to Canada.

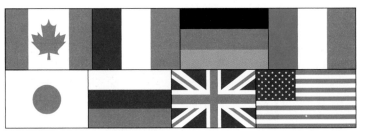

Figure 2.11 Flags of the G8 nations.

Web Link

To find out more about doing business in Canada and with Canadian companies, follow the link at
www.internationalbusiness.nelson.com.

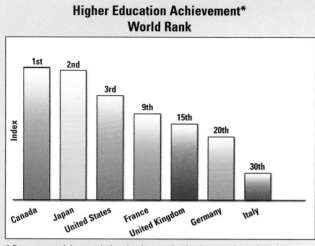

Higher Education Achievement*
World Rank

1st — Canada
2nd — Japan
3rd — United States
9th — France
15th — United Kingdom
20th — Germany
30th — Italy

Index

* Percentage of the population that has attained at least tertiary education among 36 countries considered in the World Competitiveness Yearbook, 2001.

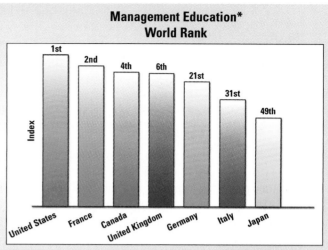

Management Education*
World Rank

1st — United States
2nd — France
4th — Canada
6th — United Kingdom
21st — Germany
31st — Italy
49th — Japan

Index

* Standing among 75 countries. Index based on the availability of Management education in first-class business schools.

Figure 2.12 The overall skill level of Canada's workforce ranks high among 36 competing countries. Canada has the highest percentage of individuals achieving at least college or university education.

Figure 2.13 Canada ranks fourth among 75 countries of locally available management education in first-class business schools.

TRADE TALK

Canada plays an important role in the new global knowledge-based economy. We are recognized the world over for our innovative capabilities and advanced technologies. Canadian companies are considered world leaders in industries from fibre optics to aerospace. These industries are the engine driving economic growth and job creation in Canada. This country also offers many compelling advantages to potential foreign investors, including a highly skilled work force, low production and research and development costs, and a high standard of living.

– *Prime Minister Jean Chrétien*

Positive Business Climate

The Economist, a British magazine specializing in matters of the economy and business, ranks Canada fourth in the world with regard to its overall **business climate**, a measure of the ease with which companies can run their businesses. A positive business climate is an environment that encourages the success of business, promotes fair competition, and welcomes foreign investment. In addition, a study by the respected International Policy Center (IPC) has Canada ranked first in the G8 countries in business ethical practices. Positive business ethics are generally understood to include such values as equality of opportunity, promotion of human rights and equitable labour standards, sound environmental stewardship, protection of workers' health and safety, and transparency in company and community relationships. Canada also has a higher rate of unionization than the United States, and its workers lose fewer person-days per capita than workers south of the border, factors that can contribute to a stable and smoothly operating business environment.

Every time you press the activator valve on top of a can of shaving cream, spray-on cooking oil, or spray-on paint, you are using a type of aerosol—a container or canister that sprays the pressurized contents into the air or onto a surface. The first commercial aerosol product in North America was an insecticide, which was used from 1941 by the U.S. military in the Second World War.

The Lang family operated an electrical products manufacturing company in Toronto. In 1949, Stuart Lang and his son Gordon were at a trade show in Chicago, where they saw an aerosol container being demonstrated by a former business associate who had founded the Connecticut Chemical Company of Bridgeport, Connecticut. They agreed that, for a percentage of the profits, the Lang family would have the exclusive rights to the aerosol technology for Canada, and that Gordon would move to Connecticut, to learn about aerosols.

A year later, Gordon Lang, an engineer educated at the University of Toronto, returned to Toronto with his knowledge of the new technology, and convinced his father and uncle to build a new plant to manufacture aerosol products—Connecticut Chemicals of Canada Ltd.—in the Toronto suburb of East York. Soon the plant was manufacturing and packaging everything from hair spray to deodorant to "chocolate in a can" for some of the largest companies in the world, including Shell, Fuller Brush, Procter & Gamble, and Heinz.

Competitors soon entered the aerosol market, and by the late 1950s the aerosol industry was booming. Conn Chem Canada bought out the U.S. parent company and pioneered a host of new aerosol products—paints, furniture polish, shoe care products, and much more. With acquisitions in the 1960s, Conn Chem acquired a new plant, new employees, and new customers. Under Lang's leadership and with his business philosophy, "Hire good people and get out of their way," the company acquired more businesses that were integrated as divisions in the Conn Chem family. Lang ensured that CCL was innovative, met or exceeded the needs and expectations of its customers, and took advantage of new market developments.

In the 1970s, widely publicized research reports stated that chlorofluorocarbons (CFCs) were harmful to the earth's ozone layer. Keeping up with research and technology, Conn Chem started removing CFCs from its products, so that by the time Canadian and U.S. legislation banned CFCs from consumer aerosol products, Conn Chem was no longer dependent on them.

The defining moment for the company came in 1989 with the North American Free Trade Agreement being prepared (for implementation in 1994). One of the company's major acquisitions had been Continental Can Canada, the Canadian operations of the huge U.S. company and more than twice the size of CCL. The company foresaw that when Canadian tariffs were dropped, large customers such as Coca-Cola and other beverage and food companies would likely consolidate their business with larger U.S. companies, putting Continental Can Canada out of business. With this in mind, the Continental Can Canada operations were sold to Crown, Cork & Seal for cash and about $150 million in CC&S stock.

This large cash infusion allowed CCL to expand into the U.S. market, acquiring manufacturing, labelling, and container plants and companies, and thus establishing itself to serve the large U.S. marketers of consumer products. Along with this aggressive management came a bit of luck. Crown, Cork & Seal stock doubled and was sold off to increase CCL's cash resources by more than $300 million. Again, this money was used to purchase other manufacturers (some with complementary specializations), to acquire more plants, and to increase CCL's presence in the United States.

By 1990, CCL Industries was the largest custom manufacturing company in North America. It soon expanded to England, becoming the largest in its product group in those markets as well. Today, CCL Industries is an international enterprise, still headquartered in Toronto, employs approximately 7000 people, and operates about 33 production facilities in North and Central America, the United Kingdom, and Europe. Donald Lang is president and CEO.

The company has four business units: the custom manufacturing division, container division, plastic packaging division, and labels division. Many of the well-known brands of personal care products and specialty food products in your home have been manufactured by CCL Industries' custom manufacturing division. The container division makes aluminum specialty containers, including recyclable aerosol cans and bottles, and aluminum tubes; the plastic packaging division makes plastic tubes, jars, press tops, and other dispensing closures; and the label division produces pressure-sensitive self-adhesive labels and promotional products.

> Work hard. Don't be afraid to take risks. Be the one leading change instead of following it.
> – Gordon Lang

1. What were some of the smart business decisions that contributed to CCL's moving ahead?
2. How did the management style of Gordon Lang contribute to the company's success?
3. Why is innovation in the packaging industry of particular importance in today's markets?

Figure 2.14 CCL Industries makes the containers, plastic packages, and labels for many consumer products around the world.

Seamless North American Market Access

Canada and the United States are the world's largest trading partners, with two-way trade valued at $502 billion in 1999 and $1.7 billion a day in cross-border trade. Most Canadian cities are within a 10-hour drive of 60 percent of the American market. One-half of the North American population (200 million) lives within a 10-hour driving distance from Toronto, and more than 60 percent are just a two-hour flight away. This proximity makes delivery costs affordable and allows businesses to fulfill orders quickly and reliably. In addition, both countries are striving to make the border as easy to cross as possible to keep this vast flow of trade moving efficiently. (In Europe, the EU has already effectively abolished borders between countries. People and goods pass from country to country as we would travel from province to province.)

Canadian business has a global presence that is recognized by all stakeholders as economically rewarding to all parties, acknowledged as being ethically, socially, and environmentally responsible, welcomed by the communities in which we operate, and that facilitates economic, human resource and community development within a stable operating environment.

– *Human Rights Research and Education Centre,* University of Ottawa

Following the attacks on New York's World Trade Center on September 11, 2001, increased security checks meant long delays at the Canada-U.S. border. This had serious economic and operational impacts on many firms, especially those awaiting raw materials or parts for just-in-time production facilities. The Canadian and U.S. governments and affected industries reacted quickly to add resources, apply new technology, and establish new procedures to restore efficiency without compromising security. The crisis at the border illustrated that it is critical for Canadian suppliers that the border not be an impediment to the flow of goods to their U.S. customers. If potential border problems are a concern for U.S. customers, their lack of confidence could put Canadian suppliers at a disadvantage in the future.

Business Infrastructure

The Infrastructure Canada Web site's list of priorities is helpful in understanding what "infrastructure" means. Its first priority is "green municipal infrastructure— projects that improve the quality of our environment and contribute to our national goals of clean air and water." Its further priority projects target "water and wastewater systems, water management, solid waste management and recycling ... local transportation, roads and bridges, affordable housing, telecommunications, and tourist, cultural, and recreational facilities." The choice of such project priorities and the quality of these infrastructures and services in Canada make the country very attractive to investors and businesses interested in operating here. Canada also favours research and development through its numerous private and public research institutes and generous tax incentives in some jurisdictions. Education systems are also considered part of a country's "infrastructure," as they contribute to the qualifications of a workforce and are vital to business competitiveness.

To find out about how the United Nations ranks countries in the world, visit the link at www.internationalbusiness.nelson.com.

The Economist Intelligence Unit, which belongs to the same organization that publishes *The Economist* newspaper, is a world leader in the provision of country intelligence. The unit helps business people to make sound decisions by providing up-to-date, reliable information on market trends and business strategies. The Economist Intelligence Unit monitors political, economic, and business conditions in almost 200 countries.

Global Outlook Country Forecast
Business Environment Scorings and Rankings
(Economist Intelligence Unit (EIU))

	EIU Country Forecast (February 2002) 2002-2006		EIU Country Forecast (November 2001) 2002-2006	
	Total Score	Rank	Total Score	Rank
Netherlands	8.88	1	8.82	1
Canada	8.73	2	8.75	3
USA	8.71	3	8.80	2
UK	8.67	4	8.65	4
Switzerland	8.59	5	8.58	5
Ireland	8.58	6	8.51	8
Denmark	8.57	7	8.49	10
Finland	8.55	8	8.52	6
Hong Kong	8.50	9	8.43	11
Singapore	8.47	10	8.52	7

Figure 2.15 The Netherlands is expected to be the best place in the world to conduct business over the next five years. The country scores particularly highly on its political stability and effectiveness, its policy towards foreign investment, and the availability of finance. Canada ranked highly as well.

In 2001, the unit forecasted that the Netherlands, Canada, and the United States would be the top three countries in which to conduct business for the next five years. Top-scoring countries attained their scores because of their political stability, political effectiveness, policy towards foreign investment, and finance availability.

Quality of Life

In the 1990s, Canada was ranked the best place to live by the United Nations for seven years in a row. In deciding the annual ranking, the UN takes average measurements for 174 countries, looking at such issues as life expectancy, adult literacy, education, and income distribution. The statistics used for UN evaluations come from data provided by the OECD. Although ranked number one overall, Canada was reminded of certain shortcomings in the areas of Aboriginal health and literacy rates; and Canada came second to Norway in its gender-empowerment ranking, lagging slightly in its proportion of female professionals. Canada also has a world reputation as a multicultural country that welcomes immigrants and has a humanitarian policy toward refugees.

ICE Activities for 2.4

Ideas	Connections	Extensions
1. (a) What does the Government of Canada believe are the selling points for doing business in Canada?	(b) Name some industries that have come to Canada. What aspects of our business climate might have attracted them?	(c) What criteria does the UN use to evaluate the quality of life in countries? What criteria would you add?
2. (a) Why did the G7 change to the G8?	(b) What issues are the G8 currently discussing? What relevance do they have, if any, to your local community?	(c) Not everyone agrees with the G8's aims. Research some opposing arguments and explain your point of view on this issue.
3. (a) Name the types of infrastructure that are especially needed to support different types of business.	(b) Examine the "code of ethics" or "core values" of a place you have worked or where you might be interested in working. Compare your findings with those of a classmate.	(c) Although Canada has high numbers of knowledge workers in the field of technology, it is short of skilled professionals in medicine, engineering, and other disciplines. Why? How difficult is it for talented newcomers to practise in their fields?

2.5 Preparing for the International Workplace

As opportunities have grown for domestic businesses to expand into the international market, so have opportunities for students to get experience in international business or education by spending a work or study term abroad. Not only can students get useful work experience, but they can also live in a new culture, perhaps learn a new language, and see how international firms operate—all of which will increase their employment opportunities when they graduate.

Even if you are not interested in working in another country, you may be involved in international business without ever leaving Canada. Today, many Canadian companies need employees who have international business knowledge and skills, to work, for example, as distributors who supply products to—or buy services from—companies in other countries, or as marketers in companies that do business internationally. You may work with entrepreneurs who are setting up their own businesses and need people knowledgeable about import or export markets, or with Canadian companies that face competition in any way from international markets.

Getting Experience Abroad

Gaining international work experience offers you a number of benefits including the opportunity to

- experience how business is conducted among people of different cultures
- understand the world's resources and the nature of the global economy
- improve your skills in communicating cross-culturally
- acquire business skills that will help you survive in the global marketplace
- become more confident in dealing with people from other cultures

TRADE TIPS

The most successful candidates for overseas work or study terms are:
- flexible
- communicative
- knowledgeable
- informed
- motivated, committed to quality work
- open-minded
- patient
- organized
- mannered
- cooperative
- positive
- assertive
- enthusiastic

Dr. Alex Murray, a professor of international business in the School of Business and Economics at Wilfrid Laurier University, suggests that students who are thinking about going abroad to work measure their "cultural IQ" first. You can measure your cultural IQ by asking yourself questions such as the following: Am I flexible and able to adapt to doing things completely differently? Can I adapt easily to cultural customs I have never experienced before? Can I respect people who have a different set of values than I have?

Canadian post-secondary students have a number of options for gaining international business experience in companies. For example, the Atlantic Canada Opportunities Agency, in co-operation with universities in the Atlantic provinces, offers internship programs for small- and medium-sized companies in the Atlantic region. The Dalhousie University Centre for International Business Studies and the Canada/Atlantic Provinces Cooperation Agreement on International Business Development fund a program for Dalhousie MBA students who are interested in an international business career. The program's goal is to help companies in the Atlantic region prepare for doing business in international markets. Each student in the program is matched with two Canadian companies in his or her province who will pay $1000 for the student's services. Before they leave on assignment, the students meet with their companies and find out what their tasks will be. Students might be asked to do market research; investigate competitors, their products, and prices; investigate foreign government regulations, duties, and tax laws; obtain information about bidding opportunities; help a company representative who wants to visit the market; identify potential partners or joint venture opportunities; or conduct interviews or meet with firms on the company's behalf.

Dierdre Evans was a Dalhousie MBA student when she joined the international business internship program. She was assigned to work with Charlottetown Metal Products, a Prince Edward Island company that manufactures mussel processing equipment. The company was interested in investigating business prospects in Chile, which was on the verge of automating its mussel industry. After meeting with Wendell MacDonald, the manager of Charlottetown Metal Products, Dierdre went to Chile where she stayed at the Canadian embassy in Santiago. She identified the key mussel processors in the country, made contacts and distributed Charlottetown Metal Products brochures, and identified potential business opportunities for the company. During her second month in Chile, Dierdre worked for another Prince Edward Island company, Durabelt Inc., which manufactures a belted chain used on vegetable harvesting equipment. For Durabelt, she researched issues such as the level of mechanization in the food harvesting industry and identified potential customers. For Dierdre, the first-hand experience in another company was invaluable: "When you're actually on the spot doing market research, it's completely different from working on case studies at the university."

Some Canadian high schools offer exchange programs with other countries. One example is the work experience exchange organized in 1997 by the District School Board of Niagara between Grimsby Secondary School in Ontario and Sir Joseph Williamson's Mathematical School in Rochester, Kent, England. Canadian and British students each had an opportunity to experience the culture, work ethic, education, and family life of the other country for two weeks. The ten senior students from Grimsby stayed with the British students' families over their midwinter break, and the British students visited Grimsby in the Ontario March break. The British school arranged the work placements through their central school office, and the Grimsby teacher arranged the placements for the English students with the help of the local Chamber of Commerce.

Lindsay Slessor was one of the participants in that exchange. Because of her interest in digital design and programming languages, she was matched with Gillingham Graphics in Rochester, Kent, a small firm that designs images for logos on vehicles and signs. Lindsay was more than just an apprentice; she helped the owner learn HTML (Hypertext Markup Language) so that he could prepare a company Web site.

By visiting a different country, Lindsay had a positive experience through which she gained independence and confidence. She was able to confirm that the computer skills she already had were valuable, and went on to continue her studies in multimedia at Humber College for Applied Arts and Technology in Toronto with an important addition to her resumé.

Getting Experience at Home

Although experience in a foreign country can be helpful for someone interested in going into international business, you can also do a lot of research at home to find out about international careers or occupations that require an understanding of international business. Resources for your research could include the following:

- Your school library and local public library, where you can read books about cross-cultural management or doing business in the country in which you are interested. Investigate global demographic trends, geographic influences, economic conditions, and industry trends in the countries where you might like to work.

- The news media, which often publish articles about job-search planning and career trends, including international careers. For example, newspaper stories and television programs can give you news about Canadian companies that are expanding into another country or international companies that operate in Canada.

- Personal and business contacts that you may have. Find people who are involved in international business and ask them for an information interview, for example, people in the human resources departments of international companies. Use your interview questions to find out as much as you can about international careers or about countries you might be interested in.

- Community organizations, such as your local chamber of commerce or the Junior Team Canada branch in your area, where you can gain valuable skills and find out about future opportunities to work abroad. Also investigate any professional associations in your area that have international components.

- Web sites of international companies, especially those that include descriptions of their international business and foreign job openings. Also investigate periodicals and newspapers from the country you are interested in. Many foreign newspapers now have English-language versions available on their Web sites each day.

- The International Business Career Profiles in this book, which offer a wide range of career possibilities and descriptions of the educational and skills background of the subjects of the profiles.

There are also ways to gain experience and improve your business skills in international affairs and business without leaving Canada. You could join an international organization or committee, volunteer to work with refugees or with non-governmental organizations (NGOs) in Canada, or take on leadership roles in local committees and projects. Once you are in college or university, you can work as a volunteer with the International Students' Office and act as a host for students coming to Canada from other countries. You can take post-secondary courses in international business, politics, or contemporary cultural history. Work for companies in Canada that have offices abroad and find out as much as you can about the overseas work of the company.

Figure 2.16 CIDA's goal is to support sustainable development activities in the world's poorest regions.

Knowledge and Skills for International Business

Before you think about an international business career, you will need to understand yourself to be sure that you would be comfortable living abroad. You'll have to be willing to increase your understanding of cultures other than your own. You'll need problem-solving and critical thinking skills and be able to use those skills in circumstances that might be new to you. You'll also need leadership skills, and to be able to resolve conflicts and negotiate agreements in sometimes challenging circumstances. You will need strong written and spoken language skills. Clear communication will be especially important in these circumstances because you may be dealing with translations or with people for whom English is not a first language. A second language would, of course, be very helpful. Being able to speak the language of the people with whom you are doing business allows you to have direct communication with those who don't speak English.

Web Link

Follow the link at
www.internationalbusiness.nelson.com
to investigate the Canadian International Development Agency's student opportunities for working in other countries.

According to the Canadian Association of Career Educators and Employers, your international skills inventory should include the following:

- **General traits:** enjoy change; have a sense of adventure; desire to seek out challenges; be open-minded, patient, and curious

- **Adaptation and coping skills:** be emotionally stable and have the ability to deal with stress; know what culture shock is; have observation and adaptation skills; be flexible; have a sense of humour; and know yourself

- **Intercultural communications skills and traits:** be tolerant of and sensitive to others; have good listening and observation skills; understand and be able to use non-verbal communication skills; know a second language

- **Overseas work effectiveness skills:** independence and self-discipline; experience in training people; resourcefulness; versatility; persistence; organizational and people skills; leadership; energy; project planning skills; writing skills; verbal communication skills; loyalty and tenacity; tact; philosophical commitment to field of work

To work in international business, you will need a good general education. Post-secondary studies in anthropology, English, foreign languages, geography, history, mathematics, politics, psychology, and sociology will be helpful. There are also a wide range of business education branches that can be used in international business: accounting, business communications, business statistics, economics, finance, human resources, information systems, law, management, marketing, and production and operations management.

Many post-secondary institutions in Canada now offer specific international business programs, such as the Dalhousie international business MBA that Dierdre Evans was working towards. Examples of such schools and their varied programs include the following:

- Grant MacEwan College in Alberta, which offers a diploma in Asia-Pacific Management (with an internship period in Asia) and a Bachelor of Applied International Business and Supply Chain Management degree.

- Humber College in Toronto, which works with organizations to offer certificates geared to specific areas of international business, such as the International Freight Forwarding Certificate, which is sponsored by the Canadian International Freight Forwarders Association. The college also offers diploma programs in International Marketing and International Project Management programs.

- Richard Ivey School of Business at the University of Western Ontario, which offers both undergraduate courses and graduate programs in international business. The Richard Ivey School was the first North American business school to open a permanent campus in Hong Kong.

- Faculty of Business at the University of Victoria, B.C., which says that "every aspect of the University of Victoria (UVic) Faculty of Business is designed with an international focus." As well as international business courses in many fields, the school offers international exchange programs, cultural liaison programs, and summer international conferences in the fields related to international business.

ICE Activities for 2.5

Ideas	Connections	Extensions
1. (a) Briefly describe one secondary and one post-secondary program that helps Canadian students gain international business experience.	(b) Using the profile of Dierdre Evans (page 67), list the international business skills she would have needed for her internship in Chile.	(c) Create a plan for developing the international business skills you would need to become a candidate for an international internship program.
2. (a) Chart the ways you can gain international business knowledge and experience without leaving Canada.	(b) Find five resources you could use to help you research international business opportunities.	(c) Write a paragraph explaining how the five resources you found in 2. (b) could help you pursue an international career.
3. (a) Describe some of the educational courses that might help you in your international career.	(b) Write a brief description of one of the international business programs offered at a Canadian college or university.	(c) Working with a partner, review the list of skills on page 69. Select one skill and role-play a job interview in which you explain to your prospective employer how you demonstrate that skill.

Canada's Trading Partners:
Focus on the United States of America

Canada and the United States share, with Mexico, the great landmass known as North America.

By 1846, even before Canada had become a country, the current border between Canada and the United States had been established. To this day it is known as the longest undefended border in the world, a testimony to the friendly relations between the two countries.

In spite of a shared and generally peaceful history, trade relations between the two countries have sometimes been contentious. Canada's first prime minister, John A. Macdonald, instituted a policy of protection by charging tariffs on goods imported from the United States. Subsequent leaders carried on with this policy at least to some extent until January 1989, when the first-ever Free Trade Agreement (FTA) between Canada and the United States came into effect. Under its terms, tariffs would gradually be eliminated on goods traded between the two countries. In 1994, in an expanded version of the FTA, the North American Free Trade Agreement (NAFTA), Mexico joined Canada and the United States. The total NAFTA market is 400 million consumers. (For a more detailed discussion of NAFTA, see Chapter 5.)

Trade and business dealings between the two countries illustrate their close relationship. The United States is the largest foreign investor in Canada: during 1994-1999, U.S. direct investment in Canada rose five times the previous five-year period to $16.5 billion CAD. The United States is also the most popular destination for Canadian exports and investment. Companies from each country have subsidiaries in the other country. Most of Canada's exports and imports flow across the Canada-United States border. Our trade relationship with the United States amounts to over $1.3 billion a day.

Of Canada's 20 largest cities, 17 are within a 90-minute drive from the United States. There are fast, efficient, and integrated transportation services that focus on just-in-time delivery. Deregulation, commercialization, and privatization have increased interest in both countries, and now Canada and the United States connect as well as any two countries in the world. Many people feel that we now have one North American market rather than two completely separate markets.

Since 1994, large numbers of Canadian and American companies have been opening locations across the border. Wal-Mart, a large American retail chain, opened stores across Canada in 1994. Since then, many American retailers have decided to bring their products to Canada—Old Navy, Best Buy, and American Eagle Outfitters, for example. Canadian retailers, such as Aldo (shoes) and Roots, have the same opportunities to do business in the United States.

Although our countries seem similar and have close ties, Canada and the United States sometimes respond differently to world conditions and the issue of global free trade. In addition, disputes still arise between the two countries. For example, in 2001, a conflict arose between the two countries about the appropriate price for the softwood lumber that Canada exports to the United States. At the heart of the matter was the question of whether Canada unfairly subsidized Canadian lumber companies by not charging them a market rate for the right to cut timber on Crown (government-owned) land. There will probably continue to be disputes on some trade issues.

Still, there are enormous opportunities for businesses to take advantage of the economic partnership between Canada and the United States. Trade has doubled since NAFTA came into effect. The Canada–United States trading relationship supports more than 2 million jobs in each country.

A SNAPSHOT OF THE UNITED STATES OF AMERICA

Size: 9 372 614 sq. km

World Region: North America

Capital City: Washington, D.C.

Language: English

Currency: U.S. dollar

Population: 280.5 million

Time: Noon in Ottawa (EST) is noon in Washington, D.C.

Climate: Ranges from subtropical rainforest in Hawaii and tropical savanna in southern Florida to subarctic and tundra climates in Alaska.

Type of Government: Federal republic

Labour Force by Occupation: 24 percent services, 21 percent manufacturing, 16 percent retail and hospitality (1999 est.)

Figure 2.17 The Statue of Liberty and the American flag are well-known symbols of American patriotism.

Membership in World Organizations: APEC, WTO, OECD, NATO and others. The United States is party to two free trade agreements: one with Canada and Mexico (NAFTA), and the other with Israel.

Importing Partners and Products:
Partners: Canada, Mexico, Japan, China, and Germany.
Products: Machinery, automobiles, consumer goods, industrial raw materials, food and beverages.

Exporting Partners and Products:
Partners: Canada, Mexico, Japan, and United Kingdom.
Products: Automobiles, industrial supplies and raw materials, consumer goods, agricultural products.

Travel Advisory: Canadians need a minimum of valid photo identification and proof of citizenship, but a valid passport is recommended. Information about temporary (non-immigrant) and permanent (immigrant) visas, or green cards, is available from the U.S. Immigration Services. People with a criminal record are generally not eligible to enter the United States. It is advisable to purchase health insurance and travellers' cheques before entering the United States.

Business Etiquette: Conventions in business are very similar to those in Canada with a few differences that vary from region to region. Before going on a business trip to the United States, check about American business holidays.

Country Link

For more information on Canada's trade with the United States, follow the link at www.internationalbusiness.nelson.com

Chapter Challenges

Knowledge/Understanding

1. Match each of the following terms to the correct definition or description below:
   - (a) products
   - (b) goods
   - (c) services
   - (d) importing
   - (e) exporting
   - (f) direct foreign investment
   - (g) portfolio investment
   - (h) international business

   - (i) selling goods or services to another region or country
   - (ii) control or own production, distribution, services, or other facilities outside the country in which they are based
   - (iii) include both goods and services
   - (iv) buying a share of a foreign company but not having a controlling interest or say in the running of the company
   - (v) buying goods or services from another region or country
   - (vi) activities that individuals or groups perform to assist other individuals, organizations, or companies
   - (vii) activities needed to create, ship, and sell goods and services from a business in one country to a business in another country
   - (viii) raw materials, semi-manufactured items, manufactured merchandise

2. Name and describe three types of international business activity.

3. How have recent improvements in communication technology helped international business to expand?

4. What are six of the skills that international businesses want in their employees? What are some ways that future employees could acquire those skills?

Thinking/Inquiry

1. Canada "fast-tracks" immigration for people with technology skills. Some immigrants are from countries that may lack the ability to provide their citizens with technological training; some immigrants could not afford the training even if it were available; and some countries may discourage or even prevent women from accessing such training. Prepare a brief oral presentation to respond to the following questions: How do you think these immigrants would react to Canada's fast-track policy? How might Canada defend its policy? How could Canada address their concerns?

2. Why has international trade become less risky, less costly, and less time-consuming than in the past? Do you think business confidence will likely grow even more in the future? Write a paragraph or a brief editorial summarizing your point of view on these questions. Include evidence to support your opinion.

3. Many Canadian sports figures and entertainers have found success internationally. Are people such as Wayne Gretzky and Celine Dion exporting services? What happens when Canadian entertainers move to the United States, for example, but you still buy their CDs or go to see their movies in Canada? Are you buying a good or a service under such circumstances?

4. Review the data in Figures 2.10 and 2.11. In a small group, brainstorm the benefits that the businesses in a country gain from a high ranking in each of these categories and the disadvantages to those businesses if the ranking fell.

Communication

1. Create a timeline to show the details of one Canadian company's expansion into international trade. In a caption to your timeline, explain the benefits and disadvantages of the expansion for the company through the years.

2. Research a recent Team Canada trade mission, and write a report in which you a) describe the reason for the mission, b) explain the potential benefits to Canadian businesses that might result from the mission, and c) identify the goals of at least three of the participants in the mission.

3. Working with a partner, select two of the possible international business research categories described on page 68. Find at least ten useful, accessible resources in your categories. Prepare a one- or two-page annotated bibliography of your findings. Then collect all of the findings from your classmates and bind the pages together into an International Resource publication.

Application

1. Create a graphic organizer in which you compare international business programs in at least three post-secondary educational institutions in Canada. Focus your search on an aspect of international business that you are interested in. What are the educational prerequisites for the program? What kinds of courses are offered? Does the school have any international internship programs? What kinds of businesses do graduates from the program usually work for?

2. The Canada's Trading Partners feature for this chapter focuses on trade between Canada and the United States. The author of the feature states, "In spite of a shared and generally peaceful history, trade relations between the two countries have sometimes been contentious." Research a current or historical trade dispute between Canada and the United States, and create an illustrated report or multimedia presentation in which you explain the causes of the dispute and the effects it had (or is likely to have) on Canadian-U.S. trade.

3. From local newspapers, Web sites, television or radio broadcasts, or personal interviews, collect at least three stories of how a local domestic business is competing with international businesses. Select the story that appeals to you most, and prepare a 3-minute presentation in which you explain to your classmates—in role as the owner or manager of the business—how international competition has affected your business.

International Business Portfolio

A Snapshot of Your IBP Country

After you complete this assignment, you will have a good overview of your chosen country. You will also be familiar with some of the reference tools available to you and which you will find useful throughout the course.

Activities

1. Provide a map of your country, with major cities and physical characteristics (mountains, rivers, etc.) marked.

2. List:
   Size relative to Canada   World region
   Population   Capital city
   Language(s) spoken   Currency
   GDP per capita ($) (converted to Canadian dollars)

3. Time: When it is noon in Ottawa, it is _____ in _____.

4. Briefly describe the climate.

5. Briefly describe the size and typical occupations of the labour force.

6. Briefly describe the type of government—for example, constitutional monarchy, republic, parliamentary democracy, etc.

7. List examples of exports to and imports from Canada.

8. Identify and describe at least one brand name product, company, or multinational enterprise that originates in your IBP country.

9. List major post-secondary institutions (colleges, universities, or technical schools) in your IBP country. Is there a post-secondary program you would like to take? Would you consider pursuing post-secondary studies in this country? Why or why not? Focus on the advantages and disadvantages.

Chapter 3

International Competitiveness, Productivity, and Quality

Today, countries and businesses face the challenge of competing in the global marketplace. Intense competition places increasing demands on everyone who is involved in international business. Canadian governments and businesses have to know the factors that will contribute to their international competitiveness; to their positive global presence; and to an increase in Canadian business productivity, intellectual capital, innovative capacity, and quality control.

Chapter Topics

➤ 3.1 – Establishing a Global Presence 78

➤ 3.2 – Achieving Competitive Advantage 82

➤ 3.3 – The Meaning of Productivity 86

➤ 3.4 – Canada's Global Challenge 90

➤ 3.5 – Quality Control and Continual Improvement 99

➤ *Canada's Trading Partners: Focus on* Vietnam 104

➤ Chapter Challenges 106

Prior Knowledge

- Why do countries compete to try to get international businesses to locate in their countries?
- What kinds of economic and social factors would attract international business to Canada?
- How can an unprofitable international business improve its chances of becoming profitable?

Inquiries/Expectations

- What are some of the advantages to Canadians of our country's international business relationships and activities?
- What factors motivate companies to engage in international business?
- How does the state of Canada's economy and industries affect international businesses operating in Canada?
- What factors affect the international competitiveness of Canadian businesses?
- What does rationalization mean as it applies to business and industry?
- What impact does global business have on rationalization in Canadian business?

Important Terms

absolute advantage
capital
comparative advantage
competitive advantage
developed nations
developing nations
economies of scale
gross domestic product (GDP)
intellectual capital
International Organization for
   Standardization (ISO)

knowledge economy
less developed nations
market-driven organizations
opportunity cost
productivity
rationalization
standard of living
total quality management (TQM)
utility

3.1 Establishing a Global Presence

Global Presence and Canada

The globalization of the world economy has been underway for several decades. When a country has a global presence, it is recognized internationally for its reliability, the fairness and integrity of its business dealings, and the standards of its companies' goods and services. Although the term global presence is usually used in a positive way, a country can also be known for its negative qualities. Some countries with a negative global presence are known for non-democratic governments, unsafe and unfair working environments, lack of environmental protection, and political upheaval.

Canada's global presence is important because it means other countries are aware of the products, standards, and reliability we offer. Our global presence also gives us access to capital and markets from around the world, and Canadian companies can benefit from this access. **Capital** is the money or other assets that are available for investment purposes.

A company expanding internationally needs to develop a strong international or global presence. (A company is considered to be international, rather than global, if it operates and sources its needs in only a few countries.) Just because a company has a presence in another country, however, does not guarantee competitive success—"going global (or international)" can often make or break an organization.

In the chapters ahead, you will discover more about the strategies required to achieve international success. For many companies, becoming an international business means establishing distribution arrangements, offices, and possibly manufacturing premises in other countries, as well as hiring local staff. An international presence may also be established with a toll-free telephone number, a Web site, and a focus on e-commerce, which is business conducted over the Internet. Some companies can secure a global presence through the marketing power of the Internet. For example, when the large Dutch banking group ING, entered the Canadian market, it purposely did not spend a great deal on staff, overhead, or buildings. ING banking is conducted over the phone or online. As a result, ING is able to pass along attractive banking services to Canadian customers, since it can offer higher interest rates and lower service charges than other banks.

On the other hand, expansion internationally does not always translate into growth and profitability. For example, PepsiCo Inc., a large American beverage company, withdrew from some major markets, such as South Africa, after facing significant losses from its international beverage operations. What makes the difference between success and failure for companies seeking to compete internationally?

GLOBAL THOUGHT

It is the older generation that remains loyal to nationally produced goods. The British buy British, the French buy French, and the Americans buy American out of long-held habit. It is an expression of patriotism. The young couldn't care less. Today, it's made by BMW, made by Nokia, made by Alessi, made by Sony. What matters is who—not where. It's "made by"— not "made in."

– *Kjell Nordstrom* and *Jonas Ridderstrale*

To build a global or international presence that minimizes risk and maximizes profits, a company should develop a plan that answers the following four questions:

- Which product will lead the way as the company launches or "rolls out" an international business initiative?
- Which markets should be entered first?
- What is the best way to enter these markets?
- How rapidly should the company expand internationally?

Turning global presence into global competitive advantage requires companies to pursue opportunities and to meet the related challenges. To be successful globally, companies must be able to adapt to local markets in other countries. In Japan, for example, Baskin-Robbins sells green tea flavoured ice cream. Green tea is a staple in the Japanese diet. Therefore, when considering whether to expand into Japan, Baskin-Robbins had to research the flavours of ice cream that might be popular there. Perhaps you can think of some other ways companies adapt to international markets.

Competitive Advantage

The ultimate goal for companies in the international marketplace is to increase sales and profits; a key means of doing this is through achieving **competitive advantage**. Competitive advantage is achieved when companies and countries outperform their competitors around the world by improved or superior products (goods or services), better pricing, higher quality, better service, uniqueness, or profit. Access to markets and distribution channels is an important factor as well.

Competitive advantage can be measured in a variety of ways: by market share and performance (compared to key competitors), partnerships with suppliers, customer demand, customer loyalty, distribution, service, and basic resources such as support systems and skilled and knowledgeable workers. There are important financial indices as well.

Canada is eighth among 80 countries measured for their competitive growth according to the World Economic Forum's Global Competitiveness Report released in 2002. The authors of the report state that the Growth Competitiveness Index is made up of "hard data and unique survey data to assess competitiveness in a large sample of countries" and to assess different countries' potential for economic growth. The forum's survey records the opinions of business leaders around the world by asking them to compare aspects of their local business environment with global standards.

Growth Competitiveness Index Ranking of Top 25 Countries

Country	Growth Competitiveness Ranking 2002	Growth Competitiveness Ranking 2001
United States	1	2
Finland	2	1
Taiwan	3	7
Singapore	4	4
Sweden	5	9
Switzerland	6	15
Australia	7	5
Canada	8	3
Norway	9	6
Denmark	10	14
United Kingdom	11	12
Iceland	12	16
Japan	13	21
Germany	14	17
Netherlands	15	8
New Zealand	16	10
Hong Kong SAR	17	13
Austria	18	18
Israel	19	24
Chile	20	27
Korea	21	23
Spain	22	22
Portugal	23	25
Ireland	24	11
Belgium	25	19

Figure 3.1 According to World Economic Forum's analysis of statistical data and responses to its executive survey, Canada's competitive advantage was lower in 2002 than it was in 2001.

Web Link

Follow the link at www.internationalbusiness.nelson.com to find out more about the World Economic Forum.

GDP per Capita (Selected Countries)

Country	Population (millions)	GDP ($billions USD)	GDP per Capita ($000 USD)
Australia	19.2	416.2	21.7
Canada	31.3	722.3	23.1
France	59.3	1 373.0	23.1
Germany	82.8	1 864.0	22.5
Italy	57.6	1 212.0	21.0
Japan	126.5	2 950.0	23.3
Netherlands	15.9	365.1	23.0
South Korea	47.5	625.7	13.2
Sweden	8.9	184.0	20.7
Switzerland	7.3	197.0	27.1
United Kingdom	59.5	1 290.0	21.7
United States	275.6	9 255.0	33.6

Figure 3.2 Rank the 12 countries from high to low according to GDP per capita. Do the rankings surprise you?

Canada's gross domestic product and income per capita have slipped relative to the United States and a number of European and other countries. **Gross domestic product (GDP)** is the total value of all goods and services produced in a country during a specific period. GDP includes items produced by foreign-owned companies. GDP per capita (per person) is the total GDP divided by the number of people in the country. Canada's lower GDP means that a number of other countries are being more productive and are in a better position to compete internationally. The lower Canadian productivity is the result of a number of factors. Economic critics have suggested that Canada's manufacturing sector has lagged and that Canada's lack of investment in research and development (R&D) is evident in this showing. The figure may also result from a slower move to adopt new technologies compared with our American counterparts. In addition, Canada's economy has become increasingly dependent on services rather than manufactured goods. While the need for services or support products in all areas will grow and remain important, the manufacture and, more importantly, the consumption of tangible or actual products will continue to be the driving force behind most economies. These factors explain why some countries are improving their prosperity faster than others.

Competitiveness is linked to the research and development (R&D) spending of both governments and private business. Companies and countries must use productive management strategies to encourage innovation. The development of new technologies and processes can add a great deal to the capabilities and competitiveness of a company and of a country. In 1916, the federal government established the National Research Council (called at that time the Honorary Advisory Council for Scientific and Industrial Research). It now has a large "campus" and many buildings, each of which has ongoing research in a special area of science and social science.

Governments also often support the research and development of industries and of private companies. This was true of the development by MD Robotics (formerly Spar Aerospace) of the Canadarm for the NASA space shuttle program. The success of that innovative tool has given Canada significant stature and competitive advantage in the area of space technology.

Governments also usually insist on high product and process standards for any major items that they order, thus stimulating companies to update their performance standards and their environmental controls.

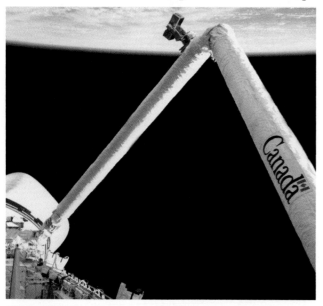

Figure 3.3 The Canadian government supported the development of the Canadarm. The success of the Canadarm has given Canada a competitive advantage in space technology.

TRADE TALK

Hewers of quality goods...if only the world knew: New study suggests exporters should associate products with Canada

A new study out of Carleton University in Ottawa suggests the stereotype of the quiet, polite Canadian has extended into marketing and hindered the sale of Canadian products overseas. Professors Nicolas Papadopoulos and Louise Heslop of Carleton's business department say while Canada's image as a country ranked first among 18 examined, Canadian products are falling woefully behind because companies don't use that stellar image in promoting products in foreign markets.

"What this tells us is that there is a real risk that we could be lost in the shuffle of globalization," said Mr. Papadopoulos, who specializes in marketing and international business. "The presence of other countries has increased. There are so many products floating around out there that you have to run twice as fast to keep up."

The Carleton researchers led a one-year study from July 1997 to July 1998, assisted by an international research group. About 6100 consumers, 300 in each of 13 countries, and 600 in the United States and 1500 from across Canada, were asked to evaluate 18 countries on their image and people, and on the quality and visibility of their products.

What they found is such countries as Germany, Japan, and Sweden have cultivated reputations in certain products—luxury cars, electronics and furniture—which manufacturers exploit in their advertising. Thus, Canadian audiences associate IKEA furniture with Sweden or fine chocolate with Belgium.

The study suggests the Canadian reputation for natural resources and little else hasn't evolved with the global market. Product awareness has not changed since their last study, conducted ten years before.

There are exceptions. Brand names like Tilley Endurables and Roots, which have promoted themselves in international markets by associating themselves with the Canadian nature and outdoors image, have benefited by reaping high sales. Ms. Heslop cited beer and children's books as popular Canadian exports.

"People like us and think we're nice," she said, "but when you grow up and become more sophisticated maybe we're not there yet [in terms of image]."

Consumers in the study gave Canadian workmanship a higher score than they did their knowledge of Canadian products, suggesting overseas consumers think highly of Canadian goods, even if they don't know exactly what they are.

"Hands down, we are rated first in trustworthiness in the world," Mr. Papadopoulos said. "If you're a manufacturer, what does this mean for you? You can turn it around into reliability in manufacturing or delivering, for example."

The study hasn't been embraced by the Canadian manufacturing industry, where Greg MacDonald, an Alliance of Manufacturers and Exporters Canada spokesman, said it's important to remember many of Canada's exports are components of other products.

"The products that we make are among the finest in the world. But you're not going to buy a Canadian television," Mr. MacDonald said, citing automobiles and parts, telecommunications, aerospace products and furniture as among Canada's largest exports.

"Canadian products have a reputation for reliability, so they're well known. They must be very good because companies keep coming back," Mr. MacDonald said. "There's always a need to promote better. I think that will always exist."

There is a bright spot in the study. Mr. Papadopoulos said Canadian companies are doing a better job of selling their products at home, and Canadian-made products enjoy a higher reputation for quality than they did ten years ago.

At the same time, the Canadian reputation in the United States is lower among young Americans than it is among their parents, suggesting Canadian manufacturers and marketers have to make up lost ground before the gap widens.

– *Carolynne Wheeler*, The Ottawa Citizen, *August 26, 2000*

ICE Activities for 3.1

Ideas	Connections	Extensions
1. (a) What is meant by the term "global presence"?	(b) Identify an organization (for-profit or nonprofit) in or near your community that has a global presence. List three strategies it used to achieve its global presence.	(c) What are the implications of foreign companies establishing a presence in your community?
2. (a) List four measures of competitive advantage.	(b) Why is GDP an important measure of competitiveness?	(c) What are the implications of Canada losing its competitive position in the global economy?
3. (a) According to those quoted in the article on page 81, why are overseas sales of Canadian products lagging behind?	(b) Conduct a survey of 10 people (fellow students, friends, co-workers, family). Ask the question "What is your opinion of products made in Canada?" Present a summary of your findings and conclusions.	(c) In your opinion, how can Canadians improve the way other countries perceive our products?

3.2 Achieving Competitive Advantage

Companies that achieve a competitive advantage manufacture products or provide services that have greater economic utility, or usefulness, than products or services supplied by their competitors.

Economic **utility** is a product's ability to satisfy the needs and wants of the customer. Utility can be found in a variety of ways. For example, form utility is created when raw materials are converted into a finished product. Wheat by itself is least useful, but when made into flour and then bread it is most useful. Similarly, place utility means that a product, such as ice cream, has the most value when it is in the freezer at home, ready for consumption, rather than far away, at the dairy, where it is made.

Factors Affecting Canada's Competitiveness

Many factors influence a country's ability to achieve competitive advantage in the global marketplace. Think about a team in which you are a member—perhaps you are a member of a work team in your part-time job or maybe you belong to a school team. What makes your team competitive? What makes your team better than the competition? What are your strengths and weaknesses? These same characteristics, and others, can be applied to a country's business climate to assess its potential for success at home and abroad.

There are a number of factors to consider when assessing any country's competitive strength or position. Criteria such as per capita income and employment statistics are used as measures, but so are other factors. As the following list shows, sometimes the same factor has both positive and negative ramifications for Canadian competitiveness.

Figure 3.4 More than 80 percent of Canada's exports go to the United States. Proximity to the U.S. market is one of Canada's competitive advantages.

Figure 3.5 Members of Canada's gold medal-winning women's hockey team celebrating a goal at the 2002 Olympic Games in Salt Lake City. Some of the qualities that make a sports team competitive can also be used to make a country or a company competitive.

- **quality and quantity of natural resources:** Canada's abundant natural resources in oil and gas, forest products, minerals, and water are competitive advantages. Canada's proximity to the United States and the relatively open borders between the two countries allow many of these natural resources to be exported to the United States. On the other hand, the great distances between domestic Canadian markets—and between Canada and other world markets—can be a disadvantage when transport costs and delivery time are taken into account.

- **strength of the country's currency and its exchange rate:** Over the last decade, Canada's currency has been relatively weak against the U.S. dollar. While this encourages foreign investment and increases the number of Canadian exports, it also means that Canadian companies have to pay more to import machinery, components, and new technology into the country.

- **infrastructure in the country:** Canada has strong transportation and communication systems that support Canadian business production by allowing companies to get their products to market efficiently and by helping businesses communicate with customers and suppliers around the world.

- **research and development:** The level and scope of research and development—which fosters innovation in a country—can affect its competitive position. Canada's record on research and development spending varies according to sector with R&D in information technology and telecommunications infrastructure sectors leading the way.

- **workforce characteristics:** The level of education and the extent of training in the workforce are also factors in a country's competitiveness. Although the Canadian workforce is fewer in number than those of some other countries, relative to most countries, Canada has a well-educated workforce and a high level of literacy. On the other hand, international and multinational businesses are interested in knowing the number of days lost due to union-management problems in a country.

THINK ABOUT IT

What examples can you find in your community that illustrate one or more of Canada's competitive advantages? Have there been situations in your community where the lack of one or more of these advantages has affected the local economy?

- **societal characteristics:** Factors such as the value a country's citizens place on quality and productivity at work, the level of health care and standard of living, and the tolerance and diversity of a country's population give Canada an edge in attracting foreign investment and people from around the world.

- **entrepreneurship:** The quality and quantity of entrepreneurship in a country affects its competitiveness, as well as new venture start-ups and the general environment for entrepreneurs. Canadian entrepreneurs help the Canadian economy and our international competitiveness by providing business solutions to both Canadian and global consumers' needs and wants.

- **government involvement:** A country's tax environment (for example, in Canada the GST and PST) also affects its economy and its competitive business position relative to other countries. The Canadian government's participation in free trade agreements in North America, its membership in the G8, and its efforts to expand trade partnerships around the world are competitive advantages. On the other hand, the uncertainty of the political situation in Quebec sometimes adversely affects Canada's international trade and foreign investors' confidence in Canada.

Opportunity Cost, and Absolute and Comparative Advantage

One of the keys to understanding international business and competitive advantage is understanding the economic concept of **opportunity cost**. Whenever one opportunity is chosen or pursued by a company or an organization, others are sacrificed. Opportunity cost calculates, usually in financial terms, the benefits of the value of the next best opportunity that was foregone or not taken.

A simple example is the cost of giving up a job with an annual salary of $25 000 to go back to university to study law, medicine, or engineering. The basic opportunity cost of taking the four-year course is (4 x $25 000 = $100 000). Many times, a community has to choose between building a hospital or a school. The opportunity cost of either choice is the cost that would have been incurred in building the other, which must be measured against the priorities of the community.

In business, opportunity cost is expressed in dollars, calculating the costs involved in not implementing a real alternative in favour of the alternative chosen. In a thorough analysis, a company would calculate the costs of other production not undertaken compared to those of the alternative chosen, the costs of employing labour, inventory, and resources, the cost of capital, and operating costs for plants and equipment. The company may have to move employees from one area or product line, thereby reducing the output there, to the alternative chosen. The owner's resources (time, effort, and money) could also have been employed elsewhere.

GLOBAL THOUGHT

A market is a social system in which individuals pursue their own self-interest through the exchange with others whenever these trades are mutually beneficial. Suppose that I like ice cream but have a dozen apples, and you have a pint of ice cream but prefer apples. We could trade, and we would both be happier. Apples may be better for me, but I really do prefer ice cream, and that is what matters. In a market, people pursue their self-interest, however they define it for themselves.

– Janice Gross Stein

When one country has a lower cost in producing a product at a lower opportunity cost than another country, it is said to have a **comparative advantage**. When a country has a comparative advantage, it can specialize in what it does well and at a reasonable cost. It can then trade with other countries or export its products to them.

In the early 1990s, the consumption of Canadian salmon heads in southern China grew at a rapid rate. Canada specializes in salmon and, therefore, had a comparative advantage over China in providing salmon heads. Previously, this resource had been discarded as waste. Southern China has a comparative advantage in the production of toys and textiles because it uses comparatively inexpensive labour to produce them. Each country enjoys the benefits of consumption or use of these products—Canada buys toys and China buys salmon heads for their respective consumers.

A country has an **absolute advantage** in the production of a good relative to another country if it can produce the good at lower cost or with a higher rate of productivity. In other words, a country that can produce a good with lower production costs (by more efficient machinery or techniques, and/or fewer labour resources or costs) can obviously compete more strongly with another country.

Figure 3.6 Canada has a comparative advantage in telecommunications and wireless technology.

ICE Activities for 3.2

Ideas	Connections	Extensions
1. (a) How does a country achieve competitive advantage?	(b) Prepare a brief summary showing how your community is affected by one of Canada's competitive advantages and one of its disadvantages.	(c) Imagine your community without the competitive advantage and disadvantage you identified in 1. (b). How would your community be different?
2. (a) What is economic utility?	(b) Choose a Canadian raw material, such as wood, and describe how it is developed to have both form and place utility.	(c) How can you develop competitive advantage in your career? Start by considering your short- and long-term goals. Develop an action plan for achieving those goals. Write a report and keep it in your portfolio for future reference.
3. (a) Define the terms "opportunity cost," "absolute advantage," and "comparative advantage."	(b) Choose a Canadian company, product, or industry sector and explain how it helps provide Canada with absolute and/or comparative advantage.	(c) Choose a Canadian company, product, or industry sector that lacks a comparative advantage. Suggest three ways that it could develop a comparative advantage.

3.3 The Meaning of Productivity

What does it mean to be productive? When you have a number of tasks to perform in a day—handing in an essay, making a phone call about a part-time job, getting your bicycle repaired, and raking the leaves—you know the satisfaction that comes from completing those tasks on time. You've had a productive day.

Businesses, too, are interested in productivity. The factors of production are land, labour, capital, technology, and entrepreneurship. **Productivity** refers to the amount of work that is accomplished in a unit of time using the factors of production. Productivity can sometimes be increased by making relatively simple changes such as revising the way employees work on an assembly line to increase the number of products they can finish in an hour. At other times, an increase in productivity requires the investment of significant amounts of capital such as when a factory installs new technology that increases automation on the assembly line.

Business Purpose and Goals

The goal of any business is to make a profit. But what is the purpose of a business? This is usually expressed in a company's mission statement. Thomson Corporation's states, in part: "To…empower our people to help customers become more successful by providing them with indispensable information, insight, and solutions."

Two simple, common purposes for a business are to fulfill a need or to solve a problem. For example, when planning the 2000 Olympics in Sydney, Australia, it was determined that the sand for the beach volleyball event may not be satisfactory. Hutcheson Sand and Mixes, of Huntsville, Ontario, the "Official Consulting Firm for the Fédération Internationale de Volleyball (FIVB)," has a reputation for expertise in perfecting sand products (filling a need), and it was called upon to assess the quality of the sand in Sydney. Hutcheson has also gained recognition internationally, and its consulting services have been used throughout North America for golf courses and around the world for beach volleyball.

Figure 3.7 Hutcheson Sand and Mixes supplied the sand for this FIVB tournament in 1998 in Toronto.

Imagine you are writing
an essay on productivity
for your International
Business course.
What is your purpose?
How is this different
from your goal?

Achieving goals and targets requires organizations to be productive. With a car, you can measure the fuel efficiency (how many litres of gasoline it takes to drive 100 km) and have a mechanic advise on what work or new parts will be needed to increase the car's fuel efficiency. In industry, performance efficiency ratings are part of measuring productivity. If a machine or a production line is working at less than capacity, its performance efficiency generally can be improved. In any business, productivity is measured in some way. Even customer service is measured. For example, call centres track the number of calls a representative can handle in an hour. To become more productive, an individual, department, or business has to determine what it would take to do more, produce more, or reduce machine downtime (when a machine needs repair or maintenance).

Efficiency is a value. And whether we realize it or not, it is the central value in Canadian society. It has largely displaced religion, ethnicity, and language as a source of public loyalty.

– Joseph Heath

Action on these items will increase efficiency and productivity (which may be one goal, or a department goal), which will help achieve the company's overall goals.

For a company, productivity measures the relationship between "inputs" and "outputs," or how well a company uses the resources it has (people, machines, production lines, parts supplies, or raw materials) to perform more profitably or more competitively. Such measures can be adapted to any kind of organization.

Factors Influencing a Country's Productivity

TRADE TALK

Nearly eight million Canadian workers are online at work. A study has shown that the Internet can have a negative effect on productivity. According to an Angus Reid Group Inc. survey, 78 percent of Canadians with Internet access at work admit they regularly use it for personal reasons (for personal e-mail, checking the headlines, tracking investments, and so on).

Many factors affect a country's productivity:
- efficient use of human and physical resources
- costs associated with labour (for example, wages and salaries, benefits, workers' safety and insurance costs, payroll administration)
- accessibility and quantity of a country's usable natural resources
- quality and availability of a nation's technology
- quality of education and of government services
- quality of business leadership and strategy
- general work ethic and healthy lifestyle
- efficiency of plants and of organizational structures
- size of both domestic and international markets for a country's products and services
- amount of support given to research and development

Let's look at just one of these factors, the quality of a nation's technology, as an example of how it affects productivity. When Henry Ford introduced the assembly line in the early part of the twentieth century, it became possible to mass-produce automobiles, making them affordable for the average family. At the time, the assembly line was what we now call "cutting-edge" technology. But if a car manufacturer used these same assembly-line methods at the beginning of the twenty-first century, it would soon go out of business. Today, the automobile assembly line still exists, but it is highly mechanized, using robotic machines to do much of the work formerly done by people. By using the latest in technology, a car manufacturer can continue Ford's tradition: supplying automobiles for the mass market. In a country whose businesses cannot afford to install this new technology, the productivity cannot match that of countries with the new technology.

A country's standard of living and quality of life are determined by its productivity. If Canadians are competitive and productive, they will enjoy the "fruits of their labour." But maintaining efficiency and high productivity is an ongoing pursuit, as you can see from the examples of the Ford assembly line from the turn of the century and the General Motors assembly line shown in the early 2000s. Therefore, continuing to measure such items as a country's GDP, either in total or per capita, is an important way to determine the value or productivity of each country involved in global trade.

GLOBAL THOUGHT

Business journalist David Crane made this observation in an article in the *Toronto Star* in 2000:

In recent years, we have had to watch with envy as Americans enjoyed the benefits from a sharp rise in productivity performance and a widening gap between ourselves and our neighbours to the south in living standards. While Americans are now generating about $34 268 USD in per capita income, Canadians are generating $26 375 USD— a gap of nearly $8 000 USD or nearly $12 000 CAD.

THINK ABOUT IT

What do you think accounts for the difference in the per capita income between Canada and the United States? Has the gap changed since the author wrote his article?

Figure 3.8 Ford assembly line in the early 1900s.

Figure 3.9 General Motors of Canada robot-driven assembly line in the early 2000s.

The World of 100 People

If we could shrink the earth's population to a village of precisely 100 people, with all the existing human ratios remaining the same, it would look something like the following:

There would be 57 Asians, 21 Europeans, 14 from the Western Hemisphere, both North and South, 8 Africans.

52 would be female, 48 would be male.

70 would be non-white, 30 would be white.

70 would be non-Christian, 30 would be Christian.

89 would be heterosexual, 11 would be homosexual.

6 people would possess 59% of the entire world's wealth—and all 6 would be from the United States.

80 would live in substandard housing.

70 would be unable to read.

50 would suffer malnutrition.

1 would be near death, 1 would be pregnant.

1 (yes, only 1) would have a college/university education.

1 would own a computer.

– Donella Meadows

Figure 3.10 The demographics (or characteristics) of the world's human populations.

For a country, high rates of productivity can be reflected in higher wage and salary levels, increased profits to reinvest in innovation and research, and greater tax revenues to finance health, education, and the needs of an aging society. Productivity growth is evident in innovation in information technologies, strong machinery, equipment and plant investment, and low unemployment. Productivity performance is one of the best indicators of economic performance. Improved productivity is necessary to improve living standards.

ICE Activities for 3.3

Ideas	Connections	Extensions
1. (a) Identify the difference between the purpose and the goal of an organization.	(b) Identify one goal that ties in to your career aspirations. How might you go about achieving that goal?	(c) In your opinion, how does going through life without identifying a purpose and goals affect a person's productivity?
2. (a) Explain what productivity means in business terms.	(b) Refer to the list of factors affecting a country's productivity on page 87. How could any of these factors account for the difference in per capita income between Canada and the United States?	(c) How could an organization such as the following use its resources differently to become more productive: your school team or club, your favourite professional sports team, your municipal government.
3. (a) List three factors that influence a country's productivity.	(b) Working with a partner, research one of the factors you selected in 3. (a), and present a brief oral presentation explaining how that factor affects business productivity in your region of Canada.	(c) Imagine that you are an entrepreneur interested in exporting to an international market. How might you overcome any disadvantages associated with the factor you researched in 3. (b)?

3.4 Canada's Global Challenge

Improved levels of productivity in one nation will result in more competition among all countries engaged in international business or global trade. In an increasingly "shrinking" world, Canada's small domestic market, normally seen as a drawback, may also be its greatest strength. With few customers close at hand, many Canadian companies must be innovative, entrepreneurial, and export-driven. Canadian businesses need to respond to the challenges of an international market by focusing on producing high-quality products and investing in training and education. Businesses and government need to encourage innovation along with research and development.

More than 40 percent of our gross domestic product and one-third of our jobs now depend on international trade, and this is likely to increase in the future if Canada can create a positive presence internationally.

GLOBAL THOUGHT

International competition is more than ever about people. What people know and can do determines whether a company can earn profits and expand and whether a country can attract investment and grow its economy.... It is impossible to talk about human capital without reference to its principal incubator— the education system....We continue to invest more in the education of our citizens than most industrialized countries.

– *Thomas Paul D'Aquino* and
David Stewart-Patterson

Another challenge facing Canada is maintaining our standard of living. **Standard of living** is the way people live as measured by the kinds and quality of goods and services they can afford. Major economic indicators of standard of living include average family income and expenditures, household ownership of durable goods (such as the number of telephones and personal computers), number of physicians per 1000 people, and literacy rate of the population.

Canada has consistently scored high on standard-of-living assessments, often in the top 10 of most surveys. Maintaining a good standard of living will help Canada retain and attract talented, educated people who will maintain and increase our productivity as a nation. Especially important are people who work in what is called the "knowledge economy."

TRADE TALK

Knowledge and Development

The World Bank is concerned with promoting growth and reducing poverty in the developing world....Today the World Bank has shifted much of its emphasis to the intangibles of knowledge, institutions, and culture in an attempt to forge a more comprehensive New Development Framework for our work.

– *Joseph Stiglitz*, Senior Vice President and Chief Economist, The World Bank Group

The Knowledge Economy

The term **knowledge economy** refers to the increased reliance of business, labour, and government on knowledge, information, and ideas—and information technology to put them to practical use. Its importance underscores the growing importance of "brain over brawn" or mental over physical labour. In the knowledge economy, workers are paid to think and to employ state-of-the-art information technology in many areas. They can access more information and ideas, and their ability to process, adapt, and implement yields results that are then incorporated as improvements to existing systems and processes.

The industrial revolution transformed the economy from agriculture to industry, and from rural to urban. Then the scientific revolution moved us to research laboratories and to research and development programs, as well as exploited the potential of innovation and inventions.

Sarah Brennan-Peeters

Vice-President of International Sales, Spin Master Toys

If you have heard of Air Hogs, Devil Sticks, or Earth Buddy, you'll know about Spin Master Toys of Toronto. It's the job of Sarah Brennan-Peeters, vice-president of international sales, to make sure people in other countries know about these products too.

Brennan-Peeters joined this young Canadian company in 1996, right out of university. "I graduated from York University, Glendon College, with a degree in International Relations," says Brennan-Peeters. "I wanted to be a diplomat, but I really didn't have enough languages." By directing the global effort at Spin Master Toys, however, she has gained valuable skills in managing international relations.

Brennan-Peeters' first job in the company was as an executive assistant. In this position, she learned much of the detail she would need to know in sales and marketing, including pricing, shipping, distributor relations, and promotion. The company was growing quickly, and Brennan-Peeters was soon catapulted into international sales. Spin Master Toys began its international efforts in Germany, Austria, and Switzerland, using a distributor. Next came Australia and Scandinavia. Currently, the company is re-thinking its strategy and hopes to take a direct sales approach to retailers in select countries.

Brennan-Peeters loves the travel (even though it can be demanding and tiring) and meeting people. She is constantly learning new approaches to business—an important ability, since the firm can be focusing on 10–20 countries at once, each with its own customs, preferences, and trends.

"I think I would consider our positioning of the Air Hog [a toy airplane] in the Japanese market as one of my greatest challenges. Young Japanese consumers are very technically oriented. They are demanding and prefer products that are sophisticated and animated. Very few North American toy products ever make it onto Japanese retail shelves. However, flight is universal and our Air Hog product, with a little modification in packaging, won them over!"

Today, China produces 85 percent of the world's toys, according to Brennan-Peeters; Taiwan and Germany are also important producers. Spin Master Toys now uses five factories to produce its toys, benefiting from China's abundance of labour, which produces quality product at low cost. All this production is anchored by the Hong Kong office of 17 staff, which is able to manage the factory relationships and global shipping.

Brennan-Peeters's advice to young people considering a career with an international organization is that "companies of all sizes are now beginning to realize the business potential of going global. To work internationally means you have to be patient, open to new experiences and, of course, willing to travel on your own."

Brennan-Peeters is quick to point out that markets are shrinking. The toy industry in particular is very competitive. Young people have more sophisticated tastes and are enticed by video and DVD games and other high-tech products. She also points out that Spin Master Toys keeps its competitive advantage by innovating constantly and keeping the entrepreneurial spirit alive. "We are always investing in new product ideas and developing brands as we go. In fact, we hire engineers for this very purpose," says Brennan-Peeters. The company also has the ability to get new products to market quickly. Responding to markets, and doing so swiftly, is paramount.

• •

1. How did awareness of the target Japanese market help Sarah Brennan-Peeters successfully position the Air Hog?

2. What advice does Brennan-Peeters propose for individuals and companies planning to go global?

Improvements or changes are welcomed in most industries. The greatest rate of change appears to be taking place in the application of information technology (IT). Today, IT influences all sectors of the economy.

Canadian author Nuala Beck has categorized North America's industries as follows:

High-Knowledge Industries: More than 40 percent of these industries' employees are knowledge workers. Examples include information technology, education, government, microelectronics, biotechnology, telecommunications, and computers.

Moderate-Knowledge Industries: Between 20 percent and 40 percent of these industries' employees are knowledge workers. Examples include job-training services and real estate sales, customer service, sales representatives, and financial services.

Low-Knowledge Industries: Less than 20 percent of these industries' employees are knowledge workers. Examples include retail sales, meat processing, truck driving, and any type of manual labour.

Intellectual Capital

Intellectual capital is the sum of knowledge, information, intellectual property, talent, and experience within a country or an organization. Intellectual capital includes ideas, is part of a company's human capital, and is a factor in a company's or a country's competitiveness and its ability to create wealth. It can be argued that intellectual capital has become more important than natural resources as a source of wealth. However, intellectual capital is not measured or accounted for in the way that land and financial capital are.

An example of intellectual capital at work can be found in the medical field. A number of medical discoveries have recently occurred in the field of biotechnology, where most of the workers are considered to be knowledge workers. Some of these discoveries relate to treatments for conditions such as high blood pressure, cancer, and Alzheimer's disease. It takes years of research and experimentation to perfect these treatments, but once the treatment, in the form of a product, reaches the consumer, the producer usually profits.

Today's world economy requires companies to be innovative and creative, and to bring to market products that are unique and superior to those of competitors. Companies that are built on intellectual capital have become powerful and important components of the world's economy.

For example, when the company Netscape decided to go public (become a public company listed on the stock market) in 1995, it had $17 million USD in sales

Figure 3.11 Into which category of knowledge industries do medical workers fit? Why?

with 50 employees. After the first day of trading, the stock market in the United States valued Netscape at $3 billion! Individuals and institutions had invested in the value of Netscape's people and their knowledge. Many information technology companies multiplied their financial worth dramatically because of this trend, but much of this was unrealistically inflated and some company stocks later declined substantially in value.

A company's brains, the know-how, intellectual property, trade secrets, and collective knowledge of its employees all define its competitive advantage today. However, brainpower, which will continue to be a more valuable asset than muscle, mechanical, or technical power in many fields, cannot always protect a company from the dangers of a volatile economy. High-risk enterprises in the IT field may reap large rewards or may face major failures. In the economic downturn of 2001, a number of IT companies collapsed.

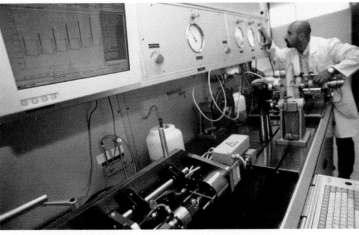

Figure 3.12 The research laboratory is a place where many scientists have made discoveries.

THINK ABOUT IT

New products are invented to meet needs and wants. Here are some products you may see one day:
- Cars with built-in sensors that would record information about accidents in which the car is involved.
- Self-cleaning clothes.
- Dog collars that contain a small digital recorder on which the dog's owner can record the dog's name, the owner's name, and the owner's phone number.

Do these inventions meet needs or wants? Are there existing methods to deal with the problems they solve?

Thriving in the Knowledge Economy

There are plenty of stories of missing the boat on great new knowledge. The Swiss invented a mechanism that counted time in digits but couldn't see how it applied to watches. The Japanese saw the mechanism in an exhibit of interesting curiosities and the rest, as they say, is history. Talk to Xerox people and they'll freely admit— in fact it's part of their folklore—that their research facility at Palo Alto came up with truly breakthrough technology (for example, the mouse, icon technology, laptops). None of it was exploited because Xerox management couldn't see its market value. Apple did.

According to Frances Horibe in *Managing Knowledge Workers*, the 3M Corporation's discovery of Post-it notes was "the result of a scientist creating a glue that didn't stick well." 3M is a multinational corporation with more than 40 business units, with operations in more than 60 countries, and with a reputation for innovation. As Horibe explains, "The genius was not just that scientist, but in the company's ability to recognize usefulness. In hindsight, it's easy to shake our heads and say, 'How stupid, how short-sighted,' and to believe we're more like the 3M manager who gave the go-ahead for the Post-it notes.... Great ideas are great because they don't fit into our current way of thinking."

Knowledge is the prime source of competitive advantage in the global economy. Managers of organizations must deal with this reality. They must learn to develop, share, use, and measure knowledge to create more value for customers, employees, and shareholders. One key idea in the knowledge economy is that knowledge is developed when people work with one another. Knowledge must be connected to existing knowledge or information. Existing knowledge leads to new knowledge. Knowledge develops when companies make connections or networks. The more and better the connections, the more and better the information that can be shared, in turn developing more knowledge.

The knowledge economy requires members of organizations to share information openly. This sharing within a company, known as transparency, helps ensure productivity by avoiding duplication of effort or reinventing a successful solution that already exists. Such solutions may be found down the street, around the world, or in the next cubicle. Organizational knowledge is all the knowledge stored within the boundaries of a company. For a global company, the development of a worldwide network is imperative. Your personal career success will likely depend on your ability to create and develop your own network. For Canadian businesses, the challenge is to foster a sense of teamwork throughout the entire organization.

GLOBAL THOUGHT

Knowledge is infinitely renewable and expandable, and it is also increasingly specialized and customized. We think very differently about "product" today than we have in the past. For example, at first it was those who grew tea and sold it abroad who reaped economic gain. Later, it was those who manufactured the teacup, mass-produced for a mass market, who profited even more.

– Janice Gross Stein

Innovation and Quality

Innovation refers not only to technological and scientific breakthroughs you read about in newspapers and magazines. It also includes constant improvements in the way businesses adopt new processes and adapt to new markets. To capture the emerging opportunities on the international scene, Canadians must seek improved technology wherever it is available. No country alone can develop all the technology it needs.

There are two major ways to ensure international competitiveness: by price and by the uniqueness of the product or service. In both cases, quality and innovation will give Canada a competitive edge.

Perhaps the most important aspect of competing through innovation and quality is that it gives the producer the capability to change often. Innovation forces competitors to struggle to catch up. A good example is the computer software market. Microsoft Windows programs are constantly changing and improving to help users become more efficient and adapt to an ever-changing hardware market.

Innovation is the key to finding new ways of increasing productivity and goes beyond investment in research. Since there are always ways to improve, innovation requires consistent dedication. Regardless of past performance, individuals, organizations, and countries can always ask the question, "How can I (we) make it better?"

TRADE TALK

To deliver the high-value jobs and rising incomes that flow from productivity and innovation, Canadian companies must compete globally both in selling their products and in attracting investors. To ignore the world, to remain content with being a big fish in the Canadian pond, can at best provide an illusion of stability in the short term and a guarantee of declining fortunes for Canadian investors and employees alike over the longer term.

– Thomas Paul D'Aquino and David Stewart-Patterson

Taxation and Innovation

Taxation is the method used to generate the finances required to run the country. The money collected by municipal, provincial, and federal governments from individuals and businesses is spent on a variety of programs and projects, both domestically and internationally.

Canadians have come to rely on the infrastructure provided by many of these programs, such as health care, education, and a good transportation system. However, when compared to a range of other countries, Canada's corporate tax rate is higher than many of its global competitors. As a result, Canada may have more difficulty attracting foreign investment than other countries. Companies tend to target their investment in countries that support them with lower taxes. However, when companies look to other countries for investment opportunities, they take more than taxes into account. For example, companies deciding where to locate need to balance lower labour costs against higher tax rates. In 1999, for example, Canada's manufacturing labour costs were the lowest of the G7, according to the U.S. Bureau of Labor Statistics.

Some people believe that lowering taxes on individuals and companies can stimulate the economy by encouraging business and consumer spending, foreign investment, and employment. When businesses have greater net profits because they pay lower taxes, they may decide to build inventory or to invest in other ways, including research, improved productivity, and increased staff. When people have more money in their paycheques because they are sending less to the government, they may spend it on goods they otherwise would not have bought. This starts a cycle of increased consumption, increased production, and increased employment, meaning that more people are now earning a paycheque and paying taxes. Thus the total amount of taxes received may increase, even though the taxation rate has decreased.

THINK ABOUT IT

A tax on personal income was introduced in Canada in 1917 to pay for the costs of Canada's participation in World War I. The tax was meant as a temporary measure. However, Canadians still pay income tax. How do you think the government raised money before 1917?

Rationalization

Rationalization is the process used by an organization or company to change its organizational structure, its product line, or its production process to become more efficient, productive, and competitive. The process may result in relatively straightforward changes such as combining departments or product lines into a new division, refocusing or changing business priorities, downsizing some aspects of the business, or closing down some product lines.

Rationalization can also involve larger changes: building new factories, developing new technologies, starting up new businesses or acquiring existing businesses. On the other hand, it may also result in closing factories or divisions, discarding outmoded technologies, or specializing production by product line in different parts of the world to take advantage of lower labour costs, available investment capital, or raw materials.

Figure 3.13 During 2000, lower consumer demand for automobiles resulted in rationalization in the North American automobile industry as General Motors, Ford, and Daimler Chrysler closed production facilities and cut jobs around the world.

Causes and Effects of Rationalization

A company may have to rationalize various aspects of its business because of changes in consumer demand for its products. Some companies buy up or merge with other companies to bring more profits into the parent company and to contribute to economies of scale. **Economies of scale** refer to the tendency of the cost per item to go down when items are bought or produced in large quantities. Less productive factories can be closed or downsized, and more productive ones can take up the slack. In this process, employees are often laid off when their services become redundant; a single factory can perform the functions that were previously performed in many factories. Such closures also affect the businesses that supplied goods or services to the rationalized business. A supply company may have depended on the downsized company, and so the supply company and its employees may be adversely affected by the rationalization process.

In difficult economic times, companies sometimes rationalize their production facilities to try to regain the confidence of investors and of the financial institutions that lend them money. For example, in January 2001, after a slowdown in the U.S. economy and increased competition from foreign imports led to a year of poor profits, the Ford Motor Company announced profits were down $692 million in the third quarter of 2000. As a result, the company decided to lay off 35 000 workers around the world and close five plants in North America over the next few years. Ford's Ontario plant in Oakville would close by 2004. In the same month, Daimler Chrysler announced it would cut 20 percent of its workforce—26 000 jobs—in the United States, Canada, Mexico, Argentina, and Brazil. Daimler Chrysler had become increasingly unprofitable since the merger of the two companies in 1998. The company's stock had fallen to $48 USD from a high of $103 in January 1999. These closures caused job losses and rationalization in businesses that depend on the auto industry: their parts suppliers and automobile dealerships, as well as the local retail stores and other businesses that serviced the laid-off automotive workers.

As companies, or even industries, make decisions about rationalizing their business internationally, they look at various factors in different countries: consumer demand, a country's trade balance and business climate, and the situation that has resulted from mergers and acquisitions. As the following examples show, the interrelationship among these factors can be complex.

- **The demand for the industry's products in Canada:** While there has been growth in some of the industries that market products to older Canadians, this growth doesn't always mean more jobs for Canadians. The demand for products may have increased, but so has productivity in many industries. For example, according to the Industry Canada / Price Waterhouse "Study of the Pharmaceutical

Industry" published in 2001, the number of employees working in the pharmaceutical industry in Canada decreased 10 percent from 1987 to 1994. This decrease occurred even though the demand for pharmaceutical products worldwide increased by 8 percent a year during the same time period.

- **The trade balance between Canada and other countries:** Canada imports more of certain types of products than it manufactures and exports. For example, according to Statistics Canada, Canada imported $28 194.4 million in industrial and agricultural machinery in 2001 and exported $19 230.8 million of the same type of product. However, even if Canadian exports were to increase, the economies of scale and increased automation in this industry might mean that there would not be many more jobs for Canadians.

- **Organizational change:** In many countries, companies that are developing new technologies have had to make organizational changes to stay in business. For example, Ballard Power Systems of Vancouver, which develops, manufactures, and markets zero-emission fuel cells for automobiles, announced in December 2002 that it would cut its workforce by 400 in a restructuring plan to reduce its costs.

- **Canadian business activities:** The level of Canadian employment in an industry depends on a number of factors, including the likelihood of future earnings. For example, in December 2002, Canada's Parliament approved the Kyoto Protocol to reduce greenhouse gases. Early opponents of the Protocol in Alberta feared that this decision would threaten exports of oil and gas. According to Alberta Premier Ralph Klein, cutting emissions would cost multinational fuel companies too much, and they would leave Canada, resulting in substantial job and investment losses to Canadians.

Privatization is a type of rationalization. Some people argue that privatizing electrical power, prisons, health care, or highways will bring about more productive systems. Those who support privatization believe that the private sector is more efficient and effective than the public sector at running an organization. They believe that government is wasteful or inefficient, and that taxpayers do not like to see their taxes spent on poorly run services. However, there are many instances when government should control the product or service. A good example is airport security: tighter, more effective security is perhaps best placed with a government that ensures that high standards are set and enforced. In the end, consumers and producers tend to look to markets for efficiency. However, consumers also turn to government to ensure that producers maintain both quality and accountability.

THINK ABOUT IT

Using the newspaper or the Internet, identify a former government service that is being privatized in your province or community. What arguments are presented for this change? What is your opinion of the change?

Web Link

Follow the link at www.internationalbusiness.nelson.com to find out more about rationalization at Industry Canada's Strategis Web site.

Developed Nations and Economies

Canada is referred to as a developed or industrialized nation. **Developed nations** tend to have a high standard of living and produce a sophisticated range of products such as computers and automobiles. **Developing nations**, also called newly industrialized economies (NIEs), such as Vietnam and China, have made the transition to more sophisticated manufacturing. They have moved away from an economy based largely on textiles, shoes and clothing, and agricultural products. The growing number of developed nations means more international competitors. It also indicates there may be more potential markets or consumers available for producers around the world. Developing nations are also ideal settings for businesses from developed countries to manufacture products, since the cost of labour is much lower.

Finally, there are those countries that are known as **less-developed nations**. These largely agricultural-based countries have a tendency to experience political and military instability more often. However, they too may be potential sites for expanding investment, business, and trade.

As technological innovation spreads around the world, developing countries may be able to benefit by avoiding some of the negative aspects of industrial life such as smokestacks and assembly-line work. For example, is the automobile necessarily a symbol of a high standard of living if it creates gridlock on the streets and pollutes the air? This question and others will have to be answered by developing nations. They have the advantage of learning from those developed countries that have made mistakes along the way.

ICE Activities for 3.4

Ideas	Connections	Extensions
1. (a) What economic indicators are used to determine a nation's standard of living?	(b) Estimate how many of your classmates have a cell phone. List the different makes and models, and the costs per phone. If your class were a country, what would its standard of living be if based solely on the ownership of cell phones?	(c) In your opinion, what is Canada's global challenge in the twenty-first century? How do you think Canada can address this challenge? Prepare a half-page report.
2. (a) What is intellectual capital?	(b) What effect do knowledge and intellectual capital have on the competitiveness and productivity of a company? Why?	(c) Using a national or online international newspaper, research a discovery that intellectual capital made possible. Write a brief report of your findings.
3. (a) What is business rationalization?	(b) What methods of rationalization are employed to improve a company's or country's competitive position?	(c) Create a concept web or mind map to show some of the ways that a Canadian business could use the trend towards rationalization to strengthen its international competitiveness.

3.5 Quality Control and Continual Improvement

To sustain a competitive advantage, a country or business must always be on the lookout for ways to improve. The Japanese have a name for the concept of continual improvement: kaizen (ki-zan). Kaizen is the belief that to gain competitive advantage, there must be a commitment to quality. When applied to business and the workplace, kaizen promotes everyone working together to make improvements. Kaizen helps eliminate waste in all systems and processes of an organization but does not necessarily mean an increase in investments or costs.

Web Link

To learn more about Dr. Deming's valuable global contribution, follow the link at www.internationalbusiness.nelson.com.

Quality Control

After World War II ended in 1945, Japan and its economy lay in ruins as a result of its military defeat by the United States and the Allied Forces. Japan realized that to become an economic force to be reckoned with, it would have to focus on productivity, particularly with an emphasis on quality. In 1951, American management and quality expert W. Edwards Deming was invited to Japan to explain the quality control techniques that had been developed in the United States. In the 1950s and 1960s, "Made in Japan" often meant that the product was substandard and poor quality. By the early 1980s, however, Japan's economic might and products challenged the United States. By the end of that decade, Deming's ideas on quality had been adopted by many Japanese companies. Japan was able to compete with, and in some cases surpass, the United States in industries such as consumer electronics, robotics, and automobiles.

Figure 3.14 Japan adopted W. Edwards Deming's 14 management principles, and by the late 1980's, some Japanese industries surpassed their U.S. counterparts.

Deming is perhaps best known for his "14 Points for Management." Some of his ideas include the following:

- Always continuously improve the product or service to stay competitive and create jobs.

- Encourage education of the workforce, both on and off the job.

- Allow workers to take responsibility for and pride in their work.

- Remove communication barriers between management and the factory floor.

- Encourage teamwork between departments to improve product quality and to create common goals.

Rocky Mountain Bicycles

Appropriately, Rocky Mountain Bicycles, in Vancouver, is named after the rugged Rocky Mountains of western Canada. Its bikes have a reputation for standing up to demanding riding and conditions. The company's philosophy states, "We build bikes for people who love to ride. It's the core of what we do. We know there are a million different types of riders out there…. As a bike company, we've made it our mission to create a high-grade quiver of bikes that meets the needs of the myriad of off-road cyclists out there. To do this, we pay particular attention to innovation, quality, and detail."

The company was started in 1981 and in 1982 produced its first Rocky Mountain bike after travelling to Japan to seek out parts to use in this first bike. By 1984, the company's reputation was growing, and sales expanded to eastern Canada.

In 1987, the company established its slogan "Total Commitment, No Compromise." It neatly conveys the company's dedication to quality, from the shop floor to the retail outlet. This belief in quality paid off. In 1989, Rocky Mountain shipped five bikes to Germany, a country long known for its attention to quality and detail. The company has a strong following in Germany and is exploring other markets. Today, Rocky Mountain bikes are known worldwide for their performance and quality. There are distributors in over 12 countries.

Rocky Mountain's hand-built bikes have also been used by Olympic athletes like Canadian Alison Sydor. Every one of the bikes the company produces every year bears the stamp "Built in Canada."

Rocky Mountain invests major resources and many hours in research and development for their products, with an R&D facility right in their factory. Biking has grown to encompass a variety of riders— from downhill racing to urban riding. Rocky Mountain has diversified its product line to meet these needs. It is dedicated to continual innovation to improve upon its designs. To do that, it relies on an in-house team of engineers, designers, and welders. Rocky Mountain builds its bikes by hand and invests heavily in quality control and high construction standards.

Rocky Mountain Bicycles has gained considerable market share through 40 percent (1999) growth in the United States, a market that is relatively flat. And sales in Europe continue to grow. Now Rocky Mountain offers a line of clothing. That means when people go to buy, Rocky Mountain bikes are definitely top of mind!

Photo: Blake Jorgenson

Figure 3.15 Rocky Mountain bicycles are known for their ability to endure rugged riding and terrain.

In 2001, *Mountain Bike Magazine USA* readers chose Rocky Mountain as the fastest-growing bicycle company. Rocky Mountain Bicycles has sponsored teams and two of Canada's best-known racers— Andreas Hestler and Lesley Tomlinson, who have both represented Canada at the Olympics.

• •

1. How has Rocky Mountain Bicycles maintained a competitive advantage in the international bike industry?
2. What role has quality control played in the success of Rocky Mountain Bicycles?

These ideas apply to small and large organizations alike, to the service industry as well as to manufacturing. They can also apply to a struggling division within a company.

Japan adopted Deming's 14 principles, and Japanese businesses dedicated themselves to the change, or "transformation." Government, business, and labour worked together with a commitment to quality and productivity. As a result, Japan became known as Japan, Inc. However, Japan's adherence to these principles throughout the last half of the twentieth century was not enough to protect it from the Asian economic decline that began in 1997. The situation was not the result of a decrease in or lack of quality but rather of shifting market forces in the global economy.

Total Quality Management (TQM)

Another philosophy that originated with the pursuit of business excellence in the 1980s and 1990s was total quality management. **Total quality management (TQM)** is a method of managing organizations with a commitment to continuously improve the products, processes, and the work habits of employees; management also is determined to consistently meet customer needs. **Market-driven organizations** are those that respond to market needs by providing customers with high-quality goods and services that are low in cost and available when required; they may also use TQM management techniques.

To successfully compete globally and improve their competitive advantage, Canadian companies must be market-driven. They must be flexible, able to adapt and respond quickly to change, and able to use information and knowledge effectively.

Web Link

Follow the link at
www.internationalbusiness.nelson.com
to learn how the National Quality Institute enables organizations to achieve greater productivity.

The International Organization for Standardization (ISO)

The mission of the **International Organization for Standardization (ISO)** is to promote the development of voluntary standards and related activities in the world, with a view to facilitating the international exchange of goods and services, and to developing cooperation in the spheres of intellectual, scientific, technological, and economic activity. Perhaps you have seen the ISO symbol on a banner at a manufacturing facility.

The ISO is a non-governmental organization established in 1947. It is now a worldwide federation of national standards organizations from some 140 countries, with one individual member from each country. The ISO has published over 12 000 standards, the most notable of which are the ISO 9000 series of standards on quality management and quality assurance.

The ISO 9000 standard provides the requirements that an organization must meet to have its Quality Management System (QMS) verified and registered by a third-party registrar. Many organizations that have implemented a QMS and have been registered will advertise this on their facilities. In Canada and around the world, the uptake of these standards is extensive (over 400 000 certificates issued worldwide).

The Standards Council of Canada coordinates Canada's participation in the world's two leading international standards bodies—the ISO and the International Electrotechnical Commission (IEC). The Standards Council is a federal Crown corporation with the mandate to promote efficient and effective standardization. It has accredited over 300 public and private organizations to develop standards or to determine the compliance of products, services, or systems to a standard's requirements. The Standards Council oversees the National Standards System.

Many large company and government buyers both in Canada and in other countries now require that suppliers meet certain ISO standards.

Figure 3.16 Many manufacturing facilities display banners that identify them as ISO certified.

Web Link

For more information on the Standards Council of Canada and the International Organization for Standardization, follow the link at
www.internationalbusiness.nelson.com.

ICE Activities for 3.5

Ideas	Connections	Extensions
1. (a) What is *kaizen*?	(b) How can *kaizen* transform companies into superior competitors?	(c) In small teams, use the *kaizen* model to suggest ways in which the operation of your school could be improved. Share your results with the rest of the class.
2. (a) Who was W. Edwards Deming and what was his contribution to the business world?	(b) Research an organization that is market driven. Provide examples to show how it is market driven.	(c) Research Deming's "14 Points for Management." Select one of these points and explain how an organization you are in, or used to be a member of, could implement it. What do you think the implications of this change would be?
3. (a) What does the ISO symbol stand for?	(b) Why is it important that Canadian companies be ISO certified?	(c) Predict how newly industrialized countries such as China will be able to match the productivity and quality of the output of more established economies. What are the implications of such productivity for the developed countries of the G8?

Canada's Trading Partners:
Focus on Vietnam

If Coca-Cola signs can be taken as a sign of capitalism and foreign investment, then Vietnam has firmly grasped the concept. In 1986, in an effort to transform Vietnam from a centrally planned (communist) economy to a market-driven economy, the country launched the policy of *doi moi* (reconstruction). It wasn't long before the Coca-Cola logo was popping up everywhere.

In a market-driven economy, countries and companies attempt to create and to determine consumer needs and then fulfill those needs. A communist economy offers consumers little choice. Many of Vietnam's trading partners in Asia thought they would benefit from Vietnam's ability to organize, focus, and work hard. Investment poured into the country when the American trade embargo was lifted in 1984. By 1996, foreign investment had reached $8.3 billion USD a year. Between 1990 and 1997, Vietnam experienced an average GDP growth rate of 8 percent.

Vietnam remains a difficult country in which to invest. Vietnam is still in need of new infrastructure, including new telephone networks, banks, roads, hotels, sewers, bridges, dams, and improved transportation. In October 1997, Asia suffered a financial crisis, and the Vietnam market, like other Asian markets, slowed down. Investing in Vietnam is risky due to government inefficiency and corruption. Large companies like Chrysler have moved out after years of frustration and broken government promises.

In 1999, Canadian exports to Vietnam were $47.6 million (down 12.6 percent from 1998). Canadian imports from Vietnam were $194.6 million, an increase of 7 percent in the same period. Vietnam exports clothing, footwear, fish, coffee, rubber, and rice. By 1999, Vietnam had become the world's second-greatest exporter of rice and coffee.

While Vietnam encourages an entrepreneurial business mentality and has an educated workforce, more development and stability are required before Vietnam becomes a true magnet for investment facilities. Foreign investment tends to go to those countries that are changing more rapidly and progressively.

Figure 3.17 When Vietnam's economy became market-driven, Coca-Cola signs became a common sight.

A SNAPSHOT OF VIETNAM

Size: 329 560 sq. km

World Region: Southeast Asia

Capital City: Hanoi

Language: Vietnamese

Currency: New Dong

Population: 81.0 million

Time: Noon in Ottawa (EST) is midnight the next day (12 hours ahead) in Hanoi.

Climate: Tropical with monsoons and a chance of typhoons from May to January.

Type of Government: Communist state. Socialist economy with approximately one-half of all industry owned by the state.

Labour Force by Occupation: 69.2 percent agriculture, 17 percent services, 12.9 percent industry (1996 est.). Approximately 75 percent of the population is involved in subsistence farming, in which people consume most of what they grow.

Figure 3.18 A rice field in Vietnam.

Membership in World Organizations: Joined ASEAN Free Trade Area (Association of South East Asian Nations) in 1995; applied for membership in WTO and APEC

Importing Partners and Products:
Partners: Singapore, Korea, Japan, and China make up 58 percent. Canada represents 0.4 percent.
Products: Machinery, chemical fertilizers, motorcycles.

Exporting Partners and Products:
Partners: Japan, Germany, United States, and France.
Products: Footwear, textiles, rice, coffee, rubber.

Travel Advisory: Travellers need to be aware of the following:

- Roads are poor, city streets are congested, and floods occur in the rainy season.
- Travel may be restricted in some border areas. Officials may monitor some telephones, and hotel rooms may be monitored by officials.
- Visitors cannot stay with Vietnamese families without permission.
- Vaccination shots are required.
- A valid Vietnamese driver's licence is required to rent a vehicle. It's wiser to rent a vehicle with a Vietnamese driver.

Business Etiquette: The Vietnamese place a high value on politeness and have a great respect for age and position. When possible, submit a meeting agenda and issues to be discussed via fax prior to the meeting. Communication through an interpreter is advisable, though not mandatory.

Country Link

Follow the link at
www.internationalbusiness.nelson.com
to learn more about Canadian business opportunities in Vietnam.

Chapter Challenges

Knowledge/Understanding

1. Match each of the following terms to the correct definition or description below:
   (a) competitive advantage
   (b) gross domestic product
   (c) economies of scale
   (d) standard of living
   (e) transparency
   (f) capital
   (g) developed countries
   (h) developing countries
   (i) knowledge economy

   (i) the total value of goods and services produced in a country during a specific period
   (ii) an open sharing of information within an organization or company
   (iii) money or other assets that are available for investment purposes
   (iv) outperformance of competitors in a number of areas
   (v) reliance on information, ideas, and technology
   (vi) a measurement based on the kinds and quality of goods and services people can afford
   (vii) countries that are in the process of becoming industrialized
   (viii) the tendency of cost per item to go down when items are produced in large quantities
   (ix) countries with a high standard of living

2. Identify five factors that influence Canada's ability to compete in world markets.

3. What are three advantages and three disadvantages Canada has in competing globally?

4. What factors affect a nation's productivity?

Thinking/Inquiry

1. Thesis statement: Education is now the main measure of competitiveness among countries—more than capital and more than technology. We are at an important point in the life of Canada and of the world. Economic and technological transformations are completely altering the way we do business. Money today follows knowledge and people. In this environment, a strong education system and access to lifelong learning are ensuring social harmony and prosperity. A new approach to education must be flexible and focused on innovation, the needs of both the students and the economy, and performance.

   Identify at least three arguments supporting this claim using newspapers, the Internet, and books. Do you agree with the claim and the arguments? Explain.

2. Working in a small group, brainstorm some steps that you think the Vietnamese government and Vietnamese businesses could take to attract the levels of investment Vietnam enjoyed before the Asian financial crisis in the late 1990s. From the results of your brainstorming session, create at least six research questions that would help you find out more about this challenging situation.

3. Many companies announce their products as inventive or innovative and as offering a solution to consumers' problems. Research advertisements of such products in print or online media. Use a chart similar to the "Innovative Global Products" chart to record your findings and analysis. In the rating column, provide a rating from 1 to 5, with 1 being low and 5 being high, based on your assessment of the product's utility and practicality. Does it have a large potential international market? Does it solve a large or small problem? Be sure to indicate in writing where you obtained information, including the source and the date.

Innovative Global Products

Name of Innovation/ Product	Country of Origin	Company/ Organization Involved	Price/ Availability	Nature of Problem/ Solution	Potential International Market	Your Rating

Figure 3.19 A sample form for rating innovative products.

Communication

1. Debate this statement: "Water is the oil of the future. Canada has over 20 percent of the earth's fresh water. Canada will become the Saudi Arabia of 2025 due to our wealth of water in a thirsty world." Work with a partner to develop supporting and refuting arguments on this issue.

2. Conduct a Web search on one of the following business theorists: Nuala Beck, W. Edwards Deming, or Kenichi Omahae; or select another theorist whose work you are interested in investigating further. In 250 to 300 words, describe the theorist's major contribution to competitive advantage, productivity, innovation, or quality control.

Application

1. Productivity can be measured close to home:

   What would you like to accomplish through your "education plan"? What resources will you require?

   What strategies will you use to be both efficient and effective?

   How will you measure the overall success of goal attainment and resource utilization as you map out your career? What criteria will you use (money, happiness, lifestyle, security, family, and so on)?

2. Research ways that the knowledge economy has affected people who are involved in international trade. Create an illustrated report or multimedia presentation in which you explain some of the causes and effects related to this factor of international business.

3. To remain profitable many Canadian companies have had to rationalize their operations over the past few years. Use print and Internet resources to find three of these companies, and compare their approaches to rationalization. Then prepare a brief oral presentation in which you explain which company, in your opinion, used the best approach. Also explain the drawbacks of the approaches of the other two companies.

International Business Portfolio

Competitive and Absolute Advantage

In this assignment, you evaluate your IBP country's competitive advantage. For companies to gain a competitive advantage, they need to do something better, faster, or less expensively than their competition. Competitive advantages might be **comparative** or they might be **absolute**.

As you learned in this chapter, a comparative advantage means the country is *relatively* more efficient at producing something than other countries. An absolute advantage exists when a country can *always* produce a good or service at a lower cost than anyone else. For example, absolute advantages usually occur because of natural resources present within the country. Research conditions within your IBP country to determine what its competitive advantages might be.

Activities

1. Does your country have resources that can be found only there, or are resources there of a high quality? Describe the quality and quantity of natural resources.

2. List three products for which your country is best known. Describe either the competitive or absolute advantage that these products have.

3. In what ways does your country have advantages that will give it a competitive edge?

4. Is something manufactured in your country that is not manufactured elsewhere? Has your country been responsible for any major innovations? List them.

5. How do the competitive advantages offered by this country provide opportunities for rationalization of Canadian business operations? For example, is labour less expensive, making it efficient for a Canadian firm to build a plant in or source exports from this country?

Chapter 4

Changes in Canada's Global Business

In Canada, and around the world, technology has provided new products; entrepreneurs have developed new processes; and consumers' changing wants and needs have created new markets for goods and services. All these changes in the global marketplace and the workplace affect Canada and Canadian trade. This chapter looks at changes in four industries: automotive, cellular communications, information, and banking. By studying how change has affected Canada's international trade relationships in these four areas, we can analyze the concept of change and its implications in international business.

Chapter Topics

➤ 4.1 – What Is Change? 110

➤ 4.2 – The Global Marketplace 115

➤ 4.3 – The Changing Workplace 128

➤ 4.4 – Staying Domestic or Going International? 135

➤ *Canada's Trading Partners: Focus on* Brazil 138

➤ Chapter Challenges 140

Prior Knowledge

- Why do businesses change?
- Describe how the workplace that you will enter is different from the workplace of twenty years ago.
- How has the increase in world trade changed the way businesses operate in Canada?

Inquiries/Expectations

- What are the implications of changes in international business for Canadians?
- What impact has technology had on the global business environment?
- How do the activities of international companies differ from those of companies focused on domestic business activity?
- In what ways have workplaces, occupations, the nature of work, and working conditions changed as a result of the growth of a global economy?

Important Terms

Auto Pact
big box retailers
business
Canadian International
   Development Agency (CIDA)
copyright
data mining
innovation

invention
joint venture
just-in-time system
kanban
licensing
patent
telecommunication
World Bank Group

4.1 What Is Change?

Change is part of everyday life for businesses, just as it is for people. For businesses and for individuals, change can take many forms. It can be great or small, incremental or revolutionary. Ordering office supplies, selecting a health care provider, choosing a supplier, modifying a process, or hiring an employee are all examples of changes a business makes. Over the past 30 years, businesses have accommodated huge changes in information technology and telecommunications. It's difficult to imagine a workplace without a computer or voice mail.

The Changing Marketplace

Business has been defined as the manufacture and/or sale of goods and/or services to meet the needs of a marketplace and to produce a profit. This definition still holds true, even though the marketplace has changed. Some businesses do not survive the changes, others initiate change, and still others take advantage of change and become very successful. Three things that cause change in business in both the domestic and international marketplace are new technology, new processes, and new attitudes.

New Technology

TRADE TALK

In 1973, the U.S. Defense Advanced Research Projects Agency (DARPA) initiated a research program to investigate techniques and technologies for interlinking packet networks of various kinds. The objective was to develop communication protocols, which would allow networked computers to communicate transparently across multiple, linked packet networks. This was called the Internetting project, and the system of networks, which emerged from the research, was known as the "Internet." The system of protocols, which was developed over the course of this research effort, became known as the TCP/IP Protocol Suite, after the two initial protocols developed: Transmission Control Protocol (TCP) and Internet Protocol (IP).

– Internet Society

Change has sometimes come about because of inventions and innovations, which have created markets. **Inventions** are totally new products that are based on a creative idea. **Innovations** are modifications to an invention that take the inventor's initial concept even further. The telephone was an invention. Digital phones, decorator phones, and cellular phones are all innovations; however, digital technology, plastic, and cellular capabilities are inventions that helped bring about the innovations to the telephone. The two terms, invention and innovation, are closely connected and are often confused and confusing; for example, is an aluminum soft drink can an invention or an innovation on the original idea to package soft drinks for portability? Here, we will refer to all new products as inventions.

The creative inventor or the perceptive entrepreneur will see ways to adapt new technologies to useful and marketable products. As these products are introduced to the marketplace, they will often displace other products. It is very difficult to find a rotary phone, a manual typewriter, or an eight-track tape player today.

Technological change can occur on a grand scale, such as the change to personal banking caused by the adaptation of computer technology to Automated Teller Machines (ATMs). Or technological change can occur on a smaller scale and add a modest consumer benefit to an existing product (for example, re-sealable bags for snack foods).

As new technology is developed, the business or individual that owns the technology can protect the invention through patent registration and use it exclusively. The inventor can license the invention, allowing other companies to use the technology or produce and/or sell the

Figure 4.1 Communication technologies that were once revolutionary inventions have been adapted by innovators into products used in today's telecommunications industries.

new product for a fee or a percentage of sales. Patents, copyrights, and licences become valuable property, and many companies negotiate for an exclusive grant of rights, or buy them as investments or as a way to protect their own products from competition the new technology could create. Many inventors partner with another company, usually a manufacturing and/or marketing company. Some inventors allow the invention to enter "public domain," where it can be used by anyone in any way. Patents, copyrights, and licences will be examined in greater detail later in this chapter.

New Processes

Marketplace change also occurs when processes are done in different ways. Process change, often initiated by technological change, takes place in manufacturing, distribution, inventory control, accounting, and marketing.

Manufacturing: Change in the way something is made will often result in its being made better, faster, and/or less expensively. Workers in the past, for example, constructed sewers with shovels, using metal pipes that were welded together. The pipe had to be kept straight, and it was a tedious process to continually measure, then alter the position of the pipes to keep them in line. Advances in technology have changed the process. Now specifically designed earth-moving equipment does the tedious digging and earth and rock removal. Sewer pipes are now plastic or concrete, and the welding process is no longer needed. Laser equipment is used to keep the pipes straight as they are installed, saving hundreds of hours of work. As a result, sewers are more durable, road construction time and the resulting traffic disruptions are reduced, and the process is much less expensive. In Chapter 3, we also saw how much the manufacturing of vehicles has changed through technology, with similar results.

Distribution: Word processing, e-mail, and the Internet have helped businesses deal directly with their customers and sometimes eliminate intermediaries, such as the wholesaler, importer, or even the retailer. In the past, these intermediaries played an important role in getting goods to the end consumer. Today, however, businesses order from other businesses by e-mail. Consumers can visit a company's Web site, sometimes "seeing" what inventory is available and checking current prices, and then order from them directly on the Internet. Desktop publishers and Web site designers have developed new catalogue distribution methods, both online and direct-to-home, that feature a wide variety of products that customers can order from different manufacturers.

In the transportation of product and business papers, consider the impact of such firms as Federal Express on delivery times, and the faster, "seamless" cross-border movement of goods by other means. This is all made easier by using technology to track and examine goods in various ways, including chemical tracing and x-rays.

Inventory Control: This used to be a manual process, often using a card system by which individual entries were recorded and kept up to date. Now, manufacturers are linked electronically to their sources of raw materials and ingredients; retailers are connected directly to their suppliers; and service providers can track their customers. Instead of taking weeks to fill purchase orders, a supplier can anticipate its customers' needs and have the necessary inventory delivered, sometimes before it is ordered.

Just-in-time (JIT) is an inventory control system that schedules products (for example, raw materials, parts, partial assemblies, and merchandise) to arrive as they are needed for manufacturing or for supply to customers. Just-in-time inventory control systems are sometimes referred to as zero inventory systems or stockless systems. They require a full understanding and strong relationship between the purchaser and the supplier.

In traditional inventory control processes, incoming raw materials are ordered in very large shipments to protect against shortages that would mean lost sales or factory downtime. Inventory is then stored in warehouses until needed for production, sale, or providing a service. Under a JIT system, organizations connect directly to their suppliers (now often referred to as "partners"), who monitor material use or product sales, filling the gaps as needed and, more importantly, when needed. This shifts responsibility for inventory back to the supplier, enabling a firm to save money on product and storage costs and eliminate expensive inventory shortages and overages. Many North American companies have successfully implemented JIT, including Hewlett-Packard, Motorola, Black & Decker, Ford Canada, Toyota Canada, General Electric, and IBM. Magna International is a JIT supplier to many automakers.

Figure 4.2 Just-in-time delivery can be especially important to retailers who need to fill consumer demand quickly while a fad lasts. These thick-soled shoes were fashionable for a season in the early 2000s.

Kanban is a Japanese philosophy that has as a major principle the elimination of waste, especially wasted time, labour, and resources. Kanban systems are similar to JIT systems.

Accounting: New accounting systems allow for almost instantaneous reporting of profit, inventory positions and value, investment activity, and other financial data that help a company stay successful. New accounting software provides necessary data to businesses on a day-to-day basis. Many major retail chains can know precisely what stores, what departments, and what specific items increased or decreased in sales whenever this information is required. The annual physical inventory count provides a check for the online inventory management rather than being the only source of reliable inventory information.

Web Link

Follow the link at
www.internationalbusiness.nelson.com
to find out how the Business Development Bank of Canada helps small Canadian businesses use the latest technologies and processes to succeed in business.

Marketing: Changes in the retail marketplace are primarily process changes. The **big box retailers**, or "category killers," are stores that specialize in providing an overwhelming variety of one category of merchandise, such as books or hardware. Chapters, Future Shop, and Canadian Tire are located in "power centres"—shopping centres that have a number of big box retailers as tenants. The smaller retailer becomes more specialized, focusing on products or services that the larger, more powerful competitors cannot or will not provide.

Figure 4.3 Big box retailers are often found in large "power centres" where consumers can park their cars and fill a number of their needs and wants in one location.

Market research methods now include data mining. **Data mining** is a way of connecting specific customer characteristics to their purchases. Effective data-mining technology can fairly accurately predict when a customer will run out of a frozen food or cat food, for example. This research provides companies with information they can use to target marketing campaigns or distribution efforts. For example, if you were to receive a coupon in the mail for a substantial saving on a product you were going to purchase that very week, except that the coupon was for another brand than the one you normally buy, would you switch brands? The marketers who have studied your buying patterns through data-mining technology (examining your credit purchases, bank card records, or records generated by any store "savings" or loyalty cards you might have used) hope that you would.

Promotional activities are often targeted at a very specific audience. Advertisers now have a wide variety of media that reach small groups of interested buyers. The Golf Channel on cable reaches golfers, *Modern Bride* magazine is targeted at brides-to-be, and the Internet Movie Database site appeals to movie lovers. Coupons, contests, and other sales promotion methods are also used to target specific consumers, with mailings and special offers sent to people of a certain income level through specific postal codes. The accessibility of information and the wide array of new media have made the advertising and promotional activities of many businesses very different than in the past.

New Attitudes

THINK ABOUT IT

Some people don't want marketers to have access to information about their buying habits. What are their fears? Are they justified?

As people's values change, their willingness to purchase certain products changes as well. Environmental awareness may alter our willingness to purchase non-recyclable products. Concern for our health increases our willingness to purchase low-fat foods. Our social conscience prevents us from buying products made using child labour or made by companies that have used animals in their product-testing labs. Sometimes these changes are short-term style preferences that we call trends or fads. Other changes are more long term and have a more lasting effect on the marketplace.

Change seems to be initiated by technology in many of the above examples. Often that is because the new technology is the most visible form of the change. But technological change occurs most often because someone sees a need and invents something to satisfy that need. The environmental movement and the problem of garbage disposal, for example, encouraged—even demanded—that manufacturers make technological changes to develop biodegradable packaging. The desire to improve manufacturing processes for efficiency and more output has been the impetus for technological innovation since the invention of the wheel. Change, then, usually occurs as a result of a symbiosis, a coming together of a number of different elements at the right time. The Internet was invented in the 1970s, but it took 25 years until access, availability, cost, applications, and marketing led to the marketplace being ready for it and the public to accept it.

Figure 4.4 Environmental concerns in some communities resulted in regulations requiring the disposal of garden or yard waste in paper bags that decompose naturally.

ICE Activities for 4.1

Ideas	Connections	Extensions
1. (a) Describe briefly three things that initiate change in the marketplace.	(b) Ask a local manufacturer how technology, process, and attitude have affected the company's business since its inception.	(c) Find an example of a technology, a process, and an attitude that Canada has either imported or exported. Share your research with a small group. Which was the hardest example to find? Explain.
2. (a) Describe five categories of business processes that have gone through changes in recent years.	(b) Explain the business reason for one change in each of the processes you described in 2. (a).	(c) Identify some local consumer need that is not being filled. Explain how a change in current business processes might enable a company to fill that need.
3. (a) Summarize how just-in-time inventory control works.	(b) Find and describe a local business that uses just-in-time inventory control.	(c) Research the Kanban philosophy further. Do you think it would be worthwhile to incorporate some of this philosophy into your own life? Explain.

4.2 The Global Marketplace

Because Canada has increasingly become part of the global marketplace, we need to consider the changes that were outlined in Section 4.1 in a larger context. How have changes in technology, process, and attitude affected or been affected by our relationships with other countries? How has doing business in the Canadian marketplace changed as we have recognized the need for more international trade? For answers, we will examine the automobile, cellular communication, information, and banking industries in Canada.

The Automotive Industry

The automotive industry in Canada has been intertwined with the industry in the United States for the past century. The "Big Three" auto makers (Ford, General Motors, and Chrysler [now DaimlerChrysler]) have always been the foundation of the U.S. auto industry. To protect the automotive industry in Canada and to open up freer trade with the United States, both governments signed the Canada-United States Automotive Products Agreement in 1965. This agreement is usually referred to as the **Auto Pact**.

The Auto Pact encouraged Canada's relationship with U.S. automakers and made trade in vehicles and auto parts with any other country less attractive. Most importantly, it secured jobs for Canadians in the auto industry and in all of the businesses that supply the auto industry.

Then, at the beginning of the 1970s, a gasoline shortage—brought about by market manipulations of the price and supply of oil by the Organization of Petroleum Exporting Countries (OPEC)—caused North Americans to seek out smaller cars that were more fuel-efficient.

These developments turned many buyers away from North American cars to imports. Ford, Chrysler, and General Motors were said to be "driving" Canadian industry, even though the parent offices for these three companies were in the United States. However, as Canadians discovered the efficiency of the imports and their safety records, their tastes in automobiles switched to smaller, safer, more economical foreign cars.

Consumer attitudes forced the Big Three car companies to become more competitive in areas other than price. Some American cars were getting only 2.5 km/L. Their Japanese and German competitors were getting 15 km/L. Fuel conservation was a major issue, as was air pollution. Although emission controls were standard on many foreign vehicles, legislation was necessary to force North American cars to meet government-set standards. Legislation was also necessary to require seat belts, padded dashboards, and air bags on North American cars. Many imports were much safer from the beginning. The popularity of the imports occurred, not just because of price, but because of quality. The Japanese, Germans, Swedes, Italians, South Koreans, and British all "converted" many customers, who felt that these manufacturers made a better product.

TRADE TALK

Under the terms of the Canada-United States Automotive Products Agreement of 1965, vehicle manufacturers were able to import both vehicles and original equipment (OE) automotive parts duty-free from any Most-Favoured Nation (MFN) country, provided certain conditions were met:

a) Manufacturers that wanted to sell imported cars duty-free in Canada also had to build cars in Canada.

b) Assemblers had to maintain a nominal dollar amount of Canadian value added (CVA: includes direct and indirect labour, depreciation on Canadian-made machinery, eligible overhead and expenses in the cost of producing the vehicles).

– Canada-United States Automotive Products Agreement of 1965

The Russell was the first mass-produced Canadian car with an engine and chassis built in Canada. Rather than evolving from a carriage-making company, the Russell company was created by the Canada Cycle and Motor Company, popularly known as CCM. Named after Thomas Alexander Russell, later president of CCM, the first model appeared in 1905.

Why does Canada not have a Canadian-owned automobile industry today?

The Auto Pact still gave the American car companies an edge, however. No matter where in the world a car was made, if the company that made the car was U.S.-owned, it was protected by the Auto Pact, and there was no duty on any vehicle that the company shipped to Canada. As many American car companies bought up or entered into partnerships with foreign companies, the distinction between the products has become very difficult to make. General Motors imported Saab and Isuzu vehicles duty free, Ford imported Volvo and Jaguar on the same basis, and Chrysler brought in Mercedes Benz. A consumer would pay more for a car manufactured by a non-Auto Pact company—even if it were manufactured in North America using mostly North American components.

This discrepancy challenged and ultimately killed the Auto Pact. European and Japanese car manufacturers questioned the 6.1 percent tariff rate on Japanese and European auto imports into Canada. Japan and the European Union filed complaints with the World Trade Organization. The complaints focused on the right of American partnerships such as DaimlerChrysler to qualify as Auto Pact manufacturers and to export vehicles duty free into Canada from their plants in Japan and Europe, while those with no U.S. ownership were subject to the 6.1 percent tariff on the vehicles that they exported to Canada.

The WTO ruled in favour of Japan and the EU, and on February 28, 2002, Canada's Department of Finance published the final regulatory changes needed to implement the WTO ruling against provisions of the 1965 Canada-United States Auto Pact.

Figure 4.5 A Toyota hybrid. Now made by several automobile manufacturers, hybrids have a gasoline engine coupled to an electrical motor. They appeal to customers wanting a vehicle that is more environment-friendly, efficient, and economical to operate.

Cellular Communication

Canada's major contribution to the communications industry was Alexander Graham Bell's discovery of the telephone in Brantford, Ontario, between 1874 and 1876. It was Bell's telephone that began the telecommunications industry in Canada. **Telecommunication** is communication over a distance, for example, by telephone, Internet, radio, or television.

The contribution of the telephone to the business world cannot be overemphasized. But the progress of telecommunications around the world would certainly surprise Mr. Bell. The most significant communication changes in the global marketplace have been the Internet, which will be discussed in a later section of this chapter, and cellular phone technology. Cellular telephones have given rise to new Canadian businesses, new ways to do business, and global impacts that have not yet been fully analyzed.

New Businesses

Cellular phones have shown incredible growth in Canada since 1999, as Canadians found a need for cellular phones in their business and personal life. In fact, by 2001, one out of every five people in Canada owned a cellular phone, and this number was expected to increase by 50 percent within the next five years. The growth in their use also resulted from improved telephone technology, making cellular phones lighter, more portable, and less expensive. Several companies have offered improved service, along with advanced, multi-purpose wireless phones that can access e-mail, the Internet, and desktop and network drives.

Figure 4.6 By 2001, one in every five people in Canada owned a cell phone. Behind this popular communication mode is a wireless network that demands an extensive, dependable infrastructure.

For cellular phones to work, a wireless network must be established within a region. A wireless network requires the presence of three things:

- mobile units (cellular phones)
- cellular transmission/reception site—The site consists of at least one transmitter and one receiver antenna. Each antenna transmits the digital signal over a given geographical area. The site requires electrical input to power the equipment.
- mobile telephone switching office—All calls are transmitted and received by receptor sites and sent to the switching office where they are then automatically sent to the number called by the cellular customer.

Wireless networks require an expensive infrastructure to accommodate the transmission, reception, and switching of the digital signal. These sites require the leasing of land, electrical hook-ups, security, and maintenance. After acquiring and servicing the necessary land, the wireless network company arranges for the construction of cellular sites and antennas. Antennas may be constructed on various structures, such as hydro towers, monopoles (poles constructed especially for cellular transmission equipment), microwave or radar towers, trees, buildings, or lamp poles. Their placement must ensure good transmission and reception coverage over as large an area as possible. In more remote areas or where a network is not yet established, satellite phones must be used; these communicate directly through a communications satellite system.

THINK ABOUT IT

Should legislation be enacted Canada-wide to prohibit the use of cell phones in cars and other vehicles?

It is important to realize that because a wireless infrastructure is less expensive than a landline infrastructure (which needs wire, poles, and underground installations for the entire area it has to cover), parts of Canada and many countries are going directly to wireless.

Wireless technology has spawned a number of new businesses in Canada. Some of them are extensions of existing Canadian companies (Nortel Networks), and some are directly linked to international businesses (Sprint). But it is not simply the international corporate connections that have changed the Canadian business marketplace; it is the impact of cellular technology on the way business is done.

New Ways to Do Business

Satellites and wireless networks have made communication much easier than landlines and much easier for poorer nations to access. Landlines require extensive land disruption, whereas wireless networks do not. Wireless networks can provide digital services, which have more capabilities than landlines, such as text messaging. Digital phones are portable and allow online access through a cell phone from anywhere within a digital coverage area.

Countries that have had poor landline services now may acquire a communications capability they could have only imagined in the past. In many countries today—in Europe, for example—the cellular phone is the main phone for both business and home. This means that Canada, like other countries, can now communicate in a more efficient manner with company representatives, suppliers, dealers, customers, and others in countries that were formerly poorly served by older communications technology. Increased trade with less well-developed nations has become much more attractive because of the ease of communication created by this new technology.

Global Impact

Business people on a cellular phone are often seen in restaurants, in cars, on the beach, or on the street, talking to brokers and colleagues, customers and clients. As convenient as this is, there are safety issues involved. Many countries have passed or are considering passing legislation that regulates cellular phone use while driving. Wireless companies have developed better headset technology, which allows cellular phone users to talk and drive "hands free" at the same time. Innovations in automobile design or voice recognition technology may also eliminate this problem in the future.

Talking on the phone while others are trying to watch a movie, eat a meal, or relax on the beach is culturally unacceptable in many countries. Business etiquette is evolving to incorporate cellular phone use, and the international business traveller should study the customs of countries in advance of a business trip.

Figure 4.7 Trevor Baylis invented the "clockwork radio"—a reliable technology that is not dependent on electricity—to provide an inexpensive and accessible means of communication to people in Africa, where radios are the primary means of public communication but electricity is scarce and batteries are expensive.

The widespread use of cellular phones also illustrates the interdependence of one business on others. Canada is a leader in wireless technology, and numerous businesses in Canada provide both components and expertise internationally. But as Canadians increasingly adopt the use of cellular phones, the demand for components that are not made in Canada also increases. Change in the Canadian market—the increased use of cellular phones—requires the increased production of a mineral called columbite-tatanalite, also known as coltan. This particular substance is essential in the production of wireless phones, so the cellular phone boom has increased the demand and the price has gone from $66 per kilogram in 1990 to $770 per kilogram in 2001.

Coltan comes mainly from Australia, but the demand is so great and the price so high that other countries are looking for coltan deposits. The Congo, in Africa, has some very rich deposits, which are being mined on several World Heritage Sites, areas that were set aside as nature reserves. Miners working at these sites have been killing the wild animals on these nature reserves for food. The Wildlife Conservation Society estimates that thousands of elephants and gorillas have been slaughtered in the search for and mining of the mineral. As the demand for wireless phones increases, Canadians may be participating in this environmental disaster without realizing it. See Chapter 10, page 322 for more on the use of coltan and ethical implications.

Information

Acquiring, managing, and using information has brought about significant changes in the way that Canadians do business internationally. Businesses use information in two different ways: as a tool to make decisions and as a product to market. Information as a decision-making tool today owes much to the Internet and to database management; it may be organized, sometimes analyzed or correlated, and offered as a newsletter or online subscription service or in CD-ROM format. Online subscription service is important to researchers, lawyers, accountants, engineers, educators, and many other groups. Information as a commodity is also licensed or sold as patents and copyrights, licences, consulting services, and joint ventures.

Figure 4.8 The role of the library has changed dramatically because of the influence of electronic media on our daily lives.

Information as a Decision-Making Tool

The acquisition of information is relatively simple. Visiting a library, surfing the Internet, or reading an article in a new trade publication will provide information. Newspapers, television programs, radio shows, magazines, electronic highway signs, train schedules, and billboard advertisements are also sources of information. The challenge with information is how to manage it and how to use it after it has been obtained.

Businesses use information to identify consumers who may be interested in buying their product or service, both nationally and internationally. Information about foreign markets is so readily accessible that even the smallest business can analyze the feasibility of an international operation.

In Canada, two of the primary sources of international business information are Industry Canada's Strategis and the Web site for the Department of Foreign Affairs and International Trade (DFAIT).

Strategis provides information on copyrights, patents, licences, trademarks, starting a business, financing, and exporting, and research about markets, suppliers, and customers. The Web site provides extensive reports that analyze the trade opportunities available in many countries.

DFAIT provides trade data, country profiles, and market studies by sector or by country. It gives information about Team Canada and other business development missions. The DFAIT Web site contains the International Business Opportunities Centre, a listing and description of Canada's trade negotiations and agreements, including a "What's New in Trade Policy" section; profiles and links to the WTO, NAFTA, and the FTAA; and other regional and bilateral agreements. There are also trade and economic analyses, data regarding export and import controls, and details on Canadian economic sanctions against other nations.

Canadian retailers, importers, wholesalers, and manufacturers discover new customers, new suppliers, and new trends on the Internet. Any business can set up its own Web site, which will allow customers from all over the world to order products. A Canadian business operating from home now has the potential to become an international business. Those who take advantage of this opportunity are changing the Canadian marketplace dramatically.

Information as a Commodity

THINK ABOUT IT

Many students download music by their favourite artists to listen to while they're doing their homework. If they don't pay for this music, are they depriving the recording artists of their livelihood? Should songwriters and musicians expect to lose a certain amount of income by agreeing to have their music available on the Internet as a means of promotion?

Like some other countries, Canada develops technology, invents new products, and creates new processes. Often, the rights to these inventions and innovations can be granted, licensed, or sold to other businesses; this can be especially valuable to businesses in other countries that do not have the same technological expertise.

Patents and Copyrights

A **patent** is a grant of property right by law to give exclusive rights to the inventor and to protect the rights of the inventor and prevent others from making, using, or selling the invention. Under the rules of the World Trade Organization, the patent property rights exist for a period of 20 years from the date of application.

Patents are granted to inventors of any new useful process, product, or composition of matter (such as a metal alloy or chemical formula). The invention must be new (first in the world), useful (functional and operative), and it must show inventive ingenuity and not be obvious to someone skilled in that area.

The inventor can be any persons, institution, agency, or company. (A good example of a patented Canadian invention is the Robertson screw, which was invented in Milton, Ontario. See the International Company Profile in Chapter 5 on page 147.)

Like patents, copyrights, industrial designs, trademarks, and integrated circuit topographies are rights granted for intellectual creativity and are forms of intellectual property.

Patents: new technologies (process, structure, and function)

Copyrights: literary, artistic, dramatic, or musical works and computer software

Industrial designs: shape, pattern, or ornamentation applied to an industrially produced object

Trademarks: word, symbol, or picture, or combination, used to distinguish the goods or services of one person or organization from those of another

Integrated circuit topographies: three-dimensional configurations of the electronic circuits embodied in integrated circuit products or layout designs

— *World Wide Legal Information Association*

Figure 4.9 Many educational institutions and libraries have specific rules and regulations regarding what can be photocopied. It's a matter of protecting the creator's rights.

A patent is both a document protecting the rights of the inventor and a repository of useful technical information for the public. The Canadian Patent Office receives approximately 25 000 patent applications each year. An inventor can use a patent to make a profit by selling it, licensing it, or using it as an asset to negotiate funding. Patents, therefore, provide incentives for research and development.

Some foreign companies may copy an invention and use it without paying compensation to the holder of the patent. To try to prevent such activities, Canada has signed the international Patent Cooperation Treaty (PCT).

By filing one international patent application under the Patent Cooperation Treaty, Canadian companies can seek protection for an invention in more than 100 countries simultaneously throughout the world. Once an idea has been protected, the owner can sell the patent directly, license the rights to use the idea, form a joint venture, or charge a fee for consulting services.

Copyright is a form of legal protection provided to the authors of original works, including literary, dramatic, musical, artistic, and certain other intellectual works, such as software programs. Patents and copyrights are similar, in that they protect the owner of a work from having the work copied without compensation. The publishers of this textbook will make a profit only if the book is sold. If anyone who wanted a copy simply duplicated one, and this happened frequently, the publisher would not make a profit and, therefore, would no longer publish. Patents and copyrights are granted, licensed, or sold to ensure that inventors, writers, artists, publishers, designers, musicians, and other creators are compensated for their effort and their risks.

Patents and copyrights may be sold by the owner to anyone at any time. They can be bequeathed in wills, counted as assets on a company's balance sheet, or donated to a cause. Once they have been sold, however, the original owner can no longer profit from the invention, no matter how the new owner uses the patent and how much profit is made.

Web Link

Follow the link at www.internationalbusiness.nelson.com to find out more about the patents and copyrights at the Canadian Intellectual Property Office.

TRADE TALK

Licensing

A safer way to deal with patents and copyrights, but one that requires a great deal of time and effort to set up, is the licence arrangement. **Licensing** means that patent or copyright owners allow other organizations (individuals, governments, or companies) to use their idea or invention for a fee or royalty. The fee may often be expressed in the form of a fixed sum with or without a percentage of the sales or profits of the licensee (the business that pays for the right to use the invention) paid to the licensor (the owner of the patent or copyright). The licensee can also pay a negotiated amount, either all at once or at set intervals during the use of the patent or copyright. Some licensing arrangements are called franchising. Percentage or per-unit compensation for use of intellectual property is usually called a royalty.

There are also many "collectives" around the world; these are organizations or agencies that act on behalf of their members (who are usually in similar businesses or areas of creativity). The Canadian Copyright Licensing Agency, acting on behalf of publishers and creators (writers, photographers, and illustrators), is a not-for-profit agency established in 1988 by Canadian creators and publishers to license public access to copyright works. On behalf of its members collectively, it negotiates reproduction and digital licences with educational institutions, governments, libraries, organizations, and private companies to reproduce material legally and for a negotiated fee. Through bilateral agreements with similar organizations around the world, the agency also provides Canadian creators and publishers with a means to license their published works in foreign countries.

International licensing agreements are becoming increasingly popular. A business in one country licenses new technology, ideas, or processes from another country to use in its factory. For example, the licensing of the patents for the Electric Arc Furnace that allowed the conversion of old steel into new steel revolutionized steel manufacturing in North America. The Coca-Cola Company licenses its formula to local bottlers around the world and is active in nearly 200 countries. Disney licenses the images of its characters to watch makers, toy manufacturers, and clothing designers in numerous countries.

Patents and copyrights provide legal protection, but do not ensure it. On the streets of Toronto or Vancouver, sellers of fake Rolex watches, Prada handbags, or Oakley sunglasses try to convince tourists of the outstanding "value" of their counterfeit products while trying to escape the notice of the local police. In some countries, this counterfeit trade is plied openly and extends to a wide variety of products. Recent trade negotiations with countries such as China and Romania have dealt with the patent protection issue because some businesses in these two countries counterfeited products quite freely.

Figure 4.10 In 2000, the Mounted Police Foundation took over the licensing program from Walt Disney Company (Canada) Ltd. The program generates significant funds for RCMP community policing programs, such as Citizen on Patrol, youth initiatives, and aboriginal mentorship programs. The licensing program ensures that the RCMP image remains a strong Canadian symbol and that its commercial use continues to deliver tangible benefits to Canadian communities.

Joint Ventures

Often a business in one country has capital, technology, expertise, or knowledge (or a combination of these), that is needed by a business in another country. Sometimes a foreign company can only proceed, by local regulations or expectations, with a local company from that country. There are some projects in which two foreign companies wish to reduce their financial risk and schedule, or find that their skills, technology, or expertise are complementary for a specific, usually large, project. In such cases, the businesses will create a joint venture. The International Company Profile on SNC-Lavalin Group Inc. in this chapter features such a project.

A **joint venture** is an agreement between two or more companies or organizations to share assets and control of a new business for mutual gain. The businesses will often jointly set up a new company, owned by both companies, or one company will sell part interest to the other. Often, a joint venture is simply a cooperative agreement to share certain technology or manufacturing facilities. These agreements do not necessarily require a financial investment. This type of arrangement most often occurs when one company has an exceptional technology but does not have the capital or the desire to begin manufacturing, so it shares its technology with a manufacturing company that wants to produce the new product.

In some situations, negotiations between joint venture partners have to be approved by the local government, which may insist on a certain percentage of local workers, and on training and safety programs. In long-term large projects, there may also be incentives for the companies to establish support programs, such as community education or health programs, for the local communities.

International Company Profile

SNC–Lavalin Group Inc.

SNC-Lavalin is one of the leading engineering and construction companies in the world and a global player in the ownership and management of infrastructure. A business (private sector) or government (public sector) wishing to build a power dam, an aluminum smelter, an extension to a subway system, a water filtration plant, or a highway might call upon SNC-Lavalin to provide the engineering, construction, project management, and even financing. SNC-Lavalin has developed private and public sector projects in the infrastructure, petroleum, power, mining, pharmaceutical, agriculture, food processing, mass transit, defence, and facilities management industries.

One of the firm's most obvious successes is the 407 ETR (Express Toll Route) in the Greater Toronto Area, a 108 km highway equipped with sensors that electronically monitor the entry and exit of each vehicle—the world's first all-electronic, open access toll highway. 407 International Inc. owns the 407 ETR and is in turn owned by Cintra Concesiones de Infaestructuras de Transporte (a Spanish engineering company with the majority interest), and by Macquarie Infrastructure Group (an Australian company), and SNC-Lavalin, each with minority interests.

SNC-Lavalin Group Inc., as it now exists, is the result of a 1991 merger between Canada's two largest engineering firms, SNC (named after its partnership founders, Arthur Surveyer, Emil Nenniger, and Georges Chenevert) and Lavalin. The merger made two strong organizations even stronger in international markets, with a virtual supermarket of skills, expertise, and resources. SNC-Lavalin today has offices in approximately 30 other countries and is working on jobs in over 100 different nations.

The company is a leader in the innovative area of BOOT partnerships. BOOT stands for build-own-operate-transfer. A government or business that needs assistance with a project will share its vision with representatives from SNC-Lavalin. If SNC-Lavalin accepts the job, it will provide engineering and/or construction services (*build*), provide the necessary finances in an *ownership* role, *operate* and manage the project for a period of time while the business or government raises capital and/or learns how to run the project, then *transfer* the project over to the original planners.

To be successful in so many countries and so many industries, with such a large number of public and private partners, requires not only ability and knowledge, but also a sense of the global community. SNC-Lavalin has established an international division, which considers the culture and customs of the people in all the countries in which it operates and works with the indigenous population, community groups, government branches, and local businesses to provide jobs and opportunities for them. An engineering and construction firm working with dams, roads, mines, chemicals, and oil fields has an impact on the

environment of a country as well. SNC-Lavalin has a special environmental division, with experts in all fields of environmental management who assist the company in fulfilling its environmental responsibilities in connection with its projects.

The Mozal Aluminum Smelter is the largest industrial project ever undertaken in Mozambique, and it was completed on schedule despite delays due to insufficient public infrastructure, difficult geotechnical conditions, and a bout of torrential flooding in February 2000. It required the cooperation of the governments of South Africa and Mozambique, several international partners, and thousands of local workers.

Norman Morin, executive vice-president of SNC-Lavalin, said, "We are proud that our technical expertise in project management and aluminum smelters has played a pivotal role in a venture of such tremendous economic and social importance to the region." The quality of life has been improved on virtually every level. Some 740 permanent jobs were created—over 650 of which have been filled by Mozambicans—and the number of jobs created indirectly from the project is expected to reach 2500. Over 5500 Mozambicans were trained in construction skills, and all were issued certificates to help them obtain construction work on future projects. In addition, an environment management program was established, as were health education and treatment programs for AIDS, malaria, and other diseases.

SNC-Lavalin's major growth opportunities come from both Canadian and international markets. The company continues to look for project opportunities around the world and to search for innovative ways to finance and develop them.

● ●

1. What is the difference between a BOOT partnership and a joint venture?
2. How does SNC-Lavalin's sense of the international community play a role in its success?

Figure 4.11 Mozal Aluminum Smelter in Mozambique, a South African country, constructed by SNC-Lavalin and its South African joint venture partner, Murray & Roberts.
Photo: Carles Corbett

Figure 4.13 Scotiabank has been doing business internationally for over 100 years. It is the most international of the Canadian banks, having 2000 branches and offices in 50 countries spanning six continents. In June 2001, Argentina's Central Bank devalued the currency and defaulted on its debts. Many people tried to withdraw money before Argentina put a freeze on banking activities.

Web Link

Follow the link at www.internationalbusiness.nelson.com to find out more about Canadian and international banking.

ICE Activities for 4.2

Ideas	Connections	Extensions
1. (a) Why did the WTO rule against provisions of the 1965 Canada-United States Auto Pact?	(b) Working in small groups, research four recent WTO rulings on trade. Summarize the rulings, and discuss any common goals that are apparent in the different decisions.	(c) Select one of the rulings that you investigated in 1. (b), and write a paragraph in which you predict how that ruling will affect Canadian businesses in the future.
2. (a) What are four things an inventor can do with his or her idea after the patent has been registered?	(b) Prepare a brief report on a Canadian company that either licenses its products to foreign companies, or uses foreign licences to manufacture products in Canada. Explain the importance of the licensing arrangement to both the licensor and the licensee.	(c) Find current information (using print or online sources) about a patent that interests you. Speculate on how you could use the patent internationally if you owned it.
3. (a) Describe the changes that have taken place in the Canadian banking industry since the 1980s.	(b) What other financial institutions operate in Canada? Visit the Department of Finance Web site for information.	(c) Research Scotiabank's response to Argentina's devaluation of its currency. How did this response affect those banking with Scotiabank in Argentina? Write a one-page report. Share your findings with a small group.

4.3 The Changing Workplace

Figure 4.14 In the 1950s, dictaphones and typewriters were new technologies that changed the nature of office work.

Figure 4.15 As industrialization spread, increased competition meant that goods had to be made faster and with less expense.

Figure 4.16 Today, there are more Canadians employed as knowledge workers than as manual labourers.

Changing Nature of Work

The shift from hunter-gatherer society to agrarian society, which took place over a long period of time, was followed much later by a further shift, from an agrarian society to a manufacturing and mercantile society. The period from the late 1700s to the early 1800s was called the Industrial Revolution. As factories grew, so did the need for new technology and inventions to make new products faster and less expensively. Sales, marketing, advertising, and retailing developed as jobs. The more manufacturers made, the more others needed to sell.

This also became the time of the consumer. Manufacturers, service providers, stores, and advertisers became conscious of the customer or consumer (end-user). Although international trade existed on a relatively small scale for hundreds of years, prior to the industrial revolution and for many years afterwards, people were able to buy only what was available in their area. The limited ability of most manufacturers to produce products quickly meant that demand usually exceeded supply. In the industrial age, however, it became possible to make products more quickly and less expensively, and many businesses now had to compete for a share of the market. Finally, the consumer came to have choice and needed to be convinced of the advantage of one product over another. Products and stores and advertisements were made with the ultimate buyer in mind. Businesses became consumer conscious, and consumers discovered their power to create demand.

The manufacturing and mercantile society, spurred by the increasing need to know about the consumer, has caused another labour shift recently. We are now living in the information age, where much work is focused on the collection, analysis, and dissemination of data. Researchers, information analysts, and statisticians all work at collecting and analyzing information about markets, consumer preferences, available technology, and so on. Not only do the sellers want to know, but the buyers want to know as well. The consumer consumes information, too. What's in style, what's on sale, what's new? Magazines, flyers, newspapers, billboards, television programs, books, e-mails, and popup ads on the Internet—all help us make decisions about what we will buy.

Over the centuries of societal shifts, from hunters to farmers, from farmers to manufacturers, from manufacturers to marketers, and from marketers to information managers, one thing has not changed: the split between those who work with their hands and those who work with their heads. In the past, before machinery took over from the manual labourer, people who earned their living by doing hard physical labour outnumbered those who earned their living by using knowledge they had gained (lawyers, teachers, and bankers, for example). Today, the knowledge worker, who organizes, controls, and interprets or disseminates information, significantly outnumbers the physical labourer in Canada.

The Impact of Globalization

New Markets Abroad

International trade and globalization precipitated many of the shifts already discussed. The new markets created by trade spurred the development of export-based companies and import-based businesses, and created new jobs. Canadian manufacturers took primary resources such as minerals, trees, and fish and added value to them by processing them before they were exported. Processing wood into pulp and paper became a significant Canadian industry, as did steel manufacturing and fish processing.

As better communications and transportation made it easier to move goods across continents and overseas, businesses began to look farther afield in their search for new markets into which to export or from which to import goods. As a result, the marketing manager of a business would study buying patterns in Germany, for example, as diligently as he or she studied the buying patterns in Manitoba. Thirty million Canadians make up a significant market, but a market of 300 million Americans is more significant. Add the Japanese, Chinese, Mexicans, and Europeans to that number, and a Canadian business could sell products to over a billion people. Companies such as Bombardier, McCain, Domtar, and Alcan expanded into numerous other nations and developed marketing plans based on the demographics of these foreign markets.

Import Opportunities

Branch offices, sales agents, and marketing representatives set up in cities around the globe to buy foreign goods for Canadian shops as well as to sell Canadian products abroad. The marketing revolution that occurred after the Second World War brought Canadians German cars, French cheese, Belgian chocolate, Japanese radios, New Zealand lamb, Colombian coffee, and all the products that the United States could dream up. It became the era of McDonald's and Coca-Cola and Nike.

Canadian consumers have become more sophisticated. The expansion of international travel, the changing immigration patterns, and the proliferation of global media mean that Canadians have been exposed to new products from around the world. Globalization means marketing opportunities. You'll find examples with most of the Canadian companies profiled in this book.

Labour: A Variable Cost

As trade has helped Canada develop, so it has helped other nations. Many of our trading partners experience or have experienced the same shifts that Canada has experienced, as their primary-industry-based economy changes into a more manufacturing-based and knowledge-based economy. Part of this change is the result of global differences in the price of labour.

Figure 4.17 In the garment industry, labour accounts for a large percentage of the total production cost; so locating in a region where labour costs are low may mean a manufacturing company can price its goods more competitively in the global market.

Countries with a lower standard and cost of living can sometimes produce products less expensively, especially if labour is a large part of the total cost. Many international companies have followed the price of labour, setting up factories or buying from suppliers in countries where labour costs are lower, sending primary resources to these factories that use the cheap labour to convert the raw materials into finished products. The finished goods could then be sold internationally to consumers in countries that could afford to buy them. Industrialized nations have moved away somewhat from manufacturing some products, especially dry goods (textiles, clothing, household goods). Less-industrialized nations now perform this work. The ability to move manufacturing companies to places where labour was cheap was one of the most significant effects of globalization.

When labour costs are a significant part of costing a product, lower labour rates will result in a less expensive or more profitable product. Prior to globalization, a factory in Charlottetown paid wages that were comparable to other parts of Canada, once allowances for cost of living were factored into the comparison. Toronto workers are paid more than Charlottetown workers because it costs more to live in Toronto. Many Canadian companies have been encouraged by provincial and federal government grants and tax incentives to move to the Atlantic provinces to provide jobs in an area suffering high unemployment because of the decline of primary industries such as fishing and mining. Other than grants and sometimes lower tax rates, the incentive was lower wages.

In a simplified example, if Charlottetown workers receive $10 per hour, and 20 employees are needed each day, the cost of labour is $200 per hour. In some less-developed countries, workers may receive the Canadian equivalent of $1.00 per hour or less. If the same number of workers had the same productivity and quality, they would, therefore, make the same number of products for $20 per hour. When labour costs for a year are calculated, they will often be substantially lower outside Canada. Of course, quality control, and import and transportation costs have to be factored into the product cost and pricing.

This example does not necessarily mean that the workers who are earning $1.00 an hour are being exploited. It is not always fair to compare wages in Canada to those in other countries (as you can see by comparing the GDP per capita of different countries). The wages that the workers in the foreign country are paid may be higher than other wages in their country. Or the workers may have a job in a region where any paid employment is scarce. In some countries, because of climatic conditions, the cost of living may be lower: housing construction requires few materials or less insulation, heating costs are much lower, and there may be little need for seasonal clothing changes.

Companies that have access to information can make decisions that will save money or make money. Companies that do not have access to this information will be unable to compete. To be a global business, a company needs to know about wage rates, cost of living, market composition, consumer demand, sources of supply, shipping costs, tariff rates, and

GDP per Capita for Selected Countries (2001 figures and estimates in USD)

Argentina $12 000
Cambodia $1500
Congo, Democratic Republic
    (formerly Zaire) $591
Congo, Republic $900
Finland $25 800
India $2500
Kenya $1000
Netherlands $25 800
Peru $4800
Portugal $17 300
Russia $8300
Saudi Arabia $10 600
South Africa $9400

political and economic data from all over the world. This information is organized, analyzed, and used to make business decisions. Choosing transportation companies and distributors, adding a sales representative in a particular area, changing an advertisement or even modifying a product to match a cultural difference or preference, or profiling the typical teenager in a target market for a new soft drink all require information gathering and analysis. The needs of the global business community have created more demand for information and international sharing of expertise.

The developing nations buy information from the more technically advanced nations. Canada provides these nations with experts in information systems, communication systems, engineering technology, energy systems, and so on, to assist them in building the infrastructure that will allow their businesses to build new factories and start to sell products internationally. As this happens, Canadian companies, along with others, buy the goods and services the new factories produce.

For example, Kenya, which is a developing nation, has a growing cotton and textile industry. A plausible international trade sequence involving businesses from different countries might include the following steps:

1. An entrepreneur wants to open a shirt-manufacturing company in Kenya. Funding comes from local entrepreneurs, an investment from an American shirt maker, and capital from the Kenyan government.
2. A Canadian engineering firm is hired to design the factory. The Kenyan government hires Canadian energy consultants to analyze the power sources in the area and create a development plan.
3. A Kenyan construction company builds the factory, with a Canadian architect and consulting engineers on site.
4. Kenyan cotton is used in the shirt manufacture, but the shirt buttons, sewing machines, and many second-hand pieces of manufacturing equipment are purchased from Canadian textile companies that have upgraded or gone out of business.
5. The shirt manufacturer hires an agency to develop marketing campaigns for Kenya and several other African countries. Import agents from Germany, the United States, and Japan sign distribution deals. Stores in Japan, Europe, and the United States receive shipments of Kenyan shirts.
6. A U.S. sales representative sells shirts to Canadian clothing stores. Kenyan shirts arrive in the Canadian market.

The Value of Information

As the need for information increases, so does its value and the amount people are willing to pay to obtain it. Information technology (IT) is the "machinery" of the information industry and consists of satellite and cellular communication companies, research firms, data processing software designers, information managers, and anyone else whose main job consists of getting, transmitting, processing, interpreting, or organizing data. Experts in information technology are highly educated and are in high demand. Many of these IT specialists started Internet companies that manipulated data for a number of applications, then sold or leased their technology to client firms that needed it. Young IT entrepreneurs in a number of countries have sold their companies for millions of dollars.

Investors and financial analysts need the information from major investment advisers and ratings firms; this is critical to the thrust of business and the economy.

THINK ABOUT IT

Why do people move to other countries to work? What would attract you to work in another country? What would you miss about Canada?

Figure 4.18 Employment or job fairs sometimes attract specialists to companies or organizations in other countries. These are often in IT, nursing, education, health care, and other specialized fields.

Scientists, lawyers, and health care professionals subscribe to online and print information from such information providers as Carswell, CCH, Derwent Patent Services, Physician's Desk Reference, and ISI Scientific to keep up to date and be more productive.

Changes in Immigration Patterns

When Canada needed people to work the land in the 1800s, farmers came to Canada from all over Europe. When Canada needed skilled workers and highly trained manufacturing specialists in the early to mid-1900s, many well-educated people left their native country for a better opportunity in Canadian industry.

Today, the immigration pattern has changed. Canadians are finding that their education and skills have made them very popular in the international labour market. Many Canadian professionals in medicine, engineering, education, and other highly skilled fields are attracted by international work or are leaving Canada for more lucrative employment in other countries. This departure is referred to as the "brain drain," and it often is a serious problem in Canadian business.

On the other hand, skilled labourers are being given numerous opportunities in their own countries, as these nations become internationally competitive. Canada has certification requirements that can be obstacles to certain professions and trades. It is, however, attracting entrepreneurs, as Canadian immigration laws allow investors willing to start a company in Canada to qualify for landed immigrant status and to eventually become Canadian citizens.

TRADE TALK

While evidence indicates that Canada suffers from a brain drain to the United States, the issue is far more complex than first appears. Losses of highly skilled workers to the United States accelerated during the 1990s, but so too did the influx of highly skilled workers into Canada from abroad.

Canada gained four university graduates from abroad for every one it lost to the United States. As many immigrants entered Canada with a master's degree or doctorate as university graduates at all levels left for the United States.

Recent immigrant high-technology workers made an important contribution to meeting the rapidly growing demand in the high-technology sector. Immigrants in the 1990s accounted for about one-third of the increase in employment among computer engineers, systems analysts and computer programmers.

— *The Daily*

The New Office

The manager in a global company does the same job any manager would do: planning, organizing, directing, and controlling a company or one of its departments. The major difference between the manager of a domestic operation and an international one is in how the manager defines his or her office.

The domestic manager usually has an office in a fixed location. The manager of a global company may have several offices and spends a great deal of "office time" in other locations. The global manager must work in the "wired" workplace.

The Home Office

A manager of a global business must be able to talk to company plants or sales offices when they are open, which may mean 3:00 A.M. Canadian time. Stock markets in other parts of the world are open when the business day in Canada has finished. Investments and sales deals are made internationally when most Canadian offices are closed. Working from home,

Figure 4.19 A home office allows a manager of a global company to contact colleagues in other parts of the world whenever necessary.

Figure 4.20 A room in a hotel catering to business guests.

Web Link

Some Web sites offer a handy aid for business people or travellers by telling what time it is in other places in the world. For more information, follow the link at

www.internationalbusiness.nelson.com.

managers can make the international contacts whenever it is necessary and be available to talk to colleagues during their business hours. The use of faxes and e-mails has made it easier to stay in touch and up to date, because communications can be sent during the Canadian business day and be waiting when the recipient gets into the office the next day in, say, Hong Kong, Japan, Korea, or Australia.

The Travelling Office

Because the international manager usually travels a great deal, work is done while in transit. A cellular phone (sometimes a satellite phone) and a laptop computer are essential for this travelling office. Airlines and railways have provided "business class" service with more elbow room, table space, and other amenities to make the travelling office more pleasant. Many airlines provide a "business" lounge where managers can use the Internet, fax machines, copiers, and word processors.

The Hotel Office

Many international managers use their hotel room as an office, and many hotels have seen a marketing opportunity because of this use, offering business services to make the manager's task easier.

Business-class hotel rooms often include a desk, a computer port with Internet access, two or more phone lines (one for the computer modem, one for business calls), and an in-room printer and fax machine. Many hotels provide separate "business centre" office facilities that can be rented by the hour and include desks, computers, printers, fax machines, copiers, and even secretaries and translators. Many of these hotels also provide meeting rooms with boardroom-size tables and multimedia facilities. Managers can book the hotel conference facilities to set up marketing presentations, sales showrooms, and other large group events.

An Office in Another Country

As a company's business abroad grows, it often becomes necessary to have a manager on site. The company can recruit and hire a local person, who is familiar with the customs, language, and culture of the country but may not be familiar with the company's systems or operating philosophy. Or the company could promote one of its head-office managers to set up or take over the foreign office. Language, culture and customs, and local work culture may be a problem for this manager, but he or she would know the company's operations, philosophy, and procedures.

In either case, the company needs an office in a foreign country. The rental procedures, communication infrastructure (such as telephones, wiring, or Internet connections), availability of staff, and ancillary costs (such as taxes, municipal and other government permits, and licences) must all be considered. Someone from the company has to set up the office and train the staff, which means that a manager (and other staff, perhaps) will be sent to the foreign country, perhaps for several months, to make the arrangements. It is a very expensive procedure.

Eric McSweeney

Municipal Government Consultant

The old towns of Riga in Latvia, Vilnius in Lithuania, and Tallinn in Estonia have two things in common. First, UNESCO designates them as World Heritage sites. Second, Canadian management consultants and municipal government experts have shared their expertise in these areas. Eric McSweeney is one of these consultants.

With a Carleton University degree in Urban and Economic Geography, McSweeney rose through the ranks of the municipal government of the City of Ottawa, gaining experience at the operational, tactical, and strategic levels of local governance in a number of management areas.

McSweeney's first experiences in the world of international consulting came when Ottawa and other municipal governments in Canada loaned some of their experts on short assignments to developing countries through the Canadian Urban Institute (CUI), with the assistance of the CIDA capacity-building programs.

His early experiences in the Baltic countries made McSweeney realize a second career possibility existed: "Can there be a better way to travel and experience new countries, new cultures and new people, and get paid for doing it?" When municipal restructuring in Ottawa made his job disappear, he jumped into that new career. To date, McSweeney's work has taken him to the three Baltic states, Slovakia, Hungary, Poland, Bosnia and Herzegovina, Yugoslavia (Serbia), and Jamaica.

Canadian expertise and consultants are respected on the international stage. For example, McSweeney recently prepared the winning proposal for a multimillion-dollar contract to prepare and test a capacity-building program for rural local governments in Poland. The CUI led a consortium of consulting firms that won the contract over two much larger U.S. consulting firms with previous experience in Poland.

McSweeney's advice to young Canadians interested in international work is: "Seek out a field of work in which Canada is respected internationally, work hard, gain valuable experience in a number of areas, and then go for it." Some of the fields that offer exciting careers are biotechnology, education, telecommunications, engineering, property development, and banking.

McSweeney recognized that in many developing countries, power and authority are being decentralized from national to local governments. In most cases, however, local governments do not have the capacity, the know-how, or the experience to absorb and responsibly look after these recently "downloaded" authorities.

Building the capacity of local governments has been strongly supported by developed nations and institutions, such as the World Bank. This is where the Canadians come in. Local government administrations in the English-speaking countries of the world are the most advanced in Canada, Australia, the United States, and Britain. Worldwide demand for management consulting expertise in local government administration has never been greater.

• •

1. What does Eric McSweeney export?

2. What experience did McSweeney have that helped him begin his new career?

3. What steps does McSweeney recommend young Canadians interested in international work take?

4.4 Staying Domestic or Going International?

No business in Canada can be said to operate completely in a domestic arena. Each business relies to a greater or lesser degree on other businesses, both domestically and internationally. International business affects markets and competition and governments that make trade agreements with other governments and other businesses. A small potter who makes bowls and mugs and sells his or her products in the local artisan store or at craft fairs may seem a far cry from an international business. However, the artisan may be connected to international businesses in a number of ways: the clay, potter's wheel, glazes, and other supplies may come from outside Canada; the craft fair or retail store might advertise internationally and attract foreign customers; the potter might decide to create a Web site and sell his or her work online; or the potter might be competing directly with foreign imports in the marketplace. In any event, it would be very difficult for a business to remain untouched by the international marketplace today.

Many businesses, though, decide not to become international. This does not mean they are unconnected in some way to the international marketplace, only that they have chosen not to import from or export to another country. Why do these businesses choose to stay domestic?

Product Quality

Businesses that sell high-quality products might find that product quality suffers if production is increased to meet the demands of a larger market. An ice-cream parlour that makes ice cream in small batches to ensure consistency in taste and flavours cannot shift to mass production and keep producing the same type of product. Nor can the artisan glass blower or the local pastry chef maintain the high quality of their products when larger quantities are required for the international market. For many businesses, the sense of pride in the craft is the main reason for the owner to run the business, and international expansion is not required to sell the company's daily output.

Figure 4.21 Some artists and artisans who create unique products may choose to remain in their home market rather than going into international markets because large-scale production might mean a decrease in the quality of their products.

Service businesses, too, may find it difficult to become international. Local entrepreneurs who have started repair shops, cleaning services, hair salons, and child-care services, for example, could not easily transfer their particular talent to another city, let alone another country. Since the service provider is the product, the quality of his or her work depends on each individual. Unless the individual wishes to move or train others, the quality of the service is not transferable.

Complexity, Risk, and Cost

The amount of time and effort it takes to negotiate with foreign companies, arrange shipping, set up Web sites, and travel to distant places is complex, costly, and risky for many smaller businesses. Entrepreneurs who have started local businesses may wish to keep them local to avoid the time commitment and the extra financial risks involved in looking at international markets for supplies or for export opportunities. A small gift store might be able to acquire new and interesting items from trade shows in Munich or New York or Mexico City, but the costs involved in seeking out these products as well as importing them into Canada could make them unprofitable, especially without a distributor and a knowledgeable customs broker. Most local entrepreneurs need guidance and training to become successful international business people. Acquiring such assistance and training requires time that small business people may not have and includes costs and risks that they do not wish to undertake.

Quality of Life

A small business is often the dream of the owner. The business is a way of financing a hobby or passion. The music lover opening a classical music store, the skateboarder designing and building a better skateboard, the artist creating magnificent stained glass scenes can practise their craft and indulge their passions while earning an income at the same time. The fact that a book lover can be close to books is a far greater motivation for opening a bookstore than creating a global bookselling empire like Chapters/Indigo. The business itself is often secondary in the priorities of some small business people.

Most businesses recognize that extra profit can be generated by expansion into global markets. For many business people, however, the extra profit is not worth the extra effort. Even to ship products that have been ordered over the Internet to other countries takes extra time. Often, travel is necessary, and travel keeps managers or owners away from their families. When faced with the need to obtain a passport, receive a series of inoculations, hire a translator, learn a country's customs, negotiate foreign trade rules and regulations, arrange foreign financing, schedule shipping, and calculate transportation costs, currency exchange rates, and tariffs, many business owners say, "No thanks."

ICE Activities for 4.3 and 4.4

Ideas	Connections	Extensions
1. (a) Explain how increased access to information has changed today's workplace.	(b) Describe the kind of work done by someone you know. How has globalization changed the way this work is done?	(c) There is a split between manual labourers and knowledge workers. What do you think will be the future of these two types of workers? Explain your answer.
2. (a) Globalization has had an impact on the workplace in five major areas. What are they?	(b) Find and describe an example from your community that illustrates the impact of globalization on one of the five major areas of the workplace.	(c) List all the sources of information that you and your family use in an average week. What would be the implications of not having access to this information? How would this change your lives?
3. (a) What are four different "offices" that international managers may have to use?	(b) Research a Canadian hotel in your area and give examples of the business services that the hotel offers.	(c) Select a foreign country. Assume you are a manager trying to set up an office there. Report on the specific problems that you would need to consider. How would you overcome these obstacles?
4. (a) Explain why all companies are not international.	(b) List five businesses in your region that are domestic and five that are international. In a small group, brainstorm reasons these businesses have chosen to either remain domestic or to go international.	(c) Select one of the domestic businesses that you listed in 4. (b). Prepare a report on how the business could become international.

Canada's Trading Partners: Focus on Brazil

Throughout the 1990s, Brazil's economic policies emphasized market liberalization, the privatization of state enterprises, and prudent monetary policy. Inflation has been kept at levels that have raised the incomes of the lower classes, and throughout the decade, trade with Brazil has more than doubled.

Possessing large and well-developed agricultural, mining, manufacturing, and service sectors, Brazil's economy outweighs that of all other Latin American countries and is expanding its presence in world markets.

With the world's sixth-largest population, Brazil is a major exporter of coffee, fruit juice, cocoa, appliances and electrical equipment, construction steel and other metal products, mineral products, and footwear.

Brazil is Canada's largest trading partner in the South American and Caribbean markets (excluding Mexico). Brazilian companies shipped $1.5 billion of products to Canada in 2001, making Brazil the sixteenth-largest source of imports to Canada. It is also a primary destination for Canadian foreign direct investment in the hemisphere—approaching $7 billion.

However, recent trade disputes have been in the news. In 2001, for example, Canada banned imports of beef and beef products from Brazil because of concerns about mad cow disease. But after three weeks of intense criticism of Canada, and Brazil's threats of a full-scale trade war, with its trade with the United States and Mexico negatively affected (through NAFTA), Canada lifted the ban. A Canadian team of inspectors concluded that Brazil's beef was safe.

Canada was also in a dispute with Brazil over aircraft manufacturing subsidies. Montreal-based aerospace giant Bombardier Inc. is the world's third-largest commercial aircraft maker. Bombardier claimed that it had lost $7.5 billion in international jet sales to Brazilian companies in 1996-99 because of a Brazilian-government subsidy program, which supported Brazilian aircraft-maker Embraer SA. Brazil granted more than $35 million worth of illegal (according to WTO rules) subsidies to local aircraft manufacturers, giving them an unfair advantage.

(The regional jet market in Brazil is worth $8 billion a year.) Bombardier even ran an open letter in Brazilian and some other countries' newspapers explaining its position.

In December 2000, the WTO granted Canada the right to impose sanctions or penalties (tariffs) worth over $2 billion over six years to compensate for Brazil's refusal to withdraw these subsidies from its aircraft industry.

In February 2002, however, the WTO panel reported that it had found that certain financing countermeasures Canada had undertaken to preserve jobs in Canada were inconsistent with WTO rules. Canada's then International Trade Minister, Pierre Pettigrew, announced, "We are committed to a trade system based on clear rules—a priority we hope will be shared by Brazil....We have decided that, on balance, it's better to let the decision stand. We want to turn the page on this trade dispute and find a mutually acceptable solution with Brazil."

GLOBAL THOUGHT

As a regional heavyweight with global aspirations, Brazil has its own well-defined foreign and trade policy agenda. In regional and global terms, both countries [Canada and Brazil] recognize in the other a valued partner. Formal bilateral consultations are being held regularly on political, trade, international, and defence security issues. Cooperation in diverse areas such as audio-visual co-production, mutual legal assistance, extradition, nuclear cooperation, human rights, democratic institution building, international demining, and education are giving further structure to our relations.

– Department of Foreign Affairs and International Trade

A SNAPSHOT OF BRAZIL

Size: 8 511 965 sq. km

World Region: Latin America

Capital City: Brasilia

Language: Portuguese

Currency: Real

Population: 176.0 million

Time: Noon in Ottawa (EST) is 2:00 P.M. in Brasilia.

Climate: Mostly tropical but temperate in the south

Type of Government: Federal republic

Labour Force by Occupation: 53 percent services, 24 percent industry, 23 percent agriculture

Membership in World Organizations: Mercosur (the Southern Cone Common Market), WTO, OECD

Importing Partners and Products:
Partners: United States, Argentina, Germany, Japan, and Italy.
Products: Machinery and equipment, chemical products, oil, automobiles and automobile parts.

Exporting Partners and Products:
Partners: United States, Argentina, Germany, Japan, Italy, and Netherlands.
Products: Iron ore, soybeans, footwear, coffee, and automobiles.

Travel Advisory: A business visa must be obtained by a person wishing to carry equipment, catalogues, or a personal computer. Infectious diseases can occur. Serious crime, often involving violence, is high and increasing in a number of urban centres.

Business Etiquette: Business in Brazil is based on personal relationships. English is preferred over Spanish if Portuguese is not available when conducting business. Professional dress is conservative. Motto on the Brazilian flag: Ordem e Progresso (Order and Progress).

Figure 4.22 According to *Cincinnati Enquirer* writer Michael Astor and some financial analysts, Brazil's winning the World Cup of Soccer in 2002 may boost the country's economy. A study by HSBC Bank (one of the world's largest banks) found that the stock markets of developed countries that have won the World Cup of Soccer since 1966 outperformed the global average by 9 percent.

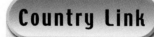

Country Link

For further material on Brazil, links to the Canadian embassy in Brazil, trade figures, and links to other important sites, follow the link at
www.internationalbusiness.nelson.com.

Chapter Challenges

Knowledge/Understanding

1. Match each of the following terms to the correct definition or description below:
   - (a) invention
   - (b) innovation
   - (c) just-in-time inventory system
   - (d) kanban
   - (e) big box retailer
   - (f) data mining
   - (g) telecommunication
   - (h) joint venture

   - (i) a Japanese philosophy focused on eliminating waste
   - (ii) business that specializes in offering a huge variety of one category of merchandise
   - (iii) a marketing research method
   - (iv) a change that extends an initial concept
   - (v) communication across distances
   - (vi) two or more businesses combining assets for mutual gain
   - (vii) a new product based on a new creative idea
   - (viii) products scheduled to arrive as they are needed

2. Explain how inventors and software creators benefit from patents and copyrights.

3. Create a cause-and-effect organizer to show the relationship between one of the following industries and the development of international business in Canada: automotive, cellular communications, information, or banking.

4. List three reasons that some businesses decide to stay domestic rather than enter international markets.

Thinking/Inquiry

1. How has the trade relationship between Canada and Brazil changed over the past decade? Why have these changes taken place?

2. Coffee, cocoa, beef, diamonds, sugar, oil, and minerals are resources that are in great demand in North America. The development of trade to acquire these resources has caused hardships in other countries. Select one of these resources (or use a resource assigned by your teacher) and discuss how the exploitation of that resource has caused problems. Suggest a way to help solve the problem.

3. Napster was a controversial online music-swapping company that allowed Internet users to download popular music for free. Napster was forced offline in July 2001 after major record companies launched successful lawsuits against it, citing music piracy. What do you think? Did Napster provide a much-needed service? Or did its service damage the recording artists, musicians, songwriters, and others involved in producing pop music?

Communication

1. **The Global Debate**
   Topic: Globalization means Americanization.

   Possible Supporting Statements
   - The United States is the only world superpower and wields great influence over much of the world's commerce, politics, and information.
   - One of the barriers to any other country trying to enter the global marketplace is that the U.S. companies are already there. Most of the top 50 global brands are American.

   Possible Refuting Statements
   - Many countries, such as Japan, France, and England, have strong cultural identities and economies based on their own identities.
   - More and more countries are celebrating their uniqueness and rejecting U.S. culture.

   Work with a partner to develop other supporting and refuting arguments.

2. Select one product with which you are familiar. Create a timeline that demonstrates how the product has changed since its invention. Include the changes that have occurred in North America and in the global marketplace.

3. Write a case study of a company (one that is not profiled in this book) that has been successful in international trade. Explain the reasons for the company's success. Identify changes in technology, process, or attitudes that have affected this company. Share your case study with other students in the class.

Application

1. Lower labour costs in other countries may attract Canadian international businesses, but the wages paid to workers in those countries may not be enough for the workers to live on. In addition, it may be virtually impossible for workers in some countries to establish unions to ensure fair wages, safe working conditions, and job security. In small groups, discuss what you think Canadians should do about these complex human rights issues.

2. The widespread use of cellular phones illustrates the interdependence of businesses around the world. Research Canadian companies that provide cellular communications components or consultants to other countries. Prepare an illustrated report (using diagrams, maps, photos, tables, or graphs) to show how these companies are contributing to the expansion of Canada's global business presence.

3. Working with a partner, investigate the Strategis Web site for current information on export opportunities; research on markets; potential suppliers, partners, and customers; use of technology opportunities; issues regarding business and the environment; or one of its other information categories. Analyze the content of one of these categories and prepare a brief oral presentation in which you explain to your classmates how the availability of this information online creates new opportunities for Canadian international businesses.

International Business Portfolio

Working in Your IBP Country

In your IBP country, you will conduct business in the airport or a hotel, or you may even set up an office in this country. Here are some of the things you should consider before you go:
• airport and airline facilities
• business hotels
• office space
• human resources
• recent changes in the political, economic, or cultural life of your country

Activities

1. Gather illustrations and descriptions of the work area facilities provided in airports, airlines, and hotels. Include rates, brochures, or Web sites.

2. Using the Internet or a newspaper from your country, describe three possible office spaces currently available, and include the rent in Canadian dollars. List the equipment, supplies, phone lines, and other tools you would need to get connected.

3. Check the classified advertisements or Internet job-search sites to obtain an example of an ad for an office worker such as a receptionist, executive assistant, or office manager. As well as a job description, the ad could include salary offered, educational background, and skill level required.

4. List recent changes in this country that may have an impact on business relationships there; for example, significant currency fluctuation or a change in government.

Chapter 5

International Agreements, Organizations, and Policies

Organizations, companies—and countries— must position themselves to conduct effective international trade and commerce. Positioning requires an awareness of global and national trade organizations, agreements, and policies. By increasing communication and collaboration among nations, trade agreements and organizations help develop a more stable business climate. In turn, this may lead to a healthier, more peaceful world that can seek out ways for globalization to benefit less-developed nations.

Chapter Topics

➤ 5.1 – Positioning in the Global Economy 144

➤ 5.2 – Corporate Globalization 150

➤ 5.3 – International Trade Agreements 157

➤ 5.4 – Organizations Influencing Global Trade 168

➤ *Canada's Trading Partners: Focus on* Belgium 174

➤ Chapter Challenges 176

Prior Knowledge

- If Canada traded only with the United States, what would be the advantages and disadvantages of such a trade arrangement?
- With which trade agreements and international organizations are you already familiar? What are their principles, members, and mandates?
- What is Canada's reputation in the global marketplace? What is its image? How do these terms differ?

Inquiries/Expectations

- What are some of the reasons for the growth of the number and size of multinational companies over time?
- How can multinational companies have both positive and negative effects on the countries in which they operate?
- What international agreements and organizations have influenced global business activity, and what is Canada's involvement in those agreements and organizations?
- What are some arguments for and against freer international trade for Canada?

Important Terms

Agreement on Internal Trade (AIT)
Asia-Pacific Economic Cooperation (APEC)
Association of South East Asian Nations (ASEAN)
bilateral trade
ethnocentric MNC
European Union (EU)
franchise
Free Trade Area of the Americas (FTAA)
free-trade zones
G-20
geocentric MNC
globalization

International Chamber of Commerce (ICC)
International Monetary Fund (IMF)
multilateral trade
multinational company (MNC)
North American Free Trade Agreement (NAFTA)
Organization for Economic Cooperation and Development (OECD)
polycentric MNC
strategic alliance
trading bloc
World Economic Forum (WEF)

5.1 Positioning in the Global Economy

Figure 5.1 Satellites, like the one shown above, relay information to countries around the world.

Communication satellites orbit the globe high above the earth, transmitting and receiving signals far beyond national political boundaries. These satellites, from a number of nations, relay images and information to the world below. They have transformed communications in recent times and opened up vast new opportunities for international relationships and global trade. Images conveyed by satellite are the technical basis of video-conferencing and the Internet, allowing individuals and organizations around the globe to exchange messages instantaneously. Ventures such as the International Space Station have been launched through the cooperation of groups of nations, including Japan, the United States, and Canada, to benefit global space discovery and experimentation. All this technology is ready to service today's businesses.

The global positioning system (GPS) is a satellite-based navigational system that is funded and controlled by the U.S. Department of Defense. The 24 GPS satellites transmit specially coded satellite signals, enabling the receiver to compute position, velocity, and time. The exact position of the GPS receiver can be determined within a few metres anywhere on Earth. The GPS is dependent on technology; likewise, global traders are dependent on international communications and require expertise in the use of all the available tools and technical knowledge to ensure success.

GPS may help people position themselves in geographic terms, but companies trying to secure world markets also need to have systems that will position them in the global marketplace, the mind of the consumer, and the competition they face in their target countries. Companies engaged in international business want to lead consumers to think of them and their products first. As you will learn in Chapter 11, companies use specific techniques to learn their position in global markets and other techniques to boost that position in the minds of their customers and trading partners in business and in government.

To position itself in world markets, a business must establish what makes its products and services unique, different, or superior. Well-positioned and well-run companies know where they and their products—and their image and reputation—are at all times.

Figure 5.2 The Official Web site of the Canadian Tourism Commission provides practical tips, a personal Travel Notebook for planning a trip, and links to various local tourism Web sites.

Part of Canada's challenge is to spread the word internationally that we as a country are both open for business and have the technical knowledge when it comes to doing business with our major trade partners. Creating this image depends on our visibility among our trading partners. To raise visibility, we need a plan to communicate with these partners, and others, what Canada has to offer.

A strong example of what Canada has to offer can be found on the Canadian Tourism Commission's Web site. Designed to motivate international and Canadian travellers to explore Canada, the Commission's consumer-oriented Web site offers great travel ideas and itineraries for our country's diverse regions and distinct seasons.

Strategies toward Global Positioning

Whether companies are large or small, they may use the following strategies to position themselves internationally or globally.

When starting out to do business beyond their national borders, companies are most likely to enter the international arena by either exporting (selling) their products to other countries, or importing (buying) products from other countries. One form of exporting and importing is the licensing agreement, whereby a business pays a fee to a company from another country to produce or sell that company's products (see Chapter 4).

Another way to achieve a global presence is to franchise a business operation. A **franchise** is a type of business in which a company authorizes a group or an individual to sell its goods and services. These formal agreements usually involve the franchisee (the one who buys the rights) paying the franchisor (the one who sells the rights) a fee and a percentage of revenue or profits. In this arrangement, the franchisee pays for being able to ride on the success of the franchisor, following its "formula," and gaining benefits from its brand name and image. Franchise operations require each franchisee to use the same type of equipment, physical layout, systems, operations, marketing, training, staffing, and customer service model. The goals are to have the franchisee replicate the proven, successful "formula" of the franchisor, and for the domestic and foreign consumer to enjoy the same experience.

For example, when the Vancouver-based company Boston Pizza expanded to the United States, it was able to quickly set up franchises on a North American basis, supplying franchisees with real estate, construction, startup procedures, fixtures, operations systems, signage, equipment, marketing programs, training, and menus, all based on its successful development of the concept in Canada. In fact, the only change that was made for the U.S. market was a modification of

Figure 5.3 *Boston's, the Gourmet Pizza* restaurant in Dallas, Texas. Except for the name, this store completely mirrors the Boston Pizza restaurants in Canada.

the name to Boston's, the Gourmet Pizza in order to acquire federal trademark protection for the brand in the United States. As with other types of franchise, protection and positioning of the brand are paramount, so franchisee screening, training, ongoing supervision and communication are required. Once everything is set up, however, the franchisee follows the operations manual, and it is expected that good results will follow. Experience teaches that financial failure can be the cost of not following the franchise concept closely, though minor adjustments are expected in some cultures.

A company may enter a foreign country by starting up a wholly owned subsidiary that it operates in the host country. A subsidiary may bear, and operate under, a different name or be owned by a company's larger subsidiary in a similar area of business. (See the profile of Robertson Screws in this chapter.) Canada has historically been largely dependent on the investment that foreign subsidiaries have brought into this country from a variety of nations.

Another popular international market entry strategy is to purchase in foreign markets the parts or materials required for manufacturing a product in the home market. This method is common in the automotive, furniture, and computer industries in which components arrive from other countries to be installed at the assembly site.

Another international strategy (which you learned about in Chapter 4) is to establish a joint venture with a company from another country to produce a new product. An automobile manufacturer may choose to combine parts, expertise, and complementary technologies from different countries to produce a vehicle. In the 1990s, for example, a number of the major international automobile producers from countries like Japan, the United States, and Germany proposed ideas for a car for Chinese consumers. Major Japanese and American automobile firms have frequently used this approach. The recently introduced Nummi, produced jointly by General Motors and Toyota, is an example of a joint venture.

Another type of international partnership is referred to as a **strategic alliance,** in which two or more firms cooperate to co-develop, co-produce, or co-market their products. In Japan and South Korea, national alliances cooperate, or networks of businesses link large manufacturers, suppliers, and finance companies with common interests. Sometimes such partners also cross-invest; that is, they buy each others' shares, usually to ensure supply or to share risk and profit.

The Japanese term for these mutually supporting alliances is *keiretsu*; in South Korea, similar strategic alliances are known as *chaebol*. These conglomerates merge expertise from government, business, and education. In Western nations, this process of multilevel cooperation has been referred to as "Japan Inc."

International Company Profile

Robertson Inc.

Think of all the products that depend on screws to hold them together. Now think of all of the different types of screws and screwdrivers that are available. It wasn't always that way.

By 1906, Peter Lymburner Robertson had decided that improvements over the old slotted screw were needed. He found a way to make a socket head screw and applied for a patent. In 1908, he set up shop in Milton, Ontario, just west of Toronto, to begin manufacturing square-headed screwdrivers and screw systems. The process involved punching a pointed square impression into the head of the metal fasteners. Robertson's innovation made it easier to loosen or tighten a screw and less likely to strip the screw head. Today, this type of screw is still called a "Robertson."

Anyone who has ever used a screwdriver will appreciate the difference. Robertson supposedly liked to say that his product was "the biggest little invention of the twentieth century … so far."

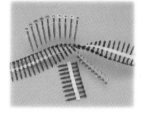

Robertson's Milton factory radically changed the local economy, which had up to then relied on farming, retail, and a failing brickyard. By the 1930s, the company staff accounted for about 20 percent of the town's workforce, and the company continued

Figure 5.4 Robertson's factory in Montreal, Quebec, manufactures the square-headed screws.

to diversify its product selection. The Robertson screw became a fixture on the bodywork of Henry Ford's Model T automobile and in the ships built by the British navy during the Second World War.

Robertson ran the company until his death in 1951. In the 1960s, the company was purchased by Trans Union, a multi-faceted company whose businesses included railroad tank cars (Procor). Through acquisition in 1981, Trans Union and its affiliated businesses joined The Marmon Group, one of America's largest private business enterprises. Today, Robertson Inc. is a member of The Marmon Group, an international association of manufacturing and service companies with collective sales of 6 billion USD.

Robertson's president lives in the United States, but most of the company's direction is taken by the Milton-based vice-president and general manager, and about 100 employees staff the Milton head office. North American and international sales and distribution go through the company facilities in Montreal, Calgary, and Milton, but most production happens in the Montreal operation.

One exciting development was the 2002 opening of a production facility in Jiashan near Shanghai, China, with about 50 workers and a general manager of Canadian-Chinese origin. The company has positioned itself strategically to compete with comparable manufacturers from countries such as Taiwan. Competitors have the right to make a square-headed product but they cannot use the Robertson name (which is protected by trademark). With the growth in China and many surrounding Asian nations, Robertson is establishing its presence globally.

. . . .

1. How did Robertson change the market for screws and screwdrivers?
2. What steps led to Robertson establishing a global presence?
3. Identify one product or service for which your community is well known. How important is it to the local economy? Explain.

International and Global Companies

We live in an age characterized by interdependence among nations and economies. Today's trend toward the globalization of business influences everyone. The global economy is based on the interdependence of competitors, markets, and resources. Individuals everywhere must be able to work with people of different cultures and keep informed about international events.

As we have already seen, companies expand internationally to increase sales and profit, and for a variety of other reasons. Once a Canadian company sells its products outside Canada, it gains international status. If it ships its products through Buffalo, New York, for American distribution, it can be described as international. What does it take for a company to be considered global? Consider a few of the characteristics that distinguish "international" from "global" company operations.

Some international companies think of their foreign operations as appendages, which usually produce and sell products designed and engineered in the domestic market and sometimes adapted for local needs, culture, and tastes. Decisions, strategies, and technology come from corporate headquarters, and executives of the home country often fill at least one of the subsidiary's top management positions. In many cases, the company pursues a centrally directed strategy designed to bring the bulk of profits back to the corporate headquarters.

Figure 5.5 In global companies, members of the management team enrich their companies with the variety of skills, knowledge, and aptitudes that they bring from their different countries and cultures.

A *global* company is one in which top management makes decisions to maximize worldwide revenues, income, and profits. Global companies encourage employees to move from country to country, and they promote foreign nationals to top management positions. Global companies encourage research and development in the most expedient location available. Their goal is to create a "stateless" corporation that operates relatively freely across international borders, although it must respect the regulations of the countries in which it operates.

As cross-border free trade and investment become more accessible, growing numbers of companies are developing into global companies to compete in the global marketplace.

Benefits and Challenges in Global Companies

Here are a few advantages of developing a truly global company:

- savings in raw materials and labour by moving production facilities to locations where wages are lower
- creation of more knowledgeable and powerful leadership through a team of managers from different countries
- worldwide access to the most innovative ideas and designs
- ability to market a product to meet worldwide needs and wants
- job creation in developing nations

TRADE TALK

Asuransi Jiwa ManuLife Indonesia, the largest foreign joint-venture insurer in that country, was declared bankrupt by the Jakarta Commercial Court head judge in June 2002, for non-payment of shareholder dividends. But the Supreme Court overturned the bankruptcy verdict in July, confirming that this was a private shareholder matter and that shareholders had agreed not to declare or distribute dividends for the year 1999.

- transfer of technology and training across national borders
- easier access to foreign investment, joint ventures, and strategic alliances
- potential recognition as an outstanding "global corporate citizen," observing the culture and laws of the nations that the company enters

There are also a number of challenges and costs in developing a global company:

- cost of creating and maintaining a global presence
- challenge of maintaining quality product standards throughout the company's facilities
- time required for sourcing decisions and manufacturing processes
- need for home-government approval of the actions of global companies; regulations and taxes may be imposed
- challenge of gaining understanding of many nations and their business, political, and cultural environments
- risk of unfair treatment by local justice system or government (see Trade Talk)
- political, economic, commercial, and foreign currency exchange risks

ICE Activities for 5.1

Ideas	Connections	Extensions
1. (a) What is "positioning" in business terms?	(b) What is the value to Canada of promoting its image?	(c) Imagine it is your job to "sell" Canada to the world. In groups, prepare a plan to position Canada in the global marketplace.
2. (a) Explain the advantages and challenges of a global company.	(b) Select one of the points you listed in 2. (a) for further research. Write five research questions that you might use as a starting point in your investigation.	(c) Review the list of advantages and challenges in 2. (a). If you were the owner of a successful Canadian company, would you go global or would you remain domestic? Explain the reasons for your decision.
3. (a) Outline three different strategies a company can use to enter a foreign market.	(b) How does an international company differ from a global company?	(c) Identify a foreign subsidiary in your community. Profile the operation by researching: name of company, name of parent company, country of origin, main product(s), and number of employees.

5.2 Corporate Globalization

Globalization refers to the growth and spread of interactive international economies and businesses around the world. Over the past few decades, there has been a growing trend toward families of interrelated and cooperating companies operating throughout the world. As companies become more multinational, nationality and borders become less important. When you buy a Ricky Martin CD, for example, you are participating in globalization as a consumer. Martin is a singer from Puerto Rico. His CDs are produced by Sony Music Entertainment in Holland, but are manufactured and distributed by Sony Music Entertainment (Canada) Inc. for Canadian consumers.

Another example of multinational collaboration is the Airbus. The production of Airbus commercial airliners spans several countries in Europe and draws upon a global network of suppliers. Airbus was established in 1970 as a European consortium of French, German, and, later, Spanish and British companies; the goal of the consortium was to compete against the large U.S. aircraft manufacturers. The company is based in Toulouse, France, and the consortium that builds the Airbus now consists of companies from Britain, France, Germany, Spain, and Belgium, with training and support centres in China, Japan, and North America. Many international airlines use Airbus models; Airbus now boasts a 50 percent world market share.

THINK ABOUT IT

What would be some of the consequences that developing nations would face as a result of global corporations having such a high degree of economic power?

Some global corporations have more economic power (and, occasionally, political power) than some of the countries across whose borders they operate. A simple indicator of the power of corporations over governments is the amount of wealth that each type of economy generates. As discussed earlier, this wealth is measured by comparing a corporation's sales and a country's gross domestic product. By this measure, of the largest economies in the world—including both countries and corporations—more than half are corporations rather than countries. For example, the economy of the Ford Motor Company is larger than the economies of Saudi Arabia and Norway. Philip Morris, a large American corporation that sells food, cigarettes, and other consumer products, has annual sales that exceed the gross domestic product of New Zealand.

Multinational Companies

A **multinational company (MNC)** (also known as a transnational company) is a business enterprise that conducts business in several countries. MNCs operate worldwide on a borderless basis while still observing national regulations and policies in the countries where they operate.

The global influence of these economic giants is illustrated by their dominance in the following areas:

- They extract, refine, and distribute most of the world's oil and gasoline.
- They build most of the world's hydroelectric and nuclear plants.
- They mine and extract from the ground most of the world's minerals.
- They manufacture and sell most of the world's automobiles, airplanes, communication satellites, computers, home electronics, chemicals, medicines, and biotechnology products.

- They harvest much of the world's wood and make most of its paper.
- They grow many of the world's agricultural crops, and process and distribute much of its food.

These MNCs account for more than 70 percent of world trade. Global economic power is clearly established in the northern hemisphere, where over 90 percent of the parent companies of MNCs are based. They operate according to multilateral agreements established among countries to regulate international trade. There are about 40 000 multinational companies in the world today that have subsidiaries in countries other than their own. This seems like a large number of such companies, until you realize that there are 90 000 companies in Canada. And Ontario alone is home to over 1100 multinational corporations. Notable examples are Roots and Nortel Networks.

Multinational companies usually have their international headquarters in a major city and operate on a global basis in one of the following three ways:

- An **ethnocentric MNC** operates internationally, in much the same way as it does at home. It usually has tight control over its foreign operations from head office.

  An example of an ethnocentric MNC is Coca-Cola Company. Founded in 1886, it is now the world's leading manufacturer, marketer, and distributor of non-alcoholic beverages, concentrates, and syrups, which are used to produce nearly 300 beverage brands. Headquartered in Atlanta, Georgia, it controls product specifications and many other aspects of international operations, and it has local operations in nearly 200 countries. Seventy percent of Coca-Cola's income is from operations outside the United States.

  As a country, Japan has had a history of being an ambitious exporter to the world but somewhat "closed" to products from other countries, often being very selective in the products it chooses to import. Japanese MNCs have gained a reputation for being ethnocentric.

- A **polycentric MNC** understands the market differences from country to country and gives its foreign operations greater autonomy.

  An example of a polycentric MNC is 3M Corp., with over 50 percent of its $16 billion USD in sales coming from outside the United States. Of the 35 000 employees outside the United States, only 300 are foreign-service employees not residing in their own countries. Each of the four regions outside the United States has its own management structure.

  Colgate-Palmolive operates in 200 countries with its management functions dispersed and with facilities in many locations that serve internal and external customers across regional boundaries.

- A **geocentric MNC** takes a multinational approach and seeks total integration of its global operations. Both polycentric and geocentric MNCs tend to describe the position held by North American and European companies. A truly global MNC is hard to find. Colgate-Palmolive and the accounting and consulting firm Deloitte & Touche are possible examples.

Historically, international trade required a company to make a product in its own country and then sell it to customers in other nations. Consumers today buy products that are made of components from many countries. It is sometimes challenging to determine how to complete the required "Made in…" to indicate the origin of a product. Canadian companies are part of the global supply chain. Regardless of their international structure, companies must source raw materials, semi-manufactured and manufactured goods, research, and many other services worldwide. (For example, the screws used to hold your furniture together may be Canadian even though the chair is made in the United States.)

One very dominant world grouping is the so-called *Triad*, whose three players are the United States, the European Union, and Japan. The Triad can be seen as an economic power structure of multinational corporate "states" or regions, at times cooperating, at times competing with one another around the globe. Their "tri-polar" economic power is so great that some nations are "taking a backseat" to the multinational companies that are in one or more of these centres of economic activity. To remain relevant, governments of many countries have had to adjust to this global reality; freer and more flexible trade agreements were needed, and several were agreed to in the later years of the twentieth century. By facilitating freer movement of goods, services, labour, and capital across borders—liberalizing market access and encouraging "going global"—new economic agreements have given countries and companies much wider economic reach and influence. In political terms, this process of economic domination of certain nations or groups of nations over other countries is often referred to as imperialism.

Challenges to Multinational Organizations

As these huge multinational organizations spread their influence around the world, they bring with them money, technology, know-how, and skills. When a corporation invests in another country, the benefits are usually evident in jobs, the transfer of technology, and training. As always, however, there is another side to the story.

In his book *The End of Globalization*, economist and scholar Alan Rugman contends that the majority of manufacturing and service-based multinational enterprises have actually been organized regionally for their own benefit. The world's 500 largest multinational enterprises account for more than 50 percent of world trade. Yet, he suggests, these enterprises are not really global; they operate primarily within the Triad—regional markets consisting of Europe, North America, and Japan.

GLOBAL THOUGHT

Although U.S. corporations have profound political influence, Japan is perhaps the most classic example of the traditional corporate state. *Sei-kan-zai ittaikiko*, the Japanese amalgamation of politics, bureaucracy, and big business, has come to be known in the West as "Japan Inc." This fusing of elements is reinforced by a series of interfamily ties that link the government and corporate leadership of the country (*kei batsu*), by "old boy" university networks (*gaku batsu*), by a powerful corporate lobby, and by the system of *amakudari* (descent from heaven), which resembles the "revolving door" of the Western nations, where high-ranking government officials slip right into corporate boards of directors upon retirement. Such tight relationships, combined with a foreign aid program that subsidizes investment abroad, provide a solid base from which Japan's corporations project themselves into the world economy.

– Joshua Karliner

Honda of Canada Manufacturing was the first Japanese manufacturer to produce vehicles in Canada, starting operations in Alliston, Ontario, in November 1986. It is a private company that does not publicly trade shares, but it is a significant part of the Canadian economy. In the July 2002 *Report on Business Magazine's* 100 Biggest Private Companies, Honda ranked third with more than $12 billion in revenue.

Honda of Canada produces automobiles mainly for the North American market and some export markets, including South America, and even a limited number of Honda Odysseys for the Japanese market. Honda has established a number of Japanese work structures and organizational designs, reflecting the organizational philosophy that is standard in Japan.

The three regions in the Triad tend to work to the advantage of countries within their region, says Rugman, rather than encouraging true globalization by integrating with other nations. For example, over 85 percent of the world's automobile production takes place in these three regional markets, and 90 percent of the cars made in Europe are sold to Europeans. The challenge to Canadian companies may now be to develop global customers beyond the Triad. At the moment, the great majority of our exports travel only as far as the United States.

According to Rugman, it is also important for multinationals to be accountable and responsible for their actions. This means that the jobs they create, as well as the technology, profits, and skills that they access in a host country, should stay in that country. As trade barriers and impediments to investment disappear and as new technologies are introduced, multinationals have much greater freedom to serve the needs of foreign countries. However, some foreign countries complain about the ways in which some multinationals dominate their economies and try to influence their governments.

Rugman points out another drawback to the way multinationals sometimes do business. Multinationals are creating global production systems, with parts, components, and assembly located in different countries. However, by deciding which jobs will be located in which parts of the world, they are creating new international divisions of labour. The Canadian auto industry provides a good example. Both American and Japanese auto companies have decided that Canada is a good place to assemble automobiles, using some parts made elsewhere. In Canada, Honda and Toyota use over 75 percent local content. However, they provide only a limited amount of automobile design work and research and development opportunities for personnel in Canada.

Figure 5.6 Honda Canada Manufacturing: Odysseys coming off the line at Plant 2, with a white plastic to protect the paint surface during transit. While Canada assembles many Honda vehicles, Honda provides few design and research and development opportunities for Canadians.

Global Organizational Structure

The international marketplace is extremely unpredictable. It is very different from the familiar comfort of domestic markets and customers. The stakes are high. International business experts agree that the question to ask is not "if" something will go wrong, but "when." Caution, along with good planning and organization, can help to minimize global problems. After all, international activities affect every department in a company.

Large companies tend to be like large ships—it takes a long time to manoeuvre or change course. Therefore, it takes longer for them to analyze information and alternatives, and to manoeuvre around barriers and obstacles. This gives smaller, more responsive companies an actual advantage in the international market-place. When this advantage is combined with the benefits of technology, smaller companies can be very competitive with the bigger ones.

Companies that are expanding internationally require an organizational structure that will accommodate their wider vision. The next section describes five ways (with some variations) to organize people and resources for international business.

Separate International Divisions

International staff are isolated and function separately from the company. The international department has its own systems for sales, marketing, customer support, and logistics. This department handles all products going to all foreign markets. This structure can be quite efficient but has the potential disadvantage of requiring special plans for communication with the main operations of the company, which can cause delays.

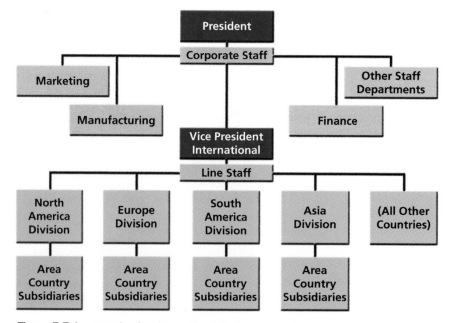

Figure 5.7 An example of an international division organization chart.

Functional Divisions

The company maintains separate departments in sales, accounting, logistics, and research and development, with one or more individuals in each department responsible for handling international activities. An advantage of this structure is that international requirements are less likely to be neglected when international representatives are part of the functional processes.

With this structure, companies are assured that their employees work in their assigned professional or technical specialty and capacity. However, communication barriers sometimes arise across functions, making management more complex and difficult. As a result, a discipline of consultation, collaboration, and planning must be kept up.

Product Divisions

International and domestic activities are separated by product groupings. In this model, the division usually shares support or staff functions, such as accounting, with other divisions.

General Motors built its automotive success using this approach. Having a series of product divisions within the company can create a healthy sense of competition and a focus on production. However, it can be detrimental in the allocation of a company's financial, human, and material resources.

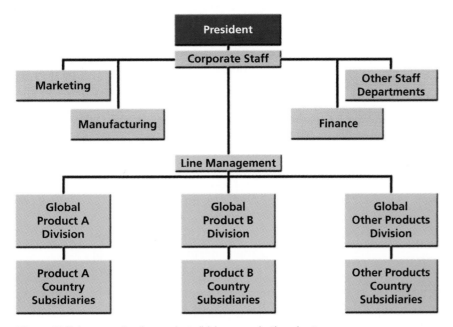

Figure 5.8 An example of a product division organization chart.

Geographic Divisions

International staff are grouped according to the global markets or regions they support and represent—South America, Australia, or Japan, for example. Many publishing and media companies are structured this way. A foreign market division allows a company to concentrate its efforts by establishing a true presence in a region. It is a major investment, but one that often must be made to position products—original or customized—overseas.

Matrix Organization

Though international staff may be separated according to function, product, or market responsibility, their reporting flows across all departments. Matrix management allows more meaningful, more frequent, and more informal communication among staff and departments, but it is difficult to implement.

Companies can choose among several possible models to develop a structure that will suit their needs, size, and markets. The key to organizing is to choose a structure that will allow companies to respond as efficiently and decisively as possible to changes in the international situation that may affect them. Responsiveness is paramount.

ICE Activities for 5.2

Ideas	Connections	Extensions
1. (a) Explain what a multi-national company is.	(b) Select a Canadian multi-national company and describe what makes it multinational.	(c) In small groups, discuss why global economic power is strongly established in the northern hemisphere. What are some of the consequences of this fact for countries in the southern hemisphere?
2. (a) What is the "Triad"?	(b) How is the alliance among Triad members influential in the global economy?	(c) In your opinion, how would the Triad affect a small Canadian business that is trying to establish itself internationally?
3. (a) Describe four global business organizational structures.	(b) Select one of the structures you described in 3. (a). Describe an international business scenario (real or imagined) that would cause problems for a multinational company with that structure.	(c) For the problem you described in 3. (b), suggest a possible business solution.

5.3 International Trade Agreements

As countries and companies have expanded their thinking beyond their borders to seek out international opportunities, the need for trade agreements has become more urgent. Most recently, negotiated trade agreements have been developed in the spirit of "free trade." Some of these agreements lead to the establishment of a number of **trading blocs** or regions in which countries agree to support mutual economic growth by opening their markets to cross-border trade and business development. Free trade supports the free flow of goods and services, workers, and investments within a region. This means eliminating or reducing tariffs, duties, and other barriers.

Historically, free trade has often been referred to as **reciprocity**. In other words, trade is reciprocal according to the terms mutually agreed upon by countries. Even though governments may have agreed on reciprocity or free trade, not everyone agrees with the concept. For example, opposition to NAFTA, the North American Free Trade Agreement, arose in Canada because of fear of job losses. Both Mexico and Canada also feared that American culture and values would erode their national identity.

The opposite of free trade is protectionism, a government's effort to protect domestic industries from foreign competition. For example, for years Japan was very selective with its imports and sought to block the entry of many foreign products that might compete with Japanese products. Today, trade with Japan is more open. The present trading blocs will likely continue to change over the years as countries agree to either permit or restrict the flow of products.

Trade between two countries—Canada and the United States, for example—is referred to as **bilateral trade**. Trade among more than two nations is referred to as **multilateral trade**. Canada trades with many nations and, therefore, has many bilateral and multilateral trade relations. Countries have increasingly entered into trade alliances and in some cases have created trading blocs based on common regional interests. The agreements and trade alliances discussed in the following section make up the three dominant trading regions or blocs whose member countries together account for over 90 percent of global trade:

- North American Free Trade Agreement (NAFTA)
- European Union (EU)
- Asia-Pacific Economic Cooperation (APEC)

THINK ABOUT IT

In 2000, *Maclean's* published the results of a national survey on what Canadians value both now and for the future. One of the many questions was, "Should Canada have free-trade agreements with many countries?" Seventy-one percent of respondents agreed with the statement; seventeen percent disagreed. In which category would you have cast your vote?

Canada's Trade with the World, 2000 ($ billions)

Region	Exports	Change %	Imports	Change %	Trade	Change %
United States	333.7	16.5	229.3	6.4	563.1	12.2
Europe	20.2	14.4	44.9	20.1	65.1	18.3
Asia/Oceania	21.0	12.2	51.6	18.3	72.6	16.5
South America	5.0	17.0	17.2	25.2	22.2	23.4
Other	4.2	0.7	13.4	33.7	17.6	24.1
TOTAL	**384.1**	**15.9**	**356.5**	**11.3**	**740.6**	**13.7**

Figure 5.9 Canada's trade by region in 2000, compared with the previous year. In real terms, except for trade with the United States, imports increased more rapidly than exports, resulting in shrinkage of the goods surplus.

TRADE TALK

"Free Trade Is a Good Thing. A Global Perspective."

Like most kids, I collected hockey cards. And I learned early on to leave my "keepers" at home but to carry my "traders" or duplicates. There was always potential for a free exchange of cards that would improve both my collection and that of someone else.

This simple logic applies directly to international trade. We produce certain goods or services, more than we need, and sell the extra in the global market. Other countries do the same, and we all use the proceeds to buy the things we do not produce from other countries. This makes more sense than trying to produce everything ourselves, including things we are not good at. Trade, whether domestic or international, and whether in goods, services, or financial capital, is the most basic building block of prosperity.

This sounds like economic theory, which some regard as akin to science fiction. But the costs associated with trade barriers have been rigorously studied. The OECD (Organization for Economic Cooperation and Development) estimates that the trade liberalization that took place during the Uruguay Round (named after the country in which meetings started), which took years of meetings and negotiations among 117 countries, delivered the equivalent of a world tax cut of more than $200 billion per year. This is free money: the extra income results from improved efficiency through specialization. In other words, trade liberalization is a positive-sum game in which everyone wins. In contrast, trade protectionism is a negative-sum game in which everyone loses. If we put a tariff on imports to protect jobs, then every consumer in Canada pays more for those goods. That is why removing the protection is like a tax cut.

The OECD calculates that the average cost to consumers of a job protected this way exceeds the income of the protected worker.

Then why is it so difficult for us to negotiate free trade between countries? And why do trade negotiations attract hordes of protesters? Two main reasons.

First, in the short term, there are both winners and losers from free trade, and the losers don't like it. Allowing full foreign competition means [some] local companies will fail, and [some] workers will lose their jobs. But what economics tells us is that other companies will thrive, eventually creating replacement jobs and increased spending power, which will create even more jobs in other sectors. [Government intervention through] income support and retraining programs can be easily developed to smooth these transitions.

Second, some fear that free trade will lead to compromises of environmental or labour fairness standards. But a key ingredient of improving environmental and labour standards is higher living standards, which in turn will be generated by free trade. Separate agreements can be negotiated to ensure respect of environmental and labour issues, but they can be dealt with most effectively under a free trade umbrella.

The bottom line? Free trade is worth pursuing, whether bilaterally, regionally, or globally. All three negotiating agendas should be pushed to the maximum, for we all stand to gain from them. Maintaining or raising trade barriers is like telling kids they cannot trade their extra hockey cards—forcing them to buy pack after pack to fill the holes in their collections. In short, protectionism hurts everybody.

– *Stephen S. Poloz*, Vice-President and Chief Economist, Export Development Canada

TRADE TALK

The Free Trade Area of the Americas and the Threat to Social Programs, Environmental Sustainability, and Social Justice in Canada and the Americas

The Free Trade Area of the Americas (FTAA), currently being negotiated by 34 countries of the Americas, is intended by its architects to be the most far-reaching trade agreement in history. Although it is based on the model of the North American Free Trade Agreement (NAFTA), it goes far beyond NAFTA in its scope and power. The FTAA, as it now stands, would introduce into the Western Hemisphere all the disciplines of the proposed services agreement of the World Trade Organization (WTO)—the General Agreement on Trade in Services (GATS)—with the powers of the failed Multilateral Agreement on Investment (MAI), to create a new trade powerhouse with sweeping new authority over every aspect of life in Canada and the Americas.

The GATS, now being negotiated in Geneva, is mandated to liberalize the global trade in services, including all public programs, and gradually phase out all government "barriers" to international competition in the services sector. The Trade Negotiations Committee of the FTAA, led by Canada in the crucial formative months when the first draft was written, is proposing a similar, even expanded, services agreement in the hemispheric pact. It is also proposing to retain, and perhaps expand, the "investor-state" provisions of NAFTA, which give corporations unprecedented rights to pursue their trade interests through legally binding trade tribunals.

Combining these two powers into one agreement will give unequaled new rights to the transnational corporations of the hemisphere to compete for and even challenge every publicly funded service of its governments, including health care, education, social security, culture, and environmental protection.

As well, the proposed FTAA contains new provisions on competition policy, government procurement, market access, and dispute settlement that, together with the inclusion of services and investment, could remove the ability of all the governments of the Americas to create or maintain laws, standards, and regulations to protect the health, safety, and well-being of their citizens and the environment they share. Moreover, the FTAA negotiators appear to have chosen to emulate the WTO rather than NAFTA in key areas of standard-setting and dispute settlement, where the WTO rules are tougher.

Essentially, what the FTAA negotiators have done, urged on by the big business community in every country, is to take the most ambitious elements of every global trade and investment agreement—existing or proposed—and put them all together in this openly ambitious hemispheric pact.

Once again, as in former trade agreements like NAFTA and the WTO, this free trade agreement will contain no safeguards in the body of the text to protect workers, human rights, social security, or health and environmental standards. Once again, civil society and the majority of citizens who want a different kind of trade agreement have been excluded from the negotiations. . . .

However, the stakes for the peoples of the Americas have never been higher, and it appears a confrontation is inevitable. . . .

If the terms and recommendations of the FTAA Negotiating Groups are the substantive basis for a hemisphere trade pact, the whole process is totally unacceptable, and the citizens of the Americas must work to defeat it entirely. In spite of government protestations that they have negotiated these new trade and investment rules in full collaboration with their citizens, the proposed FTAA reflects none of the concerns voiced by civil society and contains all of the provisions considered most egregious by environmentalists, human rights and social justice groups, farmers, indigenous peoples, artists, workers, and many others. Every single social program, environmental regulation, and natural resource is at risk under the proposed FTAA. As it appears to stand now, there is no possible collaboration to make this trade pact acceptable.

— *Maude Barlow*, Chairperson, Council of Canadians

North American Free Trade Agreement (NAFTA)

On January 1, 1994, the **North American Free Trade Agreement** created a free-trade zone consisting of Canada, Mexico, and the United States. The objective of NAFTA is to increase trade, reduce prices and costs through increased production, and meet the challenges of global competition. (NAFTA was preceded by the Free Trade Agreement (FTA) between the United States and Canada in 1989.) The entire region has a combined population of almost 400 million consumers and a total GDP of more than $9 trillion. Trade among NAFTA countries makes up about one-third of all international trade.

NAFTA covers trade in goods and services as well as investment, and it has provisions for the protection of intellectual property (copyright and patents, for example), fair competition, and dispute resolution. The agreement eliminates duties, barriers, and restrictions on almost all products and services traded (softwood lumber, the subject of cross-border disputes, is not included). For example, NAFTA has made it possible for financial services such as banks to operate across North American borders more freely.

Web Link

Follow the link at www.internationalbusiness.nelson.com to learn more about the contents and provisions of NAFTA.

For customs officials to determine whether import tariff charges are applicable, a certificate of origin is required with shipments. Products produced outside of NAFTA may incur a duty. For example, a chair produced in the United States can be shipped to Canada duty-free. A chair shipped from China to Canada, however, would have a duty applied.

If companies make incorrect statements on the certificate of origin, their NAFTA privileges may be suspended. Here are a few important terms used in the NAFTA certificate of origin:

- American products enter Canada with a *zero tariff*, whereas products from Europe into Canada are assessed an import duty. In this respect, American products receive preferential treatment in Canada.

- *Originating material* refers to parts, raw materials, components, or finished products originating in a NAFTA country (for example, wheat from Canada). Non-originating material refers to material that originally came from a non-NAFTA country (for example, rice from China).

- When parts for a product come together in the manufacturing process, this process is known as *transformation*. If transformation occurs in Canada, then the product is considered to be of Canadian manufacture.

For a product to qualify as a NAFTA product, it must have been at least 50 percent produced at a manufacturing plant in the region and be composed of materials or components from the region. If a company's products qualify for NAFTA treatment, then those products will benefit from lower tariff rates.

THINK ABOUT IT

What are some of the benefits and drawbacks of having a region largely dependent on one main industry?

Canada is still the United States' largest export market; each minute of the day, we do $1 million of business with the United States. Being a major trading partner also helps to resolve issues other than trade; for example, Canada and the United States work together to provide defence of the continent and facilitate smoother border-point processing of people, services, and goods. Recently, however, concerns have been expressed about Canada's trade position with the United States: complaints that border points and traffic were congested and slow following the events of September 11, 2001, or that Canada's manufacturing capability may not be as productive as required by the agreement. There are predictions that Mexico could surpass Canada as the primary trading partner of the United States by as early as 2010. Mexico has been able to build upon lower wage and production costs to capture a larger share of the American market. As of 2002, Canada's share of two-way trade was about double Mexico's and exceeds more than $1 billion a day.

More than 80 percent of Canadian exports go to the United States. The United States brings 19 percent of its imports from Canada and 10 percent from Mexico. Canada's current annual exports to Mexico are worth $2 billion and imports from Mexico are worth $12 billion. Canada must find ways to maintain our current export levels to the United States.

NAFTA sets the stage for a potential North-South alliance from Alaska to Chile. While not yet in place, this potential trade zone is already being referred to as the Free Trade Area of the Americas (FTAA). Other economic unions already exist in the Western hemisphere. For example, the Mercosur agreement links the South American countries of Bolivia, Brazil, Paraguay, Uruguay, and Argentina. Another union, called Caricom, influences trade among the Caribbean countries.

Free Trade Area of the Americas (FTAA)

Discussions initiated at the 1994 Summit of the Americas in Miami are being pursued with an aim to integrate the economies of the western hemisphere into a single free trade zone, an extension of NAFTA to be known as the **Free Trade Area of the Americas (FTAA)**. The hope is to reach an agreement by 2005. The potential FTAA is considered to be as important for the Americas as the

Figure 5.10 At the signing ceremony of Summit of the Americas. Quebec City, April 2001: Colombia's President Andreas Pastrana, Prime Minister Jean Chrétien, and Prime Minister Denzil Douglas of St. Kitts and Nevis.

creation of the European Union was for the countries of Europe. Finalizing such a treaty will require significant debate and negotiations (as with all treaties and agreements) around issues dealing with the environment, human rights, culture, and labour. It is proposed that the FTAA include 34 countries from North, Central, and South America. The main objectives of the treaty are to continue to lower trade barriers among the countries and to promote investment without government interference or preferential treatment.

Between 1990 and 2000, Canada, the United States, and our 32 Latin American and Caribbean partners saw our combined GDP output grow to $11.4 trillion from $7.1 trillion. Output in the Latin and Caribbean countries increased to $2.4 trillion by 2000, from $1 trillion. The affluent or wealthy nations reaped most of the benefits, however, while the number of people living in poverty grew.

The European Union (EU)

The **European Union (EU)** is a political and economic alliance in Europe consisting of 15 countries (with 10 candidate countries), formerly known as the European Community. These nations eliminated trade barriers among the members. The EU represents a new Europe. One of its most significant economic changes occurred in 1998 when the majority of the EU countries became an economic and monetary union sharing a common currency known as the euro. (Britain kept its currency.) The fact that the EU has a common currency is unique and distinguishes it from NAFTA and the countries of the Asia-Pacific region. Many of the countries bordering Europe (for example, Cyprus, Malta, Turkey, and former communist countries in Eastern and Central Europe) are now considering the standards adopted by the EU.

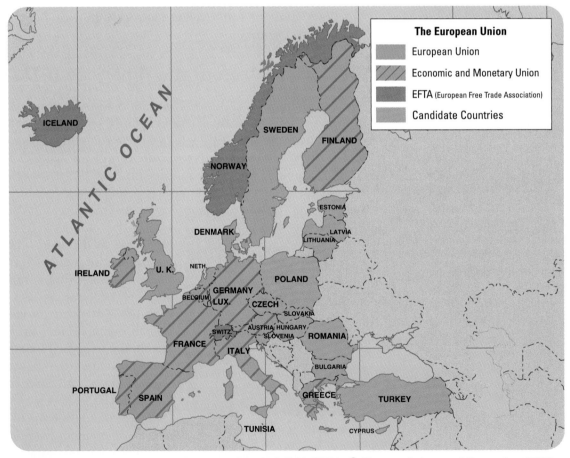

Figure 5.11 The total area of the European Union is 3 241 380 km². The population as of September 2002 was 377 million, and GDP per capita was $32 467 CAD (2001). In 2000, the European Union exported $1 282 billion CAD to the world and imported $1 404 billion CAD from the world.

The European Union has many advantages for the countries that belong. One is size; its member countries now have access to nearly 380 million consumers. Another advantage is that its manufacturers have uniform standards for technical products in an attempt to ensure greater quality and productivity. Monetary union also encourages higher economic performance among its members. If Germany has a strong economy and trade, the hope is that it will act as a strong team member to encourage and boost a weaker member. These 15 EU countries have a combined GDP of nearly $7.5 trillion USD.

Now the world's largest single market, the EU has surpassed the United States in both gross domestic product and population, and ranks as Canada's second most important trading and investment partner (after the United States). According to the Canadian Department of Foreign Affairs and International Trade, in 2001 Canada exported $17.3 billion CAD to, and imported $38.4 billion CAD from, the EU. Canadians also spent $75 billion CAD in foreign direct investment in countries of the EU, about the same amount that Europeans invested in Canada.

A possible future direction proposed by experts in free trade is that Britain should join NAFTA, thereby creating a North Atlantic Free Trade Area. Closer NAFTA-EU relationships will inevitably be part of future discussions and negotiations, as they are in the WTO.

THINK ABOUT IT

In 1994, Norway held a vote to decide whether to join the European Union. The Norwegians decided not to join because many felt that joining would mean uprooting too much of their Norwegian identity and way of life.

How has Norway been affected by this decision?

Economics and technology are bringing down the "fences" (tariffs, protectionism, currency exchange, and government regulations) that used to "surround" countries. For the success of free trade arrangements in a trading bloc such as the EU, citizens of different countries will have to learn to work well with people who may be very different from their own cultural or ethnic group. National regulations in Europe that were designed to protect local industries have been replaced by Europe-wide rules. This change has promoted trade and investment based on economies of scale. As a result, the overall average cost of some products per unit has decreased, because production has increased.

The integrated European Union represents one of the world's largest markets. It has a currency that can compete with the U.S. dollar and the Japanese yen. People and products can move more freely within the region. This flexibility should help EU companies and countries to strengthen their position in the global marketplace.

Asia-Pacific Economic Cooperation (APEC)

The **Asia-Pacific Economic Cooperation (APEC)** is a forum for ministers and senior government officials of countries bordering the Pacific Ocean to discuss regional policy. APEC was formed in 1989 to promote trade among its members. It is not a trade agreement or pact, and it has no formal institutional structure. However, as a result of the cooperation that APEC has encouraged, a number of regional economic alliances among Asian and Pacific Rim countries have evolved. Its long-term purpose is to foster greater economic cooperation in the Pacific Rim in the hope that such cooperation will spill over into the entire international community.

Laraine Kaminsky

Laraine Kaminsky first experienced "culture shock," the challenges of dealing with new cultures, when she left her native South Africa at age 22 and travelled to England and Canada.

Here she began teaching English as a Second Language, and realized that while her students were learning the language, they could be learning about the culture of Canada. From this observation, MALKAM Cross-Cultural Training was born in 1989. "I started as an ESL teacher," said Kaminsky, "and built my knowledge and contacts in the area of cross-cultural awareness and diversity—and my company grew from there."

Kaminsky was pleasantly surprised with the positive response when she approached Ottawa employers with her ideas. Her service? For a fee she would provide their new employees from other countries with the communication skills they needed for their duties in Canada. While many had solid technical skills, they needed help with language and Canadian culture.

Kaminsky has also developed programs in cultural awareness and diversity for employers: "The Cultural Components of International Trade," and "Cross-Cultural Training for Women in Exporting," for example. Her aim is to create inclusive workplaces where people are valued and respected regardless of their differences.

"Globalization and the removal of many tariffs and protectionist policies have been generally good for MALKAM," says Kaminsky. MALKAM now provides pre-departure orientations for companies sending individuals and teams on assignments to other countries. The need for cultural awareness and understanding is now a major part of Canadian society and a necessary feature in conducting international business.

Kaminsky now has over 20 years of experience in training, consulting, and presenting to clients in Canada and abroad. She has speaking engagements as far away as Australia and Africa, some of which DFAIT has helped arrange. She admits that part of the excitement of such business travel is exploring other places and cultures.

Kaminsky's overall goal is to help organizations and individuals succeed in their local environment and the global marketplace through workplace harmony and productivity—and to minimize the effects of culture shock! Her commitment has been recognized by her selection as a finalist for the Women's Business Achievement Award.

"Working with different companies and different cultures is my passion," says Kaminsky. "Helping people overcome challenges and work together in the growing international economy is very rewarding."

If you're interested in pursuing international business as a career, she advises, "Go for it! As the world's economies become more global, the concept of domestic business will begin to fade and international business will continue to grow. It will be a great discipline for young people to focus their interest and energy."

GLOBAL THOUGHT

As business becomes more global and national borders begin to disappear, from a business and trade perspective, it is the cultural barriers that organizations need to be more concerned with.

– Laraine Kaminsky

1. Identify a time when you felt you experienced "culture shock." Describe the experience in a paragraph.

2. What services and programs does Laraine Kaminsky offer?

3. Why do you think globalization and a reduction in protectionism has helped Kaminsky's business?

The term "Pacific Rim" is used by geologists to describe the "ring of fire," the circle of earthquake zones and volcanoes that surrounds the Pacific Ocean. More recently, however, the term has come to refer to the vast, powerful, and interconnected economic and cultural community that borders on the Pacific Ocean. It encompasses southeast Asia, northeast Asia, Australia and the South Pacific, New Zealand, Papua New Guinea, and North and South America.

Today APEC has more than 20 participating countries, or economies. The map of this region clearly shows how prominent it is on a global scale. Because of the inclusion of China, APEC countries are well on their way to representing half of the world's marketplace, on the basis of their population and output. These countries represent the world's top market for such products as automotive and telecommunications equipment. Many APEC countries attract business because they are able to offer "low-cost" labour. However, the region now offers increasing numbers of highly skilled workers.

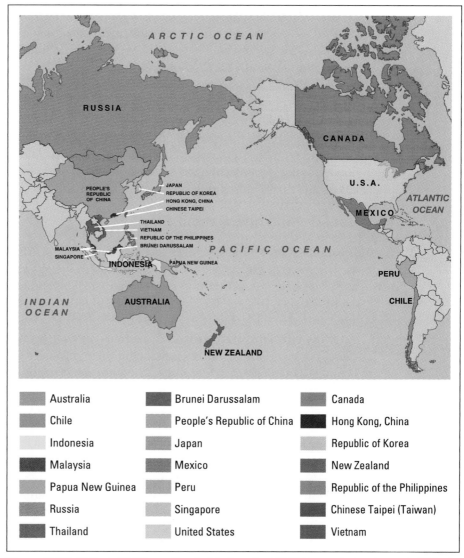

	Australia		Brunei Darussalam		Canada
	Chile		People's Republic of China		Hong Kong, China
	Indonesia		Japan		Republic of Korea
	Malaysia		Mexico		New Zealand
	Papua New Guinea		Peru		Republic of the Philippines
	Russia		Singapore		Chinese Taipei (Taiwan)
	Thailand		United States		Vietnam

Figure 5.12 At their 2002 meeting in Mexico, the APEC Economic Leaders established a program to improve security against terrorist attacks and committed themselves to promoting shared global prosperity.

One of the original questions facing APEC was, "Who should belong to this organization?" The member countries are very different from one another in many respects—size, political system, stage of economic development, language, culture, and history. In the final analysis, the main thing that APEC countries have in common is that they are geographically on the Pacific Rim. Any country that borders on the Pacific Ocean may apply for membership.

In the fall of 1997, several of the Asian countries in this group experienced an economic crisis, and some of their currencies were devalued overnight. However, APEC countries continue to grow and influence the rest of the world. China, particularly, has emerged as a dominant economic force, and it still represents the world's largest potential consumer market. Japan continues to be a major economy both in APEC and globally. It is evident that countries within the region are joining more than one alliance.

Several APEC countries have elected to take the bilateral free-trade route. Since bilateral trade is more efficient to organize than multilateral trade, many countries are arranging bilateral agreements. For example, Singapore, Australia, and New Zealand have announced free-trade agreements that they hope will eventually become APEC-wide. There is another Asian regional trade agreement called the **Association of South East Asian Nations (ASEAN)**. This free-trade area currently includes Brunei, Indonesia, Malaysia, the Philippines, Singapore, Thailand, and Vietnam. Its combined population is over 450 million with a total GDP of about $1.8 trillion USD.

In a recent APEC initiative, efforts are being made to narrow the economic gap between members, particularly with regard to the level of digital and information technology. Many countries in the region have large subsistence farming populations and are still struggling to wipe out poverty.

Canada and the Pacific Rim

There is also a movement to raise Canada's image and position in Pacific Rim countries. Some economists believe Ottawa should move toward an even greater free-trade agreement with Japan to reduce Canada's dependence on the American export market. In 1999, Canada imported $15 billion worth of goods from Japan, almost double the value of its exports to that country. This represents a substantial trade imbalance. Since the 1997 currency crisis in Pacific Rim countries, Canadian businesses have been reducing their emphasis on Asia. However, since Japan is Canada's second-largest trading partner, turning our attention toward Asia again would recognize the evolution of the global economy. The Asian Development Bank (ADB) has forecast that by 2025, Asia's share of world GDP will climb to 57 percent from its 2002 level of 37 percent.

In examining Canada's response to globalization, a recent annual survey by the Asia–Pacific Foundation, the Vancouver-based think tank on Canada–Asia relations, says that Canada has been missing out on opportunities to trade and invest in Asia because it is too focused on the American market. It calls on Ottawa to provide a more level playing field for Canada's other trade partners. The Canadian stake in globalization has been largely defined by the terms of the Canada–United States Free Trade Agreement and NAFTA. These free-trade deals have been good for Canadian manufacturing and finance. However, the Foundation said, concentration on the United States has left Canada economically vulnerable because of its dependence on a single, if gigantic, market. Since the beginning of the Canada-United States Free Trade Agreement, Canadian investment in the United States has risen nearly 150 percent. Since both Canadian and American economies follow similar business cycles, any downturn in the American economy will have an adverse effect in Canada. This concentration also means that Canada may be overlooking business opportunities elsewhere in the world.

THINK ABOUT IT

Do existing trade barriers within Canada affect the ability of Canadian companies to compete internationally? How?

Agreement on Internal Trade (AIT)

As international trade barriers disappear and as Canada participates in the global economy, there are still a number of protectionist policies within our own national borders. Interprovincial trade barriers make it difficult, particularly for agricultural producers, to sell products across provincial borders. These barriers are set up to protect regional interests. For example, Nova Scotia dairy producers cannot distribute their milk in Prince Edward Island. Without the possibility of healthy interprovincial competition, however, businesses are often forced to look south of the border for new markets.

Web Link

Follow the link at www.internationalbusiness.nelson.com for more information about Canada's Agreement on Internal Trade.

In 1995, the provincial and federal governments signed the **Agreement on Internal Trade (AIT)**. This agreement attempts to harmonize regulations and standards from province to province in areas such as transportation and consumer protection. Its ultimate goal is to eliminate barriers to trade, investment, and product mobility within Canada.

Free Trade or Duty-Free Zones

Until recently, Canada has lost billions of investment dollars to the United States, which imposes no goods and services tax and has more favourable customs regulations.

Starting in 2001, however, Canadian customs and tax rules have encouraged free-trade zones. Foreign companies are allowed to bring goods into Canada and then ship them to the United States and elsewhere without paying duty or tax. This strategy should create jobs for Canadians in the high-tech sector. For example, a foreign computer-maker is now able to ship products to Canada and then have add-ons such as additional memory or other components customized for consumers. It is hoped that foreign companies will now be more likely to use Canada as the gateway to the American market. Port cities like Vancouver and Halifax will benefit from their proximity to the Asian, European, and North American markets.

ICE Activities for 5.3

Ideas	Connections	Extensions
1. (a) Explain the purpose of international trade agreements.	(b) Summarize the arguments for and against free trade in the two Trade Talk features on pages 158 and 159.	(c) In your opinion, which of the features you analyzed in 1. (b) presents the stronger arguments? Explain why you have drawn this conclusion.
2. (a) List the 15 countries in the EU.	(b) Work with a partner to create a chart or graphic organizer in which you explain the value of belonging to the European Union for each of the countries in your list from 2. (a).	(c) What might be some of the implications for Canada, the United States, and Mexico if the three countries were to form a North American Union along the lines of the European Union?
3. (a) Explain the function that APEC serves for its members.	(b) What would be the advantages and disadvantages of increasing Canada's trade with Asia?	(c) Do you think that Canada should eliminate inter-provincial trade barriers? In your answer, consider whether you think this change would affect all regions of Canada equally.

5.4 Organizations Influencing Global Trade

In 1999, the creation of the **G20**—an international forum of finance ministers and central bank governors—was announced. At their second meeting, in Montreal in 2000, they decided that, in addition to promoting international financial and economic stability (their original agenda), they would work on addressing the challenges of globalization. At their 2001 meeting, they also included a plan to combat the financing of terrorism. The G20 is designed to complement the activities of other international organizations, and, unlike larger organizations such as the World Bank, has a size and structure that allow informal exchange and consensus-building. Participating countries represent about 87 percent of the world's gross domestic product and 65 percent of the world's population. In being responsive to world events, this group of countries aims to find an equitable way to integrate the world's economies through globalization and mitigate the effects of financial and global crises.

As more and more nations reach "developed" status, global and national organizations become increasingly necessary, and it is important that they work together to solve the problems facing all countries.

THINK ABOUT IT

How many countries are involved in the G20?

Which countries are they?

GLOBAL THOUGHT

World Trade Organization (WTO)

Formerly known as the General Agreement on Tariffs and Trade (GATT), the WTO has been active for over 50 years. Its members agree to ongoing negotiations and to reducing tariffs and trade restrictions. Because of today's economic globalization, no nation can operate in isolation. Since legal, political, economic, and cultural environments vary widely, members are expected to abide by the laws of the host country in which they operate.

The WTO has described itself in the following terms:

- It is member-driven.
- It is not an advocate of free trade at any cost.
- It supports sustainable (controlled) development.
- Commerce does not take priority over the environment.
- It does not widen the gap between rich and poor.

The activities of the WTO have faced much opposition. However, in describing its response to its mandate, the WTO reported that its agreements have contributed positively to globalization in the following ways:

- It contributes to world peace.
- It allows disputes to be handled constructively.
- It is a system based on rules, not power.
- Free trade cuts the cost of living.
- It gives consumers a broader range of qualities and products from which to choose.
- Trade raises incomes.
- Trade stimulates economic growth.
- The basic principles make the system economically more efficient (non-discrimination, transparency, trading conditions, standardization, trade facilitation).
- The system shields governments from narrow interests (protectionists).
- The system encourages good government and reduces opportunities for corruption.

World Economic Forum (WEF)

The **World Economic Forum (WEF)** is an independent not-for-profit foundation, formed in 1971, which is committed to raising the level of corporate citizenship in its member countries. As a global partnership of business, political, and intellectual leaders of society, it works to define and discuss key issues on the global agenda. In a recent annual conference of the WEF, for example, the theme, "Bridging the Divides: Creating a Roadmap for the Global Future," reflected the organization's concern to bridge the "digital divide." The 2002 conference, held in South Africa, focused on the most important steps that African government, business, civil society, and the international community must take to support NEPAD, the New Partnership for Africa's Development, in its efforts to help African countries take control of their own economic destiny. This initiative was brought forward at the 2002 G8 summit, hosted by Canada in Kananaskis, Alberta.

The 2002 World Economic Federation "Summit" focused primarily on the following themes:

- The Role of Africa: Good Governance, Stability for Development and Investment
- The Response of Africa's International Partners: Market Access and Debt Relief
- Business Engages NEPAD: Seizing the Opportunities Presented
- The Way Forward: Collaborative Strategies for Success
- Bridging the Digital Divide
- The Global Health Initiative

Organization for Economic Cooperation and Development (OECD)

The **Organization for Economic Cooperation and Development (OECD)** is a multilateral organization of developed and developing countries that helps formulate social, economic, trade, development, education, and scientific policies.

The OECD has been called a think tank or monitoring agency. It offers governments a setting in which to discuss, develop, and perfect economic and social policy by comparing their countries' experiences and answers to common problems. The OECD also works to coordinate domestic and international policies so that they form a web of even practice across nations. It is hoped that the type of communication that the OECD fosters will lead to agreements that cut down on bribery and corruption in world markets. The OECD is financed by member countries according to the weight—or size—of their economy; the United States is the largest contributor and Japan the second largest.

World Bank Group

As you learned in Chapter 4, the World Bank, as it is commonly called, is the world's largest source of development assistance, providing nearly $16 billion USD in loans annually to its client countries. Its slogan is "Our dream is a world free of poverty." The World Bank uses its financial resources, staff, and knowledge base to help developing countries onto a path of stable, sustainable growth in the fight against poverty. It does this by supporting countries with financial assistance and partnerships. According to the president of the World Bank Group, James D. Wolfensohn, "The World Bank Group is repositioning itself to meet the demands of a new millennium—an institution committed to results, partnerships, and inclusive development. The 4.8 billion people who are our ultimate clients deserve nothing less." The World Bank's goals for the millennium include targets for reduction in poverty, improvements in health and education, and protection of the environment.

International Chamber of Commerce (ICC)

The **International Chamber of Commerce (ICC)** is a world business organization that promotes an open international trade and investment system and market economy. The ICC was established in 1919 and since then has become a voice for its thousands of member companies and associations around the world. Its policy is that trade in the market economy is a powerful force for peace and prosperity. In fact, the founders of the ICC referred to themselves as "the merchants of peace." The organization makes rules that govern the conduct of businesses across borders, including regulations governing shipments and payments. The first international code of conduct for international companies was created by the ICC in 1937.

Although acceptance of ICC rules is voluntary, those rules are observed in thousands of free-trade transactions every day. The ICC handles issues involving financial services, information technologies, telecommunications, marketing ethics, the environment, transportation, competition law, and intellectual property. The ICC has worked with the United Nations to judge and settle trade disputes since the United Nations was founded. The ICC International Court of Arbitration recommends guidelines and rules of conduct in a wide range of business activities: for example, anti-corruption, biosociety, business law, commercial crime, customs and trade regulations, e-business, environment and energy, and trade and investment policies.

International Monetary Fund (IMF)

The **International Monetary Fund (IMF)** is a multigovernmental organization that focuses on international monetary cooperation and stability in foreign exchange. The IMF has 182 member countries and a staff of 2700 from 110 countries. Since 1946, it has collaborated with its member countries to foster economic growth and high levels of employment. The IMF also provides temporary financial assistance to countries to help ease economic difficulties resulting from a variety of problems. Members include the former centrally planned economies of Eastern Europe and the former Soviet Union. Members can leave the IMF whenever they wish. Cuba, the Czech Republic, Indonesia, and Poland have done so in the past. (All but Cuba eventually rejoined the institution.)

National Organizations

There are many Canadian organizations to assist those who are engaged in international business. Two that provide links to other useful Web sites are the C.D. Howe Institute and the Forum for International Trade Training Inc. (FITT).

The C.D. Howe Institute, a Canadian think tank, was formed in 1973 as an independent, nonprofit research institution specializing in analysis of economic and social policy. It is named after Clarence Decatur Howe, who served as Canada's Minister of Trade and Commerce in the 1950s. The Institute identifies emerging national problems and explores solutions that take Canadian regional perspectives into account. It focuses on issues such as international and interprovincial trade, the environment, and monetary policy. Overall, the C.D. Howe Institute attempts to reduce uncertainty in economic policy in Canada.

As its name suggests, the Forum for International Trade Training is an organization that prepares training programs and services to educate businesses and individuals in ways of competing successfully in international trade. It has also set up country-wide standards and certification to ensure continuing professional development in the practice of international trade. It was founded in 1992 by both industry and government, with the philosophy that Canada's economic well-being hinges on the improved performance of Canadian business people and companies in the global marketplace.

Another important source of government assistance in international commerce is Team Canada Inc. (See Chapters 2 and 10.) This government-industry partnership facilitates access to the international business services offered in Canada.

ExportSource is a partnership of federal and provincial governments and other organizations that provides information and services for individuals and companies interested in international business. Its Web site is an excellent online resource for export information. The services of ExportSource include skills development, export counselling and financing, and market-entry support. Details on trade shows, business-trip preparation and planning, and international sales are also available. The Web site recounts a number of "success stories" by inspired successful ventures.

GLOBAL THOUGHT

After two days of talks at Kananaskis [June 2002], the Group of Eight agreed on additional aid to Africa, outlined a new way of distributing that aid, and called for economic reforms on that continent.

But the leaders announced no new initiatives to expedite the WTO's current negotiations, nor toward removing the trade barriers that threaten economic growth, especially industrialized-country barriers to developing-country exports....

The commitment to make the [next] trade talks a 'development' round was especially encouraging to people in the developing countries, where exports of farm products and textiles will be the key to climbing out of poverty and hopelessness....

Africa produces only two percent of the world's exports, but even that income far outweighs the continent's aid from all sources. Its only hope for lasting economic growth is through additional exports. In other words, the best answer to the world's worst problems is not aid. It is trade.

– *Richard D. McCormick*, President, International Chamber of Commerce

Web Link

Follow the link at www.internationalbusiness.nelson.com to investigate some of the organizations that influence global trade.

ICE Activities for 5.4

Ideas	Connections	Extensions
1. (a) According to the WTO, how does it contribute to economic globalization?	(b) Working with a small group, investigate some of the organizations and groups that oppose the policies of the WTO. Create a list of arguments for and against WTO policies.	(c) From the list of arguments in 1. (b), select one that you agree with. Research the issue further and write an editorial expressing your viewpoint on the issue.
2. (a) Review the Global Thought on page 169. Select the three most compelling points on the "wish list" and explain why you consider them most important.	(b) What does Global Exchange want the WTO and International Monetary Fund to do? Choose an item from Global Exchange's wish list. Give an example of how this wish could be implemented.	(c) You have been appointed a mediator between the WTO and Global Exchange. How would you suggest the two groups find a "middle ground" on an issue that divides them?
3. (a) Explain the role of the OECD.	(b) Explain how the relationship between domestic and international policies might "form a web of even practice" among different nations.	(c) Research the ways that Canada participates in the OECD. What are some of the implications of these types of participation for Canada's future international trade?

Canada's Trading Partners: Focus on Belgium

The European Union was created when 12 European countries ratified the Maastricht Treaty in the Dutch city of Maastricht in 1993. It was an appropriate choice as a location for the signing of such an important treaty, because one of the first European free trade agreements had started in this region. In 1944, the Benelux was created by the economic union of

Figure 5.15 Paul-Henri Spaak in the mid 1950s.

Figure 5.16 The European Union flag.

Belgium, the Netherlands, and Luxembourg.

Benelux had been initiated by a Belgian, Paul-Henri Spaak, who was called Mr. Europe because he was instrumental in creating the European Union, even though he never lived to see it (he died in 1972). He was the first president of the United Nations General Assembly in 1946 and served as chairman of the European Economic Community (1948–1950) and the European Coal and Steel Community (1952–1954); these were early European efforts to achieve freer trade

within the community of Western Europe. Germany, France, Italy, and the Benelux countries developed the idea of an economic union even further at the Messina Conference in 1955. The Six, as they were called, appointed Paul-Henri Spaak as chairman of the committee that produced the 1957 Treaty of Rome.

Spaak's Treaty of Rome amalgamated the European Coal and Steel Community and the European Atomic Energy Community into the European Economic Community (the EEC), known at the time as the European Common Market. The Maastricht Treaty amended the Treaty of Rome to officially become the Treaty on European Union in 1992. European union was a reality.

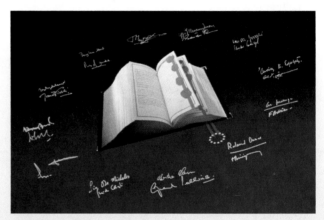

Figure 5.17 Signatures on the Maastricht Treaty.

Spaak would be proud of his work and his country. What centuries of war could never achieve, free trade achieved. A united Europe now exists, with a common market and a common currency. It is fitting and proper that the European Union has made Brussels, Belgium's capital and Paul-Henri Spaak's home, its capital city.

Belgium is Canada's seventh largest export market and its third largest in the EU. Belgium is the centre of the world's diamond trade, where 80 percent of the world's rough diamonds are traded; it is Canada's most important partner in the growing Canadian diamond industry. Diamond exploration companies rush their discoveries to Antwerp for a market assessment, as the world price of diamonds is set there. The majority of Canada's rough diamonds are sent there for international marketing. Belgian investors have been an important source of advice and assistance in developing the diamond industry in Canada.

A SNAPSHOT OF BELGIUM

Size: 30 510 sq. km

World Region: Central Europe

Capital City: Brussels (home to NATO and the European Union)

Languages: Dutch (Flemish is a mixture of Dutch dialects) French, German

Currency: Euro

Population: 10.2 million

Time: Noon in Ottawa (EST) is 6:00 P.M. in Brussels.

Climate: Temperate; mild winters, cool summers

Type of Government: Federal parliamentary democracy under constitutional monarchy

Labour Force by Occupation: 73 percent services, 25 percent industry, 2 percent agriculture

Membership in World Organizations: Benelux, G8, EU, NATO, WTO, and Francophonie

GDP per capita: $35 938

Importing Products and Partners:
Partners: Germany, France, Netherlands, and United Kingdom.
Products: Automobiles, automotive parts, uncut diamonds, polymerization products, medical equipment, computers, metals, and metal products.

Exporting Products and Partners:
Partners: Germany, France, Netherlands, United Kingdom, and United States.
Products: Machinery, equipment, chemicals, diamonds, tractors, petroleum products.

Investments: Belgian investments in Canada $3 billion; Canadian investments in Belgium $3.5 billion

Travel Advisory: Belgium is considered the crossroads of Europe; a majority of the West European capitals are within 1000 km of Brussels.

Figure 5.18 Waffles and chocolates are among Belgium's exports to the rest of the world.

Country Link

For more information on Belgium, follow the link at www.internationalbusiness.nelson.com.

Chapter Challenges

Knowledge/Understanding

1. Match each of the following terms to the correct definition or description below:
   (a) AIT
   (b) strategic alliance
   (c) APEC
   (d) globalization
   (e) NAFTA
   (f) trading blocs
   (g) FTAA
   (h) franchise
   (i) EU

   (i) a business in which a company authorizes a group or an individual to sell its goods and services
   (ii) a free-trade zone among Canada, Mexico, and the United States
   (iii) countries that have agreed to open their markets to cross-border trade
   (iv) a trade forum for officials of countries bordering the Pacific Ocean
   (v) agreement between Canadian provincial and federal governments to harmonize trade regulations and standards
   (vi) a free-trade zone among North and South American nations
   (vii) a political and economic alliance among European countries
   (viii) two or more companies cooperate to develop, produce, or market products
   (ix) the growth and spread of international economies and businesses around the world

2. Distinguish between bilateral trade and multi-lateral trade.

3. Why have some Canadian cities been designated as "free-trade zones"?

4. Briefly describe the type of problem that the Agreement on Internal Trade attempts to solve.

Thinking/Inquiry

1. Working in a small group, review the types of challenges that a business faces when it becomes a global company (see page 149). Decide which category the members of your group would like to focus on. Then work together to suggest possible solutions to five specific challenges that a global Canadian business is likely to face within that category.

2. Over half of the largest economies (GDP) in the world are companies. What does this mean for nations and the way they function both now and in the future?

3. What is the connection between Canada's diamond industry and Antwerp, a city in the north of Belgium? Research the concern about "blood diamonds." As more information is revealed about this issue, predict how it could affect Canada–Belgium trade relations.

Communication

1. Which type of global organizational structure do you think would be most effective for a large, multinational Canadian auto parts supplier? Explain the reasons for your choice in a paragraph with a strong thesis statement and at least three pieces of evidence.

2. Use a mind map or concept web (or other form of graphic organizer) to demonstrate the potential advantages or disadvantages of a free trade policy among the countries that belong to APEC.

3. Debate this statement:

   The United States–Canada border is on its way to becoming irrelevant, and people and goods will soon move between the two countries with little or no hindrance. In fact, the border is likely to disappear altogether.

   Work with a partner to develop supporting and refuting arguments.

Application

1. Visit the Web site for the Forum for International Trade Training and look at their "Guide to Careers." Complete a one-page report on an international job found under one of the following categories:

   - international marketing
   - international sales and procurement
   - international operations management
   - international logistics
   - international financial services
   - foreign trade and investment accounting
   - international law
   - international electronic infrastructure specialists
   - market access and trade promotion
   - activities related to international affairs

   Include a brief job description, trends in the job, qualifications, skills, aptitude, and knowledge required.

2. Research the life and work of Paul-Henri Spaak, the Belgian who is credited with initiating the move toward an economic union in Europe. After you have collected your data, plan, draft, and revise an International Business Career Profile on Spaak. Use the profiles throughout the chapters of this book as models for your profile.

3. Work with two other students to prepare a role-play based on an FTAA, NAFTA, WTO, or World Bank meeting. Research a current issue that is of concern to proponents or opponents of one of these agreements or organizations. Your roles are a) an official delegate to the meeting, b) an unofficial delegate to the meeting, and c) a television interviewer who is interested in presenting both sides of an issue. Work together to script a five-minute interview and present it to the other members of your class.

International Business Portfolio

International Agreements

It is important to know what trade relationships already exist between Canada and your IBP country. It is also important to understand how international organizations such as the World Trade Organization and the International Monetary Fund affect the relationship.

Activities

1. Identify the trade agreements between Canada and your country.

2. Find an example of a partnership or joint venture between a business in your selected country and a Canadian business.

3. Using the links at **www.internationalbusiness. nelson.com**, find out your country's membership status in the following international organizations:
   - World Trade Organization
   - World Economic Forum
   - Organization for Economic Cooperation and Development
   - World Bank Group
   - International Monetary Fund

4. What other trade agreements or organizations are part of your selected country's trading arrangements (for example, APEC, NAFTA, EU, or bilateral trade agreements)? How do these agreements affect Canada's status as a trading partner?

Chapter 6

International Business Opportunities and Trends

Exciting opportunities are available for Canadians who want to participate in international businesses and organizations, who can identify and analyze those opportunities, and who can set realistic goals for going international. The global marketplace has created opportunities for those small and large businesses that are aware of global trends and that know which of those trends are likely to develop into growth markets. To seize such market opportunities, businesses need creative, innovative employees who are flexible enough to adapt to rapidly changing market circumstances.

Chapter Topics

➤ 6.1 – Understanding International Opportunities 180

➤ 6.2 – Identifying International Opportunities and Trends 189

➤ 6.3 – Mapping International Trends 193

➤ *Canada's Trading Partners: Focus on* Ireland 210

➤ Chapter Challenges 212

Prior Knowledge

- As a class, list products that are available in other countries but not in Canada.
- What are some of the major trends influencing products and services around the world today?
- Identify a Canadian company that enjoyed a market relatively free from competition until it was challenged by a foreign interest.

Inquiries/Expectations

- What are the characteristics of innovative international companies?
- How will increases in global business affect the strength of businesses, industries, and sectors in Canada's economy in the next decade?
- What are characteristics of growing international markets?
- How has the global marketplace changed the ways people run businesses today?
- How does the global marketplace create business opportunities for small businesses?

Important Terms

business opportunity
chief executive officer (CEO)
deliverables
entrepreneur
global brand
global mindset
growth market
hyper-competition

life cycle (trend or product)
mission statement
monopoly
request for proposal (RFP)
small- and medium-sized
    enterprises (SMEs)
technological convergence
trend

6.1 Understanding International Opportunities

Developing Ideas, Solutions, and Opportunities

International markets are not necessarily the right place for every company. With careful research and planning, however, international markets have the potential to provide individuals and companies with excellent opportunities to grow and flourish. Many preliminary questions need to be addressed. Here are some examples:

- Does the company have the product, the talent, and the skills to be successful internationally?
- Can the company meet the estimated demand for the product in international markets? Will there be enough capacity or ability to produce what is ordered?
- Can the company meet market entry costs as well as the costs required to sustain a position in the foreign market? Is the investment justified?
- How will the company's ability to serve its current customer base be affected?
- How will a company's decision to enter an international market affect its competitive position in its already established markets?
- Does the new international market have long-term potential?
- Will entry into the new international market help the company to achieve its strategic business goals?

How can a company distinguish between a business idea and a **business opportunity** in the international arena? A good idea may, in fact, not present a good opportunity. The timing may not be right or implementing the idea may be too expensive; perhaps the business climate in the target country is not hospitable or transportation difficulties are insurmountable. Market research may indicate that someone else has already introduced a competitive product to the intended market. However, once the potential of an idea has been assessed, selling to or expanding into foreign markets might be a beneficial move for a business. How can a business recognize a good opportunity? The first step is to ensure that the company's products will meet a need or solve a problem in another country.

In some cases, rather than having goods to export, a company may have expertise or technology that another country needs. Sometimes, organizations are sought out and asked to do a job in a foreign country on the basis of their international reputation.

GLOBAL THOUGHT

Figure 6.1 Prime Minister Pierre Trudeau knew that Canadians needed to develop entrepreneurial attitudes before they could succeed in developing international markets.

After years in office, I eventually came to the conclusion that Canadian businesspeople have it so easy with the United States—where they already know the customers, the techniques, the language, and the geography —that they are a little lazier and less inclined towards initiatives in Asia or Africa or other parts of the world, even Europe. I think they are entrepreneurs with a difference. You see the Germans or the Americans or the French in the most faraway corners, but my successive ministers of international trade used to tell me that you have to kick Canadians in the pants to get them to go to a new market. And so our trade expanded, but it did not diversify.

– *Pierre Trudeau*

Web Link

Follow the link at www.internationalbusiness.nelson.com to learn more about how Canadian companies are solving international business problems.

For example, a country or a foreign company may have an environmental problem and may therefore negotiate a contract with a Canadian company that can solve that problem.

Companies develop experience and expertise in industries as diverse as management consulting, firefighting, power generation, marine biology, or specialty industrial hardware, and they bring their core experience and personnel quickly and flexibly to new situations. Because ideas fuel solutions, any problem provides a challenge and opportunities. After studying a problem or potential need, learning all of its circumstances, and understanding it thoroughly, companies can suggest or provide a solution. Their customers may be industrial or government, business or retail.

The first company to enter a market often does well if it fully understands the opportunity. If it finds that it does not, however, it must modify its solution or actions, or other companies may capitalize on its mistakes and capture a larger part of the market that has been identified or created.

Today, we live in the age of information where ideas and research abilities are key resources. Usually, professionals need to brainstorm many ideas and build on or combine their thoughts as they seek a solution to a problem. Evaluating, discarding, and perhaps even starting again with different ideas may be required to develop a good solution. Companies with good ideas as well as in-depth knowledge and special expertise—that is, companies that are good problem-solvers—have many opportunities in the international marketplace.

GLOBAL THOUGHT

Figure 6.2 In 2000, Prime Minister Jean Chrétien suggested that, as long as national governments take steps to promote home-grown artists and keep their traditions alive, people around the world need not fear the "Americanization" of world culture.

It's not a problem, as long as every nation has a way to make sure that people are comfortable with themselves, they know who they are, they know their roots and they work to have their arts and culture well inside themselves.

– *Prime Minister Jean Chrétien* on global culture

International Company Profile

Magna International

The automotive industry is in the midst of fierce global competition, ongoing consolidation and the continuous challenge of producing a better quality product at a better price. To remain profitable and competitive, Magna continues to refine its structure to meet changing conditions in the global economy and within our industry. Our operating structure has always evolved in anticipation of the needs of our customers and to keep ahead of changes within the industry. It will continue to do so.

– *Frank Stronach*, Chairman, Magna International Inc., 2001 Annual Report

Frank Stronach is the founder and Chairman of Magna International Inc. Magna, with headquarters in Aurora, Ontario, is one of the most diversified automotive suppliers in the world. Magna designs, develops, and manufactures automotive systems, assemblies, modules and components, and engineers and assembles complete vehicles, primarily for sale to Original Equipment Manufacturers (OEMs). The company employs over 72 000 people at 197 manufacturing divisions and 44 product development and engineering centres throughout 22 countries. Magna is recognized for its innovative technology, product design, and total vehicle program management.

Back in 1957, Frank Stronach, who had immigrated from Austria in 1954, had just opened his first tool and die shop called Multimatic. Tool and die makers make machine-shop tools and devices to hold tools and make "dies" to stamp, cut, or mould materials into specific shapes. By 1960, Multimatic had its first contract with General Motors to supply sun-visor brackets. The small company grew throughout the 1960s as it seized business opportunities and won more contracts to supply parts to car makers. When Multimatic merged with Magna Electronics in 1969, the combined company added electronic mechanical components to its roster of products. Magna continued to develop new ideas, to offer customers solutions to their manufacturing problems, to beat out competitors, and to win more and more contracts to supply the automotive industry. In 1973, the company became Magna International Inc.

Research, development, engineering, and design weren't the only areas in which Frank Stronach was an innovator. In 1984, the company adopted Magna's Corporate Constitution, which is based on a "Fair Enterprise" philosophy and commits to sharing the company's profits with stakeholders, management, and employees.

Figure 6.3 Frank and Belinda Stronach at the company's annual meeting in 2001.

In 1988, the Employee's Charter was formally adopted by the company. Magna believes that, especially in today's global market, every employee has an important role to play in making sure the company stays competitive by making quality products for better prices and by delivering those products on time. The Charter commits to a number of principles, such as job security by providing job counselling, training, and employee assistance programs, as well as a safe and healthful workplace, fair treatment, competitive wages and benefits, employee equity and profit participation, and ongoing communication. To be sure that the Charter is put into effect, Magna has a telephone hotline where employees can forward their concerns in strict confidence. All employee concerns are carefully investigated and resolved by Magna's Employee Relations Department.

Throughout the 1980s, Magna continued to innovate and provide solutions for its customers in the automotive industry. For example, in 1989, the company co-designed and co-developed a built-in child safety seat that has been recognized by the U.S. Smithsonian Institute as one of the great innovations of the 1980s. By the 1990s, the company was managing complete interior and exterior systems for automobiles. In 1995, Magna developed hydroforming technology, which is a unique manufacturing process that uses water pressure to bend and form metal. During the late 1990s and early 2000s, Magna began to spin off its automotive systems groups as separate public companies to focus on individual product categories to better meet the needs of their customers.

Belinda Stronach, Frank Stronach's daughter, is now President and Chief Executive Officer of Magna International. She continues the traditions of the company founded by her father nearly half a century ago. As she says of Magna today,

> "Magna has a track record of anticipating change, and moving quickly to capitalize on that change. We have a clear idea of where the automotive industry is headed, and how we can help our customers get there more quickly, more competitively, and more cost-effectively."
>
> – *Belinda Stronach*, President and Chief Executive Officer, 2001 Annual Report

1. Create a timeline to show the business opportunities that Magna has taken advantage of through the years.

2. What characteristics of Magna show that it is an innovative international company?

Creativity, Change, and Innovation

Creative people use their imagination and technical know-how to solve problems. Companies depend on those employees who can apply their creativity to generate ideas that will provide innovative solutions. As you learned in Chapter 3, innovation is very important to the success of business today, and this is especially true for international business. Innovative employees find better ways of doing things: they create new products or improve existing products to better fill consumer needs and wants.

John R. Schermerhorn, in *Management*, outlines the four steps of the product innovation process:

1. **Idea Creation:** New knowledge forms around basic discoveries, extensions of existing understanding, or spontaneous creativity made possible by individual ingenuity and communication with others.

2. **Initial Experimentation:** Ideas are initially tested in concept by discussions with others, referrals to customers, clients, or technical experts; and/or in the form of prototypes or samples.

3. **Feasibility Determination:** Practicality and financial value are examined in formal feasibility studies, which identify potential costs and benefits as well as potential markets or applications.

4. **Final Application:** A new product is finally commercialized or put on sale in the open market, or a new process is implemented as part of normal operating routines.

In countries like Japan, Germany, and the United States, which are considered "high-wage" countries, industries need to use innovation to stay competitive in a global marketplace. Innovation can lead to more economical and sustainable production processes, artful designs, or enhanced product performance. If a company can manufacture a more durable and attractive product or produce it more responsibly or economically, then it will attract customers. Innovation provides the advantage that high-wage countries need if they are to remain competitive with countries that offer lower-priced labour.

Figure 6.4 POSCO's Pohang Works, located in South Korea.

On the southeast coast of South Korea, there is an internationally known steel mill called POSCO. Since South Korea has access to very few mineral resources domestically, POSCO imports the iron ore it needs to make the steel used in the manufacture of Korean-built ships and automobiles for domestic use and for export around the world. At the entrance to POSCO's Pohang Works, there is a sign that captures the spirit of opportunity. It reads: "Resources are limited, creativity is unlimited." This statement suggests that creative and innovative companies can compete globally even if their physical resources are not readily available.

Characteristics of Innovative International Companies

Successful managers and business owners know the value of having creative, high-calibre employees. In the study, "Beyond the Bottom Line: What CEOs Are Thinking," conducted by Ipsos-Reid, Canadian chief executive officers (CEOs) were asked to list their "most important" business priorities. **Chief executive officers** are the most senior managers in a company; they are responsible for the company's attainment of business goals, performance, financial results, general conduct, and financial return to shareholders. In the Ipsos-Reid study, CEOs said that their second-highest priority, after higher profitability, was the need to attract and retain the best people they could get as employees.

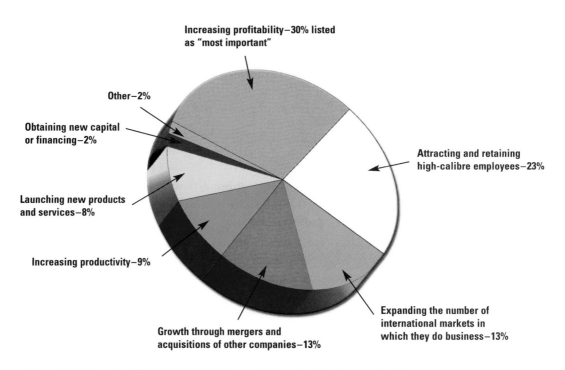

Increasing profitability—30% listed as "most important"

Other—2%

Obtaining new capital or financing—2%

Launching new products and services—8%

Increasing productivity—9%

Growth through mergers and acquisitions of other companies—13%

Attracting and retaining high-calibre employees—23%

Expanding the number of international markets in which they do business—13%

Figure 6.5 Canadian CEOs identified their most important business priorities.

Successful businesses have a clear vision of where they are going and of the role that innovation plays in their success. A company's mission statement often captures this vision. A **mission statement** should answer the question "Where are we going?" The global company Hewlett-Packard, for example, uses a statement that describes its mission to satisfy consumer needs and wants with innovative processes and products.

Global companies recognize that with effective planning and strategy, they can design and shape their future. For a company to make its vision become reality, it needs both leadership and creativity from everyone in the organization.

What are the characteristics of innovative organizations? Typically, innovative organizations promote the following atmosphere or culture:

- Innovation is expected and failure is acceptable (just as long as mistakes are not repeated).
- The organization is willing to take risks.
- People from different functions (for example, marketing, finance, production) work together to arrive at solutions.
- Large organizations create smaller, more manageable teams to get work done.
- Ideas for improvement are welcomed and rewarded.

Today's international organizations, those that today's students may eventually work for, need people who can share their ideas, promote innovation, and manage the innovative projects that are initiated. In the international business environment, speed, innovation, and systems capabilities are critical to developing and sustaining competitive advantage. The new wealth generation process in Canada is being created by innovations in products and systems of business.

A good example is Torstar's Harlequin Books, publishers of highly popular romance fiction. From local beginnings, the company widened its target audience so that it now has operations in over 20 countries and sells in approximately 100 countries on six continents. Harlequin enters new markets by integrating with local offices or through joint ventures in other countries. The decision to enter a country is based on the existence of an established distribution system, the development of print and television advertising, and the anticipated ability to profit from its market entry.

Harlequin took its successful romance formula and, adapting it to changing gender roles and international cultures, successfully proved that it had universal appeal with millions of readers in countries around the globe, such as in Japan, France, and Poland, as well as in the United States and Canada.

Figure 6.6 Harlequin publishes in 23 languages and has 50 million readers worldwide. In 2001, Harlequin sold 160 million books—more than 5.5 books a second.

Finding Opportunities

To take advantage of opportunities in foreign markets and to position their products globally, companies must assess the market before they enter it. As you will learn in Chapter 11, international marketers spend a great deal of effort on learning as much as they can about the markets they wish to enter. International business opportunities are recognized and addressed in a number of ways.

One way the Canadian government helps Canadians find international business opportunities is through its International Business Opportunities Centre. The centre, which opened in 1995, provides a "matching" service. It helps connect foreign buyers with Canadian companies, through its partnership with Canadian trade officers in Canada's embassies and consulates around the world. When a business opportunity comes to the attention of a trade officer, the officer passes on the request to the International Business Opportunities Centre, and consultants at the centre then try to make a match with a Canadian company. The team of specialists at the centre seeks out and contacts potential Canadian exporters or service-providers that have registered with its database. In this way, the centre provides timely, relevant, and targeted business leads, or prospects for business, from the desks of foreign buyers right to the doorsteps of Canadian companies. This is one effective way a Canadian company can target an international opportunity.

Business leads provide both import and export sales opportunities for Canadian companies. They might also translate into future business, new partners, new suppliers, and even new products that will meet the needs of the foreign buyer. For committed exporters, responding to these leads is a vital strategy for engaging in the international marketplace. And, as Canadian businesses target more and more markets around the world, our capacity or ability to buy the products of other nations increases. The key for companies is to analyze the opportunity or lead and then decide whether to target it.

International business opportunities are identified in a variety of ways. In recent years, the Internet has become a particularly powerful force in communicating opportunities worldwide, changing trade across borders through electronic commerce or e-commerce. There are several ways in which organizations or individuals can obtain global opportunities—by winning contracts, by taking initiative, or by being invited on the basis of their international reputation, to name a few.

Figure 6.7 Industry Canada's International Business Opportunities Centre tries to match Canadian companies with business opportunities in other countries.

Figure 6.8 Hawaiians, and perhaps even ancient Egyptians, used a form of the hula hoop. But it was Arthur Melin and Richard Kerr who seized the opportunity to make the hula hoop a commercial success. In 1958, an Australian told them about Australian children using a bamboo hoop while dancing. Melin and Kerr worked with scientists to design a hoop made with polyethylene. They marketed it around the world, and 25 million hoops were sold in the first four months.

International contracting functions in much the same way as local contracting does. Imagine that your house needs a new roof. You would likely call two or three roofing contractors to provide you with quotes to supply and install a roof. Once the quotes are in, you would analyze each one and choose the contractor you felt would do the best job for the best price. Your decision would be influenced by the contractor's reputation for quality work, the price, the starting date, and a variety of other factors. International business works similarly, but on a wider scale. Companies from around the world compete for contracts. When Beijing won the international competition to hold the 2008 Summer Olympics, for instance, many North American firms saw the opportunity to secure contracts helping to build infrastructures for the Games. More and more international opportunities will become available as large organizations outsource work, or contract out projects to companies in other countries. As discussed earlier, in today's interdependent world, no nation can operate in complete self-sufficiency.

To start the process of seeking the right contractor, an organization requests that contractors respond in writing to a **request for proposal** (**RFP**). The RFP outlines the cost and time guidelines for the work to be done or the service to be provided. Competing contractors have an opportunity to propose ways they would "deliver" the solution. The solutions, services, or end-products developed are referred to as **deliverables**.

The RFP process is seen as a fair method because every contractor submitting a proposal has a chance to win the contract. However, not all companies are aware of opportunities to present proposals—and, in certain cases, companies may not meet criteria for submission or be invited to submit an RFP. To seek and secure international contracts, companies must be proactive and have a visible presence in the markets where contracts are to be found. Often, such opportunities are identified through embassies and other government agencies. Getting a local or international contract is similar to getting a job after the short list of candidates has been interviewed.

Personal initiative or "seizing the moment" can also create exciting possibilities. Have you ever travelled abroad and found a great product that is not available in Canada? Or have you ever had a foreign visitor bring a novelty into your home? Perhaps there is an opportunity to import and distribute that product. Finding international opportunities often happens this way.

One classic example of a company seizing the moment is the story of Ken Hakuta and the "Taco" (which means octopus in Japanese). As he tells in his book, *How to Create Your Own Fad and Make a Million Dollars*, in 1982, Hakuta's parents sent a box of gifts from Japan for his sons.

Tucked in among the picture books and toy soldiers was a gummy piece of rubber with eight little sprouts sticking out...I asked my kids to let me look at the Taco. I threw it against the wall. It took to the wall and stuck there for a second. Then it came alive, shuddered, let go, flipped over, grabbed the wall again, wriggled, lurched downward, shimmied, and expired.

THINK ABOUT IT

Do innovative products respond to a need or create a need?

Hakuta was already exporting Teflon ironing board covers to Japan and importing karate uniforms from Korea. Intrigued by the Taco, he contacted the manufacturer in Japan, made a $120 000 investment, secured the United States rights, and began importing Taco under the new name, Wacky Wallwalker. The fad caught on and Hakuta made $20 million from its sales. Keep your eyes open for opportunities the next time you travel outside Canada. Perhaps you have a relative living in another country who can send you something new, unique, or "hot" in their market to sell in your area.

Another way to create new opportunities is through research and observation of existing problems. Recently, George Roter and Parker Mitchell, then 24-year-old University of Waterloo engineers, formed Engineers Without Borders (EWB), a non-governmental organization modelled after the Nobel Prize-winning Doctors Without Borders. Founders Roter and Mitchell hoped to use technology to solve problems in developing countries. Their goal was to provide these countries with technologies inexpensive enough to be suitable. For example, they designed a light bulb powered by a pedal generator to replace dangerous light sources such as burning dung or oil-soaked twigs. Another of their projects is a water-purification system that uses the rays of the sun to heat water and kill bacteria, a method that is less expensive and more environmentally sensitive than chlorine filtration. Their work focuses on countries like India, Nepal, and the Philippines.

The organization is establishing its roots on university campuses worldwide. Engineers Without Borders hopes to attract financing from a variety of sponsors. At present, the organization has 2500 members on 25 university campuses and 500 active volunteers. These enterprising young Canadians are leading the way by being proactive, taking direct action to seek and solve problems.

Opportunities are all around us, waiting for us to recognize and address them.

Figure 6.9 Parker Mitchell (left) and George Roter (centre), founding members of Engineers Without Borders, with Matthew Phillips, who interned on a project in India.

ICE Activities for 6.1

Ideas	Connections	Extensions
1. (a) In your own words, explain the questions that a company needs to address as it looks for new business opportunities.	(b) In role as the head of a Canadian international company, explain how you would go about finding an answer to one of the questions you explained in 1. (a).	(c) Reread the two comments from Canadian prime ministers regarding international trade (pages 180 and 181). What aspects of these quotations could be used in a strategy to help Canadians be more successful in the global marketplace?
2. (a) Describe the four steps of the product innovation process.	(b) Explain how an innovative employee at a specific Canadian company might follow the four steps of the product innovation process to develop a new product.	(c) In groups, brainstorm ideas for your community to become more "global." Take one of these ideas and, following the product innovation process, describe how you might go about implementing your idea.
3. (a) Explain three ways that a Canadian company might find international opportunities.	(b) Describe one potential international business opportunity that you see in your community.	(c) Prepare at least three research questions that would help you find out more about the business opportunity that you described in 3. (b).

6.2 Identifying International Opportunities and Trends

The Global Entrepreneur and Global Entrepreneurship

A true global entrepreneur is not just an individual selling or buying goods internationally. It is not limited to a one-person shop. A true global entrepreneur can work in a one-person shop, a ten-person small company, a 500-person manufacturing company, or a giant Fortune 500 corporation.

– James F. Foley

Global entrepreneurs pursue international opportunities beyond the resources they currently control. An **entrepreneur** is a person who organizes, manages, and assumes the risk of starting and running a business. After global entrepreneurs have identified these opportunities, they assemble the resources and the plans they will need to take advantage of them, taking into account their awareness of the trends affecting world trade.

Global entrepreneurs are business leaders who have the vision to see opportunities to sell or to purchase goods or expertise internationally to enhance their business. And they have the knowledge of how to involve their company in the global market. Entrepreneurs on this scale understand the possibilities of international business and never underestimate their personal abilities or their company's potential. Global entrepreneurs know how to rally their employees to act and think in an entrepreneurial fashion. Their leadership allows the company to develop a method of approaching business called a **global mindset**.

Here is a checklist of criteria for developing a global mindset in companies:

- Be open to ideas from other countries and cultures. New cultural settings should motivate you rather than hinder you.
- When visiting or working in another culture, be sensitive to cultural differences but not fearful of those differences.
- View the international market as a source of ideas and technology.
- When working with others, treat people equally regardless of their national origin.
- Be a leader in discovering and pursuing emerging international market opportunities.
- Treat international customers, regardless of their home country, with the same respect as domestic customers.
- When researching the competition, check all regions of the world thoroughly.
- Strive to have a universal identity rather than a national identity.
- Employ a worldwide selection of workers and be sure they all have the same opportunity to move up the career ladder.
- Ensure that the board of directors, executives, and general managers represent a mix of nationalities, international experience, and language skills.

A global mindset is a chief ingredient of the type of business intelligence required to pursue and secure global opportunities. With a global mindset, a company has the possibility of becoming global, rather than just international.

Business leaders are sometimes of two minds about encouraging initiative among their employees. Executives claim to want employees to have the "entrepreneurial spirit." At the same time, however, some top managers are hesitant to give employees too much freedom to act, suggesting that it is possible for employees to become too entrepreneurial. Some Canadian executives believe that overly entrepreneurial employees only create more problems. According to a survey by consulting firm Accenture, about 70 percent of global business leaders feel that their employees do not possess entrepreneurial traits. However, 95 percent of Canadian executives said their organization actively encourages staff to be creative (compared to the global average of 86 percent).

Models for Entrepreneurship

The United States is usually considered the world's most entrepreneurial country, with Japan being a distant second. Accenture's research suggests that, no matter where in the world a company is headquartered or does business, certain basic elements must be in place for an entrepreneurial climate to grow. These include access to capital, the right regulatory and tax environment, and positive social and cultural attitudes toward entrepreneurship.

According to Accenture, entrepreneurial behaviour differs from one country to another, as the following three models demonstrate:

- The **Free Market Model** emphasizes minimal government intervention in the economy and deregulation as the best way to provide incentives for entrepreneurial behaviour. The United States is a prime example of a free market model.

- The **Guided Individualism Model**, as followed in Taiwan and Singapore, encourages individual enterprise but emphasizes the use of public policy and government to influence the direction of entrepreneurial activity.

- The **Social Democratic Model**, used in countries such as Germany, the Netherlands, and Sweden, makes government a key player, along with other partners, in setting the framework in which enterprise can flourish.

All individuals, companies, or countries that are interested in expanding markets need to find an entrepreneurial model that suits their political and cultural patterns.

Identifying Global Trends

In the world of business, a **trend** is seen as a general direction or movement of the marketplace that is occurring now or is expected to occur in the immediate future. Global trends are those that affect people worldwide and that are expected to influence the development and sale of products and hold the attention of consumers over an extended period of time. Trends should not be confused with fads that come and go quickly and have little usefulness or utility. A fad has been described as something everyone wanted yesterday and no one wants tomorrow. Trends tend to indicate **growth markets** and opportunities for producers and consumers. Growth markets or segments usually identify the direction of the market and where people are spending their time and money. Global entrepreneurs study, respond to, and become sensitive to these trends.

The Life Cycle Concept

By looking at a product **life cycle**, it is possible to identify whether a trend is rising or descending. The life cycle of a product, business, location, or industry typically follows a similar cycle, which includes four stages from birth to decline: embryo, growth, maturity, and death.

Emerging trends and businesses are sometimes referred to as *sunrise opportunities*. Those in decline or at the end of their life cycle are referred to as *sunset opportunities*.

Newly identified trends are said to be in the *embryo stage*. As suggested by the name, the trend is just beginning, or "hatching." Once the trend or product takes off and gains popularity, it is in the *growth stage*. When a large number of people have had a chance to take advantage of the trend, its use or sales begin to slow. The *maturity stage* identifies this cooling-off phase of a trend. When most of the market is captured and the market is "saturated" or full, a product loses its trendiness. Finally, the *decline stage* is evident when the trend ceases to be popular and production stops, or the

Web Link

Follow the link at
www.internationalbusiness.nelson.com
to learn about likely future international
business trends.

Popular products today may not be popular tomorrow. Here are some examples of products in each stage of the product life cycle.

1. Embryo Stage – Alternatives to the internal combustion engine for cars (fuel cells, hydrogen fuel)
2. Growth Stage – The Internet
3. Maturity Stage – Snowboards, Personal Computers
4. Decline Stage – Department Stores (replaced by big box stores)

In other countries, some of these examples may not exist, or they may be at different stages of development. This is what the global entrepreneur needs to know. Observation and research are essential to understanding trends.

business has to close its doors. Following a product through its life cycle can provide global entrepreneurs with *market signals*. Sometimes, a trend can return to popularity, even in a revised format. This phase is called the *rebirth stage*.

Products and trends constantly move through these stages. Successful companies go through a process known as "re-inventing" themselves or their products to capitalize on developing trends. For many Canadian companies, launching products internationally has been a source of this type of renewal.

Figure 6.10 The Volkswagen "Bug" has experienced all stages of the product life cycle and now is enjoying a rebirth. These photos show the models from 1958 (black), 1981 (white), and 2002 (blue).

An interesting illustration is that of the toothbrush in China. Approximately half the people in China do not brush their teeth, and each person buys fewer than two tubes of toothpaste per year. According to Western dental habits, it is said that an annual average of at least five regular-size tubes is needed to maintain basic oral hygiene. A tooth-brushing survey in a northern Chinese province found that about 95 percent of peasant families did not have toothbrushes or toothpaste. Even in cities, no more than 60 percent of people brush their teeth.

Seizing what it saw as a huge potential market, Gillette introduced its Oral-B brand of toothbrush in China. Even if it only obtained a 10 percent market share in China, Gillette would sell more toothbrushes than it does in the United States. Gillette is speculating that, as with many other cultural norms and consumer products, China's population will gravitate to these "Western practices."

ICE Activities for 6.2

Ideas	Connections	Extensions
1. (a) Identify three ways global entrepreneurs can achieve a "global mindset."	(b) What effect does a global mindset have on your school, place of work, or family?	(c) How could you develop a global mindset? Describe three specific steps that you could take to achieve this goal.
2. (a) What are the basic elements that foster an entrepreneurial climate in a company?	(b) How would you describe the difference between the free market model and the guided individualism models of entrepreneurship?	(c) Multinational companies are sometimes criticized for pushing their products on people of other cultures and showing disrespect for local customs. Do you think Gillette's plan to market its toothbrush in China presents a problem in terms of culture? Do the potential benefits outweigh any concerns? Explain your answers.
3. (a) Explain the steps in the life cycle of a product.	(b) Estimate where the following products are in their life cycles: a three-year-old cell phone, a one-year-old textbook, a television sitcom that has been running for five years.	(c) Identify an international product that you think is in its maturity stage. Predict when the product will move to its decline stage. In your opinion, does this product have the potential for rebirth? Explain the reasons for your responses.

6.3 Mapping International Trends

With close observation of world activities, it is possible to see that a number of major trends affect the way we live and do business. The following are six key international trends to observe and follow:

1. the global workplace
2. increased global competition
3. global information technology, convergence, and infrastructure
4. Asia's global impact
5. global consumer, global culture
6. global companies versus nations

Trend #1: The Global Workplace

Chances are strong that in the course of their lives, today's students will work for a global organization. The forces of globalization and the expansion of Canadian trade have led to an increase in the demand for globally aware and well-trained staff for companies wishing to support the higher volume and changing nature of international trade. Career opportunities are becoming more and more available in international business and in activities related to international affairs, such as education, environmental research, and social development. These changes point to a growing trend or market for Canadians to sell and export not just goods but professional services as well.

The sale of services is playing an expanding international role. Canada is very competitive with other developed countries in selling services to the world. Canada will need young people to be involved in the sale and implementation of Canadian services in other countries. The future looks bright for Canada, since there is great potential in selling services.

One effect of international economic instability and change is the decline of lifetime employment. It is a worldwide trend that workers must be prepared to retrain and expect more than one career during their lifetime. Flexibility and skill portability will be increasingly needed as individuals and enterprises adapt to the changing workplace, both domestically and internationally.

Someone who lives and works in a foreign country for an extended period is known as an **expatriate**. Expatriate employees may have short- or long-term assignments, and need special qualities if they are to make their international experience into a positive career move. Global workers must be culturally sensitive, flexible, and technically competent. They must also have family support and a true desire to live and work internationally.

International careers may appear full of adventure, but there are considerable risks. One career danger is that international workers may be so eager to discover new places that they will change jobs frequently to get the location they want. This random mobility can create a scattered work history that may have a negative effect on their career portfolio when they look for new opportunities later on. Living the international lifestyle and being separated from home and family, sometimes for lengthy periods, often turns a person into a "nomad." Here are a few tips for "global nomads":

- **Take care of yourself:** Adapting to different customs and foods can be unsettling and affect one's health negatively.

- **Find a mentor:** Look for someone with international experience with whom you can openly and regularly consult.

- **Start investing:** Put money into a home base, preferably in a favourite place, and begin planning for ultimate retirement.

- **Be attentive to children:** The children of international nomads will experience an interesting life but may need special care due to the constant change.

- **Continue learning:** International exposure does not make you superior to others.

Figure 6.11 One of the costs of an international lifestyle is the separation from home and family.

It is important for international workers to organize themselves to cope with potentially disorganized lives. Most progressive companies provide preparation and on-site assistance plans to help their employees ease into their international assignments. Once there, families may also face the stress of being apart for significant periods of time.

Trend #2: Increased Global Competition

Since the early 1980s, there have been major changes in the nature of international competition. With the recent reductions in trade barriers and the liberalization of trade, competition across borders has increased. The disruption of existing markets by flexible, creative, and fast-moving firms is known as **hyper-competition**. Hyper-competitive companies succeed through rapid product innovation, shorter design and product life cycle, aggressive pricing, and new approaches to serving customer needs. Canadian companies need to be on the offensive to succeed in global markets. Hyper-competition has been caused by four factors:

- Customers worldwide demand better quality products, often at lower prices.

- Rapid technological changes in the information revolution have made it easier to enter markets or achieve global "reach" in marketing.

- Competitors are more aggressive and better-financed; they are planning for the long term and are willing to lose money in the short term to enter new markets.

- Government policies collapse entry barriers. With globalization and through multilateral negotiations, countries are reducing tariffs, deregulating, and essentially saying: "We are open for business."

In future international business, the boldest, fastest-moving firms are likely to win. There will likely be more products, shorter life cycles, more markets, more people, and, of course, more competition worldwide. Consider the following indicators of increased productivity: Aircraft manufacturer Boeing reduces its time to build a 747 by 50 percent, Microsoft launches software around the globe in a single day, and McDonald's establishes three new restaurants per day, every week, around the world.

A look at the business section of a national newspaper reveals that Canada is an active participant in this increased global competition. Here are some examples:

Growing Entertainment Industry in British Columbia and Ontario:
The automotive industry has been considered Ontario's "economic engine." However, the movie and television business is fast challenging it as the province's most important industry sector. Film and television industries directly employ about 10 000 people and spend about $1 billion in Ontario annually. American and Japanese car companies, on the other hand, employ 50 000 people in Ontario, and auto suppliers and dealerships provide about six times as many jobs. While the entertainment industry has not overtaken the automotive sector, it is growing faster. The development of the entertainment industry in Ontario and British Columbia has largely been a result of American film and television producers' efforts to keep production costs lower due to a weaker Canadian dollar. Productions filmed in Canadian locations are less expensive and ultimately spell larger profits at the box office.

Expanding in the United States: The Jean Coutu Group Inc. of Quebec is the second-largest pharmacy company in Canada. It owns the 242-store Brooks Pharmacy chain in six northeastern American states and employs 4500 people. Coutu plans to invest about $1 billion in a major expansion in the United States. Coutu previously had a chance to purchase Shoppers Drug Mart, the number one pharmacy chain in Canada, but considered the sale price too high.

Figure 6.12 Krispy Kreme opened its first Canadian doughnut shop in Mississauga, Ontario, on December 11, 2001.

American Companies Coming to Canada: Since the onset of NAFTA, Canadians have witnessed the arrival of several American companies. For example, Wal-Mart provided Canadian Tire and other Canadian retailers with significant competition when it arrived in the 1990s. In a more recent move, Krispy Kreme Doughnuts Inc., a large and popular North Carolina–based chain, developed plans to open stores in Ontario, Quebec, and the Atlantic provinces, in addition to its already existing British Columbia outlets. Krispy Kreme will have to compete with popular doughnut outlets already in place, such as Tim Hortons. When asked about the reason for expansion into Canada, an executive of Krispy Kreme replied that there was plenty of room for everybody in the market.

Overseas Companies Coming to Canada: Many other countries are targeting Canada for their expansion and are seeking market entry. For example, Air Canada feels the competition from foreign airlines, which are likely to have increasing access to Canada for the lucrative Trans-Atlantic and Trans-Pacific routes, as well as the North American and the North America–South America routes. Some airlines may tap profitable market niches, which could be specific routes or the provision of particular specialties, such as in-flight manicures and massages.

Clearly, competition is everywhere. *Global Trends 2015*, a 59-page American-government–sponsored document that forecasts the future, presents an optimistic picture for developed countries. However, it predicts that the gap between rich and poor will widen. It expresses the opinion that the Information Technology Revolution represents the most significant transformation in the world since the Industrial Revolution. The document profiles a number of countries. The forecast for Canada is positive: "Canada will be a full participant in the globalization process in 2015 and a leading player in the Americas after the United States, along with Mexico and Brazil. Ottawa will still be grappling with the political, demographic, and cultural impact of heavy Asian immigration in the West, as well as residual nationalist sentiment in French-speaking Quebec. The vast and diverse country, however, will remain stable amidst constant, dynamic change...the question of Quebec's place in the country will continue to stir national debate."

Web Link

For more information on **Global Trends 2015**, follow the link at www.internationalbusiness.nelson.com.

Trend #3: Global Information Technology, Convergence, and Infrastructure

TRADE TALK

The two great engines of our age—technology and travel (now the largest industry in the world)—give fuel to each other, our machines prompting us to prize speed as an end in itself, and the longing for speed quickening a hunger for new technologies.

– Pico Iyer

Figure 6.13 Companies involved in international business must recognize the needs of international markets. For example, products must often come with instructions in several languages.

Rapid technological changes and the information revolution have made it easier to enter foreign markets. Technology—in the form of biotechnology, information technology, and transportation technology—is reshaping our world. Technology is bringing together (converging) information, communication, and people. As the benefits of technology make it easier and faster to communicate, find, and exchange information, world history is becoming a story of increasing interconnection.

Technological convergence enables companies in the telecommunications, consumer electronics, software, computer, and entertainment industries to enter each other's markets. For example, computer companies like Dell, Compaq, Intel, and Microsoft have emerged to challenge IBM. IBM, in turn, has redefined itself as a provider of "e-business on demand" solutions. Technology and information are also changing the rules of distribution, order taking, financial services, and product customization. And technological trends are breaking down the barriers to market entry that used to protect leading nations and industries. Many protectionist policies, regulations, and language barriers are disappearing as more and more companies have access to the required technologies in economies that are now more open.

Communication and convergence are linked, and the world has been "shrinking." In the mid-1700s, for example, it took 12 days to get a message from New York to Boston; a century later it took 12 hours. Today, in 12 hours you can fly from London to Tokyo, and you can send a fax or e-mail to the other side of the world in 12 seconds. Satellites are merging the world's media. With information transfer and communication occurring at the speed of light, it appears that we are closer to our global neighbours than at any previous time in human history.

For companies conducting international business, it is essential not only to understand the cultures of different countries but also to tailor or modify products to meet the demands of these different markets. The ability of international companies to create products that recognize the preferences and needs of individual markets requires highly developed multicultural understanding as well. In addition, products must come with instructions in appropriate languages and be packaged sensitively.

Figure 6.14 The portable digital assistant offers wireless e-mail or Internet access in the palm of your hand.

Figure 6.15 Bombardier MKII vehicles, Rapid Transit Millennium Line, Vancouver, BC.

THINK ABOUT IT

Can you imagine a paperless world? Consider some of the lifestyle changes that this would involve.

Wireless communications technology, which does not require plugging in and a stationary position, is now available to both individuals and companies. Innovative technology further liberates people from their offices and allows them to work virtually anywhere or everywhere. Wireless technology provides immediate connectivity, mobility, and access to information in almost any location. One popular form of wireless device is the PDA, or personal digital assistant, which provides access to e-mail and the Internet in the palm of your hand wherever you may be.

To support the increase in urban development and international travel that accompanies globalization, new infrastructure will be needed. Today's infrastructure represents the systems that support modern transportation and communication. A super-jumbo airliner (the A380 from European aircraft-maker Airbus Industrie) has been developed to carry 555 passengers. Imagine how larger airplanes will change the features of present-day airports. Future adaptations to existing infrastructure will be necessary to accommodate planes of this size and capacity.

Canadian companies are also active in developing infrastructure projects around the world. From aircraft, to airport development, to sewage and waste management, to subway cars, to safe nuclear power, Canada has developed an international reputation for a wide range of quality products.

In addition to Canada's traditional economic role as a provider of primary resources through mining, fishing, logging, and oil and natural gas exploration, this country has earned an international reputation for its world-class expertise in the design, construction, and operation of information technology, mines, refineries, gas plants, and pipeline systems.

Canadians make greater per-capita use of the Internet than citizens of any other country. According to the American market research company Computer Industry Almanac Inc., on a per capita basis in 1999, Canada had more Internet users than any other country in the world. Ipsos-Reid reported that 75 percent of Canadians have access to the Internet, and 15.1 million Canadians use the Internet at home. In 2001, Statistics Canada found that Internet use at home had jumped 42 percent from 1999. According to a 1999 Almanac study, nearly 43 percent of Canadians used the Internet at least once a month. (The global average was lower than 5 percent.) Sweden was second, Finland was third, and the United States was fourth. Canada has moved into first place very quickly, from being seventh in 1997. Economic signs indicate that Canadian investment in technology has been instrumental in boosting Canada's productivity and prosperity.

The forecast is that as Internet use in other nations grows, the Internet dominance of the more developed countries will decrease. Even developing countries are experiencing a growth of Internet cafés—outlets where people can use computer Internet services and send e-mail. For example, from a small town in the Bolivian Andes, a father can connect to his daughter in the United States for a half-hour Internet "chat" that will cost him less than a dollar. This price is a fraction of what he would have to pay for a long distance telephone call of the same length. In many developing countries, consumers opt to use Internet cafés rather than actually buy their own system for home use. The cafés have become a new hub of social life for many communities. There are indications that the number of Internet users worldwide will soon approach one billion.

Figure 6.16 CyberCafé in Sao Paulo, Brazil.

Trend #4: Asia's Global Impact

The last 20 years of the twentieth century witnessed an incredible growth in the Asia–Pacific nations, a growth trend that points to Asia's dominating the twenty-first century. Asia's huge markets are as different from each other as those in Europe or the western hemisphere.

At the beginning of the twentieth century, approximately 14 percent of the world's population were urban dwellers. By 2000, this global statistic had risen to 50 percent, with many cities reaching "megacity" status. In 2020, China could have a middle class as large as the population of the entire United States (approximately 300 million), with a similarly growing consumer appetite. And India recently passed the one billion population mark.

At current growth rates, by 2050 Asia will make up half of the world's population and will comprise 40 percent of the global economy. And Asia will have more than half of the world's information technology industry. The future of trade and global governance (the way systems are controlled and ruled) will increasingly be shaped by the great Asian trading powers.

In his book *Megatrends Asia: Eight Megatrends That Are Shaping Our World*, futurist John Naisbitt has defined some of the major trends or shifts that are taking place as Asia modernizes. These trends are important for companies wishing to seek market entry in Asia.

Among the major trends in some Asian countries, Naisbitt includes the movement from export-led to consumer-driven economies, from government-controlled to market-driven, from farms to supercities, and from labour-intensive to high-technology industries. Naisbitt also believes that Japan's economic position in Asia is on a gradual decline and that "considerations about China and expatriate Chinese now drive decision-making in Asia, as China becomes central to the total Pacific region."

According to Donald A. Ball and his fellow authors, in *International Business: The Challenge of Global Competition*, much of the competition that Japan now faces in the Asian region is the result of Japanese firms moving their production to other Asian countries in the mid-1990s. After World War II, Japan began an economic recovery based on making products for export. Since then, Japan's standard of living grew until it became one of the highest in the world. The reason for the decision to move production out of Japan was the lower labour and production costs in other less-developed Asian countries. Ball cites the following example: Japan produced "38.2 million videocassette recorders (VCRs) in 1989, which accounted for most of the world's markets." However, by 1998, Japan was producing only 9.6 million VCRs, which was a 66 percent decline. Of the 3.3 million machines that the Sanyo Electric Co. Ltd. produced annually, only 600 000 were Japanese-made; the remainder were produced in Indonesia, China, and Germany.

China is Asia's largest country and is the oldest continuous civilization in the world. According to the U.S. Central Intelligence Agency's *The World Factbook 2002*, China covers an area of 9 596 960 sq. km. and had an estimated population of 1 284 303 705 in July 2002. This means that the country not only has a very large labour force, but also many potential consumers. In terms of its economy, since 1978 the trend in China has been away from central planning and towards a more market-oriented system (for more information on economic systems, see Chapter 9). Although communist control is still strong, non-state organizations and small entrepreneurs are gaining more influence, and the country is opening to more foreign trade and investment. Since 1978, China's GDP has quadrupled, even though the 2001 GDP per capita was only $4300 USD. Workers' incomes in Asian countries can vary widely depending on the countries' stage of development. For example, in 2001 per capita GDP (all figures are in U.S. dollars) was $281 in Cambodia, $2500 in India, $684 in Indonesia, $886 in the Philippines, and $27 200 in Japan.

In 1997, a financial crisis in Thailand spread throughout Asia and caused a loss of value of local currencies and stock values. Some Asian currencies lost 80 percent of their value. Prices rose, sometimes by as much as 70 percent, and stock markets closed. There was civil unrest, and even the downfall of some governments, such as Indonesia's in 1998. Many countries in the region have recovered since that time, with the support of the International Monetary Fund. The IMF loaned over $35 billion to the affected countries and helped them to restructure operations of their financial institutions.

John Naisbitt believes that global trends are forcing Western countries "to confront the reality of the rise of the East" in terms of economic power. In his opinion, "Thousands of years ago, Asia was the centre of the world, and it is taking up that role again."

International Business Career Profile

Wonderful International Digital Quest

Brady Gilchrist is busy living the digital life with a natural twist. The 34-year-old business consultant from Toronto believes that by going digital, many aspects of our lives will be fundamentally changed. Over the past two years, his mission has been to prove just that by exploring, documenting, and integrating digital media and equipment into his life. Says Brady, "We keep hearing about this movement to an Internet and wireless world—through this adventure I'm going to see exactly what it means."

In April 2000, he initiated a six-month experiment. He put virtually everything he owned in storage except his clothes and, with about $50,000 worth of technology, moved onto a 30-foot (9-metre) sailboat docked in Toronto harbour. He did without all traditional forms of media like newspapers, books, and television, preferring to explore how the same information, and more, could be accessed from his digital tools. He set out to prove that he could live digitally and that he could master, converge, and merge his digital tools. He also banked on a few supporting sponsors to help finance his dream. While the adventure was isolating at times, he remained connected digitally and discovered a broad range of business opportunities.

As a result of his story being broadcast internationally, Gilchrist received an invitation to be a part of an even greater adventure.

Figure 6.17 Gilchrist relied on digital connections for six months while living on a boat. Gilchrist posted reflections about leading a digital life on his Web site.

During the winter of 2000–2001, he responded to an invitation to join the boat Starship, a German-backed expedition that had set out to make a multimedia record of the planet during a 1000-day trip around the globe. Brady reached the boat near Madagascar off the east coast of Africa. The journey further convinced him of the ability to lead a digital life.

By the summer of 2001, he had returned to Canada and was exploring the Great Lakes on his own boat once again. He was also adding journal accounts of his adventures and reflections on his Web site.

For the immediate future, Gilchrist has returned to the world of advertising and marketing, something he did full-time before he went to sea. He has temporarily shelved a few of his ambitions and goals. On reflection, he says, "The digital life has been an excellent research and development lab. It was all about understanding convergence."

Here are a few of Brady Gilchrist's predictions:
- The Internet will surpass television as the most important mass communications medium in western society.
- Electronic books will become a raging success.
- Portable computing devices like handhelds will become central to how we live our lives and consume entertainment.
- Most long distance telephone calls will be almost free.
- Distance education will be a component of everything we do.
- Web consumers will redefine the traditional rules of marketing and targeting markets.
- Work will be done on demand, and contracts will be defined by need and past performance, not solely by interpersonal relationship.

1. Which of these predictions do you think are most likely to have an impact on your life in the next few years?

2. Do you agree with Brady Gilchrist that we can live digitally? Explain.

Trend #5: Global Consumer, Global Culture

As companies and countries engage in trade with each other, the world appears to be merging and forming a single culture or *monoculture*, a society that has a lack of diversity in values and beliefs. This trend toward a monoculture has resulted from the fact that consumers worldwide are gaining the buying power to acquire products. Rising wealth and per-capita incomes around the world promote the creation of a larger middle class, an improved standard of living, and the ability to spend income. When consumers can afford more material wealth, they are said to be more affluent. The conditions that encourage affluence in a society are a high productivity and a low birthrate.

Multinational companies have the greatest investment, or stake, in encouraging consumers to support the development of this monoculture in which everyone is a potential consumer. Some organizations even avoid using the word "foreign" since it implies the strange and unknown, and suggests barriers to trade. One aspect of globalization is that the world is considered to be one large market.

Sweden's IKEA furniture company moved into China recently, just at a time when the Chinese government was urging its citizens to buy their own homes (which until then had been provided by the state or by public corporations). As they become homeowners, growing numbers of Chinese consumers are discovering IKEA's innovative furnishings. However, while IKEA boasts low prices, only the more affluent Chinese can afford IKEA's products. The company is responding to the Chinese market with new products designed specifically for the spatial and living needs of 1.3 billion potential consumers. These market initiatives raise a question that the company must look at: "Is IKEA in the process of changing China or is China changing IKEA?"

Figure 6.18 IKEA store in Beijing, China

GLOBAL THOUGHT

Globalization also refers to the development of shared thought, language, and symbols among people who increasingly work wherever they want and live in no one place for very long. We usually think of scientific, technological, commercial, and financial elites as globalized minds, but members of humanitarian non-governmental organizations (NGOs) and human-rights organizations share this global sensibility, even though they give it very different meaning. The sense of home as place diminishes among these people, who increasingly think of themselves as global citizens, with global interests and values.

I think about globalization as the shrinking of distance through thickening networks of connections. It is the economic, technological, environmental, social, cultural, and political processes that work together first to connect and then to integrate the layers of societies.

– *Janice Gross Stein*

Another area where monoculture is occurring is language. Many countries are embracing English because they recognize its importance in promoting economic growth and even survival. It makes sense to encourage proficiency in a language like English, which links bankers, business people, politicians, educators, and consumers the world over. Asian nations like Japan, Taiwan, and South Korea have sought to make their people competent in English. Three-quarters of the world's mail, and four-fifths of its electronic information, is now transmitted in English. The bulk of existing know-how in science and technology is written in English. Even taxi drivers in Beijing are learning English to prepare for the 2008 Summer Olympics. For many, not knowing English can mean losing opportunities.

People still prefer to buy in their own language, however. Language is like software. Compatibility is essential for economic utility. Some employers claim that an "English-only" workplace promotes harmony, productivity, and safety. Jobs in such venues as a hospital, a nuclear power plant, or an air-traffic tower require instant comprehension of the situation. However, there are legitimate concerns about a monolingual workplace, especially one that is enforced. Workers face the possibility of discrimination. It is an excellent career strategy to learn one or two other languages. Applying the skill to speak two languages interchangeably is referred to as "code switching." No matter how fluent Hindi or Chinese speakers are in English, when they do business with foreigners, the deals often go to those who speak their languages.

Producers must research and analyze the **demographic profile** of the target market. This means looking at the income, gender, and age of the population. There are a number of global consumer trends to consider. For example, in developed countries such as Japan and Canada, birth rates are dropping, and the average age of the "baby boomers" population, born after the Second World War, is increasing. When travel clothing designer Tilley Endurables, which outfits the "mature" consumer, ventured into Japan, it hired an intermediary, or agent, to help decide on a product offering for a Japanese catalogue.

At the same time, global goods are making their way into once-remote regions of developing countries. Production often crosses traditional cultural stereotypes, and less expensive imports are within the reach of almost everybody. A good example is chopsticks, which are now made from birch trees in Minnesota and then shipped to huge markets in Asia. Ontario and British Columbia produce world-class wines to compete with those of France and Germany. There appear to be no boundaries to international opportunities.

Here are other demographic ideas to consider:

- While there are three billion people in Asia, half of them are under the age of 25. Many countries have a large population of seniors, and marketers are acting on such demographic trends.

- Women around the world are working more outside the home. They are earning and, therefore, consuming more—something producers and advertisers need to consider. More women are travelling both for business and for pleasure. One of the biggest hurdles for business women in organizations has been the *glass border*, the notion that women are prevented from travelling on business because of the stereotypes that perceive women to be staying at home. Many business women want to travel. They can see through the glass border to recognize global opportunities. However, they are often overlooked for foreign postings. Again, this is changing as more and more women travel globally on behalf of their companies, and hotels cater to the needs of female travellers.

- As cultures merge with one another, companies are responding with new and unique products, particularly in clothing and food. For example, Thailand plans to develop global Thai food franchises similar to Western hamburger chains. The three Thai food franchises are called Golden Leaf, Cool Basil, and Elephant Jump. Thai food leads the global food trends, as it is healthy low-fat food with many interesting herbal seasonings. There are about 5000 Thai restaurants outside Thailand, and this number should soon increase to 8000.

- It is apparent that world population will continue to grow in the twenty-first century. It is anticipated that it will increase from 6 billion in 2000 to approximately 8.5 billion by 2025. This growth will for the most part be favourable to the development of international business. Growth rates will range widely: we can expect high growth in Asia, Latin America, and Africa, slow growth in North America, and no growth in Europe and Japan. It is the high-growth areas that will create major opportunities for consumer products.

- Canada is thought to be undergoing a crisis of under-population. Some people express the opinion that its 31 million people, spread thinly over a vast expanse, cannot maintain the institutions needed in a global culture. Canada's market is considered too small and its infrastructure too expensive to support a voice of its own. According to Canadian Metropolis, since the United States reached one hundred million people in 1920, it has been suggested that Canada might also try for one hundred million. There are positive aspects to increasing Canada's population through immigration. The arrival of new immigrants could mean more new Canadians with skills required by the economy, and greater numbers of taxpayers could provide a tax benefit for the government.

Web Link

For more information on Canadian Metropolis, follow the link at www.internationalbusiness.nelson.com.

I'm glad that they have McDonald's in Japan, and I am glad that I have a sushi bar near my home in Bethesda (Maryland, USA). I'm glad that a little Japanese girl likes McDonald's, just as I am glad my girls like sushi. But it is important that this Japanese girl like it because it is different, not because she is fooled into thinking that it is actually Japanese. When that happens, homogenization is just around the corner. When that happens, there is every chance that this Japanese girl will eventually lose touch with what is really Japanese, and one day she will wake up...and discover that she has been invaded and there's nothing left of her original self and culture.

– *Thomas L. Friedman*

TRADE TIPS

Futurist Frank Feather coined the phrase: "Think globally, act locally." Feather claims that the Web will command 30 percent of consumer spending by 2010. This will have an adverse effect on retailers who do not sell online. Feather says online sales will top $1 trillion. People already buy everything from automobiles to prescription drugs online, and by 2010, he says, most shopping will be done online.

The increased use of television around the world has, through advertising, promoted worldwide consumption of consumer products. The resulting demand has in turn led to the development of North American-style malls far from North America. Global companies have a tendency to sell the same product in the same way everywhere, leaving them open to the criticism that they push their products upon other cultures and show disrespect to local customs. If this is true, then it is yet another example of how global products and companies are making the world more homogeneous, almost like one large global shopping mall.

With the current spotlight on rising economies in Asia, it is important to remember that three-quarters of the world's population live in poorer countries in Asia, Latin America, and Africa, where steady jobs and incomes do not exist. As people move to cities around the world, exposure to advertising messages and the urge to consume global brands will increase. Some critics suggest that global marketers are like religious missionaries. The consumers of less industrialized societies are seen as future converts to commercialism and materialism.

Product brand names and logos represent "global banners" that are instantly recognizable by millions of consumers. These products are referred to as **global brands**. As a result, Tokyo, Japan, and New York are starting to resemble each other more and more. Consumers around the world recognize a product brand or logo but may not know the colour of the United Nations flag. Coca-Cola is so widely recognized that it sells nearly half of all the soft drinks consumed on the planet.

Figure 6.19 McDonald's in Tokyo, Japan.

Technology also creates a monoculture where everything, everywhere is exactly the same. If we wire up everybody and interconnect countries, everyone ends up having similar wants and needs. By 2015, we could see a mass culture worldwide.

Understanding and researching the global consumer by region will still be important. It is important to know that four times as much yogurt is consumed in France as in Britain, or that the British eat more canned food than Americans, or that beef is three times more popular in Germany than in Sweden. Teenagers in Paris have more in common with teenagers in Ottawa than with their own parents. They buy the same products, see the same movies, listen to the same music, and sip the same beverages.

Trend #6: Global Companies versus Nations

As countries interconnect more and more, and as multinational companies amass greater wealth and revenue than many countries, political governing bodies suddenly find themselves losing control. An international, virtual community has been established, which national governments have difficulty regulating. Short of banning products for import and prohibiting advertising of products, governments can do very little to stop people from wanting to become global consumers.

What role can governments play in the new world economy? Their role might be reduced to intervening when a technology proves itself harmful, or using their powers to curb the rise of technology-based crime. As the number of people flying internationally doubles within the next ten years, it is expected that there will be a rise in smuggling and illegal migration. Wireless communications make it more difficult to track criminals. "Hackers" are able to unleash increasingly sophisticated and destructive computer viruses from anywhere in the world.

Of necessity, there will be a trend toward more alliances between business and government. For business this means sharing suppliers and distributors. Governments will be faced with the challenge of dealing with the creation of *monopolies*. A monopoly occurs when one company is favoured over others and corners the marketplace with its products, thereby preventing the distribution of other products. For many high-tech companies, however, it is the ability to create such a dominant position that earns extreme profits. Governments can help prepare their citizens to be competitive, but they may need to intervene when the dominance of monopolies prevents constructive solutions to problems, and stands in the way of innovation and progress. Achieving a global presence and a global mindset allows a country to increase its potential purchasing power as a country specifically and for its citizens generally.

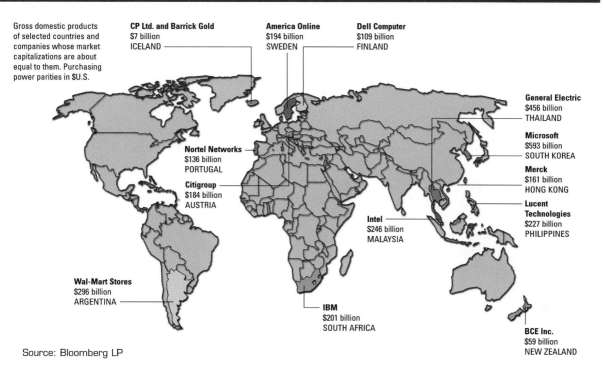

Gross domestic products of selected countries and companies whose market capitalizations are about equal to them. Purchasing power parities in $U.S.

CP Ltd. and Barrick Gold
$7 billion
ICELAND

America Online
$194 billion
SWEDEN

Dell Computer
$109 billion
FINLAND

General Electric
$456 billion
THAILAND

Microsoft
$593 billion
SOUTH KOREA

Merck
$161 billion
HONG KONG

Nortel Networks
$136 billion
PORTUGAL

Citigroup
$184 billion
AUSTRIA

Lucent Technologies
$227 billion
PHILIPPINES

Intel
$246 billion
MALAYSIA

Wal-Mart Stores
$296 billion
ARGENTINA

IBM
$201 billion
SOUTH AFRICA

BCE Inc.
$59 billion
NEW ZEALAND

Source: Bloomberg LP

Figure 6.20 Some multinational companies are as wealthy as some countries.

Global Opportunities for Smaller Businesses

While the removal of trade barriers all over the world seemed at first to present big opportunities primarily for big companies, it has actually opened the way for many **small-** and **medium-sized enterprises (SMEs)** to enter new markets. In the past, only large firms could afford new, powerful technology. Now, almost any business can have state-of-the-art technology that provides for innovation and speed to market. Small firms (in terms of people and sales) will need software that enables them to compete and conduct business outside their national borders. Small is big. Small businesses are increasingly respected internationally.

In a study conducted on behalf of Scotiabank and the Canadian Federation of Independent Business, 1800 people from Canada, the United States, Japan, Germany, and Brazil were asked to rate small businesses in terms of their contribution and respectability. Small businesses ranked first, ahead of large companies. One positive feature was that small companies are responsible for most employment growth. Many opportunities will exist in the developing world in places like Russia, Eastern Europe, China, Indonesia, Vietnam, South Africa, and a unified (North and South) Korea.

The Internet has changed business conduct, enabling both small and large businesses from any part of the world to compete. However, to remain competitive, small firms will require assistance. No longer can small firms compete for business based solely in their local area. Today a small business can anticipate that distant firms will be doing business in what was once their territory and doing it through the Internet.

When the 76-year-old family-based company Braun's Bicycle and Fitness launched its e-commerce Web site, for example, the company quickly obtained international sales. To achieve the power of the Web, Braun contracted the services of a technology partner called Emerge2 Digital, whose strategy took them from a "bricks and mortar" operation to a truly global business. Every time Braun's makes an online sale, its new customers are identified with a coloured pushpin on a world map. The Kitchener store now takes orders from around the world and, with more than 75 e-mails a day, its online sales make up approximately 10 percent of its annual revenue. Customers from the United States form its biggest online market, but orders have come from as far away as Australia and New Zealand. Much of Braun's merchandise is now shipped rather than being ridden out of the store, and they can serve customers in areas where bike products are not available. With Internet sales, Braun's can conduct business year-round, shipping products to global customers.

As opportunities for international business become more accessible, the time it takes between the decision to go international to the creation of a truly global company will be shortened for companies of all sizes.

Figure 6.21 Robert Braun, general manager of Braun's Bicycles, Kitchener, Ontario.

Web Link

Follow the link at www.internationalbusiness.nelson.com to review the contents and structure of Braun's Bicycle and Fitness Web site.

ICE Activities for 6.3

Ideas	Connections	Extensions
1. (a) Summarize the six global trends influencing present and future international trade.	(b) Using an example from your own experience, describe how one of these six global trends has personally affected you or a member of your family.	(c) Choose one of the trends on page 200 and discuss how it might affect companies wishing to do business in Asia.
2. (a) What is "hyper-competition"?	(b) Explain the relationship between hyper-competition and international trade.	(c) Work with a partner to brainstorm a list of resources you would need to start a successful Internet café. Estimate the start-up costs including rent, insurance, equipment, and advertising. Try to forecast your sales for a year based on the service you provide.
3. (a) Briefly describe Naisbitt's megatrends occurring in the shifting Asian market.	(b) Research your community or your region and profile a company conducting international trade via e-commerce.	(c) Consider the advantages and disadvantages of Canada increasing its population from 31 million to 100 million over the next 15 to 20 years. Do you think Canada should strive for this? Explain your answer.

Figure 6.22 Mary Robinson, former Prime Minister of Ireland and United Nations High Commissioner for Human Rights.

We are at the edge of a big idea—the shaping of ethical globalization ... The task is to create the momentum to make globalization a positive force for all the world's people, to make it inclusive and equitable.

– *Mary Robinson*, Second Global Ethics Lecture, Tübingen University, Jan. 12, 2002

Ireland's economy was affected by unemployment and emigration for several generations. However, the newly prosperous Ireland has embarked on a global recruitment drive as it ran out of workers to fill the jobs created by its flourishing economy. This job bonanza was one product of an economic boom dating back to the mid-1990s that earned Ireland the title the "Celtic Tiger."

In 1992, unemployment was running from 17 to 18 percent. Irish workers were looking for work outside the country in places like Germany. Then the tables turned: employment agencies went to cities in Germany to lure people to Ireland.

The boom, which has seen the Irish economy grow at an average rate of 9 percent, has been fuelled by massive investment by foreign companies, many in the high-tech sector. Attracted by Ireland's well-educated English-speaking workforce, low corporate tax rates, and relatively low wages, companies such as Microsoft and Intel have established key European operations in Ireland. Close to 7 percent of Ireland's labour market (about 110 000 workers) is currently employed by American high-tech firms.

Ireland produces one-third of Europe's PCs and half of the world's Pentium chips. There is also a significant health-care products market.

Although an increase in the number of women working has expanded the labour pool, unemployment is now at a record low of 3.7 percent. There are upward of 40 000 unfilled vacancies in Ireland, and a stroll around central Dublin reveals "Staff Wanted" signs in most eateries and shops.

Ireland now faces the challenge of managing and maintaining success. To sustain the pace of economic progress it enjoys, it will have to add as many as 200 000 people to the labour force between 2000 and 2005. One solution is to conduct trade missions for companies to recruit workers from other countries.

Many young, educated Irish who went to Britain or the United States to escape hard times during the 1980s may no longer be interested in returning. Ireland has targeted the EU nations to fill the need, but the United States, Canada, New Zealand, Australia, and Eastern European countries are also being tapped. Applicants can even submit their resumes via a Web site, allowing prospective employers to search online for workers.

With a population of 3.8 million, Ireland might be said to be an "importer of people." A number of challenges come with economic progress:

- Personal taxes have increased.
- Housing prices have increased dramatically.
- There is a shortage of childcare.
- The transport system is struggling to cope with traffic increases.
- With growing numbers of non-white foreign workers, racism in the workplace has increased.

By March of 2001, the Celtic Tiger's economy had "overheated," by growing so fast and falling into the pattern of an economic cycle that affects and governs growth and slowdowns. When the United States' economy slowed down in the early part of 2001, Ireland's economy was directly affected since many of the companies that located there were of American origin. Employment opportunities have been somewhat reduced.

TRADE TIPS

National economies can heat up and cool down. "Hot" economies cause incomes and the cost of living to increase while they drive down unemployment.

A SNAPSHOT OF IRELAND

Size: 68 890 sq. km

World Region: Europe

Capital City: Dublin

Languages: English, Gaelic

Currency: Euro

Population: 3.8 million

Time: Noon in Ottawa (EST) is 5:00 P.M. in Dublin.

Climate: Temperate maritime

Type of Government: Republic—Parliamentary democracy

Labour Force by Occupation: 63 percent services, 28 percent industry, 9 percent agriculture

Membership in World Organizations: EU, WTO, OECD, WEF

Importing Partners and Products:
Partners: United Kingdom, United States, Germany, France, and Japan.
Products: Machinery and equipment, chemicals, petroleum and petroleum products, textiles, and clothing.

Exporting Partners and Products:
Partners: United Kingdom, United States, Germany, France, and Netherlands.
Products: Machinery and equipment, computers, chemicals and pharmaceuticals.

Investments: Canadian direct investment in Ireland is $7 billion. Irish direct investment in Canada is $560 million.

Travel Advisory: Medical care can be expensive. Economy is dominated by foreign multinationals attracted by tax breaks.

Business Etiquette: Ireland is very similar to North America; less formal than many EU countries; promptness in business dealings is important.

Figure 6.23 Dublin, Ireland's capital city, has proven to be an attractive location to many high-tech companies.

Country Link

For trade and travel information about Ireland, follow the links at www.internationalbusiness.nelson.com.

Chapter Challenges

Knowledge/Understanding

1. Match each of the following terms to the correct definition or description below:

   (a) creativity

   (b) vision

   (c) mission statement

   (d) entrepreneur

   (e) business leads

   (f) request for proposal

   (g) deliverables

   (h) chief executive officer

   (i) trend

   (j) growth markets

   (i) a person who organizes, manages, and assumes the risk of starting and running a business

   (ii) outlines the cost and time guidelines for the work to be done or the service to be provided

   (iii) prospects for business

   (iv) the most senior manager in a company

   (v) an organization's sense of the future and its understanding of how to get there

   (vi) solutions, services, or end-products developed to respond to requests for proposals

   (vii) the use of imagination and technical know-how to solve a problem

   (viii) explains where a company is going

   (ix) usually shows the direction of the market and where people spend their time and money

   (x) a current or expected general direction of the marketplace

2. Explain how a company can foster global entrepreneurship and help employees develop a global mindset.

3. List and explain three characteristics of an innovative international company.

4. What are four causes of hyper-competition?

Thinking/Inquiry

1. Working with a partner, create a chart in which you list and explain at least six international trends that affect the way people do business today. Then, for each trend, suggest one way that small Canadian businesses or entrepreneurs might take advantage of that trend to develop a product or service that could be sold internationally. Be sure to explain the rationale for each of your decisions.

2. While some multinational companies have more spending power than entire counties, *Global Trends 2015*, a document sponsored by the U.S. government, predicts a widening gap between rich and poor. How do you think it is possible for both things to happen at the same time? Propose an idea that might address part of the problem.

Communication

1. Research local or international newspaper stories (using print and online resources) to find current stories about a Canadian who has found an international business opportunity and has used that opportunity to either create or to expand his or her business. Prepare either an oral or a multimedia presentation in which you explain

   a) the consumer problem that was solved by the Canadian's action

   b) the ways that the person took advantage of the opportunity that existed in the problem

   c) any business partners that were involved in the venture

   d) the personal initiative and innovation that the story demonstrates

2. Imagine that you have an idea for a product that you believe would have genuine international market potential. Identify the four steps that you could use as you explore producing your product. Use those steps for further investigation of your product. Then review the international trends section of this chapter. Which of those trends might help you position your product for the international market? After you have collected all of your data and done your analysis of your

product and the market situation, plan, draft, and revise a report on the feasibility of following up this business opportunity.

3. **Global Debate**

   As a class debate, this statement: Globalization will provide opportunities for Canadians.

Application

1. As you learned in the Canada's Trading Partners feature in this chapter, Ireland has capitalized on the global trend toward increasingly sophisticated computer technologies. Ireland has finally become an importer rather than an exporter of people. Research the current state of technology companies and employment in Ireland. Do you see any risks associated with the country's focus on attracting branch plants of multinational computer companies? Write an editorial in which you argue for or against expanding the computer industries in Ireland.

2. Queen's University professor Tom Courchene, who is also a senior scholar at the Institute for Research on Public Policy, predicts that by 2030 the world will have only two major currencies—the euro and the U.S. dollar, with one or the other being used by most regions of the world. Conduct a class or team "think tank" for 15–20 minutes to brainstorm your predictions of what the world will be like in 2030. Try to think about how your daily life might change—with a focus on an aspect such as work, money, sports, entertainment, technology, or travel. Try to generate as many ideas or predictions as you can in the time period.

3. Innovations in the News – Many new discoveries, innovations, product launches, and trends from around the world are pictured and described in newspapers or magazines. Searching through a print media publication, your job is to find five innovations that will affect the way we live in the near future. Use a chart to organize your data.

International Business Portfolio

Pursuing Opportunities and Recognizing Trends

The focus in this chapter is **pursuing opportunities** and **recognizing trends**. Opportunities and trends are linked: trends often point or lead to opportunities. In this activity, you will examine the methods by which Canadian businesses choose to operate internationally, and identify the trends that provide these opportunities.

Activities

1. Define the following methods for getting involved in international business:
   - direct exporting
   - management consulting
   - licensing
   - franchising
   - joint venture
   - foreign direct investment
   - wholly owned subsidiary
   - economic development activities (such as those undertaken by the Canadian Economic Development Corporation)

   As your research progresses, you should be able to find examples of Canadian businesses operating in your IBP country using many of the above methods.

2. Give examples of major trends listed in the textbook or elsewhere that support any of the above opportunities in your IBP country. Do any of the trends negate any of the above opportunities? (For example, economic development activities are often directed at developing nations rather than developed nations.)

Chapter 7

Avoiding and Managing Common Mistakes and Problems

This chapter highlights the major types of difficulties that can arise in international business. Many businesses experience setbacks or failure when they attempt to move into international markets. Lack of success is often caused by errors in pricing, distribution, market analysis, or packaging, but sometimes results from an insufficient understanding of the infrastructure and culture of the trading nation. Examples of the most notable problems illustrate how knowledge, research, planning, preparation, and consultants can help companies avoid the most serious pitfalls.

Chapter Topics

➤ 7.1 – Common Pitfalls 216

➤ 7.2 – Problems with Standards 224

➤ 7.3 – Realistic Marketing 228

➤ 7.4 – Infrastructure and Services 235

➤ *Canada's Trading Partners: Focus on* China 240

➤ Chapter Challenges 242

Prior Knowledge

- Have you ever shopped in the United States? If so, what did you buy? Why did you purchase the item in the United States rather than in Canada?
- What are some of the difficulties or unexpected costs you might experience if you purchase from foreign TV or Internet sources?
- Have you ever had problems with warranties, instruction manuals, or service agreements when you purchased an imported product? Why might problems arise in these areas?

Inquiries/Expectations

- What are the most common mistakes that companies make when they enter foreign markets?
- What kinds of problems have some companies experienced when they exported or imported goods and services?
- Why have some products imported into Canada not sold well?

Important Terms

advising bank
boycott
business-to-business
   relationships (B2B)
buy forward
containerization
hard currency

infrastructure
issuing bank
landed cost
letter of credit
soft currency
tariffs

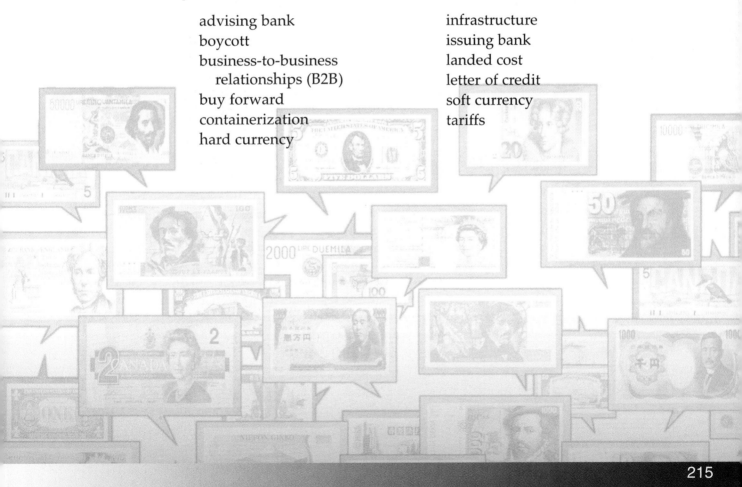

7.1 Common Pitfalls

The errors that many businesses make when they attempt to trade internationally can be grouped into four main categories, each of which will be treated in depth in this chapter.

- **Costing:** Correctly calculating the full landed cost of a product is essential for any business. The **landed cost** is the cost of a product after all transportation, handling, currency exchange rates, and import charges have been added. A distributor or wholesaler must figure out this cost when determining a suggested local retail price for either imports or exports. A manufacturer requires the full landed cost of supplies, parts, and machinery when developing a budget, proposal, or cost analysis.

- **Standards:** Many nations have standards for manufacturing, sizing, labelling, and packaging that are different from Canadian standards. Failure to recognize the differences and adapt to them can cause costly errors. Other countries may also have different regulations for a variety of services and products, or for the manner in which they are supplied.

- **Marketing:** Exporting companies sometimes fail to research and, therefore, do not understand their target foreign market, its distribution channels, its types of consumer marketing, the time it requires to arrange deals and introduce products, and its local sensitivities and preferences.

- **Infrastructure:** Companies often do not consider the problems that may arise as a result of the infrastructure of the target country. Internal transportation, human and material resources, communication systems, health and safety, bureaucracy—and, in some cases, corruption and bribery in businesses or government—all can be potential obstacles to international business.

Figure 7.1 Costing, standards, marketing, and infrastructure all influence how a product is exported.

Potential Costing Errors

Let's look at a typical international trade scenario. A Canadian purchasing agent is acting on behalf of a Canadian retail chain that wants a new and interesting line of preserves for its upscale customers. The agent visits a trade show in France to look for suitable European suppliers. One booth at the show displays a dozen different jams, jellies, and compotes that are not available in Canada. All look delicious and are beautifully packaged. The buyer knows that these products would be perfect for the client. The price of each jar of jam is marked at 1.50 EUR.

To make a profit, a retailer must sell a product at a standard markup, which is usually twice the product's actual cost.

The opportunities for error in determining this actual cost are considerable. Besides the price of the product, which is 1.50 EUR for the jam, the buyer must take into consideration tariffs and duties, brokerage fees, transportation costs, insurance costs for goods in transit, currency exchange rates, currency fluctuations, and any hidden costs, as well as arrangements to finance the order. A costing error can negate any advantage provided by the foreign trade.

Figure 7.2 A display of jams and other specialties from Provence in the south of France. Provençal foods, perfumes, and other specialties are enjoyed around the world.

Exchange Rates and Currency Strategies

The first step in pricing a product is to convert its cost from its own currency into the present equivalent in Canadian dollars. If the euro is worth $1.39 in Canadian currency, then the wholesale price of each jar of jam in Canada is $2.09 ($1.39 CAD x 1.50 EUR).

Like the Canadian dollar, the euro is considered a **hard currency**, which means that it is widely accepted on the foreign currency exchange market and can easily be converted to another currency by most banks. Many countries—China, Russia, or Ukraine, for example—have a **soft currency**. Soft currencies are those that fluctuate in value and are not considered stable. As a result, they are not easily converted into Canadian dollars.

Currency is rated from AAA (triple-A, the highest rating, for a particularly hard currency) down to D (indicates a very soft currency that is difficult to exchange). Between the highest rating and the lowest are AA, A, BBB, BB, B, and C. A currency's rating is a measure of the degree of confidence that world markets have in its country's political and economic stability. Hard currencies are those rated at BBB and above. Financial research companies such as Moody's and Standard and Poor's make these ratings and publish them to their subscribers for a fee. Canada's rating has recently been re-established in the triple-A category.

TRADE TALK

The Currency Exchange Market

The major currency exchange dealing centres today are London, New York, Tokyo, Zurich, Frankfurt, Hong Kong, and Singapore, followed by Paris and Sydney.

In terms of trading volume, the currency exchange market is the world's largest market, with daily trading volumes in excess of $1.5 trillion USD. This makes it impossible for individuals or companies to affect the exchange rates. Even central banks and governments find it increasingly difficult to affect the exchange rates of the most liquid currencies, such as the U.S. dollar, Japanese yen, euro, Swiss franc, Canadian dollar, or Australian dollar.

The currency exchange market is a true 24-hour market, five days a week. There are dealers in every major time zone. Trading begins Monday morning in Sydney (3 P.M. EST Sunday) and then moves around the world through the various trading centres until closing Friday evening at 4.30 P.M. EST in New York.

Businesses usually deal only in hard currencies; that is, they will accept only hard currency as payment. If a country has restrictions on the amount of foreign currency that its people can own or purchase, then restricting business to hard currency limits the amount of trade that can take place. Canadian firms that conduct business in China are reluctant to accept the yuan renminbi, the Chinese currency, as it is very "soft"; they prefer, even insist on, payment in U.S. dollars. Yet American dollars are very difficult for Chinese businesses to obtain, because the Chinese government has strict quotas for the amount of foreign exchange that each business may possess.

This section explains some of the complexities in paying for imports into Canada. A foreign company paying for exports from Canada experiences some of the same issues, plus its own country's regulations.

Figure 7.3 Moscow residents line up to exchange soft currency for hard currency so that they can purchase foreign products.

Protection against Currency Fluctuations

To secure the price of a product, businesses often **buy forward**. When a business buys forward, it purchases the foreign currency required for an order at the time the order is placed. This enables the company to avoid potential fluctuations in exchange rates. Another less-popular method is to fix an agreed exchange rate in the purchase agreement; then either the seller or the purchaser can gain or lose on currency exchange.

Let's return to the purchasing agent at the trade fair who decides to place a trial order for 12 assorted cases of jam, with 24 jars in a case. If each jar costs 1.50 EUR, the order will total 432.00 EUR. At an exchange rate $1.39 CAD for each euro, the Canadian dollar equivalent is $600.48 for the order or $2.085 CAD per jar. If, after the order is placed, the exchange rate becomes $1.50 CAD for each euro, the cost of the order will increase to $648.00. Each jar will now cost $2.25 CAD.

To minimize the effect of currency fluctuation and guarantee the cost of the product, the Canadian importing company can buy euros at the $1.39 CAD exchange rate when the jam order is placed. Then, if the exchange value of the euro increases, the price of the order will not be affected, the cost of the jam for the Canadian market will not change, and the purchaser will come out ahead. If, on the other hand, the euro decreases in value, the purchaser will not obtain any savings.

The seller makes the same revenue, regardless, because the price is fixed in its currency, and it does not have to concern itself with currency exchange rates.

Importers, however, are in business to sell products for a profit, not to speculate in currency. With good cost management, an importer accurately calculates the final Canadian dollar purchase price, which will enable it to make competitive pricing decisions for the Canadian market.

Letters of Credit

The French jam manufacturer will want to be sure that it will be paid when the transaction is completed. Banks play a crucial role at this stage. A bank can issue a **letter of credit** that assures the French company that the Canadian business has enough money on deposit in a French bank to complete the payment.

TRADE TALK

Letters of credit have been in use for more than 400 years. They were first instituted because of the difficulty in securing payment for goods shipped to the "new world." They help to simplify financial dealings between an importer's home bank (the issuing bank) and an exporter's bank (the advising bank).

Letters of credit are an important method of reducing risk in international business. They allow an importer (buyer) to provide secure terms to an exporter (seller). After the jam deal has been made, for example, and all costs have been calculated, the importer applies to its bank, the **issuing bank**, for a letter of credit in the full amount of the invoice. The importer must assign business assets as collateral for the letter; cash on deposit is not used for this purpose. The assets are usually stocks, bonds, or other financial assets that can be assigned to the issuing bank without tying up a business's cash.

If the issuing bank approves the buyer's credit, it sends the letter of credit ("Confirmation of funds available") to the exporter's bank, the **advising bank**, which then informs the seller that the letter of credit has arrived. As soon as the jam manufacturer is advised of the letter of credit, it can process the order and ship the jam to Canada. The advising bank monitors the shipment, and when the Canadian buyer receives it, the advising bank pays the jam manufacturer. The issuing bank then pays the advising bank and collects from the buyer. After the buyer has paid, the issuing bank provides the documentation that the buyer requires to collect the jam and complete the transaction.

If the country of one of the parties in the transaction has a poorly developed banking system, it may be very difficult or impossible to arrange a letter of credit, or it may not be useful to obtain one. Without a letter of credit, a great deal of trust would be required to complete the jam transaction. The exporting business might ask for cash before shipping but then take the money and never ship the product. Or, if terms are arranged so that the importing company could send payment after the goods are received, the importing company might keep the product and not pay for it. Few businesses are willing to trust one another to this extent. Most international businesses will trade only with foreign countries that have a solid banking system that is able to work with letters of credit.

Tariffs and Duties

Very good jams are available in Canada from companies such as E.D. Smith & Sons Ltd., a family-owned Canadian company that has been selling jams since 1882. The import of foreign jams could affect the domestic sales of E.D. Smith & Sons. To protect Canadian businesses, the government of Canada levies taxes on imports that compete with comparable Canadian-made goods. These taxes are called tariffs or duties. **Tariffs** increase the price of an imported product, which enables existing Canadian product to be priced more competitively and, therefore, be more profitable. Any importer that is unaware of applicable tariffs may find that unexpected extra costs make the imported product too expensive to compete with Canadian products.

Tariff rates depend on product being imported and on Canada's relationship with the source country. Jam from France enters Canada under a Most-Favoured-Nation (MFN) tariff. According to the Canada Customs and Revenue Agency, the tariff rate on jam from France in 2002 is 8.5 percent. If each jar of imported jam cost the buyer $2.25, the duty on each jar would be 19 cents and the landed cost of each jar of jam would rise to $2.44.

The World Trade Organization (WTO) facilitates discussions among countries regarding the setting of import tariff rates for each product. There is always much discussion and negotiation about these, and each member country must agree. Countries can negotiate lower tariff rates with each other if they have historic ties or are interested in regular trade with each other. Where free trade exists, as in the case of the North American Free Trade Agreement (NAFTA) among Canada, the United States, and Mexico, tariffs between nations are removed. (Tariffs on qualifying goods traded between Canada and the United States became duty-free on January 1, 1998; however, certain goods—softwood lumber, for example—were not included, and negotiations continued on these long after NAFTA was proclaimed.)

Figure 7.4 Canada, the United States, and Mexico are all member countries of the North American Free Trade Agreement (NAFTA).

Transportation

Charges for transporting goods are affected by five factors:

1. the agent and shipping company or freight forwarder
2. the shipment method
3. the weight of the goods
4. the size or volume of the goods
5. the distance to their final destination

Shipping companies and freight forwarders are very competitive. Many specialize in particular destinations and offer attractive rates for shipments to those destinations. Some offer special rates for large shipments, while others specialize in smaller, more delicate shipments or shipments that have special requirements, such as refrigeration. Many small and medium-sized businesses use a shipping agent that is knowledgeable about the local transportation companies and their rates and can help the exporter or importer select the most appropriate firm. An agent's commission is based on the values of the goods shipped.

The cost of shipping goods is one of the largest components of the landed cost. Air freight is far more expensive than ocean or land transport. Obviously, goods shipped from overseas countries must travel either by air or by water during a portion of the journey, and importers must weigh cost against speed. The faster the shipping method, the more expensive it is. To take advantage of cheaper, but slower, ocean freight, many companies order goods well in advance of when they actually need them. Goods that are to be shipped by air, sea, or rail are first trucked from the factory to an airport, port, or rail terminal. Then, they are picked up by truck at the arrival point for delivery to their ultimate destination.

Estimated Transportation Costs for Jam from Paris to Toronto

Quantity of Cases (24 jars/case)	Method	Weight	Volume	Cost	Cost/Jar
12	Air	96 kg	4.8 m³	$96	$0.33
12	Ocean	96 kg	4.8 m³	$48	$0.16
80	Shared Container	640 kg	32 m³	$160	$0.08

Figure 7.5 Eighty cases of jam would not fill a container, so the space must be shared with another exporter.

THINK ABOUT IT

Officials in many countries are considering reversing the traditional customs practices by examining containers in the country of origin before they are sealed. What implications could such a change have for international trade?

Containerization is the stowage of freight in sealed, reusable containers of uniform size and shape. It substantially lowers the cost of shipping. Logistics experts can consolidate multiple small shipments in a container so that smaller shippers can obtain similar security and cost advantages as larger shippers.

Sizes and Capacities of Two Standard Containers

Type	Length (m)	Width (m)	Height (m)	Volume (cu. m)
20′ Dry Cargo	5.89	2.35	2.38	33
40′ Dry Cargo	12.00	2.34	2.28	67

Figure 7.6 Containers are a standard size, which makes handling them easier and less expensive.

The use of standard-sized containers and equipment reduces the handling of cargo pieces and provides protection for the shipment. Because containers are locked when they are filled and are usually not opened again until they arrive at their final destination, cargo theft and damage are also minimized. Container shipments are, therefore, more efficient, faster, and much more economical. See Chapter 12 for more information on international transportation of goods.

Figure 7.7 Container ships such as this heavily laden one in Halifax Harbour expedite international shipments in the most cost-effective way.

Hidden Costs

Failure to anticipate the so-called hidden costs can be the largest costing error in importing goods. Importers may have to travel to find the right merchandise and make shipment arrangements, and travel has its costs. Letters of credit and currency conversion come at a price, and insurance against loss or damage may be expensive. Businesses are sometimes taken by surprise by the costs of translation services, phone charges, interest charges, labelling costs (to conform to Canada's bilingual and metric labelling requirements, for example), local taxes, and government charges. Importers need to estimate the hidden costs and add them to the expected charges for a shipment to calculate the total landed cost per item or unit. Only then can they arrive at an accurate price for the product in the Canadian market.

TRADE TALK

The more a shipment weighs and the greater its volume, the more it costs to ship. A shipment of pillows that weighs 100 kg will cost more to ship than an order of jam that weighs the same amount, as the pillows take up more space. Also, the farther a shipment travels, the more it costs to ship.

E.D. Smith & Sons, Inc.

Figure 7.8 Pie fillings are one of many E.D. Smith products.

Ernest D'Israeli Smith started the E.D. Smith & Sons, Inc. business in 1882 as a fruit production firm. The company became the first commercial manufacturer of jams in Canada. Prior to this, jams on most Canadian tables had been either homemade or made in England and imported to Canada. They were considered luxury items, because import costs, especially transportation costs, were very high. E.D. Smith made an affordable and high-quality jam, and its business grew rapidly.

Soon, the E.D. Smith brand name was seen on other products such as pie fillings, ketchup, sauces, toppings, and syrups. The firm purchased products from all over the world to help expand its product line: sugar, fruits, berries, and other ingredients not grown in Canada or not grown in sufficient quantity to meet manufacturing needs. The company also expanded its sales throughout North America, and received many honours, including being named one of "Canada's Top 50 Best-Managed Private Companies" in 1999.

In 1992, E.D. Smith opened a factory in Byhalia, Mississippi. Loblaws had been urging E.D. Smith and its other top Canadian suppliers—those making its popular President's Choice brand products—to set up in the United States after it was unable to find satisfactory suppliers there. Wal-Mart was seeking new U.S.-based suppliers as well. E.D. Smith was a privately held company, with Llewellyn Smith as both the president and the fourth generation of Smiths in a management role. Difficulties arose, however, within the first three years because the head office in Canada and the U.S. subsidiary did not have the same dedication and work culture. The executives at E.D. Smith admitted that they had not researched the area carefully enough before deciding to build their factory there, and in 1996 it became clear that they would have to close the Mississippi plant.

E.D. Smith then began concentrating instead on its exports and on transportation management. The firm was one of the founding members of a transportation consortium called Cross Canada Logistics Inc. (CCL), put together in 1995 by 12 members of the food industry in Canada. Cross Canada Logistics pools the purchasing power of 12 major food companies to negotiate greatly reduced transportation costs, and has begun to explore new opportunities, such as co-shipping products. Co-shipping enables manufacturers to consolidate their loads, thereby allowing the participants to benefit from truckload rates (as opposed to the higher "less than truckload rate") without a third-party business managing this service. CCL's members are rethinking the way they conduct business in the field of logistics and transportation, and are actually considering co-shipping with competitive companies that may be shipping to the same customers.

After having remained a family-owned business for over a century, E.D. Smith was sold in January 2002 to a Toronto merchant bank, the Imperial Capital Corporation.

• •

1. What mistakes does E.D. Smith appear to have made in its expansion into the United States?

2. In your opinion, what ingredients would E.D. Smith need to import into Canada? Select one of these ingredients and determine its foreign source. Outline any difficulties E.D. Smith may encounter in importing this item.

3. As the new owner of E.D. Smith, explain how you might plan to expand the company's international markets.

ICE Activities for 7.1

Ideas	Connections	Extensions
1. (a) Identify the common costing errors that some businesses make going into international markets.	(b) Profile a shipping company or freight forwarder. Be sure to outline all the services that it provides.	(c) Select a hidden cost discussed in this chapter. Report on the effects of that hidden cost for a business importing to Canada.
2. (a) How can currency conversion affect costs?	(b) Make a list of the current Canadian exchange rates of five foreign currencies. What were their exchange rates a year ago? Compare your lists with those of others in the class.	(c) Using the list you prepared, decide whether you should have "bought forward" in the currencies from the countries you chose, if you had ordered products from them last year.
3. (a) What are some ways of managing costs when exporting products to another country?	(b) Choose one imported product. Find out the tariff rate charged on its importation into Canada. Estimate the per-item (per-unit) dollar cost to you as a result of this tariff. Report your findings to other class members.	(c) Do you think you could sell the French jam in Canada and make a profit? Explain your answer.

7.2 Problems with Standards

Another common error that businesses make when they enter foreign markets is to assume that all countries use the same standards. Whether it is production standards, service standards, quality standards, or ethical standards, many countries have entirely different codes and principles from those in Canada. A mistake in this area can be very inconvenient and costly. When imported or exported products do not meet consumer expectations, customers may reject them, and the importer or exporter will be unsuccessful. In practice, therefore, businesses are well advised to examine and meet standards long before a product reaches its market.

When a country's market is large enough, importers can manage differences in standards by dealing with reputable international firms that have adapted—or are able to adapt—their factories to make products to local standards. Appliances, clothing, automobiles, and many other products are manufactured for specific markets. British clothing manufacturers, for example, produce apparel for North American markets using the North American size chart and for their domestic market using the British size chart. To ensure that imported manufactured goods are well received in the market, importers must have trained technical staff and service centres available to provide parts and make repairs to damaged products and to honour warranties and guarantees.

Production Standards

An episode from the life of a teenaged traveller will give an example of the consequences of variation in international standards. When Emily visited the United Kingdom last summer, she was delighted to find a videotape of *Gregory's Girl*, a British film that she really liked. However, when she tried to play the tape after she got home, she discovered that British videotapes will not play on Canadian VCRs. NTSC (National Television System Committee) is the broadcast standard used in the United States, Canada, Mexico, and Japan. PAL (Phase Alternating Line) is the broadcast standard for Australia, the United Kingdom, much of Europe, Singapore, and Hong Kong. A third set of standards, the SECAM (Système Électronique Couleur Avec Mémoire) format, is used in France, Greece, the Middle East, and most of Eastern Europe. Any importer or exporter of videotapes, DVDs, VCRs, television sets, DVD players, or other television-related entertainment systems needs to be aware of the different standards for each country.

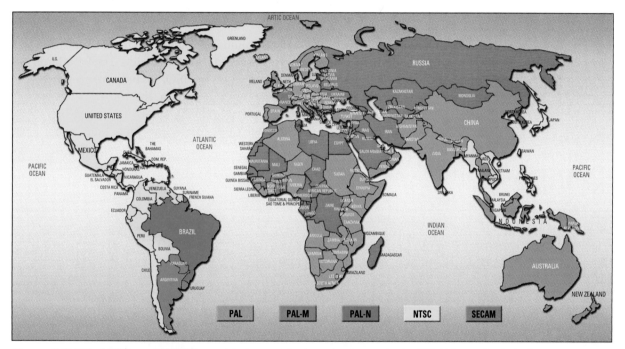

Figure 7.9 PAL, NTSC, and SECAM are the three major broadcast standards. PAL-N is used only in Argentina, Uruguay, and Paraguay. PAL-M is used only in Brazil.

Countries also have a variety of electrical standards. In some cases, the difference means that Canadian electrical appliances will not work in those countries. For example, the household standard in Canada is a 120-volt electrical current. Denmark uses 220 volts, Great Britain 230 volts, and Hawaii 110 volts. Besides the different voltages, countries have a number of different plug configurations. Even though an appliance imported into Canada from Guatemala, for example, has the same voltage (120) as the Canadian standard, its plug will not fit into standard Canadian receptacles. For travelling North Americans, there are adapter plugs for use with our standard electrical appliances in other countries.

Size standards for clothing are another issue in the world of import and export. Size-10 jeans, size-8 shoes, and size-15 shirts mean something to Canadian consumers. However, Canadian size-10 jeans are size 77 in Korea. A size-8 woman's shoe is a size 55 in Japan, and a size-15 man's shirt is a size-38 in most European countries. Hats, socks, and jackets also are sized differently in many countries. The cut of a piece of clothing may also be different. Even though a garment manufactured elsewhere may technically be the same size as a Canadian garment, the tailoring standard in the other nation may require a much tighter fit around the hips or a fuller cut in the back.

Some Comparative Women's Clothing Sizes

Country	Size						
Japan	9	11	13	15	17	19	21
United States	10	12	14	16	18	20	22
England	32	34	36	38	40	42	44

Figure 7.10 Clothing and shoes have different size standards in different countries.

As you learned in Chapter 3, the International Organization for Standardization (ISO) was formed to help establish technical standards worldwide. The Standards Council of Canada is Canada's representative on the ISO. By helping member countries agree to standards for specifications and criteria, the ISO facilitates the exchange of goods and ideas around the world. Toy safety, water quality, window glass, and insulation are just a few of the many products that have been standardized.

TRADE TALK

According to the ISO, standards are "documented agreements containing technical specifications or other precise criteria to be used consistently as rules, guidelines, or definitions of characteristics, to ensure that materials, products, processes and services are fit for their purpose.

"For example, the format of the credit cards, phone cards, and "smart" cards that have become commonplace is derived from an ISO International Standard. Adhering to the standard, which defines such features as an optimal thickness (0.76 mm), means that the cards can be used worldwide.

"International Standards thus contribute to making life simpler, and to increasing the reliability and effectiveness of the goods and services we use."

Figure 7.11 The ISO was responsible for setting a standard thickness for bank cards, making it possible for travellers to access their accounts in many different countries.

Ethical Standards

Some companies try to save money and cut corners by importing from or investing in foreign factories whose ethical standards are different from Canadian standards. Such supplier relationships or direct investments can be risky to a company's reputation. Many Canadians, for example, prefer not to deal with companies that they believe buy from or invest in foreign businesses that use child labour, have inadequate health and safety standards for their workers, have a reputation for being environmentally destructive, or are located in countries with governments perceived as corrupt. Some Canadians avoid trading with companies that use animals in product-testing labs or businesses that provide military equipment to other nations. It is important to keep in mind that some other countries have different values and have different ethical standards. For example, there are countries where it is common to see workers on a construction site without safety shoes, helmets, or harnesses, and where children are expected to contribute to family labour.

Although many companies have tried to lower their costs by importing from countries with lower ethical standards or by setting up manufacturing operations in these countries, the media and ethical consumers groups are on the lookout for them and will expose them to the public. Investigative television programs such as *Fifth Estate*, *W5*, and *60 Minutes* feature this type of story frequently, and the **boycotts** (organized campaigns to refuse purchasing a company's or a country's products) that sometimes result can affect even multinational corporations. Consumers are able to influence the ethical practices of the corporate world.

The topics of business ethics and corporate responsibility are covered in greater depth in Chapter 10.

Figure 7.12 A cosmetic boutique guarantees its customers cruelty-free products.

ICE Activities for 7.2

Ideas	Connections	Extensions
1. (a) Describe briefly the three main types of standards that may be different in other countries from Canadian standards.	(b) Research the different standards governing broadcast, electrical products, and clothing sizes in countries outside North America. Compare your list with those of others in your class.	(c) How could the different standards that you learned about in 1. (b) be a challenge for Canadian exporters?
2. (a) Describe the rationale for using ISO production standards.	(b) Select one ISO area of standardization and describe it in detail.	(c) Choose one product or service that you think should be standardized internationally, and research the standards that exist for it. If standards do not exist, suggest standards that would improve the chances for its international use.
3. (a) What may happen if a Canadian company does business with an international company with less rigorous ethical standards?	(b) Collect news articles (a series, if possible) that describe an ethical problem faced by a specific company. How has this ethical problem affected this company's sales?	(c) Discuss, and support with examples, your views on whether Canadian businesses have high ethical standards.

7.3 Realistic Marketing

There are 1.3 billion people in China. If only one percent of that number were consumers of your company's toaster or tracksuit, and if each person bought one of the items you were selling, your business would sell (theoretically) 10 million toasters or 10 million tracksuits. The market appears so vast that many businesses have attempted to sell toasters and tracksuits and countless other products to the Chinese. Most have not succeeded, however, because they have made errors in marketing.

Marketing failures occur primarily because of three interrelated types of errors:

- miscalculation of the composition, size, and distribution channels of the target market
- lack of research in branding, packaging, and timing of product introduction
- misunderstanding of the culture, customs, and appropriate advertising and promotion among potential consumers

For example, a company trying to sell toasters in China is not likely to have much success, as China's staple of choice is rice, not bread. Another type of cultural misunderstanding may occur if a company tries to market its product using its traditional brand name, not realizing that the name sounds or looks like a word that is culturally offensive and in fact will alienate the target market. A good example is the popular Japanese beverage called Pocari Sweat, which is similar to Gatorade in its appeal. Just as the Japanese might avoid Gatorade, perhaps thinking that it might have something to do with alligators, Canadians would likely not be attracted to a beverage with "sweat" in the name. A lot of research and preparation is needed to avoid the problem of misreading the target market, the brand, and the culture. Exxon, the giant petroleum company, did extensive testing and surveys to select a name that had no negative connotations in other countries.

Figure 7.13 Gatorade was named after a Florida football team, the Gators. The drink was developed to keep the players properly hydrated in the sometimes intense Florida heat.

Companies with consumer products that were not successful in China looked at its population of 1.3 billion people and saw only huge potential for their products, not realizing that consumer purchasing power and business practices in China make doing business there very different from doing business in Canada. According to a study by analyst A.T. Kearney (*New Yorker*, July 16, 2001), as of 1999, only 40 percent of the multinationals doing business in China were making a profit there. Although many of these companies may have been in the initial stages of establishing their presence in China and still investing in building up relationships and customer loyalty, their lack of profit may have been attributable to misjudging their markets. For the most part, the 1.3 billion Chinese do not have hard currency to spend on the consumer products that other nations wish to sell them. The real consumer population in China—the population of consumers with purchasing power—is approximately the same size as that of the United States, 275 million people.

Many Canadian business success stories come from **business-to-business relationships (B2B)**. A Canadian company will set up a joint venture with a Chinese firm to manufacture products in China (14 joint ventures, worth over $100 million, exist with Canadian companies in China's Guizhou province alone). These goods are then distributed all over the world from the Chinese plant. The Chinese and Canadian partners share the costs and the profit. Other B2B transactions involve sales of Canadian raw material and processed goods to Chinese manufacturers who convert the Canadian products into finished goods in China and sell them on world markets. For example, the Chinese DVD player, Apex, may contain some Canadian plastic. As the Chinese manufacturing base is growing, Canadian suppliers have an excellent B2B opportunity.

TRADE TIPS

To Chinese people, *quanxi* are webs of ongoing obligation and loyalty. Participants are expected to perform favours upon request as a sign of loyalty and good faith.

TRADE TALK

Nortel's Success in China

Nortel Networks serves communication service providers, carriers, small and medium-sized businesses, and large corporations in more than 150 countries and territories around the world.

A report prepared for the federal Department of Foreign Affairs and International Trade (DFAIT) in 1995 stated that Nortel was then very successful in China, with more than 50 percent of the market share for telephone switching systems. Nortel is still experiencing success in China, winning recent contracts for wireless infrastructure for high-speed Internet services in 17 of China's 31 provinces and serving more than 11.6 million subscribers. In Canada and elsewhere in the world, however, Nortel has cut jobs and experienced record losses.

Nortel's success in China can be attributed mainly to the fact that it researched and is familiar with the Chinese market and took the time to establish important relationships first.

The potential offered by China's large market has not escaped the Japanese, the Americans, the Finns, and numerous other foreign competitors. According to a study by Janet X. Ai and Dr. Neil Abramson called "Readjusting the Focus of Doing Business in China," other foreign businesses are better prepared than most Canadian companies to do business in China. This fact has also not escaped the notice of Chinese businesses, which are certainly in a better position to sell to their own people. Nortel Networks is one company that has managed to overcome the bureaucracy, the infrastructure, and the cultural differences between Canada and China to build a profitable relationship with the Chinese through patience, experience, and understanding. Businesses that are looking for a quick profit in this export market may do better to consider markets other than China. International marketing is discussed in more detail in Chapter 11.

Size and Composition of the Market

Perhaps the most significant error a company can make when thinking about international markets is to overestimate consumer demand. Businesses have to answer two questions before they import or export a product. The first question is, "Will anyone buy it?" If the answer to that question is "Yes," the next question should be, "Is anyone else already selling a similar product?" A market of 500 million people is a significant market only if it is composed of people who actually need or want your product or service or who may reasonably be persuaded to want or need it through marketing efforts. Far too often, the manufacturer of a successful North American product will assume that the product will be successful elsewhere without doing the research required to verify the market.

To properly research a product in a foreign market, it is a good idea for businesses to hire marketing research companies that are familiar with the market composition of the target country. Good local marketing research done upfront can help manufacturers or distributors avoid many costly errors. Any Canadian who has had a cup of coffee in a British restaurant, for example, might think that Tim Hortons would do very well in Great Britain. However, the British still prefer tea, and unless a potential Tim Hortons franchisee conducted comprehensive market research that included taste tests and preference surveys in the target community, he or she might spend a lot of time, effort, and money on a business that had relatively little chance of success.

TRADE TALK

In Britain, tea accounts for around 43 percent of all beverage consumption. Nearly 80 percent of the country's population drink tea daily in the home. Britons drink twice as much tea as coffee. What is the history of that preference?

The British trading presence in India and Ceylon (now Sri Lanka) through the East India Company in the 18th and 19th centuries certainly provided a source for the beverage for Britain, whereas North American trade was dominated by the Dutch West Indian Company, which brought coffee to the United States (and from there to Canada).

The "Boston Tea Party," when anti-British rebels threw a shipment of tea into Boston harbour, is remembered as one of the first American acts of opposition to British rule and taxation that led to the American Revolution in 1776.

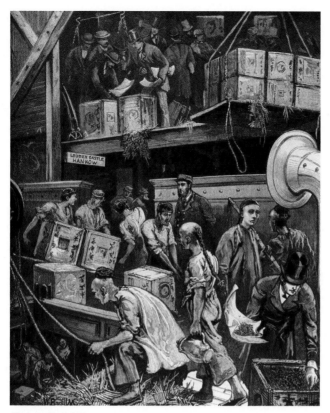

Figure 7.14 British traders inspecting tea at the port of London, 1877.

Figure 7.15 Prince Charles delights in a cup of tea in Ottawa, 2001. Are tea or coffee sales more successful in Canada?

The preferences of foreign markets are often misunderstood. For example, there are two million female teens in France. Canadian clothing manufacturers might expect that French girls would love their casual clothing, such as sweatshirts or T-shirts, but French teenagers prefer very different styles from those worn by Canadian teenagers. Without market research, Canadian manufacturers would be attempting to sell products that too few consumers want to buy.

John Gruetzner

International Business Consultant for Asia

Intercedent

It is not uncommon for John Gruetzner to fly to a different country several times a week. He has a home in Toronto but spends two-thirds of his time in Asia.

Gruetzner is the executive vice-president and chief operating officer of Intercedent Limited, a leading Canadian business and marketing development organization with offices in Toronto, Beijing, and Singapore. Founded in 1988 in Toronto, Intercedent Limited is the parent company of the Intercedent Group, a consulting company that advises clients in worldwide markets in the areas of strategic planning, trade management, market research, law, and investment banking.

In his role as international business consultant, Gruetzner proposes business development strategies for high technology companies, and gives advice on financial services and telecommunications to clients who are doing business in Asia or exploring the possibility of doing so. He also helps his clients analyze and research markets and choose the most advantageous locations and countries for their businesses. If companies need environment assessments, an evaluation of their competitors, or an analysis of distribution channels, they can use his consulting services. Gruetzner is also a business contributor to a number of publications.

While Gruetzner was working on his BA in Political Science at the University of Toronto, he attended the University of Nankai in the People's Republic of China. He has now lived and worked in China for close to 20 years. Before joining Intercedent, he was the manager of the Canada Trade Council in Beijing and worked in feature film production.

What are the major requirements for a career in international consulting? Gruetzner's answer: knowledge of international business practices, an expertise in one or more foreign cultures, a fluency in a variety of foreign languages, and a willingness to travel anywhere.

Gruetzner says that being outside Canada so often gives him a unique perspective on this country and helps him appreciate what a special place we live in. "We have created a country that is unique. We should not squander this. We should care about this country and not only take from it, but contribute to it as well. Living a portion of your life in another country is a privilege! No matter what business you are in or profession you have chosen, the benefit of seeing how a person in another country runs a business, a restaurant, or a society will only make you more aware that you are a member of a global society. But there are days on the road when you would rather just be by a lake in northern Ontario, waiting for the sun to go down."

1. In what ways can a business consultant help a company avoid common pitfalls in conducting international business?

2. In your opinion, how would living outside Canada provide a unique perspective on Canada?

Branding, Packaging, and Labelling

THINK ABOUT IT

Timothy's Coffees of the World, Canadian Tire Corporation, and retailer Harry Rosen (upscale men's apparel) have all tried, unsuccessfully, to enter the U.S. market. Why do you think these companies were not successful in the United States?

Companies that have struggled for decades to develop a brand awareness and brand identity in their own country cannot expect to transfer that brand identity directly to another country. One mistake that some companies make is to spend too little money on marketing efforts to develop awareness of their brand in the foreign market. The exporting company must examine the brand name, logo, and slogan already attached to its brand to ensure that the brand identification is appropriate for the new market and can be translated. Certain Japanese products would not be successful in Canada, for example, because of their names: a fruit candy that is branded in English as Dew-Dew, a snack product with the English brand name "Baked Chunk," or a chocolate cookie named "Collon." North American businesses sometimes make similar errors when attempting to sell their products in foreign markets. One example is a 1980s Coca-Cola slogan that was translated as "I Feel Coke."

Even a product's packaging must be carefully researched. The Japanese, for example, prefer lavish packaging, as their culture requires a great deal of gift-giving. The Japanese consumer looks for elaborately packaged goods that speak well of the gift-giver. Even fruits such as melons and oranges are individually packaged. Companies that enter the Japanese market with simple packages that have little style will have a hard sell among merchandise buyers for Japanese shops.

Many countries have different environmental standards from those required for products sold in Canada. Even though there may be no regulations in Canadian law that require packages to be reusable or recyclable, companies wishing to enter the Canadian marketplace should package their products in environmentally friendly containers. Otherwise, the companies risk consumer rejection on the shelf. Surveys have revealed that consumers are concerned about the environmental qualities of the products they purchase. Potential purchasers refer to product packaging for information on these qualities, and they will buy products that make "green" claims over other products. There are also government regulations that specify standard package sizes for wine, glucose/refined sugar syrups, peanut butter, and cookies.

Web Link

To find out more about environmental packaging standards, follow the link at www.internationalbusiness.nelson.com.

Packaging for imported products must conform to Canadian labelling requirements. For example, the labelling requirements for food products might make a foreign exporter think twice about entering the Canadian market. Canada's labelling requirements for packaged foods and beverages have been established in accordance with the Consumer Packaging and Labelling Act, the Weights and Measures Act, and the Canadian Agricultural Products Act. One of the roles of officials of the Canada Customs and Revenue Agency at our borders is to ensure that products entering Canada are labelled correctly. Goods improperly marked can be impounded until the labelling problem is corrected. All pre-packaged foods and beverages sold in Canada require the following content on their labels:

- country of origin, such as "Made in Thailand"
- bilingual (French and English) labelling
- product identity declaration, with the product's common or generic name as prescribed by regulations; for example, orange juice from concentrated juice, or orange drink
- declaration of net quantity or volume, specified metrically
- minimum type font size relative to the display surface of the package
- list of ingredients and their components, when appropriate, in descending order of proportion by weight. Ingredients must be identified by their generic or common name. (Spices, seasonings, food additives, vitamins, and mineral nutrients, may be shown at the end of the list in any order. Some components of ingredients are totally exempt from declaration, while others are exempt based on the amount used.)
- company identification and principal place of business (in English or French) to identify where the pre-packaged product was manufactured or produced for resale. If a Canadian company name and address are shown on an imported product that has been wholly manufactured outside Canada, the Canadian declaration must be preceded by appropriate terms such as "Imported by/Importé par."
- shelf life, when a food or beverage has a shelf life of 90 days or less. A "Best before" date and storage instructions must be indicated on the package if it requires storage that differs from normal storage-room conditions. Products packaged at the retail level should provide a "Packaged on" date instead of a "Best Before" date.
- artificial flavours when used alone or with natural flavouring agents. These must be indicated adjacent to any label markings or graphics that depict a natural source of flavour.

Labelling requirements for Canadian products entering another country are equally strict. Failure to research these requirements before negotiating a trade deal could lead to serious inconvenience and expense for a Canadian manufacturer.

Culture and Customs

Customs and culture have a major impact on buying habits and product use. Pumpkins, Christmas lights, turkeys, and Mother's Day cards, for example, are all sold in Canada to meet certain cultural needs. Many other countries would have no market for these items at all, as their population may not celebrate Halloween or Christmas, serve turkey as a meal, or recognize Mother's Day. Similarly, as Canada becomes more and more multicultural, increasingly diverse products will be needed to address the cultural needs of a wide variety of traditions. The impact of culture and customs on international business will be discussed in depth in Chapter 8.

Ideas	Connections	Extensions
1. (a) List and briefly describe the three major marketing errors some companies make.	(b) In pairs, think of and share a list of North American products that have not been successful in international markets.	(c) Select a product that you think a Canadian company could export to China. What marketing research would be necessary to avoid the common marketing errors?
2. (a) What did Nortel Networks do right to achieve success in China?	(b) Develop a short profile of a Canadian company that was either successful or unsuccessful in marketing a product outside North America. Account for the company's success or failure in marketing.	(c) From your findings, develop a list of instructions for a company preparing to sell its product internationally.
3. (a) Describe briefly the three methods of brand identification.	(b) There are numerous reports of unsuccessful branding in magazines and books, and on the Internet. Find some examples of unsuccessful branding efforts and briefly explain each one. Share your list with a small group.	(c) Find a brand-name product that is sold in your community that you think is poorly branded for the Canadian market. Give reasons for your opinion.

7.4 Infrastructure and Services

Many of the problems that a Canadian business may have in trading with another country are created by the infrastructure (or the lack of infrastructure) in the partner country. **Infrastructure** refers to the large-scale public systems, services, and facilities of a country or region that are necessary for economic activity. Infrastructure includes power and water supplies, transportation systems, telecommunications, roads, financial facilities, health-care systems, and even education systems. Before a company can trade or set up business in another country, its management must study the country's infrastructure to be sure that the necessary services and facilities are provided.

Transportation Systems

Good transportation systems are essential to move goods to the target foreign market and distribute them in that country. Import and export businesses require reliable freight forwarding companies to pick up and deliver freight around the target country. This also means that roads, docks, and freight-handling facilities must exist and be in good repair.

World Ranking of the Top Ten Airports by Total Cargo (2001)

Rank	Airport
1	Memphis (MEM)
2	Hong Kong (HKG)
3	Anchorage (ANC)
4	Los Angeles (LAX)
5	Tokyo (NRT)
6	Miami (MIA)
7	Frankfurt/main (FRA)
8	Paris (CDG)
9	Singapore (SIN)
10	Louisville (SDF)

Figure 7.16 These ten airports are ranked according to the weight of the cargo they handle.

If the target country has geographic impediments, such as widely separated urban centres or a mountainous terrain, it should have a road or rail system in place to ship goods from one urban centre to another. The trucks and trains should be able to accommodate a variety of shipments, including frozen or refrigerated goods, livestock, liquids, or standard containers. The terminals and railheads on the system should also be connected to the urban centres by good roads and a network of highways. If the country borders on an ocean, it should have at least one deep-sea port and equipment for standard-size tankers, freighters, and container ships, with facilities for handling the actual containers. If the country consists of a number of islands, it should have an efficient maritime freight forwarding system.

Airports should be near major urban centres and have efficient ground links to these centres (roads, public transit, taxis). The main airport should be able to accommodate international flights and large passenger and cargo planes, and it should have freight handling facilities.

It is important to check airport security for the freight area, as theft is a problem at many airports around the world. Insurance providers will factor a company's choice of airport into the insurance equation, charging higher fees for insuring freight that is shipped to an airport with a reputation for freight loss or damage.

Communication Systems

Businesses working abroad need to be able to communicate with their home offices. Communication methods can include phones, cellular or satellite phone systems, Internet providers, faxing capabilities, or even telex systems. Cell phones are rapidly gaining popularity as a communication tool, particularly in countries around the world where the established phone systems are very difficult to use or not up to date. However, for cell phones to work, countries must have cell towers that receive and transmit signals.

Broadcast facilities are related to communication systems. Although a business will probably be working through local wholesalers and distributors, if it is selling consumer products, it should know what media are available to carry advertising messages, the target markets for the media, the reach and circulation of the media, and the regulations that may be in place for media use. It will also be useful to know in advance what marketing and advertising costs will be in the different media, and what technical specifications and mechanical requirements are in place for advertisements. In many countries, content in newspapers and magazines and on radio and television is government-controlled or highly regulated.

Government Services

Governments vary in the extent to which they encourage and support businesses in their country. To encourage trade, some countries provide a multitude of support facilities to connect foreign buyers and investors (and those seeking a joint venture partner) with local sellers or to connect local buyers with foreign sellers. Many governments even offer financing or tax incentives, or both, if the proposed deal represents a direct capital investment opportunity for their country.

On the other hand, some nations seem to discourage business by the complexity of their bureaucracies. There are many forms to complete and numerous rules and regulations for business practices. In many countries, payoffs to business and government officials are a normal part of doing business. Because this type of information will not appear on any government-sponsored Web site, a business must use other means to find accurate and credible information about the foreign country. Web sites of the Canadian and U.S. governments provide excellent research sources for Canadian businesses contemplating trade with other nations.

Other Services

Business people planning a visit or an extended stay in a new country to build trade and capitalize on growth opportunities should research the following:

- **Accommodation:** What hotels are available for business travellers? What are their rates for short and long-term stays? Do they have ensuite bathrooms? Are they equipped with business centres or in-room wiring for computers and Internet access?

- **Food:** Are good, clean restaurants that serve "Western" cuisine available? What precautions may need to be taken with food?

- **Health:** What diseases are prevalent, and what preventive measures (for example, inoculations or medications) are needed to prevent the contraction of disease while in the country? What health-care facilities are available? Do Canadian health insurance plans cover visitors or Canadian expatriates in that country?

- **Safety:** What is the crime rate? Are the streets safe? Is kidnapping or terrorism a problem? Are efficient police, fire, and ambulance systems accessible?

- **Education:** Are there schools with acceptable international standards that will prepare trained and educated personnel for your company? Is there suitable education to accommodate your expatriate employees' children?

- **Business support services:** Are translators, shipping agents, lawyers, advertising and promotional agencies, storage facilities, sales agents, consultants, market research companies, and purchasing agents available?

- **Financial services:** Does the country have an efficient and reliable banking system? Is Canadian currency (in cash or travellers' cheques) easily convertible? Are international credit cards widely accepted?

- **Official Canadian presence:** Is there a Canadian high commission, embassy, or consulate in the country? If not, to whom should a business traveller go for Canadian services?

- **Communication and business etiquette:** How do people communicate in person? What local relationship customs should a traveller be aware of? What are the differences in business practices, decision-making, and communication?

With the increasing availability of information on the Internet, basic research into the infrastructure of countries around the world can be easily carried out. (For example, see the background information on Kenya, which was obtained from a wide variety of Internet sources by searching for specific information,

Figure 7.17 A giraffe passes by a multipurpose vehicle in Kenya. A bush plane sits on the nearby runway. How does a country's infrastructure affect its ability to transact international trade?

such as "transportation in Kenya.") There is no substitute, however, for first-hand information from people who have experienced the conditions in the country. The Canadian government's Department of Foreign Affairs and International Trade provides personal interviews for businesses that wish to get current information for countries.

To find out more about travel in Kenya, follow the link at www.internationalbusiness.nelson.com.

The Infrastructure of Kenya

Transportation
- Traffic moves on the left-hand side of the road.
- Kenya has two major airports (Jomo Kenyatta in Nairobi and Moi in Mombasa).
- Inland passengers and freight are conveyed by the road and rail network: 2652 km of track, 64 590 km of roads.
- Road conditions are poor. Only 9 percent of roads in Kenya are paved. Only 32 percent of the paved roads are in good repair.
- Kenya has two ocean ports, at Mombasa and Lamu, and an inland port at Kisumu. Ocean piracy is a real threat.

Communication
- Direct dial telephone service and fax are available throughout the country.
- There are more than 50 Internet service providers in Kenya.
- Kencell Communications Limited and Safaricom Communications Limited are two major mobile phone companies in Kenya.

Utilities
- Water and 220-volt 50-Hz single-phase and three-phase electricity are available.
- The British three-blade electrical plug is used widely.
- Power supply interruptions frequently occur, including cuts in industrial zones during evening peak hours.
- Permanent or long-term residents should consider buying standby electrical generators, because electricity demand is expected to exceed generating capacity, with frequent interruptions or "brown-outs."
- Bottled propane is available, but supply cannot be guaranteed.
- Most homes have reserve water tanks built into their roof structure.

Health
- Adequate medical services are available in Nairobi.
- Malaria is not prevalent at high elevations, but precautions must be taken in lower areas, especially in the coastal regions.

Financial
- Kenya has a developed banking system, with major world banks (Barclays, Citibank, and Bank of India) well represented. As of 2002, no Canadian banks were in Kenya.
- ATM service is provided at many banks throughout Kenya (for an updated list, visit either the VISA or the MasterCard Web sites).
- Major credit cards are accepted throughout the country.
- Canadian currency and travellers' cheques are not accepted in stores but can be exchanged at most banks for Kenyan schillings.

ICE Activities for 7.4

Ideas	Connections	Extensions
1. (a) Explain why a country's infrastructure is important to a Canadian business wanting to do business in that country.	(b) Describe the transportation infrastructure (name the specific airports, railheads, carriers, companies, ports, and so on) in a country other than Canada or Kenya or the United States.	(c) Evaluate Canada's infrastructure systems and compose an "infrastructure advisory" for a foreign business.
2. (a) Describe the major components of a country's infrastructure.	(b) Profile the infrastructure of a country other than a North American country or Kenya.	(c) Select one of the components of an infrastructure. Use that component as a basis of comparison between two possible trading partners for Canada.
3. (a) How can a country's infrastructure be either an asset or an obstacle to its trading with Canada?	(b) What infrastructure problem would be the most difficult for Canadians doing business in Kenya? Explain.	(c) Analyze the impact on trade of the changes in air service since the events of September 11, 2001.

Canada's Trading Partners: Focus on China

Figure 7.18 The head of the World Trade Organization and officials from China and Qatar share a toast during the signing ceremony for China's entry into the WTO in Doha, November 11, 2001.

Only twenty years ago, China was one of the world's poorest nations. The country seemed to be an unlikely trading partner for Canadian businesses. It had a Communist government that discouraged private ownership and competition. Its "cultural revolution" had provided a direction for the education system and intellectual community that discouraged international linkages. Human rights violations were notorious. Recent reforms, however, have opened up special economic zones that permit a free market in various sections of China.

China has not yet developed a completely free-market economy, but the world's largest country (by population count) no longer totally rejects capi-talism. Hong Kong and Macao were once considered the freest of all the free market economies in the world, and, until recently, had only a tenuous political con-nection with Communist China. In 1997, Hong Kong reverted from British to Chinese control, and, in 1999, Macao went from Portuguese to Chinese sovereignty. The government in China has recognized that these areas provide both a window on the capitalist world and a much-needed source of foreign capital. As a result, the free-wheeling capitalist economies are encouraged. Both former colonies became special economic zones and joined others (such as Shenzen and Shekou) within the Chinese mainland borders.

China joined the World Trade Organization in December 2001. Suppliers of some of Canada's top goods and services exports to China will benefit from the market liberalization that was required of China before it was accepted into the WTO. China has reduced market entry restrictions for telecommunica-tions and financial sectors, two areas of primary interest to Canadian companies. The WTO documents also clarify and improve on foreign access to the Chinese market in a range of other service sectors. China's tariffs will be cut substantially for most Canadian exports. By 2005, for example, tariffs will be eliminated on 251 information technology products. In addition, the Chinese government is gradually increasing the quota for Canadian wheat from the approximately 1 million tonnes in 2000 to 9.6 million tonnes by 2004. By 2006, the average Chinese tariff on certain motor vehicle parts originating from Canada will drop to 11.5 percent from the current 21.1 percent.

Canadians still have concerns about the "new" China. Canadian banks and insurance companies that currently have offices in China wonder about the effect of new regulations when China's financial services markets open up. Canadian manufacturers worry about the Chinese government's ability to protect intellectual property. For example, will copy-rights on Canadian software or on cast automotive parts be respected?

China is pursuing trade deals around the world. Its gradual shift toward a free market is expected to bring economic prosperity to the country and improve the overall quality of life for its people.

A SNAPSHOT OF CHINA

Size: 9 596 960 sq. km

World Region: Asia-Pacific

Capital City: Beijing

Language: Mandarin Chinese

Currency: Yuan Renminbi

Population: 1.3 billion

Time: Noon in Ottawa (EST) is midnight in Beijing.

Climate: Ranges from tropical to desert

Type of Government: One party, communist system

Labour Force by Occupation: 74 percent agriculture, 14 percent industry, 13 percent services

Membership in World Organizations: APEC, ASEAN, WTO

Importing Partners and Products:
Partners: Japan, Taiwan, United States, South Korea. China imported $2.6 billion from Canada in 1999, making Canada seventeenth in its import ranking.
Products: Wheat, machinery and equipment, mineral fuels, plastics, iron and steel, chemicals.

Exporting Partners and Products:
Partners: United States, Hong Kong, Japan, South Korea, Germany, Netherlands, United Kingdom, Singapore, Taiwan.
Products: Machinery and equipment, textiles and clothing, footwear, toys and sporting goods, mineral fuels.

Figure 7.19 Mao Tse-Tung brought Communism to China in the 1940s.

Travel Advisory: Travellers to China need a visa to enter the country and travel there. Business visitors should bring their own interpreters to supplement the services provided by the Chinese. Flights in China are often overbooked, so reconfirmation of internal and return flight reservations is essential. Be cautious and watch for pickpockets, who target passports. Report the loss of a passport to the police and to the Canadian embassy immediately.

Country Link

To find out more about China, follow the links at
www.internationalbusiness.nelson.com.

Business Etiquette: Avoid using colour in any printed material, as colours have special meanings, often negative. Collective thinking still prevails, even in sectors experimenting with free enterprise. The Communist party and government bureaucrats are responsible for all business decisions.

If a Chinese business person is embarrassed ("loses face"), even unintentionally, it could harm negotiations. Reputation and social standing are important. The Chinese like exchanging business cards. Be sure that one side is in English and the other in Chinese. Cards printed in gold ink indicate prestige and prosperity. Present the card with two hands, with the Chinese side facing the recipient.

The first Canadian to enter a meeting room is assumed to be the head of the delegation and the only person who will speak. People enter the room in hierarchical order. Foreign visitors should leave a meeting before their Chinese hosts. Rather than say "no," Chinese prefer to say "perhaps," "I'm not sure," "I'll think about it," or "we'll see." These phrases usually mean "no."

Chapter Challenges

Knowledge/Understanding

1. Match each of the following terms to the correct definition or description below:

   (a) buy forward
   (b) hard currency
   (c) soft currency
   (d) currency exchange market
   (e) landed cost
   (f) standards
   (g) boycott
   (h) local market research
   (i) labelling requirements

   (i) investigation into consumer preferences in a specific region
   (ii) the world's largest trading market
   (iii) the cost of a product after all transportation, handling, currency exchange rates, and import charges have been included
   (iv) rules governing one aspect of product packaging
   (v) to purchase foreign currency in advance
   (vi) currency that is widely accepted on foreign exchange markets
   (vii) agreements to be used as guidelines
   (viii) an organized campaign to refuse purchasing specific products
   (ix) currency that is not stable or easily converted into Canadian dollars

2. Explain the four major problem areas that businesses need to examine when planning to trade with a business in another country.

3. How can each of these four problem areas create problems? What is one way of avoiding a problem for each of the areas you described?

4. What research should businesses do before their representatives travel to another country on business?

Thinking/Inquiry

1. Visit the Web site of one of the following organizations and explain, with examples, how the organization helps set or maintain Canadian standards:

   The Canadian Standards Association (CSA)
   The Standards Council of Canada (SCC)
   The Canadian General Standards Board
   The Institute of Electronics and Electrical Engineers (IEEE)

   Links to these sites are found at **www.internationalbusiness.nelson.com**.

2. In your opinion, what would likely be some of the consequences for Canadian exporters if Canada's currency was downgraded? Write a paragraph in which you clearly state your thesis and offer at least three pieces of evidence to support that thesis.

3. Research one of the following topics and prepare a short report that outlines a few of the differences between Canada and a nation outside North America in relation to your chosen topic:

   - packaging materials
   - package design
   - vending machines
   - catalogue shopping
   - retail stores
   - shopping centres
   - print advertising
   - television advertising
   - bank cards
   - e-commerce

Communication

1. Research a current story about a problem encountered by a Canadian business in the international marketplace. As sources, use the principles discussed in this chapter and business magazines, the business section of local and online newspapers, and/or reliable Web sites. Use a problem-solution graphic organizer to outline the aspects of the problem, the possible solutions, the solution selected by the company in question, and your evaluation of that solution.

2. Working with a partner, select a product that has been successfully imported into Canada for more than 10 years. Research the company that makes the product and the history of the product. Then, prepare a 5-minute interview between a Canadian business reporter and the president of the company in which you discuss the challenges faced in costing, standards, and marketing for the Canadian market.

3. The section on production standards (page 225) mentions a number of different challenges that Canadian consumers face when buying imported goods. Research another production standard. Create a mind map to demonstrate the challenges that a Canadian retailer importing a related product should consider as regards that standard.

4. Debate this statement: "Canada is the easiest nation in the world with which to trade." Use information from this chapter to support your argument.

Application

1. Using the "Canada's Trading Partners: Focus on China" feature (page 241), work in a small group to plan and present a panel discussion on how to respond to the challenges facing a Canadian company of your choice that wants to export its products or services to China.

2. Prepare an illustrated case study that profiles a business that has not been successful in selling the products that it has imported to Canada. Account for the company's failure. Use the sections of this chapter as an aid in setting up the outline for your case study, and carefully plan your use of text, charts, tables, graphs, and photos.

3. Working with a partner, interview a representative of an export business. Ask the person to describe the process that the company went through when it first started to export. What was the biggest problem, and how did the company manage these problems? Prepare a report summarizing the interview and identifying the difficulties encountered. Compare findings in other reports, and account for the differences.

International Business Portfolio

Identifying Problem Areas in Your IBP Country

Errors made by many companies attempting to trade internationally can be grouped into four categories: costing, standards, marketing, and infrastructure. Awareness of these common mistakes can help businesses achieve higher levels of success at the international level.

Activity

1. Identify specific problems or requirements, or both, associated with the following areas in your IBP country:
   • costing
   • standards and regulations
   • marketing
   • infrastructure

Chapter 8

Culture and International Business

To trade successfully in other nations, a business must understand its trading partners. This understanding comes from an appreciation of the other nations' culture and customs. This chapter describes some of the cultural factors that have shaped the beliefs and values of nations. It then relates these cultural values and customs to the world of international trade. Culture and customs can create new markets for businesses. Cultural differences, however, can create misunderstandings between potential trading partners, especially if one does not understand and respect the values and the business customs of the other.

Chapter Topics

➤ 8.1 – Customs and Culture 246

➤ 8.2 – Culture and Consumer Needs and Wants 252

➤ 8.3 – Culture and International Business Practices 258

➤ 8.4 – Disappearing Diversity 265

➤ *Canada's Trading Partners: Focus on* Russia 268

➤ Chapter Challenges 270

Prior Knowledge

- How would you describe your culture to someone who has never been to Canada?
- How does culture influence our needs and wants as consumers?
- How does culture affect the way people conduct business in other countries?

Inquiries/Expectations

- What factors contribute to the development of a country's culture?
- What modifications are made to goods and services to adapt them to the cultures of other countries?
- What are some of the challenges that a company encounters when ethics, values, language, and business practices vary among countries and cultures?
- How do differences among cultures affect consumer needs and wants?
- How has the global market created more homogeneous consumer demand?

Important Terms

Canadian mosaic
cultural determinants
cultural imperialism
cultural marketing
cultural norms
culture

customs
natural hazards
negotiation style
protocol
silent language

8.1 Customs and Culture

A **culture** is a reflection of the values and beliefs of a community or a nation. A nation's religion, laws, language, technology, art, music, and literature define its culture. The story in the Global Thought feature on this page reflects the Turkmenistan belief that being a guest in someone's home confers upon the guest the highest possible status. This is part of Muslim religion and is, therefore, part of the culture in a Muslim home.

GLOBAL THOUGHT

The following story illustrates some of the cultural differences that an international business traveller might expect.

In Turkmenistan, as is true in most Muslim cultures, being a guest is the highest status one can have, and being a foreign guest is the greater still. Moreover, being the host of a foreign guest confers great status on the host from his fellow villagers.

When we visited the small isolated village of Kona Kassir on the Iranian border, we stayed with the high school chemistry teacher. We were seated on beautiful Turkmen carpets (the finest in the world) around a ground cloth covered with plates of bread, mounds of rice, and lamb that had been slaughtered that morning. At noon, the "Ak Sakhals" (elders), dressed in their fleecy telpek hats and homespun robes, arrived en masse and took their places after a silent handshake with the host. They ate silently, observing that we fastidiously ate with our right hands only, and that we accepted second and third portions after demurring twice. It took some convincing diplomacy to refuse the brains and eyeballs of the lamb, pleading that the more venerable elders were more deserving than we.

– The Savvy Traveler

The treatment of the guest, however, depends upon custom. **Customs** are the ways in which cultural behaviours are performed. They are the social habits of a people, the traditional behaviours that reflect cultural values, such as dress, food, and rituals. The Turkmenistan teacher sat on a carpet, considered the lamb's brains and eyeballs a delicacy, and wore special clothing. The seating, food, and dress are all examples of customs that establish the special status of the guest, a cultural value. Muslims also believe that the right hand is the "clean" hand and the left hand is the "unclean" one. It is a violation of religious beliefs (culture) to eat with the left hand (custom), which is why the elders watched the visitors "observing that [they] fastidiously ate with [their] right hands only."

To trade with a business in another country, companies must set up a trading relationship. The nature of the relationship depends on the cultural background of each trading partner. To avoid lost opportunities that arise from misunderstandings, business people must study one another's cultural background. A true understanding of another's culture begins by understanding how the culture developed. There are three **cultural determinants**—in other words, three things that shape a country's culture: its geography, its history, and its religion.

Geography

Consider the geographic features of Canada. Occupying the northern half of the North American continent, Canada's land mass is 9 976 140 km², making it the second-largest country, geographically, in the world after Russia. From east to west, Canada contains six time zones. Canada has coastlines on the Atlantic and Pacific oceans, and a third seacoast on the Arctic Ocean, giving it the longest coastline of any country. To the south, Canada shares an 8891 kilometre boundary with the United States. To the north, the Arctic islands come within 800 kilometres of the North Pole. Canada's neighbour across the Arctic Ocean is Russia.

Because of the harsh northern climate, only 12 percent of Canada's land is suitable for agriculture. Most of the population of 30 million lives within a few hundred kilometres of the southern border, where the climate is milder, in a long thin band stretching between the Atlantic and Pacific oceans. Canada has a population density of only three persons per square kilometre.

Now, compare Canada's geographic features with those of Japan. Japan is actually a group of islands, or archipelago, with a land mass slightly larger than Britain. With a total land area of 377 733 km2, this small nation of more than 123 million people (four times the population of Canada) has one of the highest population densities in the world: 325 people per square kilometre. Historically, the waters that surround Japan have served as a natural geographic barrier between the Japanese archipelago and Asia. Before the modern age, the distance across these waters kept foreign contact to a minimum and served as a barrier against foreign forces.

The Japanese islands consist predominantly of mountains formed through volcanic action. Even though many of these volcanoes are inactive, seismologists record more than 1500 earthquakes each year. People feel only two or three per month.

The distance from coast to coast is generally less than 320 kilometres. Yet the mountainous terrain and the numerous swiftly flowing rivers and streams made the distance extremely difficult to travel before modern transportation systems developed. These geographic features also limit the land space suitable for agricultural production or human habitation. Because Japan is so mountainous, only about 15 percent of the total land mass is suited to agricultural production.

Of the 651 cities in Japan, Tokyo is the largest. Most of the cities are situated on the flat coastal plains or mountain basins of the country. As the population grew, these urban areas encroached on valuable agricultural lands.

Because of the mountainous terrain, the rivers of Japan are generally not suitable for navigation. However, they are one of Japan's few natural sources of energy and serve as a valuable source of hydroelectric power; they are also a source of water for irrigation.

TRADE TALK

Canadian and Japanese toolmakers approach the same task in different ways. A saw for cutting lumber, if designed in Canada, is made so that the carpenter's stroke away from the body does the cutting. In Japan, saws are engineered so that cutting takes place as the carpenter draws the saw upward. This small detail yields a big difference. The Canadian saw can, if leaned into, generate more power, while the Japanese saw provides more control and refinement in the cut, requiring surprisingly less effort.

– *Hinduism Today*

Japan is located primarily in the Northern Temperate Zone. The climate in Japan is most comparable to the middle belt of the eastern United States and to the countries of central and southern Europe. If Japan were superimposed on the eastern side of North America, it would extend from Montreal in the north to Jacksonville, Florida, in the south. If it were superimposed on the west side, it would stretch from Vancouver, BC, to southern California.

The geographic features of Canada shaped a very different culture from that of Japan, just as Japan's geography played a major role in determining its cultural values. A country's climate, arable land, availability and ease of transportation, location, and natural hazards all contribute to the belief systems and social behaviour of its people and explain many of the customs that develop along with the culture.

Climate

Both Canada and Japan have cold winters, which influences the type of clothing worn by its people. Most of Japan, however, never gets as cold as Canada. Japanese clothing has evolved to incorporate silk and cotton, whereas Canadians used fur in the past and now rely on modern synthetic fibres for warmth. People select building materials because of climate as well: light building materials for tropical climates, heavy materials for colder climates. The style and shape of the homes in a nation or region are determined, in large measure, by the climate, too. The climate also influences features such as the placement and design of windows and doors, the design of the roof, and whether there is a fireplace.

Arable Land

The availability of food and the ability to be self-sufficient are huge cultural determinants. Productive areas become settled and develop communities that become nations. Every society in the world has developed around a source of food and water. As agricultural methods improved, fewer people were needed to produce enough food for their community, a change that allowed others to become involved in the growth of art, music, dance, and other cultural activities. Food customs developed based on the available food. For example, many Canadians consume large quantities of meat and milk, two foods that are scarce in Japan and not nearly as popular there. Canada's large land mass can support both beef and dairy cattle, as well as the grain to feed them. Japan's lack of arable land makes animal husbandry of secondary importance (with the exception of world-famous beef cattle raised by hand in the Kobe region). The Japanese are much more likely to eat fish and rice, because the sea surrounds them and the rice crop can be cultivated in small areas.

Transportation

European explorers learned from Canada's Aboriginal people how to make and use canoes. Canoe travel brought trade and settlement. The dog sled was the main form of transportation in northern Canada until the invention of the snowmobile. Dog sleds are still a part of Inuit culture today. Canadians developed or adapted these methods of transportation in response to the country's geography and the natural geographic barriers that lakes, mountains, and large distances created for the traveller. Canada's cultural identity as a nation grew when the railway was built across the Rockies to join the country from sea to sea.

The mountains of Japan and the rushing rivers they produce kept most of the Japanese people on the coast, causing them to develop a maritime culture.

Figure 8.1 The canoe has become a Canadian icon. Originally an important method of transportation, its use now is mainly recreational.

Location

Europeans encountered North America as they looked for a new spice route between Europe and Indonesia, China, and India. Its abundant resources made the great land mass a desirable place to bring both settlement and trade. From that time to the present, people from all over the world have come to Canada to build a life. The **Canadian mosaic** is a term used to describe Canada's cultural heritage, which has been composed of different "tiles" from all the various groups and nationalities that have settled here. Thus, our culture has emerged partially from our location.

Japan's culture has emerged from its location as well. Japan has one of the highest population densities in the world and does not encourage immigration. Whereas Canada needs more people because of its small population, Japan does not. Because Japan is surrounded by water and was difficult for early explorers and potential invaders to reach, Japan rarely had contact with outsiders, and its people were wary of outsiders. Because of this, the Japanese culture developed in isolation from other cultures. Only within the last century has Japan begun to engage with other cultures.

Natural Hazards

Canada does not have to worry about natural hazards as most countries do. **Natural hazards** are climatic or geological conditions that endanger human life and property. We do not usually experience hurricanes, tidal waves, earthquakes, or typhoons; nor do we have active volcanoes. However, Canada must deal with spring floods that can create considerable human misery and property damage, but not on the same scale as a major earthquake, for example. Occasionally, severe winter weather, such as the ice storm in 1998 that devastated the eastern part of Canada, can cause disruptions to daily life and business. Parts of Canada are also subject to tornadoes and minor earthquake tremors. Such occurrences are rare, however, and relatively few lives are lost. Japan experiences frequent earthquakes, and these natural disasters claim thousands of lives every generation. Severe storms also plague the Japanese islands. A country's consciousness of an ever-present danger shapes its culture, from the design of its buildings to its mythology. For example, one of the gods in Japanese mythology is the god of earthquakes, Nai-No-Kami.

Figure 8.2 A portion of the Hanshin Expressway is twisted down on its side in Nishinomiya near Kobe after a powerful earthquake jolted western Japan in January 1995.

Web Link

Follow the link at www.internationalbusiness.nelson.com to find out more about the effects of natural hazards on a country's economic and business culture.

History

THINK ABOUT IT

The Star Trek Prime Directive is "As the right of each sentient species to live in accordance with its normal cultural evolution is considered sacred, no Star Fleet personnel may interfere with the healthy development of alien life and culture."

In this directive, what does the phrase "normal cultural evolution" mean to you? Who decides what the "healthy development of ... life and culture" is in our society?

The study of a country's history is also a study of its culture, in the same way that history is about the settlement of nations and the cultural values that new inhabitants bring to their new homeland. A country's history is also inextricably connected to the challenges and advantages posed by its geography. Settlers choose to inhabit a place because it provides them with things they value, such as space, freedom, or resources. The ease of settlement and its speed and nature shape and reshape a country's culture. People move into another country either by invitation or permission as residents, immigrants, or refugees, or by colonization or conflict as conquerors.

Aboriginal peoples were the first to live in Canada. Then came the Vikings, English, and French. As settlement continued, immigrants came from Germany, Poland, Italy, Greece, Africa, the West Indies, the United States, Asia, and many other places. Each of these cultures, itself shaped by many other cultures, contributed to what was "Canadian," so that the real definition of Canadian culture became its multiculturalism, its mix of hundreds of different cultural norms and customs. **Cultural norms** are cultural expectations, appearance, observances, and behaviour that are normal (standard) in a region or country. Symbols of the cultures that make up Canada are all around us, and we now take many of them for granted. Wearing green on St. Patrick's Day, decorating a Christmas tree, or eating a bagel are examples of the influence of different cultures.

When a group or nation imposes its cultural values and customs on another, the practice is referred to as **cultural imperialism**. Many people consider that this imposition is unethical and believe that nations should be able to develop culturally on their own. However, throughout human history, conquerors have imposed one nation's cultural values on the people of other nations. The imperial nations of the past, such as Britain, France, the Netherlands, and Belgium, imposed their political, social, and economic systems and values on the nations in their empires. Many of their institutions, whether political or cultural, survive to this day.

Today, many people argue that the international media reflect cultural imperialism on the part of the United States. Certainly, the developed nations attempt to impose costly values such as conservation and anti-pollution measures on less-developed countries.

Religion

Whether a society's culture was formed by many different cultures, as Canada's was, or evolved in isolation, as Japan's did, religion usually played an enormous role in determining the cultural values of a nation. Some societies have a single religion that shapes their laws and customs. Other societies

Figure 8.3 Raffles Hotel is a symbol of Britain in Singapore.

embrace a multitude of religious beliefs, often in conflict with each other.

Religious ceremonies and celebrations are often accompanied by holidays (an amalgamation of the words "holy" and "days") or feast days. For Canadians who are Christians, the major religious holidays are Easter and Christmas. In earlier times, Halloween and Mardi Gras were also religious occasions. Islamic holy days, such as the month of fasting, Ramadan, and Eid-ul-Fitr, are observed by Canadian Muslims. The Canadian Jewish community observes Jewish holidays, such as Yom Kippur. Different holidays and festivals are part of the cultural fabric of every nation.

Follow the link at
www.internationalbusiness.nelson.com
to find out more about the festivals and
celebrations of cultures around the world.

Figure 8.4 A carioca (a native of Rio) in carnival costume performing a traditional African dance at the annual Mardi Gras festival in Rio de Janeiro, Brazil.

ICE Activities for 8.1

Ideas	Connections	Extensions
1. (a) What is the difference between culture and customs?	(b) Describe three main features of Canadian culture.	(c) What Canadian customs are associated with the cultural features you described?
2. (a) Describe briefly the three main cultural determinants.	(b) How have these determinants affected the development of Canadian culture?	(c) Compare the differences in culture between Canada and one other nation (not Japan) that are based on the three cultural determinants.
3. (a) What is cultural imperialism?	(b) Research several examples of the positive and negative aspects of cultural imperialism.	(c) Some international businesses have been accused of cultural imperialism. Select one business you feel may be guilty of this and outline how the business has been culturally imperialistic.

8.2 Culture and Consumer Needs and Wants

Culture influences consumer purchasing all over the world and creates many marketing opportunities. Just as Christmas creates opportunities for toy and decoration manufacturers in the Pacific Rim, so do the cultural habits of people in foreign countries create markets for Canadian products. However, the astute marketing manager must be aware of these markets.

The biggest problem with selling products to different cultures is a lack of awareness of that culture—how it is similar to ours and how is it is different. Canadian businesses should never assume that a product that is successful in Canada will be successful anywhere else. Canadian marketers need to know exactly why someone in another country would want their products, how they will use them, and under what circumstances they will use them.

Much of the success of products introduced into other cultures depends on a combination of consumer demand and the way the products are marketed. **Cultural marketing** uses marketing resources to create effective international marketing campaigns that will appeal to consumers in specific countries. The promotional campaign should be carefully researched to ensure that the product or service and its marketing message are relevant and positive in the cultural context of the importing country.

For example, Christmas, a Christian celebration, is a cultural event in Canada. Christmas has a number of cultural customs associated with it, notably decorating an evergreen tree with coloured lights and glittering objects, hanging long stockings (usually designed to carry weight) by a real or imagined fireplace, and giving gifts. The following is a partial list of products that are sold only during the Christmas season:

Christmas cards	Christmas decorations	Christmas crackers
Christmas gift wrap	Christmas tableware	Candy canes
Christmas trees	Christmas linens	Christmas cake
Plum pudding	Christmas jewellery	Christmas clothing
Christmas wreaths	Advent calendars	Christmas music

Although Christmas is not celebrated widely in China, Taiwan, Indonesia, South Korea, or Japan, the Christmas merchandise listed above is often manufactured in these countries. Business people in these Pacific Rim nations know consumer needs and wants in Western countries and consider the celebration of Christmas in Canada as a major sales opportunity.

Figure 8.5 North American retailers do half of their business at Christmas.

Many North American retailers do 50 percent of their business in the six weeks before Christmas. These consumer sales include products of all sorts. For example, the Canadian toy market, which is worth more than a billion dollars annually, sells more than half of its total annual sales (54 percent) at Christmas. In the United States, the toy market is worth $35 billion, and 80 percent of these toys are imported! A Canadian toy manufacturer, such as Irwin Toy Company, considers the U.S. market a great opportunity, especially now that the NAFTA agreement allows Canadian toys to be sold in the United States duty free.

Jaffa Citrus and Cultural Marketing

Although Christmas customs in North America are quite well understood by manufacturers around the world, other cultural customs and attitudes are not so well known. International marketers must know about these traditions and attitudes to be able to successfully sell their products to consumers in foreign markets.

Jaffa Citrus Fruit provides one example of cultural marketing. Jaffa is the brand name of the Citrus Marketing Board of Israel, a coalition of independent citrus growers who pool their marketing resources to create effective international marketing campaigns for consumers in different countries. Jaffa has been very successful in Europe, because the Marketing Board sees the world as composed of individualized markets, all based on unique cultures. Jaffa tailors its marketing approach to each country's specific tastes and does not assume that what is successful in one country will be successful in another. For example:

Figure 8.6 Oranges are a popular fruit in Canada, and in many other countries.

- In grocery stores in Finland, Jaffa sets up large models of Viking boats to display fruit. The marketing campaign aims to appeal to the Finnish consumers' love of mythology and tradition and to make the exotic connections to the Middle East that are part of the Viking myth.

- Because French consumers prefer red grapefruit to oranges as a citrus fruit, Jaffa's French campaign uses a play on words to appeal to these consumers. The French are asked to *"Passez au Rouge,"* which translates to "Move over to red." It also means "Go through the red light," a phrase that associates red grapefruit with an independent and slightly lawless spirit.

- Also in France, Jaffa addresses its Florida competition by emphasizing that Jaffa grapefruit look better than Florida grapefruit, thereby appealing to French consumers' interest in style and visual appeal.

- British consumers like exotic products with foreign names. They do not like to peel oranges; they usually squeeze oranges for their juice rather than eat them in sections. When Jaffa discovered this, the board marketed its Shamouti orange to the British with an advertising campaign that used the line "Jaffa Shamouti easy-peeling oranges—Let the Jaffa juice loose."

- The Italians see grapefruit as a tasty way to get fibre in their diet. Some Italians feel guilty about what they consider to be their bad eating habits, so Jaffa used the slogan *"Colpa e polpa"* which means "Guilt and pulp," a way of saying that the Italian consumer could eat a sweet fruit and still have a healthy diet.

- Norwegians use oranges as a high-energy food while skiing, so Jaffa promotes its oranges in ski resorts in Norway.

- In Japan, Jaffa promotes a special fruit called a Jaffa Sweetie, which is a cross between a grapefruit and a pomelo (a fruit related to the grapefruit). Jaffa Sweeties are individually wrapped and sell for more than $5.00 CAD. By presenting the Jaffa Sweetie in a special way, the marketers make it appropriate for gift giving, which is a popular Japanese cultural tradition. (See the section on gift giving on page 262.)

Adapting to Cultural Differences

Canadian manufacturers and producers may be able to find new markets in other countries, but they will first need to understand consumer cultural differences. Whether the businesses manufacture sporting goods or furniture, whether they produce Canadian fruit or dairy products, they have to be ready to take cultural differences into consideration when they go into international markets. Before spending money on advertising, promotion, and distribution, each company would have to look closely at the culture in each country and at how that culture affects consumer needs and wants.

For example, if a Canadian manufacturer of sweatshirts was planning to expand into China, India, or South Africa, the company would have to investigate whether consumers in its new markets would buy the casual and loose-fitting shirts and pants that are considered stylish in North America. The company would also need to learn whether consumers in those countries were familiar with its brand and logo, whether it would have to change the colours of its products to suit the tastes of consumers, and even whether the term "sweatshirt" could be translated into other languages without causing offence.

If Second Cup, a successful Canadian coffee chain, were going to expand internationally, its marketers would have to answer a number of questions about consumer needs and wants in the country they were considering venturing into. For example:

Figure 8.7 Do you think that casual clothing worn in North America appeals to people in other countries? Explain.

- Is coffee a popular beverage in this particular international market?

- If coffee is popular, is it much stronger or weaker than Second Cup's blends, and how could these blends be adapted to meet consumer demand?

- Does the Second Cup name mean anything to the consumers in this market?

- Are there cultural associations with drinking coffee in other countries that would make Second Cup products hard to sell?

- Will people buy take-out coffee, or will they prefer to sit and drink it in a coffee house?

Figure 8.8 Are coffee houses successful in other countries?

THINK ABOUT IT

To some people, Americans and Canadians are indistinguishable. Our cultures are similar, our language is the same, and we share many of the same values. Do you agree? Do you know of any products that have succeeded in one country but failed in the other? Was this because of cultural differences?

Or, suppose that the Ontario Farm Products Marketing Commission, which oversees marketing initiatives, appointed an organization to help apple growers increase their export of fresh apples to international markets. According to Statistics Canada, countries such as Israel and Finland imported few Canadian apples in 1999. So, these countries might be potential markets. However, before launching campaigns to export more apples to these countries, the marketing board would need to find out why consumers have not been buying Canadian apples by asking questions such as the following:

- Do consumers in these markets eat apples? Do they cook with them? Do they drink apple cider?

- Do consumers prefer another fruit that is grown locally because they are more accustomed to it?

- Are consumers in these countries aware of the high quality of Canadian apples? If not, how could they be made aware?

- Would consumers eat apples in public as a snack food as Canadians do?

Questions such as these that help to identify the cultural composition of the foreign target market will help Canadian businesses avoid making costly cultural mistakes. For example, if people in a certain country believe that eating in public is rude, an advertisement showing a young person biting into an apple on a bus might cause the consumers in that country to reject apples, even if they enjoy the flavour. Consumers, no matter where they live, are likely to reject any product that does not fit into their cultural norms and values.

Figure 8.9 More than half of all apples consumed in Canada are grown by Ontario's 700 commercial apple growers.

Web Link

Follow the link at
www.internationalbusiness.nelson.com
for tips for international business people when they visit various countries.

TRADE TIPS

The Australian Trade Commission runs a Web site that links you with information about various countries. Some of the countries profiled have a category called "Business Etiquette and Practices." Here are some of the tips given for doing business in Italy:

- Italians generally dress well at all times, but conservative attire is recommended for business meetings.

- Business visits in July and August are strongly discouraged because this is the Italian summer and most people and companies take their vacations at this time.

- Italy is price-conscious and competitive, so do as much preparation as possible before visiting Italy and send detailed company information in advance.

Sa-Cinn Native Enterprises Limited

Sa-Cinn Native Enterprises Ltd. is a 100 percent Native-owned company that promotes the cultural heritage of First Nations people. Sa-Cinn artisans create works of fine art, jewellery, carvings, and clothing, including Cowichan sweaters. These sweaters are known for their warmth, ability to repel water, and durability. The sweaters reflect the culture of the people who make them.

The Salish, the people who knit these sweaters, come from the Cowichan Valley on rugged Vancouver Island. They have been making these sweaters for over 100 years and have a tradition of weaving that extends much further into the past. Cowichan sweaters were initially made to protect those who wore them against the elements of the region's sometimes cold and wet climate.

To relate their products to international customers, Sa-Cinn Enterprises Ltd. has a Web site that features information on all of their product lines. To make ordering easy for all customers, Sa-Cinn has included a currency converter on their site and offers a variety of delivery and payment options. Promotional text is written to cross-cultural interests and needs. As an example, the Cowichan sweater is described as being "as warm as an overcoat and as dry as a raincoat."

The composition of target markets for products such as the Cowichan sweater can vary. To appeal to those consumers who are interested in all-natural products, the site mentions that the yarn is left in its natural colours, and that natural oils in the yarn retain the water-resistant quality of pure wool. For those consumers who want to purchase unique products, the site makes the point that no two sweaters are alike. Customers can choose design features for their sweaters, whether those features are combinations of rich traditional patterns or aspects of design such as length of the sweater or type of neckline. To make it easier for customers to envision and select these design elements, the Web site offers digital representations of designs and trim patterns.

To increase consumers' awareness of the cultural significance of the sweaters, the Web site also explains that the figures in the Cowichan designs are animals that are highly valued in the region's Native culture: the thunderbird is the chief of the supernaturals, the salmon is a symbol of renewal and abundance and was created to feed the world, and the bear is the protector of Native people on land.

Visitors to the Sa-Cinn Web site are also told that the pricing for the sweaters is established by the Cowichan knitters of the Cowichan Valley "collectively as being fair pricing for their work." Because the sweaters are sold over the Internet, customers can and do come from anywhere in the world.

For more on Sa-Cinn Enterprises, visit www.internationalbusiness.nelson.com.

1. How has Sa-Cinn Native Enterprises Ltd. taken into account the challenges they face in explaining their product to consumers who come from very different cultures around the world?

2. Explain the ways in which the marketers at Sa-Cinn Native Enterprises Ltd. have modified their sweaters to adapt them to the cultures of other countries while at the same time maintaining the traditions of their own culture.

ICE Activities for 8.2

Ideas	Connections	Extensions
1. (a) How does culture influence consumer purchasing decisions?	(b) In chart form, list five distinct Canadian cultural events. Describe a specific product associated with the event and identify a possible source of the product. Compare your list with others in the class. What import opportunities exist for Canadian businesses and foreign companies because of Canada's culture?	(c) Select a country other than Canada. Repeat question 1. (b), but this time have Canada as the supplier of the product. What opportunities exist for Canadian businesses because of the culture of your selected country?
2. (a) What questions should a company ask to help identify the cultural composition of a target market in a foreign country?	(b) Research a popular Canadian company and pick at least one country in which it does *not* do business. What cultural opportunities exist for this company's product(s) in that country?	(c) What cultural challenges would the company you selected in 2. (b) face in marketing their product in the country you picked?
3. (a) Summarize the marketing approaches used by the Citrus Marketing Board of Israel in different countries.	(b) Select one product sold in Canada that comes from a foreign country. How do that company's marketers appeal to Canadian customers?	(c) Select one Canadian product that you think could be marketed internationally. Suggest ways that the product could be marketed in at least three different countries.

8.3 Culture and International Business Practices

The customs of international consumers are not the only cultural challenges in the path to a successful business venture in a foreign nation. The business practices of other countries also present a cultural challenge. Canadian companies that want to do business in other countries need to consider the cultural norms and values of their potential business partners.

Deals can be lost when two business cultures clash. The misunderstandings that develop when one business does not research the business culture of another can cause insult, offence, and even anger. Such misunderstandings can result in the loss of business opportunities.

Negotiation Styles

To develop business relationships with other countries, Canadian businesses need to determine what type of negotiating style is typically used in that country. **Negotiating style** is the way in which people negotiate business relationships, and is particularly important in international business. Direct and factual negotiations may be preferred instead of making deals through offers and counteroffers. A cultural misinterpretation of negotiating style can be costly.

For example, Canadian business people negotiating a contract in Canada might mention that they are considering companies besides the company they are currently speaking with. This is a normal negotiating practice in this country. However, in some cultures this tactic would not work and might even be considered insulting. The representatives of the foreign company might expect that the Canadians have chosen to deal with their company because they consider it to be the best in its field.

Another error commonly made by Canadian and U.S. negotiators is to place too much emphasis on the financials at too early a stage in the negotiating process. In some cultures, there needs to be a high level of trust before financial details are revealed to potential partners. In addition, the financial traditions and accounting practices can vary widely from country to country. Sometimes, foreign businesses even keep two sets of books, a real set for company use and a false set to evade taxation in their home country or to deceive investors. Therefore, the Canadian negotiator needs to have patience, knowledge, and understanding in order to succeed.

Another mistake some Canadian business people make is to wait for the foreign representatives to contact them. Sometimes, persistence on the part of the Canadian team is necessary for both cultural and logistical reasons. For one thing, the communication infrastructure in the foreign country may be outdated. Not every company is able to use telephones, e-mails, or fax machines effectively. Also, some cultures prefer personal contact, and their business people may ignore other forms of communication. If the Canadian company is really interested in a deal, it may have to send its executives back to the foreign country to confirm the details of the contract.

A country's laws can also pose challenges for international business people. Laws reflect cultural values. Many countries' business laws—regarding taxation, employment, contracts, and other commercial areas—have serious consequences for negotiations. For example, Russia has been in economic upheaval since the fall of communism in the early 1990s. The business laws in the country are difficult to interpret, are in the process of change, and are sometimes difficult to enforce. The contract, which is a mainstay of Canadian business law, may not mean as much to a Russian entrepreneur. Some Russian executives believe that trust comes with personal relationships rather than with formal legal contracts.

Language

Language is one of the most important, subtle, and complex components of a culture; it is also one of the principal ways in which cultural values and customs are passed on from one generation to the next. Clear business communications are easier to achieve when people from one country speak the same language as those from another country. Even then, however, there can be differences in the meaning of certain words. When it is necessary to translate from one language into another, clear communication can be a challenge, especially since some concepts do not translate at all.

English has become widely accepted as the language of international business. Today, more people use English to conduct business than any other language, and English is understood in many countries. Because English has absorbed words from many other languages and has many business-related terms, ideas can be expressed in many different ways.

Major World Languages

Language	Number of Speakers	Where Language Is Used
Mandarin	885 000 000	China
Hindi	375 000 000	India
Spanish	375 000 000	Spain, Mexico, most Central and South American countries
English	347 000 000	Canada, United Kingdom, United States, Australia, India, and numerous Caribbean, African, and Asian countries
Arabic	211 000 000	Saudi Arabia, Iraq, Egypt, Libya, Algeria, Morocco, Tunisia, Jordan, Syria, numerous African and Middle Eastern countries
Bengali	210 000 000	India, Bangladesh
Portuguese	176 000 000	Portugal, Brazil
Russian	165 000 000	Russia, former republics of the Soviet Union
Japanese	125 000 000	Japan
German	100 000 000	Germany, Austria, Switzerland, numerous European countries
French	77 000 000	France, Canada, numerous European and African countries
Malay-Indonesian	58 000 000	Malaysia, Indonesia

Figure 8.10 Although English speakers are not the most numerous, English has become the language of international business. What are some reasons for this phenomenon?

Figure 8.11 Translators work with all kinds of people such as politicians, business people, and journalists.

Many business negotiations, however, still take place in languages other than English. When a company is negotiating in a foreign language and in a foreign country, a Canadian who has studied that language at school may not be the right person for the job. Translators, business consultants, researchers, and others who help a foreign company do business should normally be local people. For example, hiring an expert from Canada who can speak Russian is not the same as hiring a local Russian who is familiar with the current culture, language, and business practices in the country. A Canadian who is a native Russian speaker but who left the country years ago will not speak the language in the same way as someone who has lived in Russia through the years would. The Canadian might miss the new idioms or subtle language differences that could be very important in reading the tone of a negotiation.

Silent Language

Nonverbal communication such as body language, gestures, personal distances between people, appearance, the use of colours, and modes of greeting are all forms of what has been called **silent language**. All of these may be different in different cultures, and astute international business people are aware of these differences.

Gestures are a universal characteristic of communication. People in every culture use their hands to express joy, despair, anger, triumph, and a host of other emotions. It is important to remember, however, that even though everyone gestures, the gestures do not always mean the same thing from one culture to the next. For example, the North American sign for "okay" (forming a circle with the thumb and forefinger) means "zero" in France and is an obscene gesture in Brazil.

A Japanese person may nod up and down in the North American gesture for agreement, even when they mean "no." Many books and Web sites are dedicated to the meanings of gestures in other countries and the business traveller would be wise to research this topic thoroughly.

Personal demeanour is another important aspect of silent language: how to sit and when to sit; what to do with your hands, briefcase, or purse; how much eye contact is polite or expected or acceptable; what to do if you cough or sneeze; how to laugh and when to laugh. These and other points regarding personal behaviour during a negotiation should all be researched in advance.

Forms of Greetings

Forms of greeting are also important when dealing with people of other cultures. An inappropriate greeting can give serious offence to the recipient. For example, handshakes may be inappropriate in some cultures, where touching a stranger is forbidden. The Japanese bow indicates status. If a visitor to

Some anthropologists credit the British with introducing the concept of the handshake. In medieval times, a knight would extend his right hand (his weapon hand) to another to prove that he was unarmed. The concept became a cultural greeting of friendship. In much of the world today, people do not shake hands when they meet. They may hug formally or kiss one another on the cheek, as in Eastern Europe and Arab states. They may bow softly, eyes turned to the ground, as in Japan and China. The Hawaiian greeting, termed "honi," consists of placing the nostril gently beside that of the person greeted. For Hindus, the greeting of choice is two hands pressed together and held near the heart with the head gently bowed while saying "Namaste."

Figure 8.12 In Japan the card should be presented with both hands extended, palms up, with the business card in the middle, as if one were giving a gift.

Figure 8.13 Although the setting is quite different, these business meetings are equally serious.

Japan is greeted with a bow, he or she should return the bow at the same angle. To make a slighter bow insults the recipient. To make a deeper bow confers power upon him or her. It is important that business people research greeting protocol before visiting a foreign business. The visitor may even have to practise the greeting to make sure that it is appropriate.

A travelling business person should also have a business card. The card should be in the visitor's language on one side and the receiver's language on the other. The business visitor should present the card with the translated side facing the receiver so that he or she can read it.

Style of Dress

Different cultures have different expectations for suitable business attire. Dark business suits are considered conservative and formal. Khaki pants or skirts and an open-collared shirt or blouse are more casual and informal. In Japan, business people usually expect conservative attire for both men and women; shoes should be slip-ons, as the visitor needs to remove them frequently. A Brazilian business executive may expect casual attire from men but more conservative dress for women.

Most people travelling on business should pack at least one conservative suit and one "tailored casual" outfit. Dress protocols in the destination country should be investigated, if possible, but in general it is better to be dressed too formally than too casually. The casual may offend, the formal will not.

Business Protocol

Any business that wants to make a deal with a foreign country must research several areas to be sure that the executives visiting the foreign country do not make mistakes in **protocol** (rules of correct or appropriate behaviour to follow when meeting with officials or business people in another nation). Some considerations for correct business protocol are in the areas of gift giving, punctuality, scheduling meetings, and business entertaining.

Gift Giving

In some countries, the visiting business representative is expected to present a gift to the company representative he or she is visiting as a token of respect or friendship. The visitor who does not offer a gift shows disrespect and may be making a cultural mistake. In other countries, a gift to a company representative is seen as an attempt to bribe the recipient and is considered bad form or even illegal. Traditionally, Japanese business people expect a gift, especially during a first meeting. Managers of companies in most European countries would not expect or accept gifts. If a gift is expected, it is the task of the giver to select a gift that is appropriate. For example, the gift of a pen made from Canadian cedar wood with the Canadian company name on it might be considered an appropriate gesture. A gift can be too expensive and seem like a bribe, or it can be too inexpensive and seem like an insult. Some gifts are inappropriate for other cultural reasons. A set of four glasses might be an excellent gift for a Russian manager but not a Korean one, as the number 4 is associated with death in some Asian cultures. Many Web sites explain the gift-giving protocols for other nations to assist the baffled gift giver.

Punctuality

Cultures often clash over the issue of punctuality. If a visitor who holds punctuality as a high cultural value is meeting with someone from a culture where punctuality is not considered a virtue, both parties could be insulted by the other's behaviour. The business person who makes an appointment for 10:00 A.M. and arrives at 9:50 A.M., having negotiated major transportation problems to do so, will be offended when the manager he or she is visiting does not show up until 11:30 A.M. The issue may not be one of rudeness, but of a cultural attitude towards time. For example, German business people are likely to value punctuality highly. It would be very discourteous to arrive for a 3:00 P.M. meeting at 3:10 P.M. On the other hand, a Brazilian executive who scheduled an appointment for 3:00 P.M. might not arrive until 4:00 P.M. To be offended by the Brazilian executive's lateness is to impose one set of cultural values on another culture. Brazilians have a different cultural attitude towards time than Germans do. No offence is intended and none should be taken.

Scheduling of Meetings

Countries often vary from North American companies in hours of operation, holiday closings, and even scheduled break times. A company manager who plans to visit French businesses during August might find that many business are closed for vacation. In Great Britain, many factory towns have a half-day, which means they are closed for the afternoon. Which day is the half-day varies from town to town. Muslim businesses provide two prayer breaks during the day, when no appointments are scheduled. Business people should be aware of national and religious holidays when they are attempting to schedule appointments and meetings.

Business Entertaining

Many cultures believe that business negotiations should be more informal, and use lunches, dinners, or parties to negotiate with clients, suppliers, or potential business partners. In other cultures, business entertaining is used simply to meet foreign business visitors and create a social relationship. Once the purpose of the meal or party has been established, the visitor has the very daunting task of learning the rules of etiquette involved in eating and drinking in this country.

Figure 8.14 The Shammar tribe in Saudi Arabia eat food using their fingers from communal dishes while seated in a large tent.

Employee Management

Even after a deal has been struck and the negotiations for business in a foreign country have been completed successfully, there are still cultural rules to learn concerning work and employee management. An awareness of business practices is also necessary for the management of a foreign workforce. The Canadian manager of a foreign branch plant or retail outlet must understand the culture of his or her employees. Many cultural values have been incorporated into the employment laws of each country, such as minimum wage rates, paid vacations, health care, and so on, but a number of cultural traits exist in each foreign society that challenge the management skills of Canadian executives.

For example, in Mexico, lunch is generally expected to start between 2:00 and 3:30 P.M. and end between 4:00 and 5:30 P.M. Many businesses there stay open until 7:00 P.M. Greek businesses often close for a break between 2:00 and 4:00 P.M. These breaks from the working day may affect productivity in countries where such breaks are common. Managers should scale their expectations to accommodate this cultural issue.

Labour laws are often very protective of the country's citizens. In many countries—Mexico and Saudi Arabia are two examples—it is very difficult for a foreign business to fire a local employee for any reason. Before setting up any type of business in a foreign country, the company manager should review the labour laws for that country. The manager should also hire a local labour lawyer for labour negotiations.

TRADE TIPS

The Monkey Trap

To catch a monkey, you need a coconut and a banana. Cut a hole in the coconut large enough for a monkey's paw. Put the banana inside the coconut and leave it out where the monkey can get it. The monkey will reach in and grab the banana. The monkey will not be able to get its fist out of the coconut while holding the banana, but will not let the banana go. A monkey with a coconut on its paw is easily captured.

Moral: To achieve a particular goal, we must let go of others. Many of our cultural "bananas" trap us in our own "coconuts" and make business negotiations very difficult.

Possibly the most serious problem for a manager of a foreign plant comes from the differences in work ethic from one country to another. As already noted in this chapter, different cultures have different attitudes towards time, for example. If punctuality is a requirement for a North American business, that requirement should be modified when expanding the company into a culture that does not value punctuality. Countries that have had strong socialist or communist governments did not reward hard work with promotion or higher income. Jobs were fairly permanent and rarely did an employee "move up" a corporate ladder, as no such ladder existed. As a result, the work-force in these countries may be difficult to motivate. Foreign managers must work much harder in these work environments than at home to reward effort and encourage productivity.

Dolorès Cléroux

Translator

Dolorès Cléroux has had an interest in language all her life, but only recently has she used her linguistic abilities as a translator. The journey from learning sewing and fashion design at school to her current work as owner of Kingston Language Services has involved a number of twists and turns. The first involved moving from Quebec to Africa to teach sewing.

Her first career choice was fashion design, and when she moved to Kingston, Ontario, in 1979, she took a teaching position in fashion design at St. Lawrence College. Then she learned that the college needed her linguistic abilities as a francophone more than her fashion expertise.

Cléroux began teaching and developing her language teaching skills while attending Queen's University, and graduated with a degree in language and linguistics. From 1992 to 1995, she taught French as a Second Language with the Centre des langues at the Royal Military College in Kingston.

In 1995, while continuing to teach part-time, Cléroux decided to use her language skills as a translator. She opened her own business, Kingston Language Services. Today, her staff of mostly freelance translators works in more than 15 languages, including Chinese, Polish, Portuguese, Russian, Arabic, Dutch, and Swedish.

On typical days, Cléroux reads, translates, or proofreads many types of texts. On other days, she could arrange for a translator to accompany a Korean business leader to an important meeting; help an immigrant translate significant papers; assist a foreign student to get transcripts translated for an application to a Canadian post-graduate program; or proofread the translation of a Japanese sales brochure. Her company translates Web sites, foreign packaging and labelling, and technical articles for publications. She says, "I help people with language challenges solve their problems. Helping people achieve their goals feels great."

There are several ways to become a translator, all of which require fluency in another language. Universities and colleges offer translation courses and full-time programs. Government departments hire language experts, often directly from a post-secondary language program, to translate documents. Language teachers often turn part-time translation services into a full-time career. Anyone with a proficiency in a foreign language could work as a freelance translator for a business like Kingston Language Services.

Cléroux's advice to young people who want to become translators is to learn as much as you can about as much as you can. "Every little bit you learn," she says, "becomes part of your big puzzle, a puzzle that only you can put together. The reasons for knowing something may not be clear right away (grammar, for instance), but it could be very useful later on. I have taken pieces of my own puzzle from all of the different things I have learned and experienced, to build this business."

• •

1. Create a flow chart or a timeline to illustrate the development of Dolorès Cléroux's skills in languages and translation.

2. Select an occupation in international business that you would be interested in. Describe the skills you would need to succeed in this career and how you might go about achieving proficiency in those skills.

8.4 Disappearing Diversity

International business is creating a type of global culture. Very few places on earth are free from business travellers with cell phones and laptops. Almost all nations welcome trade and encourage it through international trade fairs, trade missions, and government-sponsored Web sites for companies and organizations wishing to do business.

When a representative from Canada explores business opportunities in Brazil one week and Nigeria the next, he or she becomes familiar with the culture of each nation and realizes that even though there are cultural differences between the nations, there are also similarities. The representative knows that every business in the world wants to earn a profit, and that this motivation crosses every culture. Successful business deals mean economic success, financial freedom, improved lifestyle, and economic benefits for entire communities. What might begin as a pragmatic tolerance of another nation's culture to ensure profit may become a real desire to understand the culture. Progressive companies now see nations as markets like any other and attempt to research and understand each market, just as they would attempt to understand any target market in Canada. With increased understanding comes the sense of connectedness, so that the "other" becomes less foreign, and more a part of the "us."

Market differentiation is increasingly hard to achieve and is increasingly important. Many large multinational companies have created homogeneous markets, making the whole world a marketplace for their hamburgers, cola drinks, and running shoes. The small competitors must find ways to be different. Companies, in searching for differentiation, often look beyond their borders. Products from other nations are less likely to be available in Canada and, therefore,

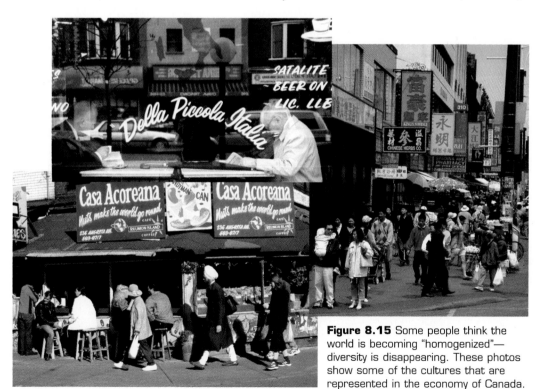

Figure 8.15 Some people think the world is becoming "homogenized"—diversity is disappearing. These photos show some of the cultures that are represented in the economy of Canada.

usually appear to be new and different—at least for a while. The pita place, the bubble teashop, and the foreign magazine dealer compete with McDonald's, Starbucks, and Chapters by appealing to customers who want something unique. Marketers welcome the new and search the world to find it. As the import finds acceptance in Canada, competitors enter the market, and the exotic becomes familiar. Soon the foreign product is considered domestic. For example, dim sum is a business lunch for thousands of Canadians, but not many years ago it was a rarity.

GLOBAL THOUGHT

We are increasingly living in a global village.
– *Marshall McLuhan*

In the past, Canada's immigrants came from Europe, but recently, most have come from Asian countries. Each immigrant group brings its culture and often creates its own immigrant community within Canada, preserving the traditions, customs, and language of the country of origin. Since most of these groups are located in urban centres, the immigrant culture soon mixes with the other cultures in the area, and the cultural richness of the community expands. Exposure to this cultural diversity gives Canadians a unique advantage in being connected to the global community.

So does travel. Canadian travellers abroad share their stories and pictures and expand the cultural experiences of their friends and neighbours as well as their own. The message many travellers bring back is that people are the same around the world. The diversity is obvious, but so are the similarities among human wants and needs, and the common denominators of family, work, and leisure.

Movies, music, the Internet, newspapers, magazines, and, most importantly, television have created a global culture. People around the world see and hear the messages from other lands, and these messages carry the countries' cultures. We are all connected through media to the thoughts, beliefs, hopes, and dreams of people from Iceland, Algeria, Peru, India, Vietnam, and every other country where people create music, make movies, or have access to the Internet. Newspapers and magazines from around the world can be read online. Radio stations around the globe stream their programs so that Canadian teenagers can listen to South African popular music while they do their homework.

GLOBAL THOUGHT

Once we surrendered our senses and nervous systems to the private manipulation of those who would try to benefit from taking a lease on our eyes and ears and nerves, we don't really have any rights left. Leasing our eyes and ears and nerves to commercial interests is like handing over the common speech to a private corporation, or like giving the earth's atmosphere to a company as a monopoly.
– *Marshall McLuhan*

Culture is central to the definition of a people, and the language, beliefs, and customs that define a culture are tenaciously preserved in all regions of the world. The diversity is still celebrated and still creates the sense of excitement and consciousness of the exotic and foreign. But central to the global community is the increasing awareness of how we are all, at heart, very similar.

ICE Activities for 8.3 and 8.4

Ideas	Connections	Extensions
1. (a) What are some factors that Canadian business people need to remember when negotiating with people from other countries?	(b) Select a country other than Canada. Prepare a report for the CEO of a Canadian company that wishes to do business in the country you selected, outlining the protocols to consider before meeting to discuss a joint venture.	(c) Prepare a similar report to the one you prepared in 1. (b), but prepare it for a foreign executive planning to do business with a Canadian firm.
2. (a) List and explain some of the challenges facing a Canadian managing employees in another country.	(b) Research news media and describe a specific situation that a Canadian manager has recently faced in a foreign country.	(c) How did the Canadian manager in 2. (b) solve the problem? Suggest two solutions that might have worked as well or better.
3. (a) What does "disappearing diversity" mean in terms of international business?	(b) In small groups, discuss the pros and cons of the disappearance of cultural boundaries around the globe.	(c) Do you agree that international business is achieving a global culture? Give at least three reasons for your opinion.

GLOBAL THOUGHT

The increasingly open Russian economy is in full expansion. The country is at last making the transition to a market economy; with demand rapidly growing for a wide range of products and services, new outlets and opportunities are emerging. There is also renewed optimism in the business community that the progress will continue.

– "Team Canada Trade Mission Targets Russia and Germany," Canada World View, Spring 2002, Department of Foreign Affairs and International Trade

Figure 8.16 In Moscow on February 13, 2002, the Russian honour guard greeted a large delegation of business leaders. These leaders met to discuss security issues and to sign several investment and trade deals.

Nortel Networks is there. So are McCain Foods, Archangel Diamonds, SNC-Lavalin, and the Royal Bank. These companies are members of the Canadian Russian Business Forum or the Canadian Business Association in Russia, or both, and they and many other Canadian firms are developing a business relationship with Russia. However, they are finding that it is not always easy.

Less than a generation ago, Russia was organized as a major communist system. Producers were told what to produce and how much of it to produce, consumers had little choice in what they could buy, and no one had the freedom to start a business to make a profit. When communism fell in Russia in the 1990s, no economic system was in place to replace it.

For several years, the country was in economic chaos. Few laws existed to protect private business, because businesses had not been allowed in Russia for decades. The business culture of the Russian people reflected the fact that the centralized government owned and operated the sources of production, and that Russia was a planned economic system rather than a free-enterprise system. The cultural values of communism are gradually being replaced by those of a free-market economy.

In February 2002, Team Canada visited Moscow to foster better business relations and economic cooperation between the two countries. Canada and Russia share a common Arctic coast and already have agreements about aspects of the Arctic: environmental monitoring, self-government, transportation, Aboriginal business, electrical utilities, and oil and gas.

Among the members of the mission were representatives of both large and small Canadian businesses—Air Canada, Alcan, Bombardier, Chilliwack Mountain Log Homes, and Polyval Coatings of Quebec. The Teslin Tlingit Council was also a member of the mission, seeking social, cultural, and economic cooperation with the indigenous peoples of Russia. The mission formed working groups made up of officials of federal and provincial governments, senior executives of Russian and Canadian companies, and industry associations related to agriculture, fuel and energy, construction and housing, and mining.

Business Information Service for Newly Independent States (BISNIS), the U.S. government's resource centre for North American companies exploring business opportunities in Russia and other newly independent states, has some cautions for businesses moving into those countries. For example, legal remedies for fraud, recovery of damages, or reimbursement of business losses are not the same as those in Canada or the United States. Differences may make it difficult to recover losses. Business cultures vary from region to region in Russia, as does infrastructure and even government regulations. Western business people still face some risk to personal safety because of the possibility of attacks by terrorist and organized crime groups.

Nevertheless, for many Canadian companies, the risks and problems are worth the effort. There are 146 million consumers in Russia, waiting for good salaries and a stable economic climate to start buying the products Canadian businesses can provide.

A SNAPSHOT OF RUSSIA

Size: 17 075 200 sq. km

World Region: Europe/Asia

Capital City: Moscow

Language: Russian

Currency: Ruble

Population: 144.9 million

Time: Noon in Ottawa is 9:00 P.M. in Moscow.

Climate: Ranges from temperate to Arctic continental.

Type of Government: Democratic federal state

Labour Force by Occupation: 61.4 percent services, 27.8 percent industry, 10.8 percent agriculture (2001 est.)

Membership in World Organizations: APEC, G8, has applied for membership in the WTO

Importing Partners and Products:
Partners: Eastern Europe, United States, New Independent States, Japan, China.
Products: Machinery and equipment, chemicals, consumer goods, medicines, meat, sugar, semi-finished metal products.

Exporting Partners and Products:
Partners: Eastern Europe, New Independent States, China, Japan.
Products: Petroleum and petroleum products, natural gas, woods and wood products, metals, chemicals

Travel Advisory: All foreigners must have an entry and exit visa. For short stays, the exit visa is issued with the entry visa. For longer stays, the exit visa must be obtained after the traveller's arrival. All travellers who spend more than three days in Russia must register their visa through their hotel or sponsor. Visitors who overstay their visa's validity even for one day or neglect to register their visa may be prevented from leaving. The role of organized crime in Russia is significant. Organized criminal groups target foreign businesses in many cities and have been known to demand protection money under threat of serious violence. Canadian business people should hire a reputable security firm for protection.

Figure 8.17 Known as the Cathedral of the Virgin of the Intercession, this historical site was built by Ivan the Terrible to commemorate the capture of the Tartar City of Kazan on the Volga, Oct. 1, 1552, and is composed of 11 religious buildings combined into one.

TRADE TIPS

Business communications systems in Russia are not yet up to Western standards, so business travellers are cautioned to expect delays in the phone system and may not necessarily be able to find fax machines and computers.

Country Link

Follow the link at
www.internationalbusiness.nelson.com.
to find out more about Canada's trade with Russia.

Chapter Challenges

Knowledge/Understanding

1. Match each of the following terms to the correct definition or description below:

   (a) culture

   (b) customs

   (c) cultural determinants

   (d) cultural imperialism

   (e) silent language

   (f) protocol

   (i) geography, history, and religion

   (ii) the rules of correct or appropriate behaviour

   (iii) a group's values, beliefs, language, art, and laws

   (iv) nonverbal communication

   (v) a group's social habits

   (vi) the imposing of cultural values by one group on another group

2. How does a country's geography influence its culture?

3. List ten cultural events in Canada and name at least five specific products that are associated with each event. Compare your list with those of other class members.

4. Create a mind map to show some of the ways in which culture influences consumer needs and wants. Then write a caption for your organizer in which you explain how international businesses have adapted their products to meet consumer demand.

Thinking/Inquiry

1. Create a list of research questions that a Canadian company of your choice should ask about the culture and consumer habits of another country before the Canadian company tries to sell its products internationally.

2. Visit a shopping mall or business area in your community. Observe the human environment for a few minutes. Explain how what you see—things such as methods of transport, how people are dressed, how people behave on the street, and types of stores—is reflective of Canadian culture.

3. Examine a current English-language version of a Russian newspaper on the Internet. Using the Country Profile in this chapter as a starting point, describe how a current political, economic, or cultural event in Russia is likely to have either a positive or negative effect on the international business environment in that country.

4. Prepare an annotated bibliography of five Web sites that a Canadian business could use to research the culture of another country. Give a brief description of each Web site's purpose and contents, including its sponsors and the usefulness of the site to international business people. Then pool your findings with those of other students to create a master bibliography of useful Web sites.

Communication

1. Using the Jaffa Citrus Fruit international marketing strategies as a model (page 253), research how one international business modifies its products to adapt them to the culture of at least three countries. Create a collage to illustrate your findings.

2. Research the cultural events of a country other than Canada. Prepare and present a short oral report on how a Canadian company might find business opportunities in the celebration of those events.

3. The Canadian media expert Marshall McLuhan said, "I find media analysis very much more exciting now simply because it affects more people than most anything. One measure of the importance of anything is: Who is affected by it?" In your opinion, how has the medium of the Internet affected the cultural diversity and homogeneity of peoples around the world? Write an editorial expressing your point of view.

Application

1. Select a Canadian product you think might be successful in Russia, Japan, Israel, Mexico, or Kenya. How would you change the product to adapt it to the culture in the selected country? Why would you make these changes?

2. Research the labour laws or work ethic in a country other than Canada. Then, outline, draft, and revise a memo for international managers in which you explain how the laws or the work ethic of that country are the same as or different from those in Canada. The purpose of your memo is to help the managers avoid any pitfalls as they manage the workforce in that country.

3. Research the current business challenges that would be faced by a specific Canadian company (of your choice) that wants to export its goods and services to Russia. Then prepare a problem-solution graphic organizer in which you recommend some practical solutions to those challenges.

International Business Portfolio

Cultural Factors and Customs

Understanding how to do business in a foreign country includes knowing the "Dos and Taboos" of that country. Dos and taboos are culturally determined. A "taboo" is a behaviour that is not considered acceptable in that culture or country. For example, in some cultures it is forbidden to touch someone on the head. In others, sticking your chopsticks upright in your food might be viewed with horror. A "do" is a behaviour that is expected or even required in the host country. For example, a Japanese business person will expect you to present a business card with both hands.

Every culture has its unique set of "Dos and Taboos." In this assignment, you will determine what will and won't "do" in your IBP country.

Activities

1. List three "Dos" and three "Taboos" in your IBP country. Indicate why a business person should or should not use those actions or behaviours.

2. Compare the culture of Canada with the culture of your IBP country using these cultural determinants: geography, history, and religion.

Chapter 9

Political and Economic Factors Affecting International Business

A Canadian company entering the international market needs to consider political factors in foreign countries. Although countries and businesses are becoming more interdependent, the different political systems around the world still pose risks that international business people have to assess and prepare for. The type of economic system in a country also has an effect on international business. Factors related to economic systems have to be understood and carefully evaluated.

Chapter Topics

➤ 9.1 – The Political Process: Government's Role in International Trade 274

➤ 9.2 – Assessing Global Political Risks 279

➤ 9.3 – Economic Factors Related to International Business 284

➤ 9.4 – Managing International Financial Risks 293

➤ *Canada's Trading Partners: Focus on* North and South Korea 298

➤ Chapter Challenges 300

Prior Knowledge

- How does a country's political system affect the country's participation in international business?
- What are some political and financial risks faced by Canadian companies in the international business world?
- How are economic systems throughout the world becoming more interdependent and more global?

Inquiries/Expectations

- How do political and economic factors influence international business methods and operations?
- Which factors make business opportunities in a more-developed country better than those in a less-developed country?
- How do different kinds of political and economic systems influence business opportunities?
- How does global business affect interdependence among countries?

Important Terms

centrally planned economy
currency devaluation
currency revaluation
democracy
economic imperialism
economic system
equilibrium
exchange controls
expropriation
floating rate
foreign investment
general instability risk
global economy
global equity market

market economy
mixed economy
operations risk
ownership risk
political risk
privatize
repatriation of earnings
think tank
supply and demand
systems
totalitarian
trade war
transfer risk

9.1 The Political Process: Government's Role in International Trade

All governments assume a role in international trade. The government of Canada promotes Canadian businesses abroad and tries to lessen the risk of doing business in foreign countries in numerous ways. The Canadian government:

- establishes import and export policies to protect Canada and Canadians

- develops trade policies and regulations to govern and encourage trade

- assists Canadian exporters in their quest to succeed internationally

- matches potential Canadian exporters with international clients

- maintains and improves relationships with other nations for the purpose of trade

- assists Canadian companies in adjusting to changing international market conditions

- fosters innovation and human resource development to enable companies to compete internationally

One of the key institutions for helping Canadian businesses is the Canadian embassy, high commission, or trade consulate located in most foreign countries. These government offices have responsibility for, among other tasks, promoting and encouraging safe and friendly trade relations. Canadian embassies and consulates help establish and manage relationships with trading partners, look after our business interests, and assist Canadians living or doing business in foreign countries. Embassies are managed by an ambassador, and trade commisions and consulates are usually managed by a trade commissioner. Embassies and consulates can also help Canadians coordinate work permits or visas in foreign countries.

Web Link

Follow the link at
www.internationalbusiness.nelson.com
to find out more about Canadian
embassies around the world.

Political Risk

All business activity, whether domestic or international, presents risks that companies must manage if they want to make a profit.

Political risk refers to political decisions, conditions, events, or activities in a country that affect the business climate. These risks may mean that investors will lose money or make less than they had anticipated when they made the investment. Losses may take many forms: financial loss, time delays, technical breakdown, loss of reputation, or loss of market share are some examples.

Political risk analysis tries to identify the causes or sources of risk and predict its impact on investment in a country. Awareness of potential political risks in a country is the first step in risk reduction or management. Risk management requires a thorough assessment of potential political situations. This assessment must then be factored into any business decisions involving a country.

Political risk arises when government policies threaten the business environment. Economic risks include government policies and controls that affect prices and currency values. Any government policy can change at any time.

Political or economic risk may be so high that a business decides to walk away from investment opportunities in a country. If, however, the business decides to proceed, it can implement different policies to protect its investment. For example, it may take out insurance. It may balance the risky investment with more secure ones in other projects or in other countries. It may build the risk factors into its prices for goods or services in the country.

Economic and financial risks will be examined in more depth later in this chapter.

Figure 9.1 A woman casts her vote during a Canadian federal election.

All over the world, the role of governments has changed dramatically in the last twenty years. Deregulation, funding cutbacks, privatization, and free trade have left governments with little to do but give more power to global economic institutions like the WTO and the World Bank and provide the security forces needed to protect the system against its detractors.

– *Maude Barlow* and *Tony Clarke*

Types of Political Systems

Countries are defined geographically by their national physical borders. Within those borders, the country's government is responsible for passing and enforcing the laws of the land—the laws that govern the country's citizens and businesses.

Most developed countries, such as Canada, have used a democratic model for their political system. **Democracy** provides government for and by the people. In democracies, the general population has the right to vote in free elections and decide on the rules that will govern them. Democratic countries allow individuals to own property and run businesses, and they permit a free press and freedom of speech. Most democratic countries have a market-oriented or capitalist economy in which the market allocates available resources: labour, capital, land, and entrepreneurship. These nations often promote free trade.

By contrast, some nations do not grant democratic freedoms to their people. **Totalitarian systems**, such as those in North Korea, Cuba, or Myanmar (formerly Burma), tend to centralize power and often use the military to control the state. Governments in such countries can be single-party rule or a dictatorship. Citizens have no elected representatives in government and have little say in how they are governed. Most totalitarian nations have a command economy, which means that the government allocates available resources.

In practice, a purely democratic or totalitarian political system is theoretical, and most countries have a mixed system of government that leans towards one end or the other of the political spectrum. In the same way, most countries have a **mixed economy**, having characteristics of both market and command economies.

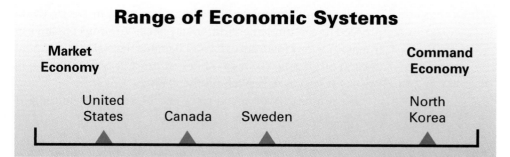

Range of Economic Systems

Market Economy   **Command Economy**

United States   Canada   Sweden   North Korea

Figure 9.2 The spectrum of political ideology.

Recent political developments in both Russia (formerly a communist country) and China (still a communist country) have led to more open markets and trade. Although Cuba remains partially closed to trade because of its political system, Canadian trade with Cuba has increased in recent years. Doing business with a country in transition from one political system to another can be risky, because all institutions—political, economic, and social—are unstable.

Political Interdependence

A country may seem independent in exercising its authority and power within its own borders, but, in fact, many countries became more interdependent in the later decades of the twentieth century. With interdependence can come pressure on countries to change their political, economic, and cultural practices. For example, for several decades, many countries refused to trade with South Africa because of the policy of *apartheid* imposed by the white minority on the Blacks, Indians, and people of mixed race of that country. Eventually, after suffering economic isolation for many years, the government bowed to international pressure, and the policy was abandoned.

Even though, in a perfect world, the Canadian government and Canadian companies might prefer to deal only with democratic countries, in practice, some companies would forgo important business opportunities if they refused to deal with non-democratic regimes such as China. From a business perspective, a strong authoritarian government under which the "rules of the game" are favourable to international trade and well understood may be preferable to a shaky democratic regime where the rules may change suddenly.

Sometimes, trade wars erupt between countries. In a **trade war**, governments act aggressively in international markets and other forums to promote their own countries' trading interests. For example, early in 2001, the Canadian government imposed a ban on the importation of beef products from Brazil. Canadian inspectors were concerned that the products might contain the mad cow disease virus. Brazilian beef products were removed from Canadian stores for more than a month.

TRADE TALK

Brazilians reacted with outrage and even protested in the streets. Critics suggested that the Canadian government served up the ban on beef products in retaliation against Brazil for a dispute that originated from competition in the sale and subsidy of Canadian and Brazilian-made aircraft. Caught in the middle of these political troubles were companies directly and marginally involved in the importation of beef food products from Brazil. For example, supermarkets and smaller grocery stores lost the income from the beef products that they might have been able to sell, and transportation companies lost business.

Interdependence also happens because of **economic imperialism**. Economic imperialism has traditionally been defined as the exploitation of developing countries by more developed countries. In this traditional definition, a developed country is driven to overseas economic expansion by both the need for markets for its manufactured goods and a need for raw materials. A less-developed country can address both these needs.

The economic power of today's multinationals often exceeds the gross domestic product of a poorer nation, and their needs are similar to those of the imperial nations of the last two centuries. In behaviour often referred to as "Coca-Colonization," a large company can exert considerable economic and cultural power over local inhabitants. Today, pressure groups and populist movements share a concern that foreign corporate or business domination can have a negative effect on the cultural identity of a nation; this is one of the causes for protests against the WTO.

Figure 9.3 A protester reacts to Canada's ban on Brazilian beef products.

Web Link

Follow the link at
www.internationalbusiness.nelson.com
to find out more about different
perspectives on world trade.

Junior Team Canada

Figure 9.4 Sean Burrowes in Taipei, Taiwan.

Junior Team Canada (JTC) is a program designed to prepare young people for careers in the worldwide workplace. Global Vision, a not-for-profit organization whose aim is to help young people become business leaders, is the official organizer of Junior Team Canada, founded in 1991.

Thirteen regional training centres across Canada hold conferences that enable both high school and post-secondary students aged 16 to 25 to meet with one another and with individuals from different industry sectors. Junior Team Canada economic missions have allowed young people to travel internationally. The program brings business, industry, and government leaders together with Canadian students to discuss careers in the international marketplace. Partners include Export Development Canada (EDC), the Canadian International Development Agency (CIDA), Industry Canada, Toshiba Canada, GlaxoSmithKline, and the Drake Foundation.

In August 2001, Sean Burrowes, a university student, was selected along with about 50 other candidates to participate in Junior Team Canada's trade mission to Asia. Sean graduated with honours from Chinguacousy Secondary School in Brampton and now studies engineering at the University of Toronto. An aspiring space scientist, he has participated in Houston's renowned International Space School Foundation in the company of astronauts such as Chris Hadfield. In fact, Sean was present in Florida in April 2001 for Hadfield's space shuttle launch and mission to install Canadarm 2 on the International Space Station.

After participating in programs at Global Vision's training centre at the Richard Ivey School of Business at the University of Western Ontario, Sean submitted a proposal for the August trip. There were two separate missions: one group would go to Japan and Korea and the other to Taiwan. Sean was selected to represent the aerospace industry on the Taiwan segment. He managed to find the necessary financial sponsors, as he was required to do, and he travelled to Ottawa for five days of training before the two-week trip.

Sean's role was to represent his sector at trade shows and business meetings in Taiwan. At the Taipei Aerospace Technology Exhibition at the Taipei World Trade Centre, Sean noticed that much of the equipment being showcased was for the defence industry. He learned about the political and military tension between China and Taiwan. He also saw that like many large, overcrowded urban areas, Taipei has some serious environmental problems. Much of the air pollution comes from mopeds powered by two-stroke engines. As well, only a small fraction of Taiwan's sewage goes through treatment facilities. The solutions to Taiwan's environmental and infrastructure problems will play a critical role in the country's future. Solving these problems may create investment opportunities for Canadian companies.

Sean learned how to adapt to a different culture. He learned very quickly that "North America is not the centre of the universe." He also added to his already solid knowledge of and experience with importing, exporting, and networking.

Web Link

Follow the link at
www.internationalbusiness.nelson.com
to find out more about the Junior Team Canada trade missions.

1. How did Sean Burrowes prepare himself to become a member of Team Canada?

2. What are the benefits of participating in the Junior Team Canada program? Give reasons why you would or would not want to be involved in a program like this.

3. Write a paragraph explaining how this profile demonstrates the advantages of political interdependence for Canadian businesses.

ICE Activities for 9.1

Ideas	Connections	Extensions
1. (a) Describe the ways in which the Canadian government assists Canadian international businesses.	(b) In pairs, identify three suggestions that you might make to the Canadian government for additional ways to help Canadian businesses abroad. Then share your ideas in a larger group.	(c) Explain how hostilities between countries interfere with the smooth running of international business.
2. (a) Explain the differences among the three political systems.	(b) In what ways is Canada a mixed political system?	(c) In your opinion, how might changes in the Canadian political system help Canadian businesses competing in the global economy?
3. (a) How does political interdependence affect international business?	(b) Differentiate between a country's political independence and its interdependence.	(c) Create a graphic organizer to demonstrate your perspective on the proper balance between a country's independence and its interdependence.

9.2 Assessing Global Political Risks

To assess political risk, companies look at the host or target country's current or future political system and examine how changes to its stability might cause a loss to investors. Clearly, international business always faces some measure of political risk. If you operate a Canadian company, your foreign customer may be unable to pay the amount owed to you in full and on time because of instability arising from currency controls imposed by government, war or military actions, civil unrest, or even government takeover of a business. There are a number of "hot spots" around the world that are unstable for international traders. For example, there is a risk of a war between China and Taiwan. Taiwan, an island east of mainland China, is modern, wealthy, democratic, and eager for recognition of its business success. Before 1949, Taiwan was part of China but, in that year, Chinese Communist troops defeated Nationalist leader Chiang Kai-shek, and he fled to Taiwan and set up his government there under U.S. protection. China has been trying to reclaim Taiwan ever since.

Types of Political Risk

When a company is analyzing the level of political risk in a country, it needs to evaluate all of these issues and areas of concern:

- risk of general political instability
- ownership risk
- operations risk
- transfer risk

All of these risks have an impact on investment in foreign countries. Companies must consider the safety of both their products and their people in unstable political situations.

- **Risk of General Political Instability:** General political instability may not be considered serious enough to cause investors to withdraw from a country. However, **general instability risk** raises uncertainty about Canadian projects overseas. Operations may be affected and profits may decline.

- **Ownership Risk:** When operations are threatened by government takeover or **expropriation**, owners may lose their offshore property. This is referred to as **ownership risk**. This risk is evident when the ideology leans towards protectionism and nationalization of business. Foreign governments may force or coerce foreign owners to sell their property or may simply expropriate it.

- **Operations Risk:** Government policies of the host country may impede business operations such as finance, marketing, or production. Uncertainty about these policies is referred to as **operations risk**. Such risk might result from new taxes, import restrictions, or government regulations in areas that affect the smooth running of an international business.

- **Transfer Risk:** Government policy may adversely affect currency exchange rates. When policies cause currency devaluation or economic downturn, they affect a company's ability to transfer capital out of the host country. Uncertainty in this case is called **transfer risk**. Under this risk, when a company creates wealth in another country, it may be forced to return a considerable amount to that country's government. This process is referred to as **repatriation of earnings**. You will learn more about this process later in the chapter.

Even if a company cannot know in advance the scope of the risks, if it can predict the possibility of risk, provide for it, and still project a profit, its venture may be ready for approval. There are a number of questions that the company should ask itself:

1. Is terrorism (using fear tactics such as kidnapping and bombings to achieve political or economic goals) part of the political landscape? Terrorism, civil unrest, and the overthrow of governments can seriously affect the international business community. For example, in the fall of 1999, seven Canadian pipeline workers from Edmonton were held for 100 days by heavily armed guerillas in the Ecuadorian jungle.

2. Could extremist groups pose a danger to the general stability of society? For example, in May 2000, Fijian armed rebels held the prime minister and members of parliament hostage, threatening to kill the captives if their demands for control of the country were not met. Although the rebels were ultimately unsuccessful, many countries boycotted Fiji's products and businesses until they returned to a democratic government. It took many months for the country to stabilize.

3. Has there been a withdrawal of freedoms (for example, curfews or restricted hours or other freedoms)? If the country's nationals are treated in this way, foreign companies doing business there could find themselves having to conform to restrictive laws. Withdrawal of freedoms is a signal of unstable government and risk. As the government tries to protect a weakening hold on power, it becomes more controlling.

4. What, if any, is the military's role in government? If it is in power, how firm is its grasp on power?

5. Is corruption (for example, bribery) part of the business ethic? Could a company find itself having to make higher and higher payments to officials?

6. Could religious or ethnic pressures (intolerance of religious belief and expression) lead to civil strife and endanger employees or your property?

Any of these conditions in a foreign host country can signal potential political risk that a business must evaluate.

Evaluating Political Risks

Managers of Canadian companies seeking to do business in other countries need to research and find answers to the following questions about the political situation in target or host countries:

- What are the chances of political and economic instability in the host country over the next three to five years?

- What agreements are in place between the Canadian government and the host government regarding Canadian investments?

- How committed is the current government to the rules of ownership rights, for example, property and business?

- When is the next election or how long will the current government stay in place?

- If a new government were to emerge, how would its platform and ideology change the current state of business affairs?

- Would a new government be likely to propose changes in policies that would affect the country's way of doing international business?

- How would changes in government affect the profitability and safety of an international project?

Consequences of Terrorism

The September 2001 destruction of the World Trade Center in New York City and damage to the Pentagon in Washington, D. C. are vivid examples of terrorism. Other examples include IRA bombs in London, England and Palestinian suicide bombers in Israel. Terrorism tends to occur when least expected and becomes a greater concern when open borders make it potentially easier for terrorists to carry out their plans. When they strike, little evidence of the terrorist perpetrator is evident. Terrorism not only instills fear in people, it has several negative consequences on a country's economy and its businesses.

Business travel is directly affected. Air traffic is disrupted and suspended; airports are closed. Security intensifies globally. Business people may have to carry more documentation to travel, and it will take longer to check in at airports. Stock markets around the world experience rapid change and volatility as some people sell off their stocks in a panic. Production slows or ceases because parts cannot be shipped when transportation systems close down. Just-in-time inventory systems, which carry only enough parts for a few hours or days of production, break down. Businesses close and workers are laid off.

Evaluating Legal Concerns

Laws and regulations or standards differ from one country to the next. Just because a law exists in Canada does not mean it exists elsewhere around the globe in exactly the same fashion. People doing business in a foreign country must obey the laws of that country. Canadians need to understand how the legal system works in the host country, evaluate its fairness (or unfairness), and decide what they would do if they had to rely on its judicial system. The following are a few common legal problems that international companies face as they conduct business with other nations.

Countries may put in place employment laws to protect their workers. These laws are in place, as they are in Canada, to prevent employees from having to work in dangerous conditions. Consumer protection laws are designed to make sure that all the products bought by the citizens of a country are safe for their use. Complying with such laws sometimes increases the cost of doing business in a country.

Taxation laws provide governments with the resources to carry out their functions. Customs duties must often be paid on products imported into the host country. Sales taxes may be imposed on the sale of products that a Canadian company is exporting into the country. Excise taxes may be imposed on specific products. There may also be payroll taxes, value-added taxes, and income taxes that must be paid by Canadians working in the country.

Figure 9.5 These Garfield toys were destroyed in Bangkok because the company that produced them did not honour copyright restrictions.

Business liability laws refer to the responsibilities, duties, and obligations that relate to debt, loss, or burden. Liability claims may be made against a Canadian company operating in a foreign country by employees (for wages), stockholders, governments (for taxes), banks (for loans), and consumers (for damages suffered because of unsafe products).

Property law includes protection of intellectual property (trademarks, trade names, patents, copyright, and industrial design), as well as physical property. Some international laws protect the property rights of companies operating in foreign countries. The World Intellectual Property Organization (WIPO), which is part of the United Nations, works with countries around the world to create treaties to protect intellectual property rights globally.

Contract law includes not only agreements among businesses but also treaties among nations. These contracts among nations impose a degree of stability and uniformity on global trade relations.

ICE Activities for 9.2

Ideas	Connections	Extensions
1. (a) Describe the four types of political risk.	(b) Using international newspapers (on the Internet), find and summarize a current report of an international company that faced one of the political risks.	(c) How could a Canadian company prepare itself to face the risk described in 1. (b)?
2. (a) What are some of the effects of terrorism on international business?	(b) Describe one effect on a Canadian international business of the September 11, 2001, terrorism attack.	(c) In your opinion, how should the Canadian business community react to the threat of terrorism?
3. (a) Explain the purpose of each of the different types of laws that relate to business.	(b) Working with a partner, research Canadian employment laws. Summarize the key laws that protect Canadian workers.	(c) Using the results of your research in 3. (b), brainstorm arguments for and against the statement that Canadian employment laws adequately protect Canadian workers.

9.3 Economic Factors Related to International Business

Economic Systems

Economic systems include all the factors of production and the rules and regulations involving production and consumption of goods and services. An economic system allows a country to decide what to produce, how to produce, and for whom to produce. Such systems include natural resources (land), labour, capital (money), and management, as well as standards or regulations for creating products.

The three most common economic systems are market (free-enterprise), centrally planned (command), and mixed economies.

Market Economies

In a **market economy**, individual companies and consumers make the decisions about what, how, and for whom goods and services are produced. In market economies,

- Ownership of private property (including businesses) is encouraged. Individuals can control property and own the means of production.

- Individuals are free to make a profit. Business is encouraged to introduce new and better products.

- Competition is encouraged as a healthy and necessary element to create quality and lower prices. Through their buying decisions, consumers influence what is produced.

- Though market-economy governments have little direct involvement with business, they create an environment in which people and businesses can develop their talents and take risks.

- Foreign investment is encouraged and self-sufficiency is not seen as an economic goal.

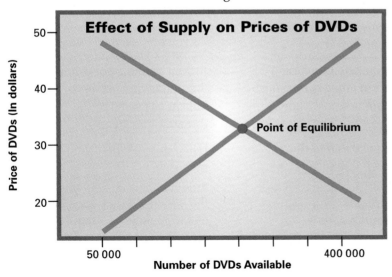

The forces of supply and demand control market economies. The "law" of **supply** states that as the price of a product increases, producers will be willing to produce more of that product. The "law" of **demand** states that as the price of a product increases, consumers will demand less of that product. Producers must find the **equilibrium** (the point at which the consumer agrees to pay the asking price and the company makes a profit). Ultimately, products are produced based on what the market (consumers) will allow.

Figure 9.6 The point of equilibrium for sales of DVDs occurs when the supply of DVDs equals the demand for DVDs.

Figure 9.7 Karl Marx wrote about the centrally planned economies.

Web Link

Follow the link at www.internationalbusiness.nelson.com to find out more about government-controlled agencies and corporations.

Centrally Planned Economies

In a **centrally planned** (**command**) **economy**, the government regulates the amount, distribution, and price of goods and services. Centrally planned economies are found in countries such as North Korea, China, and Cuba, where the government controls or restricts the ownership of private property. The needs of the entire society are considered before the individual's needs. More government control means that the profit motive is not the overriding goal of business. The state makes decisions for the citizens of the country. For example, citizens may be guaranteed a basic standard of living, health benefits, and education. However, the state makes decisions to regulate prices and wages, production quotas, and the distribution of raw materials.

There are fewer pure centrally planned economies following the collapse of communism in the former Soviet Union (Russia). The People's Republic of China (PRC) has moved closer to the market or capitalistic model. In fact, China has established "economic zones" to concentrate on the production of goods for global markets.

Mixed Economies

Many countries today have a **mixed economy** that combines government involvement and private ownership of businesses. Mixed economies have aspects of both market and centrally planned economic systems. In some countries with mixed economies, the government owns the transportation and communication businesses, as well as other industries that are important to the country's economy. In socialist mixed economies, most of the main industries are government-controlled, but citizens are free to work in other industries.

Canada has a mixed economy. Because of the country's large land mass and relatively small population, the Canadian government has had to play a major role in important industries such as transportation, health care, and communications. Government-controlled agencies and corporations include the Canadian Broadcasting Corporation (CBC), Canadian Space Agency, Federal Bridge Corporation, and Northern Pipeline Agency Canada. Countries such as Sweden, Italy, and Australia have also adopted mixed economic systems. These countries believe that the mixed system best meets the needs of their citizens.

Sometimes governments **privatize** state-owned enterprises, that is, sell them into private ownership. This can happen in market, mixed, or centrally planned economies. Privatization may occur when a country moves from a centrally planned to a market economy, but it can also happen in mixed economies, for example, when municipal governments decide to use private companies to keep roads in repair and to dispose of municipal waste. Some people believe that privatized entities are more productive than state-owned ones; other people disagree. The controversy over the privatization of Hydro One, formerly part of Ontario Hydro, demonstrates that the process is not always a smooth one.

Overall, government tends to play a greater role in the economies of developing countries. As a country's economic system matures, it tends to move closer to the market system. When a country shifts from a centrally planned economy to more of a market economy, the price of some products may rise, there is more competition, and there may be greater unemployment.

Follow the link at
www.internationalbusiness.nelson.com
to learn more about the privatization
of Hydro One.

Figure 9.8 In July 2000, Vietnam took another step towards a market economy by opening a stock trading centre in Ho Chi Minh City.

Global Economic Systems

Most nations face a number of key decisions related to goods and services. Since no country is totally self-sufficient (it cannot produce everything that it consumes) the available resources must be used to trade with others, which brings about interdependence among nations. For countries like the United States, Canada, Japan, and Germany, economic growth has meant economic stability. For example, in industrialized countries, economic stability is possible when a majority of people own a home, buy cars, take vacations, enjoy access to good health care, and have secure jobs. Such stability provides a nation with the confidence to plan for and invest in the future.

According to the International Monetary Fund:

The global economy is the world economy. It reflects the total amount of measurable economic activity going on in the world. For the global economy to exist means that a rising share of economic activity in the world is taking place between people who live in different countries. This includes all production, trade, financial flows, investment, technology, labour, and economic behaviour in nations and between nations.

TRADE TALK

In 1600, the British East India Company received from the British government its charter granting rights to trade in India. The Company came to be seen as an instrument of the British government in India. Government policy became company policy. By 1858, the British government had taken complete control of India, with the help of the British East India Company, an early form of "multinational corporation."

In the past, there existed what might be referred to as an international economy or commerce between nations, where the prevailing governments would set the rules. For example, during the 1800s Britain set many of the economic policies for the countries that were part of the British Empire. Today, more countries are becoming market or mixed economies. In today's global economy, companies treat the world as one big market. In fact, much of today's trade takes place between different parts of global companies, not just between countries. A Canadian entrepreneur can raise money anywhere in the world and can use technology, communications, management, and labour to make products anywhere and then sell them to customers worldwide.

Countries participate in the global economy to provide good jobs and a high quality of life or standard of living for their citizens. Countries use many different strategies to secure a place in this new economic order. For example, Sweden and Canada are planning to build "clusters" of high-tech industries in order to attract international investment, create and sell their products and services around the world, and provide good jobs for their citizens. When a number of companies cluster together, it appears that innovation results and interest from around the world focuses on the area. This kind of specialization in regions is not a new concept. The Ottawa region already boasts of a "silicon valley" with a number of major high-tech companies.

The Swedish Centre for Business and Policy Studies recently issued a report on clusters. The report found that this strategy is critical to Sweden's future. Clusters are considered successful if they attract foreign companies, capital, and people. The hallmarks of successful clusters include an entrepreneurial environment with a number of new company start-ups, good post-secondary institutions, capital to finance ideas, and the necessary transportation and communication infrastructure. Sweden's plan is to create about six clusters that will become internationally recognized. As Canada develops the plans for its clusters, the Swedish model could provide additional ideas.

Figure 9.9 Today's technology and global economy encourages companies to treat the world as one big market.

GLOBAL THOUGHT

The term "globalization" has acquired considerable emotive force. Some view it as a process that is beneficial—a key to world economic development—and also inevitable and irreversible. Others regard it with hostility, even fear, believing that it increases inequality within and between nations, threatens employment and living standards, and thwarts social progress.

– *International Monetary Fund*

Business Cycles

Historically, there has been a strong connection among the business cycles of the different countries around the world. In today's global economy, the effect of changes in the cycle is even more influential. Business cycles are patterned movements of the economy. The business cycle is measured by industrial growth and production in the economy, and it can have four phases:

- **Depression:** The economy slows even more. Consumers buy less. Factories shut down. Unemployment is high. In such circumstances, the government may intervene to help. However, because the main source of a government's income is taxes and both businesses and people are paying fewer taxes, the government has less money to use for social services.

- **Recovery:** The economy starts to improve. To meet new business and consumer demand, businesses begin slowly to produce more goods and provide more services. As businesses begin to hire workers to meet these demands, unemployment begins to decrease. Consumer spending increases, and prices eventually rise.

- **Prosperity:** The economy is doing well. Many goods and services are produced. Employment, wages, and profits increase. Investment is strong. For example, the period of prosperity in the 1990s in North America reflected strong advances in both the stock market and manufacturing. Raw materials and skilled labour may become scarce.

- **Recession:** The economy starts to slow. Consumers buy less. There are increases in business failures and unemployment. One sign of recession may be cutbacks in the consumption of major goods and services, such as new cars or business airline travel. A recession occurs when total economic output shrinks for at least six consecutive months (or two quarters of three months each).

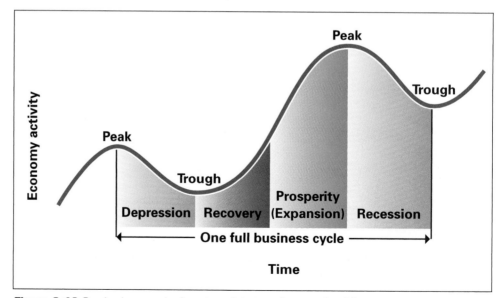

Figure 9.10 One business cycle, from trough to trough, can take eight to ten years.

The World Economic Freedom Index

One measure of a country's economic performance is its "economic freedom rating," which may be important for evaluating the risk for organizations and companies that want to do business in that country. The economic freedom rating is a measure of prosperity that relates to economic growth, per capita income, and material wealth. To calculate the rating, economies are measured according to the level of market and trade freedoms. During the 1990s, Canada's ranking slipped, not so much because economic freedom declined but because other countries had made significant improvements.

An annual report, *The Economic Freedom of the World*, is put together by more than 50 economic think tanks from around the world. A **think tank** is an organization that studies and researches specific topics and issues, often of an economic and political nature. The World Economic Freedom Index measures the following factors:

- size of government
- structure of the economy and use of markets
- monetary policy and price stability
- freedom to use alternative currencies
- legal structure and property rights
- international exchange (freedom to trade)
- freedom of exchange in capital and financial markets

Follow the link at www.internationalbusiness.nelson.com to find out more about the World Economic Freedom Index.

Canada and Global Economic Freedom Rating

2000 Summary Ratings		1990 Summary Ratings	
1. Hong Kong	8.8	1. Hong Kong	9.2
2. Singapore	8.6	2. Singapore	9.0
3. United States	8.5	3. United States	8.8
4. United Kingdom	8.4	4. Canada	8.4
5. New Zealand	8.2	4. Switzerland	8.4
5. Switzerland	8.2	4. United Kingdom	8.4
7. Ireland	8.1	7. Luxembourg	8.2
8. Australia	8.0	7. Netherlands	8.2
8. Canada	8.0	9. Germany	8.1
8. Netherlands	8.0	9. Japan	8.1
11. Finland	7.7	11. Australia	8.0
11. Iceland	7.7	11. Belgium	8.0
13. Denmark	7.6	11. New Zealand	8.0
13. Luxembourg	7.6	14. Denmark	7.7
15. Austria	7.5	14. United Arab Emirates	7.7
15. Belgium	7.5	16. Finland	7.6
15. Chile	7.5	16. France	7.6
15. Germany	7.5	16. Norway	7.6

Figure 9.11 This rating is based on a 1-20 scale according to seven factors. The lower numbers indicate countries with a great deal of economic freedom; the countries with high numbers have less economic freedom.

Canada's Global Entrepreneurs

In 2000, about 1 in 16 adults in Canada tried to start a new business. This finding was reported in a global study of entrepreneurial activity. The Global Entrepreneurship Monitor's second annual survey (GEM) ranked Canada sixth of 21 countries in entrepreneurial activity. The GEM research looks at the relationship between entrepreneurship and economic growth. Brazil was ranked first, South Korea second, and the United States third.

In many European countries, it is harder to create an entrepreneurial culture because employers provide excellent benefits, making it less attractive for people to risk starting their own businesses. Countries such as Japan and Ireland were at the low end of the list, with only 1 percent of adults (aged 18 to 64) pursuing entrepreneurial activity. For countries to be entrepreneurial, they must have both receptive governments and a flexible labour force.

Encouraging new business ventures also requires an environment free of "red tape" or bureaucratic hurdles. In 2000, Canadian entrepreneurs faced fewer hurdles and paperwork than their counterparts in any other country in the GEM survey. Australia ranked second, New Zealand third, and the United States fourth. The more hurdles, applications, or paperwork involved, the longer it takes entrepreneurs to get to market. By comparison, Russia and France tend to have the most red tape for new start-ups. In South America, Bolivia requires its entrepreneurs to follow 20 different procedures that can take nearly three months to process. Therefore, another positive aspect of a country's economic growth is its support of domestic entrepreneurs and their ventures.

Web Link

Follow the link at www.internationalbusiness.nelson.com to find out more about some Canadian entrepreneurs who are operating successful international businesses.

Around-the-Clock World Markets

Stock exchanges around the world are discussing the creation of a global market that would allow investors to trade stocks in companies around the world and around the clock. For the first time, ordinary investors would be able to trade stocks without being restricted by the hours and listings of their home market. Stock trading would join banking, grocery shopping, and a range of other services available 24 hours a day to consumers.

Figure 9.12 The major time zones of the world.

This new market has been referred to as the **global equity market**. Equity refers to something that has value or worth, such as a home or stocks. Under this new system, as each exchange closes at the end of its business day, orders are relayed to the stock market in the next time zone. Ten of the world's stock exchanges in three time zones are currently considering this set-up:

- Toronto, New York, Mexico, and Sao Paolo, Brazil, in the Americas

- Australia, Tokyo, and Hong Kong in the Asia-Pacific region

- Euronext, the combined Paris, Amsterdam, and, Brussels exchange in Europe (one of the issues to be resolved is that not all stocks are listed on each of these markets)

GLOBAL THOUGHT

First, we want as open, and growing, a free-market-oriented economy as possible, in which people are encouraged to swing free and take crazy leaps. Without risk takers and venture capitalists, there is no entrepreneurship and without entrepreneurship there is no growth. Therefore, at the heart of every healthy economy are the free-swinging trapeze of free markets.... Second, even with a growing economy every society also needs trampolines—programs that can catch workers who fall behind in this rapidly changing environment and retrain them so they can bounce back into the economy. A trampoline is strong enough to catch you before you hit the ground, but not so cushy that you can live on it forever.... Without question, the most important trampoline is lifelong learning.

– *Thomas L. Friedman*

Figure 9.13 The president of the European Central Bank unveils euro bills in August 2001.

Even without "around-the-clock" trading (a shorthand way of referring to this is 24/7—open 24 hours a day, 7 days a week), financial markets and national economies around the world are ever more interdependent. As a result, the economies of individual countries are vulnerable to events far beyond their borders. Foreign stock market uncertainties can trigger a chain of events that quickly affect the value of the Canadian dollar. For example, during the Asian financial crisis of 1997–98, foreign exchange investors sought protection in strong currencies, such as the U.S. dollar, which caused economic hardship for countries whose currencies they were selling.

Common Currency

In Europe, the euro is a new currency adopted by the countries that make up the European Union; it replaces each individual country's former currency. The euro attempts to help balance the European partners economically, with greater price stability, harmonized long-term interest rates, more stable national currencies, and a commitment to control national budget deficits and public debt.

One of the key benefits of a common currency is that it simplifies transactions. It also reduces the foreign exchange risks, as discussed earlier. The euro strengthens European companies' trading both within and outside the European Union. Tourists who travel to different countries in Europe find currency exchange easier—they only have to do it once, because the euro is used in all EU countries except Great Britain, Denmark, and Switzerland.

Some people have suggested a common currency for Canada and the United States, referred to as dollarization. Such currency integration would have a number of effects, one of them being an even closer integration of the two economies. Like many countries, Canada has already informally adopted the U.S. dollar as a "second" currency. More and more Canadian companies are listing their companies on American stock exchanges, like the NASDAQ and the New York Stock Exchange, and reporting their earnings in U.S. dollars.

THINK ABOUT IT

When the United States sneezes, Canada catches a cold. What does this mean when applied to the Canadian economy? Would a common currency change this situation?

Opponents of the plan argue that the benefits of a North American currency would not parallel the European experience. Fixing the value of the Canadian dollar to the U.S. dollar might ultimately hand control of Canada's monetary policy to the United States. It will take time to decide whether a common currency would provide easier trade and travel.

ICE Activities for 9.3

Ideas	Connections	Extensions
1. (a) Describe the characteristics of the three most common economic systems.	(b) List evidence that Canada has a mixed economy. Then discuss your findings with those of other members of a small group.	(c) In your opinion, how might a mixed economy help developing countries improve the standard of living for their citizens?
2. (a) How does the Canadian business environment encourage entrepreneurs?	(b) Research and present a short oral profile of one Canadian international entrepreneur.	(c) Propose a solution for one of the challenges faced by Canadian entrepreneurs who want to join the global economy.
3. (a) Explain the concept of a common currency between Canada and the United States.	(b) List some of the difficulties Canadian exporters face in dealing with the different currencies in Canada and the United States.	(c) What are the benefits and drawbacks of a common currency between Canada and the United States?

9.4 Managing International Financial Risks

Understanding Financial Risk

Every business and organization assumes some financial risk, but risk increases when the business enters international markets. International trade between two countries involves two legal systems, two governments, two economies, and two cultures. As a result, the likelihood for error and risk is greater than if the company were dealing with business partners in Canada. If a company does business in a number of foreign countries, then the risks are further multiplied. Financial risks and political risks are often closely related.

Canadian companies can understand and help manage international financial risk by partnering with their bank, their domestic trade agencies and resources, and their federal and provincial governments. By using such resources, a company can reduce one of the greatest risks in doing business abroad: having incomplete or unreliable information on which to base crucial business decisions.

International financial transactions are more complicated than those undertaken domestically. When a Canadian manufacturer ships its product by sea to Japan, for example, the Canadian company risks both the loss of its goods and, ultimately, the loss of the customer's sale of these products in Japan. International shipments need to be insured, which is an additional cost in international business. Also, because the legal systems that support financial systems vary greatly from country to country, the way courts operate and penalties are imposed can differ depending on the country.

Currency Risk Factors

As you learned in Chapter 7, Canadian companies doing business internationally face the challenge of fluctuating foreign exchange rates. The exchange rate is the rate at which a nation's currency can be exchanged for other currencies or gold.

In Canada, we have a **floating rate**. A floating or flexible rate is not fixed and tends to fluctuate or change over time, moving freely to seek its proper balance.

One currency risk encountered in international business transactions is currency devaluation or revaluation. **Currency devaluation** is the reduction by a government of the value of its currency relative to currencies of other nations. **Currency revaluation** occurs when a country adjusts the value of its currency upward. A currency depreciates when its price falls and appreciates when its price rises relative to another currency. Problems arise for Canadian exporters when they negotiate a sale in a foreign currency and that foreign currency is devalued or weakened. A devaluation may mean that the Canadian company may lose its profits. Devaluation may also affect the foreign buyer's ability to pay for the shipment if the devaluation is significant.

TRADE TALK

Custom House Currency Exchange is one of the largest foreign exchange brokerage firms in North America, handling more than 3 million transactions and $4 billion annually. More than 40 000 businesses rely on Custom House to handle their foreign exchange needs efficiently and securely. Custom House clients can order foreign currency for a future payment to lock into a rate, when it is anticipated that currency fluctuations will make the currency more expensive later on.

Devaluation of a nation's currency also tends to reduce the price of exports from the country whose currency has been devalued, making those goods more attractive in world markets. For example, Canadian exports are very attractive to the United States when our dollar is weaker, because the American buyer gets more product for its U.S. dollar. When the Canadian dollar is weak relative to the U.S. dollar, however, importing from the United States is more costly for Canadian businesses, and the consumer price of imported products goes up. When this happens, domestic producers are in a better position to compete against similar imported products.

Another currency risk that Canadian businesses face in international transactions is that foreign trade may be regulated by exchange controls in a foreign country. **Exchange controls** are political and economic measures used by a government to try to regulate the amount and value of its currency. One fairly common way of controlling currency flow is to restrict the amount of money that people can take out of the country. In the past, countries as diverse as Australia, France, Japan, and South Africa placed restrictions on the flow of their currency out of their countries, although this policy is usually undertaken by developing countries. Exchange controls mean that companies obtaining foreign exchange through exporting must sell their foreign exchange to the central bank in the country from which they are exporting the goods. Importers must buy their foreign exchange from the same institution.

The value of a country's currency can also be affected by individuals and financial institutions that buy and sell on the foreign exchange markets so they can profit from changes in currency values. These parties are referred to as speculators, and they affect the demand and supply of currencies and corresponding exchange rates. For example, if you receive a large sum of money in U.S. currency, you might hold on to it for a while if you believe the exchange rate will become more advantageous (you believe the U.S. dollar will become even more valuable compared to the Canadian dollar). If you believe that the Canadian dollar will strengthen, you will want to exchange your U.S. dollars now, when you will get more Canadian dollars for them. This kind of speculating is quite harmless, but large-scale speculators that buy up large quantities of a country's currency in the expectation it will weaken against the currency they are dealing in can have a detrimental effect on a somewhat unstable economy.

The value of the Canadian dollar is determined by the effects of foreign exchange between all trading countries, and Canada has little direct control over the developments that affect the value of its dollar. The Canadian dollar is not one of the world's most traded currencies and tends to be dragged along by trends in the United States and elsewhere.

TRADE TIPS

Dealing with only a single international market—"putting all your eggs in one basket"—may have more potential risk than selling in several potential markets. If the deal falls through, you lose everything. The high volatility of currency values coupled with expanded international trade and investment has increased financial risk for companies.

Strategies to Manage Financial Risk

While risk can be expected as companies expand globally, many risk management strategies are available. Most experts agree that the two essential ingredients for managing risk are to identify the risk and to take steps to minimize the risk. Some of the specific strategies by which companies can minimize their financial risk include the following.

- **Foreign Exchange Management:** Research the trading partner's currency and conduct an economic forecast of its country. Foreign exchange is beyond any single company's control since it is usually in the hands of a foreign government. However, companies can rely on outside expertise or employ their own experts. Global companies integrate foreign exchange management into every aspect of their operation. Depending on the nature of the foreign exchange risk and the currency involved, companies may decide to use different strategies to diminish risk.

- **Credit Control:** A Canadian company should know the history of its foreign buyer, the currency it does business in, and how much it owes. The international or foreign department of banks and credit companies can normally investigate a foreign buyer's credit information. The process is similar to checking a reference on a new employee and serves as a final test of the ability or capacity of the buyer to pay. As you learned in Chapter 7, companies can make a number of financial arrangements to lessen credit risk.

- **Open Accounts:** Open accounts can also be used to reduce financial risk. An open account is an agreement between the two companies that future shipments of a product will be stopped if payment is not made. An open account might cause problems if the order is rather large and expensive, because the exporting company could face added risk by not being paid on time. Credit histories can be used to lessen this risk.

- **Insurance:** A company also has the option of purchasing insurance to cover the non-payment of international invoices. If this happens, the exporter receives a majority of its invoiced amount from the insurer. With this kind of insurance in place, companies might feel more secure operating in an open account.

TRADE TIPS

The five-step process to creating a foreign exchange management strategy is as follows:

1. **Identify the Exposure to Foreign Exchange Risk.** Protecting a company against the risk of loss requires identifying risk areas, such as sales, inventory, equipment, and payments to shareholders.

2. **Identify the Size or Magnitude of the Risk.** Once the areas of risk have been identified, assess the amount of risk present so the potential loss or gain can be measured. For example, what happens if the foreign currency increases or decreases in value over the next few months?

3. **Set Foreign Exchange Objectives.** As part of overall business strategy, objectives for foreign exchange should be part of the plan. Objectives will be determined by the nature of the company's business.

4. **Implement Foreign Exchange Objectives.** The company trades in currencies for an agreed-upon rate with the assistance of a financial institution.

5. **Evaluate Performance.** Tracking performance helps a company determine whether strategies are working and are cost effective.

Analyzing Foreign Investment Climates

Over the past 50 years, Canada has removed many of the barriers to investment in Canada on the part of foreign firms. Companies invest in other countries to obtain raw materials, acquire products at a lower cost, and enter local markets. A company usually decides to invest in a company in a foreign country after it has experienced some success in export. **Foreign investment** is normally considered the purchase by non-residents of business enterprises, land, shares, and any other assets with the potential for financial return.

But international business investors need to research and analyze potential foreign investments carefully. The investment climate differs greatly from one country to another. Investors also need to determine whether a profit can be made within a given time frame. A checklist for evaluating the investment climate of a foreign country could consider the following details:

- **General political stability:** This should assess the form of government, the rivalries and conflicts present, and the past political climate.
- **Government policies towards foreign investment:** This should observe the restrictions and incentives for foreign investment, including recognition of trade agreements and attitudes.
- **Policies and legal factors:** This includes the nature of duties and restrictions, labour laws, honesty of public officials, and taxation on profits.
- **Economic environment:** This entails overall research into the host country's population, per capita income, infrastructure, and economy.
- **International payments:** This includes a look at the exchange rate of the host country's currency.

ICE Activities for 9.4

Ideas	Connections	Extensions
1. (a) Identify strategies Canadian companies can use to minimize financial risk in dealing with foreign trade partners.	(b) Work with a small group of students and research to find other strategies.	(c) What would be some of the implications of financial risk for a young entrepreneur entering the global market?
2. (a) Explain the difference between currency devaluation and currency revaluation.	(b) What are some of the reasons that a country's currency might be devalued?	(c) Write a paragraph summarizing your opinion of how the devaluation of its currency might affect a developing country.
3. (a) Explain how Canadian companies can evaluate the investment climate in a foreign country.	(b) Work with a partner to list the pros and cons of foreign investment in today's business climate.	(c) What do you think will be the effect on Canadian foreign investment as nations become more interdependent?

Political and Economic Factors Affecting International Business

Journalist

Matthew Fisher is living a boyhood dream. He travels the world and, following his father's advice, he gets someone else to pay for it. At the age of 10 or 11, he remembers that he wanted to travel. Today, Fisher travels for Canada's *National Post* newspaper. While he was still in university, he started covering sports in Europe, reporting on Canadian amateur athletes. At the age of 19, he moved on from sports to covering events in Mozambique. His job has since taken him to 148 countries.

In an interview with the magazine *campus.ca* he advised, "The best way to get a foothold as a foreign correspondent or reporter is to go abroad and try and carve out your own niche. Go to an interesting place and establish an expertise. If a war washes over the place, that's where reputations are made." True to his advice, if something is happening in the world, Fisher is there to cover it. In the past five years,

working from his home bases in London and Moscow, he has covered wars in Africa, Kosovo, and Chechnya, as well as the Olympics in Sydney. He is concerned, however, about the lack of substantive foreign news coverage done by Canadian media outlets and fears that jobs like the one he is currently doing may not exist in the future.

Not surprisingly, this is a career filled with risk. Fisher downplays it as much as possible. He says, "… no matter what type of situation I have found myself in, I have always been able to leave it. Of course there are people there who cannot. There are always other journalists who are more brave, particularly the photographers." He admits to having been in what he calls "some very bad situations." He has seen death at close quarters even though he himself was not in danger. Fisher says, "When the Hutus were killing the Tutsis I said to the driver of the vehicle in French, 'What can we do?' and he said, 'We will do nothing. If you move one millimetre, you will be dead.' I'm sure the driver was right about that."

Summing up the life of a journalist, he told *campus.ca*, "I really like my job but I don't think it is for everyone. I find a lot of people who want to do this type of work but [most] are not suited to it. Anyone who wants a nice family life had better forget it. Anybody who thinks they are going to go [overseas] and change the world had better forget it. You are there to observe and tell things as accurately and as well as you can."

Figure 9.14 A Russian soldier acts as mine sweeper in southern Chechnya. Fisher's reports on the Chechnyan conflict were read by thousands of Canadians.

Write a job advertisement that would best describe Matthew Fisher's job. What skills and knowledge would you require to fill this position? Your ad should be five to seven sentences long.

Canada's Trading Partners:
Focus on North and South Korea

North Korea names entrepreneur to lead major new foray into capitalism

Pyongyang, North Korea (AP) – A Chinese-born entrepreneur will head North Korea's first major experiment in capitalism—a walled-off region designed to draw foreign investment to the insular communist country.

Yang Bin, an orchid exporter and property developer, said Monday that the 130-square kilometre oasis of capitalism near the country's northwestern coast would be free of the staunch ideology that has been North Korea's hallmark for half a century. It reflects the government's willingness to open up to the world, he said.

– www.canada.com

Figure 9.15 South Korean president Kim Dae-jung and North Korean leader Kim Jong-il meet in June 2000.

Although Korea has been called the Land of the Morning Calm, its history has been anything but calm. Over the centuries, Korea has been invaded by the Mongols, the Chinese, and the Japanese. Korea was divided into two parts at the end of World War II in 1945. The former Soviet Union occupied the northern part, installing a communist government, and the United States set up a democratic government in the southern part. In 1950, Communist Chinese forces invaded Korea from the north. From that date until 1953, the Korean War was fought between them and the Allied forces of the West, including Canada and the United States. A ceasefire was declared in 1953 and is still in effect today. North Korea remains an isolated and totalitarian state with a centrally planned economy while South Korea is a democratic republic with a market economy. Tension between the two Koreas has erupted into a number of clashes and threats over the years.

Considerable effort has been made to reunite the two Koreas. Reunification would bring together the economic drive of the people of South Korea with the natural resource potential of the North. North Korea has a very low standard of living and often faces food shortages, during which it has to rely on international aid. As a consequence of these conditions, many people suffer from malnutrition. While South Korea has a larger population, the North has invested more in military spending. South Korea has become the world's eleventh largest trading nation, a world leader in the shipbuilding and steel industries. Its electronic sector rivals that of Japan. It is the sixth largest manufacturer of automobiles with 3.4 million vehicles produced in 2000. South Korea's plans include development of both space and telecommunications technology.

Korean leaders are meeting to try to start the reunification process, and, in 2000, Kim Dae-jung, president of South Korea, won the Nobel Peace Prize for his efforts. When and if the two Koreas are unified, there will be many challenges. The South has a per capita income about 12 times that of North Korea. In 1998, the South's trade volume was more than 150 times larger than the North's. Many families were separated as a result of the Korean War, and reunification would do more than just launch new economic development in a country torn apart by external and internal forces.

A Snapshot of North and South Korea

Size: South Korea: 98 480 sq. km; North Korea: 120 540 sq. km

World Region: Asia-Pacific

Capital Cities: South Korea: Seoul; North Korea: Pyongyang

Language: Korean

Currency: South Korean Won, North Korean Won

Population: South Korea: 48.3 million; North Korea: 22.2 million

Time: Noon in Ottawa (EST) is 2:00 A.M. the next day in Seoul and Pyongyang.

Climate: Temperate, with sometimes heavy rainfall in summer

Type of Government: South Korea: Republic; North Korea: Communist

Labour Force by Occupation: South Korea: 50 percent services, 45 percent industry, 5 percent agriculture; North Korea: 42 percent industry, 30 percent agriculture, 28 percent services

Membership in World Organizations: APEC, OECD, WTO

Importing Partners and Products: South Korea: Partners: United States, Japan, and China. **Products:** Machinery, electronics, oil, steel, textiles.
North Korea: Partners: China, Japan, Russia, South Korea, and Germany.
Products: Petroleum, coking coal, machinery and equipment, consumer goods, grains.

Exporting Partners and Products: South Korea: Partners: Korean exports to Canada outpace Canadian exports to Korea by a ratio of 3:1; South Korea also exports to the United States, China, and Japan. In the Asia-Pacific region, South Korea is Canada's third-largest export market after Japan and China. **Products:** Electronics, motor vehicles, ships, clothing, fish. **North Korea: Partners:** Japan, South Korea, China, Germany, Russia. **Products:** Minerals, metallurgical products, manufactured products including armaments, and agricultural and fishery products.

Travel Advisory: Monsoons and flooding are possible from June to August. Be sure your passport is up to date and good for at least six months beyond your departure from South Korea. Tourist facilities in North Korea are extremely limited. Food, electricity, and clean water are in short supply. The police may monitor hotel rooms, phone calls, and faxes. Access is by air or rail only, with frequent delays on the rail lines. Foreigners are not allowed to drive in North Korea. Taxis and public transit are not readily available. A North Korean official accompanies visitors at all times. You will need your passport and a visa.

Business Etiquette: Korean surnames precede given names. Koreans place more weight on verbal contracts than written ones. They show great respect for seniors and family. Tipping is not a traditional formality. Business socializing outside the work setting is normal.

Country Link

Follow the link at
www.internationalbusiness.nelson.com.
to find out more about the political and economic situation in South and North Korea.

Chapter Challenges

Knowledge/Understanding

1. Match each of the following terms to the correct definition or description below:

   (a) democracy

   (b) totalitarianism

   (c) economic imperialism

   (d) market economy

   (e) centrally planned economy

   (f) mixed economy

   (g) recession

   (h) recovery

   (i) currency devaluation

   (j) currency revaluation

   (i) individual companies and consumers decide which goods are produced

   (ii) the period when an economy slows down

   (iii) the period when an economy starts to improve

   (iv) combines government regulation and private ownership of business

   (v) government for and by the people of a country

   (vi) government regulates production of goods

   (vii) the adjustment of a currency value upwards

   (viii) extending the rule of one country over another country

   (ix) government run by a single party or by a dictator

   (x) reduction of the value of a currency relative to other currencies

2. Using a recent national newspaper, identify the name of the currency used in 10 different countries. Prepare a list in three columns, one for the country, one for the name of the currency, and the third for how much of that currency you can buy for a Canadian dollar.

3. List and explain three strategies practised by governments to ensure that their domestic businesses are competitive in the global marketplace.

4. Identify three indicators that show a country may be experiencing political or economic instability.

Thinking/Inquiry

1. You travel to England on business. While you are there, you purchase £500 worth of clothing to update your wardrobe. Calculate how much you spent in Canadian dollars. Then, as you depart from England, you submit your receipts to claim the VAT UK refund on the taxes you should not have paid. The taxes equalled £35. Calculate the refund you should receive in Canadian dollars in the next few months. Finally, given the original purchase and the refund, how much did you actually spend in Canadian dollars?

2. Create a chart to show five ways in which Canadian federal or provincial governments (or both) offer help to Canadian entrepreneurs who want to expand their business into international markets. Your chart should show (a) the name of the government department, (b) the service it offers, and (c) how an entrepreneur would benefit from the service. Use either print or online government sources for your research.

Communication

1. The idea that democracy gives rise to economic growth is commonly referred to as conventional wisdom. For the past 30 years democracy has been spreading around the globe. More people now live in democracies than under dictatorships. Will the trend towards democracy continue? Write a paragraph reflecting on your vision of the spread of democracy over the next ten years. How is this phenomenon likely to affect the political and economic climate for international business?

2. Debate this statement: "A logical objective for a global economy is a global currency." Use information from this chapter to support your argument.

3. Currency Fair: Your teacher will provide you with the name of a foreign currency. Your task is to investigate this currency and pretend it is yours. On the assigned date, you will set up a display for others in the class to see. Students will have an opportunity to travel around the

class to observe other currencies as part of a "currency fair." Students are to instruct fellow classmates on the nature of their currency by doing the following:

- Show one unit of the country's paper currency.
- Identify the characters on the currency and their significance.
- Prepare a summary of the denominations or values in which it can be purchased.
- Prepare a comparison of the exchange rate between your currency and Canada's.
- Identify the country and the capital city.
- List one type of import and one type of export this country is known for.

Application

1. Write five research questions that a Canadian exporting company (of your choice) could use as the basis for a research report on the political and economic factors that would come into play if that company were to export its product to an African country.

2. Explore the political and economic consequences of the unification of North and South Korea. Create a mind map or a concept web to illustrate how unification would affect the following:
   - the economic conditions in Korea and the prospects for international business activity
   - the likely impact of this business activity on the two main regions of the unified country
   - ways in which Canada might assist the unified Korea in terms of economic development, international business capability, and opportunities for citizens to benefit from international business
   - the challenges that North and South Korean industries would face in terms of differences in ethics, values, and business practices

International Business Portfolio

Managing International Risk

You are now becoming more expert on business matters in your IBP country. In addition to the facts and figures you have researched, you should also have newspaper and magazine articles that discuss everything from individual companies and the fiscal or monetary situation, to the popular tourist regions. It's now time to prepare a risk assessment for your IBP country. In addition to the material you have in your IB portfolio, check the Web site for Canada's Department of Foreign Affairs and International Trade. It includes travel reports and advisories on risks ranging from the weather to the political situation in different countries. Follow the link at **www.internationalbusiness.nelson.com**.

Activity

1. Prepare your IBP country's risk assessment in the following areas:
   - political risk
   - economic/financial risk (be sure to focus on the currency of your country)
   - social/cultural risk
   - technical/commercial risk
   - natural/physical risk

Using a scale of 1 to 10, with "10" being a high-risk country and "1" being a low-risk country, how would you measure your IBP country according to "risk" generally? Describe one way you can offset or deal with risks in each of the five areas.

Chapter 10

Global Business Ethics and Social Responsibility

Companies today must be concerned with more than profit, and international companies have a particular responsibility in their host countries. Conducting business around the globe requires companies to observe cultural and legal differences, and to be ethically and socially responsible. Business ethics and social responsibility have become universal concerns, and worldwide consensus is starting to emerge on internationally acceptable codes of conduct. Never before have so many companies and organizations tried to solve global problems. Both for-profit and nonprofit groups have major roles to play in designing ethical solutions.

Chapter Topics

➤ 10.1 – Understanding Business Ethics and Social Responsibility 304

➤ 10.2 – Ethical Issues Affecting the Conduct of International Business 312

➤ 10.3 – Taking Action, Ethically 321

➤ *Canada's Trading Partners: Focus on* Mexico 330

➤ Chapter Challenges 332

Prior Knowledge

- What positive and negative media stories have you heard recently about international business ethics and issues?
- To whom should multinational businesses show corporate responsibility?
- What is the role of Canadian international businesses in developing nations?

Inquiries/Expectations

- How do multinational companies cause positive and negative effects in the countries in which they operate?
- What ethical issues arise for companies competing internationally concerning consumers, employees, stockholders, and the society of the host country?
- How can Canadians help strengthen the international business potential of less-developed nations?
- What actions can individuals and non-governmental, nonprofit organizations take to solve global ethical and social problems and to be good global citizens?

Important Terms

business ethics
code of ethics
corporate social responsibility (CSR)
corporate philanthropy
Corruption Perceptions Index
cultural relativism
dumping
ethical dilemmas
ethical imperialism
Kyoto protocol

legislated codes
lobbying
non-governmental organization (NGO)
not-for-profit organization (NPO)
rule of law
social marketing
stakeholders
voluntary code of conduct

10.1 Understanding Business Ethics and Social Responsibility

The field of ethics deals with what is considered good or bad, and with moral duty and obligation. The study of ethics can lead to principles of conduct that govern the behaviour of individuals or groups. **Business ethics** are concerned with the behaviour of businesses in the treatment of employees, society, stockholders, and consumers. Especially in larger organizations, business ethics determines policies for environmental issues, social responsibility, and human rights. International or multinational corporations have a particular obligation to be clear about their ethical position, because they frequently face dilemmas related to the value systems and laws of the countries in which they operate. In this chapter, we will look at some ethical questions that arise in international business.

GLOBAL THOUGHT

The tempo of globalization is accelerating. Giant enterprises are formed through mergers. Companies are searching for overarching global values. It is now a matter of utmost urgency to raise the global skill levels of ethics officers.

– Ethics and Compliance in a Global Economy

Ethics, Business, and the Law

Homes, schools, professions, communities, and countries all have values—written or unwritten—that represent principles for the appropriate actions of their members. Organizations and companies may choose to express these principles in a **code of ethics**. The behaviour codes that come from such principles specify that particular conduct is either acceptable or unacceptable according to the group's principles. Ethical behaviour means doing the right thing according to these established guidelines. A closely related concept is morality, which may be understood to refer to more personal principles of behaviour that an individual may adopt as an overriding guide for personal actions.

A society's history and its values determine its ethical principles. Ethics may be seen as personal morality expressed toward others in a community—within families, at school, in sports and clubs, and in the workplace. Ethics also govern relationships and interactions in society as a whole, or within the larger context of international business and the global environment. For example, one common ethical standard is that you should behave toward others as you would have them behave toward you.

Many Western countries embrace the **rule of law**. These written laws, refined over centuries, establish the standards or rules that citizens are expected to follow. Consider Canadian values, for example. We place a high value on democratic principles, the fundamental freedom and dignity of each individual, the right to a high level of health care and education, and the right to be treated without discrimination. These are just a few of the values that we have determined are essential to our quality of life, and we have created laws that uphold these values. Our legal system is continually evolving to support the values of a more ethical and just society, as they have been enshrined in the *Canadian Charter of Rights and Freedoms*.

A distinction can be drawn, however, between what is legal and what is ethical. Even though legal guidelines may permit countries or companies to act in certain ways, those actions may not necessarily be ethical. Conflicting interests between two sets of values frequently arise, and solutions may require some serious critical analysis and some tough choices.

GLOBAL THOUGHT

Dilemma Paradigms for Tough Choices

The really tough choices ... don't center upon right versus wrong. They involve right versus right. They are genuine dilemmas precisely because each side is firmly rooted in one of our basic, core values. Four such dilemmas are so common to our experience that they stand as models, patterns, or paradigms. They are

- truth versus loyalty
- individual versus community
- short-term versus long-term
- justice versus mercy

The names for these patterns are less important than the ideas they reflect: whether you call it law versus love, or equity versus compassion, or fairness versus affection, you're talking about some form of justice versus mercy. So too with the others. But while the names may be flexible, the concepts are not: These four paradigms appear to be so fundamental to the right-versus-right choices all of us face that they can rightly be called dilemma paradigms.

– *Rushworth M. Kidder*

Many organizations, professions, companies, and educational institutions publish their codes of ethics to bring an awareness of their values to employees, shareholders, consumers, and society as a whole, and to provide guidelines for their members' conduct. Such ethical frameworks help guide decisions when individuals or organizations are faced with ethical dilemmas. An **ethical dilemma** arises when two or more "right" courses of action conflict; that is, when a choice between two or more options (two "fundamental rights") must be made. A code of ethics provides a framework to arrange in priority the values that support a choice. Making the right choice usually means choosing what is right or acceptable, both according to the code and according to values that are shared with the party in potential conflict.

Ethics policies also contribute to managing an organization's reputation and helping it avoid conflict of interest. In some companies, employees receive ethics training to clarify what is acceptable or unacceptable behaviour and to learn how to put the code of ethics (code of conduct) into practice.

Canadian companies that conduct business in other countries often discover that the laws, values, and ethical standards of Canada are not always the same as of other countries. International business people realize there is no single right way to behave, and ethical dilemmas arise. Executives must make decisions about their companies' actions in situations where Canadian values are not generally accepted. Will the Canadians adopt the ethical behaviour of the country in which they are doing business? Will they conduct business according to Canadian values? It is relatively easy to follow certain cultural practices, such as removing shoes in a traditional Japanese setting. But when a company's ability to compete is in question and its profits are at stake, it may be faced with more fundamental ethical dilemmas.

Cultural Relativism and Ethical Imperialism

Anyone who does business in, or travels to, a foreign country is expected to behave according to the laws and codes of that country. Ethical behaviour is determined by the norms of the host country's value system. But what if a company is considering doing business with a foreign partner that has a poor human rights record or poor business ethics? Will it do business with that partner? Two extreme positions exist in regard to decisions about ethical behaviour on the international scene: ethical imperialism and cultural relativism.

Ethical imperialism is the belief that certain forms of behaviour are categorically right or wrong. An individual, company, or country acting according to this framework may, for example, try to impose its ethical standards on another company or country. Ethical imperialists take the position that in case of conflict, their own values are right and the other party's are wrong. They believe that their understanding about what is good should be recognized universally.

Cultural relativism, on the other hand, is the belief that behaviour should be governed by what will bring about the greatest good for the greatest number of people. From the viewpoint of cultural relativism, differing values and laws do not necessarily make one country better than another—they all have equal validity. This viewpoint acknowledges a country's right to manage its affairs according to its own values, and a company with this attitude will not try to change its host country's ethics or laws.

Figure 10.1 Different countries have different attitudes toward smoking.

Attitudes toward smoking in different jurisdictions can illustrate the difference between cultural relativism and ethical imperialism. In many countries, government regulations and company policies allow smoking in public spaces and workplaces. A foreign company practising cultural relativism accepts such a policy and follows local guidelines. Many establishments in North America have banned smoking, however, since second-hand cigarette smoke has been proven hazardous to health. Although smoking is not illegal (a personal decision), smoking inside a school or workplace is now an unacceptable practice because it affects others. A company with an attitude of ethical imperialism would take the position that this policy is right and any other policy is wrong and, as a result, would attempt to impose a smoking ban in its host country workplace.

Another example of particular relevance in international business is the question of the employment of children. In certain countries, it is customary for children to start working quite long hours with their families at a very young age instead of going to school. In these communities, the practice is acceptable and should not be confused with the abuse of children. In North America, we often see this as morally wrong. What changes the perspective is the potential exploitation of such children for others' gain, including the denial of education and poor workplace health and safety.

Figure 10.2 In some countries, it is expected that children will work with their families from a young age.

The Two Extremes of Cultural Relativism and Ethical Imperialism

Cultural Relativism	Ethical Imperialism
No culture's ethics are superior.	Certain absolute truths apply everywhere.
The values and practices of the local setting determine what is right or wrong.	Universal values transcend cultures in determining what is right or wrong.

Figure 10.3 Solutions to ethical issues are often found on the continuum between these extremes.

Ethical imperialism and cultural relativism present two extremes. The solution to ethical problems between countries, however, is often found somewhere between the extremes. As the process of globalization gathers momentum, a consensus is arising that there are indeed many common values that are shared around the world. These include respect, fairness, honesty, compassion, and responsibility. Such core values of caring can override differences between individual countries. They can also be put into action without jeopardizing the long-standing traditions of a country's cultural practices.

Figure 10.4 Workers at two assembly plants, one based in Brazil and the other in Canada.

Worker safety and environmental protection are good examples of two universally respected values. One of the many effects of globalization is that it may call into question existing codes of ethics in the workplace in all nations. Conducting international business requires the development of values that apply across national boundaries and cultures. Although the actual laws may differ, the overriding principle that workers should be treated with respect becomes paramount. In searching for mutually acceptable ethical principles that underlie laws, multinational companies are finding solutions that allow their employees to work in safe and suitable conditions, no matter which country they are in.

Ecotourism and G.A.P Adventures

We have worked hard to continually develop and fine-tune our philosophy of low-impact tourism and our relationships to our travellers and local hosts. Our commitment is to supporting local people and communities and protecting the environment we travel within. In conjunction with Conservation International, we empower local people and offer travellers the opportunity to experience true ecotourism. This is not only a responsible way to travel – it is an extremely rewarding way to travel.

– Bruce Poon Tip

Bruce Poon Tip, a Canadian entrepreneur and the CEO of G.A.P Adventures, was the only tour operator invited to speak at the launch of the United Nations International Ecotourism Year 2002 in New York. According to the United Nations, ecotourism is intended to foster "better understanding among peoples everywhere. . .leading to greater awareness of the rich heritage of various civilizations and. . .bringing about a better appreciation of the inherent values of different cultures, thereby contributing to the strengthening of world peace."

As the head of G.A.P Adventures (the Great Adventure People), Poon Tip is dedicated to offering tourists the opportunity to experience "pure" travel. To Poon Tip, ecotourism means that tourists can "see, study, and understand the country and its people in their natural, day-to-day state without disturbing or changing them." G.A.P Adventurers realize it is a privilege, not a right, to visit any country. The presence of tourists "shouldn't adversely impact human, plant, or animal life, or the environments in which they live." In Poon Tip's view, the goal of ecotourism is to bring prosperity to local people and to offer a cultural exchange between the tourists and the inhabitants of different regions of the planet.

The seed for ecotours was planted years ago when Poon Tip visited Thailand on a $10-a-day budget and stayed with local hill tribes. It was not his first taste of the country, but it was the most authentic, and he has since built his company on such authentic experiences. Poon Tip believes so firmly in ecotourism that he spearheaded a post-graduate diploma program in ecotourism and adventure travel at Humber College in Toronto and helped run the program for two years. Today, his company has 85 employees and offices in 21 countries worldwide. It offers more than 800 adventure tours to more than 100 countries. About 20 percent of G.A.P's 10 000 passengers a year come from Canada. The company's gross sales in 2001 were approximately $15 million.

In June 2001, G.A.P was included in *PROFIT* magazine's list of Canada's 100 fastest-growing companies for the seventh year in a row. The company also won the Global Traders Award of Canada for leadership in exporting. But the "big one," says Poon Tip, was the Ethics in Action Award in 2000 that recognized his company's dedication to sustainable tourism and community development. That commitment was further acknowledged with an invitation from World Bank and UNESCO, for a second year running, to address the government of China in Beijing about preserving that country's cultural heritage.

• •

1. What are some of the ethical values that Bruce Poon Tip believes in regarding ecotourism?

2. Research recent Ethics in Action Awards. What criteria are used to judge candidates for the award? Which of these criteria could serve as a model for other international business practices?

Corporate Social Responsibility

Canadian companies are learning to be good corporate citizens in vastly different cultures. Every company has an obligation to a variety of stakeholders. **Stakeholders** include the community, employees, customers, suppliers, investors, and society in general. Stakeholders are the persons or groups affected by the performance of the organization. As a result of a renewed focus on all stakeholders, many business leaders today are promoting social responsibility. Socially responsible companies serve not only the financial expectations of their shareholders but also the ethical interests and demands of all their stakeholders.

One measure of corporate success is the social and environmental impact of a company, its **corporate social responsibility** (CSR). Corporate social responsibility broadly covers corporate standards and practices regarding human rights, the environment, human resources, and community relations. Socially responsible companies publish their code of ethics or behavioural guidelines, making them available to the public and to all stakeholders, such as suppliers, customers, and investors. Some companies also offer examples of their application of the guidelines and standards. This practice helps keep their practices ethical and "transparent." A company's CSR is a mark of its willingness to be accountable to its many stakeholders.

Corporate social responsibility could mean, for example, that an international trader deals only with suppliers that abide by a code of ethics that is similar to its own. Being socially responsible means listening to a wide circle of stakeholders and welcoming their feedback and ideas. Market-driven companies that listen to consumers ensure that they take their customers' and their workers' values into account and deliver what they really want and need. In foreign countries, this may extend to providing basic education and health care for the local community and the company's employees and their families. One example of such concern is the health education and AIDS and malaria treatment programs that SNC-Lavalin offered its workers in Mozambique (see Chapter 4).

GLOBAL THOUGHT

Let's talk about corporate social responsibility. It's the relationship of a company to its suppliers, its environment, its customers. It's all the aspects of doing business beyond worrying about the next quarterly profit. Companies, certainly major-sized companies, should disclose their activities in the community. Say, if you're a forestry company, how many trees are you replanting? Or, if you've got a smelter, what are you doing with the environment? If you're in a foreign country, are you using child labour? What kind of conditions do your employees live in? You should recognize certain human rights. And you should not have bribery.

– Avie Bennett

Figure 10.5 Corporate Social Responsibility (CSR) entails meeting the needs and expectations of a wide range of individuals, groups, and governments.

The 1999 "Millennium Poll on Corporate Social Responsibility" by the Conference Board of Canada and Environics International asked more than 25 000 people in 23 countries to identify the factors that influenced their impression of a company. The survey results showed that the majority named factors such as environmental impact, responsibility to society, and labour practices. Consumers are increasingly dictating acceptable corporate behaviour by supporting or boycotting companies' products in the marketplace. Even reluctant companies are being obliged to develop CSR processes.

When a company takes leadership in social responsibility and social initiatives, it initiates proactive strategies. A proactive company meets or exceeds its economic, legal, ethical, and social responsibilities. There is no law forcing a company to be proactive. However, stakeholders will recognize a company for its "good works." These good works are, in effect, a form of promotion called **social marketing**, or cause marketing. Many proactive companies decide to support an issue such as literacy, environmental protection, or poverty reduction. They commit visible amounts of their organization's human and material resources to their chosen cause. Although many companies are taking on social responsibilities and making changes in their response to ethical issues, there are still many that avoid social demands and concentrate entirely on making a profit. Making a difference in society takes time, innovation, energy, and money.

Voluntary Codes and Legislated Codes

A **voluntary code of conduct** is demonstrated in voluntary initiatives, guidelines, or non-regulatory agreements. Voluntary codes are commitments made by companies, associations, and other organizations to influence their behaviour for their own benefit and for the sake of their communities. Voluntary or discretionary codes address the needs of consumers, workers, and citizens while at the same time allowing companies to be more competitive.

One Canadian organization that has a strict, though voluntary, code of conduct is Mountain Equipment Co-op (MEC), which was established in 1971 to sell good-quality outdoor equipment that was not readily available in the Canadian marketplace. The cooperative emphasis on social and environmental responsibility has led to improved financial performance, reduced operating costs, and strong employee morale. The Mountain Equipment Co-op voluntary code focuses on four key areas:

- business operations sustainability: reduction of waste and energy consumption

- product sustainability: monitoring of labour practices and respect for local communities

- service and use of MEC products: product re-use, alternatives to buying, and rental and repair programs

- MEC as a citizen: community and environmental programs

When producing offshore, MEC has a firm policy and code in place covering employee health and safety, working hours, working conditions, and environmental issues to avoid dealing with factories that abuse their workers' rights.

Unlike a voluntary code, a **legislated code** is, in fact, law. Compliance is mandatory. A number of Canadian government agencies ensure that the legislated codes are followed, for example, at Canada's borders, in the environment, in food production, in health and safety, and in air travel. A business that fails to follow a legislated code is considered non-compliant and may face legal sanctions.

Web Link

Follow the link at www.internationalbusiness.nelson.com to find out more about voluntary codes in Canada.

ICE Activities for 10.1

Ideas	Connections	Extensions
1. (a) Explain the meaning of the term "business ethics."	(b) Investigate and report on a recent ethics issue related to international business that involved a choice between two "rights."	(c) In small groups, discuss why the really tough choices for Canadian international businesses focus on choices between one right and another right.
2. (a) Describe the difference between cultural relativism and ethical imperialism.	(b) Create a drawing in your notes to illustrate your understanding of the extremes of cultural relativism and ethical imperialism.	(c) If you were the head of an international Canadian company and faced an ethical dilemma in your host country, would your reaction tend toward cultural relativism or ethical imperialism? Explain.
3. (a) Identify three stakeholders in any international business organization.	(b) Explain the relationship between social marketing and ethical corporate behaviour.	(c) In groups, identify and record any products that you purposely buy, or the places where you purposely buy them, because the manufacturers or retailers are socially responsible. Describe the nature of their social responsibility.

10.2 Ethical Issues Affecting the Conduct of International Business

THINK ABOUT IT

While there may be an emerging global market, there is *no* evidence of an emerging global business culture defining ethically appropriate and inappropriate business practices in that market.
– *Wesley Cragg*

Do you agree or disagree with this statement?

When a Canadian company does business internationally, it must deal with many ethical issues related to its different stakeholders:

- the host country and its society
- consumers
- employees
- investors or stockholders

The company must learn about areas of dispute and determine ethical guidelines for handling such disputes. It must balance its goal of earning a profit with the need to behave ethically. Because many business people are paid according to performance, some may be tempted to bypass difficult ethical issues. However, with the constant scrutiny of current business practices by governments, the media, pressure groups, and consumers, ethical risk management has become an important factor in doing business internationally. While successful risk management can lead to the enhancement of a company's reputation, mismanagement of ethical issues may lead to business failure.

Societal Issues

Pollution of the natural environment is a universal concern, because clean air, water, and soil are necessary for human and animal life. Since such tragic events as the 1984 chemical leak from a Union Carbide Factory in Bhopal, India, which left thousands of people dead and thousands more with disabling illnesses, and the 1989 *Exxon Valdez* oil spill off the coast of Alaska, there has been a growing realization that corporations must take responsibility for the ways in which they affect the environment.

Figure 10.6 In 1989, the oil tanker *Exxon Valdez* sank, spilling oil in Prince William Sound in the Gulf of Alaska. The captain was suspected of being intoxicated.

GLOBAL THOUGHT

How does one balance the need for development with the intrinsic value of natural lands? How does one raise his or her standard of living while striving to cut back on consumption and waste production? Every environmental problem has at its base an ethical dilemma of some kind—the clashing of two fundamental "rights."
– *Abby Kidder*

Figure 10.7 Supporters of the Kyoto Accord make their views known at a meeting of energy and environment ministers in Charlottetown in May 2002.

One major source of global concern about the environment focuses on the effects of global warming. In 1997, representatives from around the world met in Kyoto, Japan, and reached an agreement on targets to combat global warming. This agreement is known as the **Kyoto Protocol (Kyoto Accord)**. This protocol would see industrialized countries, between 2008 and 2012, voluntarily reduce their carbon dioxide emissions to about 2 percent less than their 1990 levels. As of 2002, however, some countries, including the United States, have not signed the agreement. In December 2002, Canada ratified the protocol. Some governments and corporations believe that reducing carbon dioxide emissions will negatively affect their economic performance. If the Kyoto Protocol becomes law, however, polluters would not only be acting unethically, they would also be acting illegally.

Other environmental issues focus on the proper storage of hazardous materials such as nuclear waste, and on the possible wholesale export of Canada's fresh water to other countries. For example, some countries have a real need for water. The dilemma is this: it is unethical to ship water outside Canada because it could jeopardize the country's physical environment. Trying to sustain a resource by keeping it renewed is often difficult if demand for the resource outpaces regeneration. However, it could be considered unethical for Canadians, who are wasteful with water consumption, not to export water to nations in desperate need of it. It is clear that finding an appropriate stance on such issues is not easy, and they will be part of world citizenship and decision-making in the twenty-first century.

Consumer Issues

As you learned in Chapter 7, product safety standards are very important consumer issues, whether the product is a child's toy, a car tire, or a medication. Stakeholders depend on companies to deliver quality products, but quality control is sometimes difficult to maintain in products that are manufactured in international settings. When a company finds itself on the front page of the newspaper in a negative light, its public relations experts work overtime to minimize the social and financial damage to itself and to its customers. One recent example of damage to corporate reputations was the Bridgestone/Firestone August 2000 recall of 6.5 million tires in the United States following consumer complaints about defective tires on Ford Explorer sport utility vehicles. International media attention focused on both the tire company and the Ford Motor Company. The recalls and lawsuits have already cost both companies millions of dollars, but the loss of consumer confidence threatens both companies in the longer term.

More recently, consumer resistance to genetically modified foods like potatoes has increased. Monsanto Canada Inc. took its strain of Naturemark potato, genetically modified to resist the Colorado beetle, off the market. The corporation claimed it did so to concentrate on other crops. The potato industry suggested that stiff marketplace resistance was the real reason for its withdrawal.

In another recent example, Bayer AG, a large German pharmaceutical company, voluntarily pulled its drug Baycol off the market in all the countries where it had been available. While this drug had been approved for use in Canada, its use appeared to have been related to a number of deaths. Bayer's earnings were reduced in the short run, but the action was essential for the health of the public and for the long-term financial and legal interests of the company.

The safety of medications is a particularly sensitive consumer issue. One classic example is the Tylenol story from 1982. According to Heesum Wee ("Corporate Ethics: Right Makes Might," *Business Week*, April 11, 2002), someone tampered with Johnson & Johnson's Tylenol product by adding cyanide to some bottles. Seven people in the United States died from ingesting the poisoned capsules. When managers at the company learned about the poisoning, they immediately sent out orders for all Tylenol products to be recalled, for the public to be warned, and for production of the product to be halted. As Wee says, "The J&J managers ignored advice from consultants and attorneys who had argued such dramatic steps might harm the Tylenol brand." The managers agreed among themselves on the ethical course of action; based on their company's values, they had to protect consumers before any other considerations.

As a result of the Johnson & Johnson managers' swift action, lives were saved. The company was applauded for its immediate recall of the product and gained consumer respect for its handling of the incident. This event also awakened many manufacturers to the need for "tamper-proof" packaging, which was developed largely in response to the Tylenol incident.

Web Link

Follow the link at www.internationalbusiness.nelson.com to find out more about current warnings on dangerous consumer products.

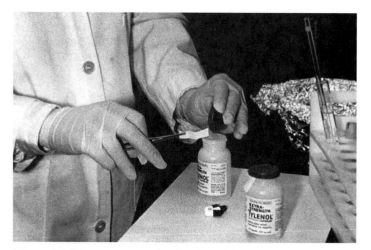

Figure 10.8 In response to the October 1982 tampering of Tylenol, the Illinois Department of Health tested bottles of the drug with a chemically treated paper that turns blue in the presence of cyanide. The tragedy resulted in the application of tamper-resistant packaging on most foods and drugs sold today.

Employee Issues

Workplace Health and Safety

Employers must ensure safe work practices for their employees. However, workplace safety standards tend to vary from country to country. If a building under construction collapses or if workers are subjected to unnecessary fumes at work, the standards have been either too lax or poorly enforced. Inadequate inspection processes and corruption of safety inspectors can be a problem in some countries.

Some multinational corporations choose not to own or operate the factories that produce their products. These companies can contract with a production facility in a foreign country rather than having to invest in their own facilities. Some companies move into developing nations with the intention of subcontracting production in work environments that have weak regulations and low labour and operating costs. Although developing nations usually welcome multinational corporations because they bring money and employment opportunities for citizens, problematic issues can arise if the companies create export industries that threaten worker safety or human rights in the workplace. Canadian companies may find themselves dealing with trade partners that condone unfair wages, child labour, and poor working conditions. Negotiating a deal to do business in some countries may also include negotiations to improve or eliminate these negative conditions.

GLOBAL THOUGHT

Overworked, untrained workers lose limbs in unsafe machines. Teen-age girls gluing soles onto shoes in unventilated workshops are poisoned by fumes. Workers locked into dormitories and factories are killed in fires ... Some factories are huge, having up to 15 000 workers who live, work, eat, and sleep there, going home just once a year.

– Anita Chan

Figure 10.9 Teenage girls inspect the soles of sport shoes as they roll by on a conveyor belt.

Equality Issues

Different countries have different understandings of the role of women and minorities in society and in the workplace, of the way they should be treated, and of the appropriate extent of their participation in a variety of levels in businesses. Education and legislation on equality issues and gender roles differ from one country to another. Canadian companies may face ethical dilemmas in their host countries in their efforts to act appropriately in issues of employee equality and affirmative action, without alienating local employees or markets.

Affirmative action refers to efforts to implement equal opportunity in employment selection and in pay. Equity, or fairness, for women, minority groups, and individuals with disabilities at work continues to be an issue in Canada and in other countries around the world. According to the World Bank, countries where women and men have equal rights enjoy higher economic growth, lower poverty rates, and less corruption than nations where women and men are treated differently.

In many countries, skilled and talented women cannot rise to positions in business or politics because of cultural barriers. As with trade barriers, however, the workplace is also experiencing a liberalization that could improve equity. The glass ceiling effect, the barrier to those who want to move ahead in their career but cannot as the result of prejudice, discrimination, and tradition, will dissolve further as governments, citizens, and multinational companies work together to increase equity in the workplace.

Human Rights Issues

You learned about Mountain Equipment Co-op (MEC) earlier in this chapter. Mountain Equipment Co-op provides an example of how to deal with potentially conflicting business practices in host countries. Its members recently debated the policy of sourcing much of its camping gear from China. They were concerned about China's poor human rights record, since China has heavy government control, no independent trade unions, no free press, and no religious freedoms. Working conditions in many Chinese factories are also poor. Mountain Equipment Co-op considered a boycott of Chinese factories in an effort to pressure the Chinese government to improve its standards and workplace health and safety.

But MEC decided that instead of a boycott, it would separate its business dealings from the area of international foreign policy. The cooperative's policy states that "MEC undertakes its business dealings with individual firms and factories, not with countries." Mountain Equipment Co-op's policy now prohibits the cooperative from dealing with sweatshop factories or with factories in special free-trade zones where it is legal to ignore minimum-wage laws and environmental protection codes. It also developed a process to review its source employers' practices relating to health and safety, employment, and the environment.

Figure 10.10 The interior of a Mountain Equipment Co-op store in Toronto, Ontario.

Is it better to provide healthy and dignified work for individual people working in independent factories or remove their opportunity to obtain work of this nature because of the country where they were born?

– Mountain Equipment Co-op's question in grappling with its ethical responsibilities in doing business in China

Company buyers now work directly with their factories, identifying weaknesses and proposing solutions. If factories do not correct their practices, they stand to lose MEC's business.

The company notes that China's standard of living has improved over the past 15 years as a result of increased trade. Although MEC is not a development agency, it believes that it can have a positive influence on the communities where its business is placed with individual firms that meet its expectations.

Labour Issues

In the changes accompanying free trade, a company can face conflicting points of view where its workers' way of life is threatened. For example, in South Korea in 2001, 20 000 labour activists staged mass demonstrations at the Daewoo Motor Company, South Korea's third-largest auto firm. They were protesting layoffs caused by the company's lagging sales and financial problems. The union objected that the layoffs were intended to help negotiations for a takeover by a U.S. auto firm. In the end, Daewoo's union reluctantly accepted the government's plan to lay off 3500 workers.

When labour feels powerless about job security, disruptions tend to occur. But, does a company have an ethical obligation to keep its workers employed? Reduced employment is often one unfortunate result of a company's loss in competitiveness. Non-union workers—more common in countries with low wages—are even more vulnerable than unionized workers. Businesses that compete in the free market still need to control risk and provide their stockholders with a fair return on their investment. Sometimes the plight of their workers is not given the highest priority. But corporations that take their social responsibility seriously have to consider their obligations to workers and their community as well as to their shareholders.

Figure 10.11 Striking workers at Daewoo Motor Company in South Korea, in 2001.

Stockholder Issues

Stockholders (shareholders) are the owners of a corporation. As owners, they have the right to earn fair dividends based on the company's performance, and they also have the right to vote on company policies and for company directors. Stockholders invest in a company in the belief that they will earn a fair return on their investment. They have a right to expect that company managers will act in their interests.

For stockholders to exercise their voting rights properly and to decide whether to continue to invest in the corporation, the corporation needs to disclose its business dealings honestly. Issues may arise about balancing sufficient disclosure with the danger of alerting the competition to business dealings.

GLOBAL THOUGHT

I define a conflict of interest as "a situation in which a person, such as a public official, an employee, or a professional, has a private or personal interest sufficient to appear to influence the objective exercise of his or her official duties."

– *Michael McDonald*

Figure 10.12 William Lerach, an attorney representing shareholders suing 29 current and former Enron Corporation executives and directors, carries a box of shredded documents into federal court in Houston, Texas.

The fall of Enron, a multinational U.S. corporation, demonstrates what happens when business dealings are hidden from stakeholders and when at least some of those dealings are dishonest. In 2000, Enron had $20 billion USD in assets and $1 billion USD in revenue. The company was one of the world's leading energy, commodities, and services companies. But by 2002, Enron was bankrupt. Examinations of Enron's management and financial practices showed that it had been engaged in self-dealing and misleading financial reporting. For example, in October 2001, the company announced a $636 million loss. After the U.S. Securities and Exchange Commission began an investigation, however, the company revised its financial statements. The loss actually extended back to the previous four years, and reduced earnings by another $586 million. The company also admitted that it had to pay $690 million in debt and that it would have to repay $6 billion by 2002.

When this news broke, stockholders labelled the Enron management as dishonest, full of conflicts of interest, and guilty of creating a culture of deception. The role and actions of Enron's auditor, the firm of Arthur Andersen, were also heavily criticized. The implications of the Enron collapse have been far-reaching and international in scope. Investors had been misled. Investments, the pensions of Enron employees, and thousands of jobs were lost. The developments brought public outrage and reduced stakeholders' confidence in the accuracy of audited financial information in general. The stock market was negatively impacted because investors rely on financial information for investment decisions.

The fall of Enron brought about much international discussion and examination of how corporations govern themselves, the role and responsibilities of corporate and outside legal counsel, and the responsibilities of both internal and external auditors. Arthur Andersen, which used to be one of the world's largest accounting and consulting firms, was abandoned by many large clients and then broken up.

Corruption and Dumping

As you saw in Chapter 8, gift giving is a vital part of some international business trips, particularly initial visits. Before engaging in discussions about sales, it is quite common to present a foreign trade partner with a gift. However, the practice of making payments to suppliers or governments to win a contract—or to gain priority in releasing a shipment, or to have an inspector come promptly—is both unethical and illegal under Canadian law. Canadian companies are subject to criminal charges if they are found guilty of bribery. In some countries, however, such payments are common and, in fact, a cost of doing business. A company that does not make provision for such "special payments" may not even be in the running for certain contracts.

Corruption is one of the greatest challenges of the contemporary world. It undermines good government, fundamentally distorts public policy, leads to the misallocation of resources, harms the private sector and private sector development, and particularly hurts the poor. Controlling it is only possible with the cooperation of a wide range of stakeholders in the integrity system, including most importantly the state, civil society, and the private sector. There is also a crucial role to be played by international institutions.

– Transparency International

In the 2002 **Corruption Perceptions Index**, published by the German group Transparency International, 102 countries were scored and ranked according to their degree of corruption as seen by business people, academics, and risk analysts. Scores range from 10 (highly clean) to 0 (highly corrupt). Russia is an interesting example, because it is a country that has been undergoing great change since the fall of the Soviet Union. Russia scored 2.7 out of 10. The country has tried to transform itself into a capitalist state, but its economy has been infiltrated by criminal groups. Because of Russia's current reputation for corruption, few foreign companies are willing to move into the Russian market. For example, 10 years ago there were 35 Alberta-based companies active in Russia; in 2002, there were two. Corruption has included seizure of bank accounts and takeovers of company offices at gunpoint.

2002 Corruption Perceptions Index (Top 10 Countries)

Rank	Country	Score
1	Finland	9.7
2	Denmark	9.5
	New Zealand	9.5
4	Iceland	9.4
5	Singapore	9.3
	Sweden	9.3
7	Canada	9.0
	Luxembourg	9.0
	Netherlands	9.0
10	United Kingdom	8.7

Figure 10.13 Each score relates to perceptions of the degree of corruption as seen by business people, academics, and risk analysts. The United States ranked number 16 with a score of 7.7.

2002 Corruption Perceptions Index (Bottom 10 Countries)

Rank	Country	Score
93	Moldova	2.1
	Uganda	2.1
95	Azerbaijan	2.0
96	Indonesia	1.9
	Kenya	1.9
98	Angola	1.7
	Madagascar	1.7
	Paraguay	1.7
101	Nigeria	1.6
102	Bangladesh	1.2

Figure 10.14 This chart shows the lowest-ranking countries in the 2002 index. Corruption was perceived as rampant in these countries, among the poorest nations in the world.

TRADE TALK

The Wilfrid Laurier University School of Business and Economics, with the help of Compas Inc., conducted a survey that ranked ethical issues facing Canadian companies. The views of 361 corporate chief executive officers were canvassed across Canada. The majority of survey respondents (76 percent) said Canada should speak up about human rights abuses abroad despite the potential loss of business opportunities. Only 17 percent said Canada should be silent on the subject.

While business leaders seem to value the concept of fair play, some suggest that successful companies operating overseas pay bribes when the need arises. In such cases, payments are paid through advisors and consultants.

Business executives look to their own family values, lawyers, business associations, public relations advisers, and even marketing research firms for advice on ethics. The survey is a sign that new policies on conducting trade and workplace behaviour are underway.

– CEO Ethics Survey

Dumping is another business issue that is controversial and considered unethical. **Dumping** is the practice of selling goods in a foreign country at a price that is lower than in the country in which they were manufactured. In a recent case, the Canadian steel industry won a battle against foreign importers of steel who had been found guilty of dumping underpriced or outdated products on the Canadian market. The Canadian International Trade Tribunal found that nine countries were selling hot-rolled carbon and alloy sheet steel at below-market prices in the Canadian market. How were foreign producers able to undercut Canadian-produced steel for the automobile industry? They received direct financial subsidies from their own governments. Developing countries complain that anti-dumping legislation is a form of protectionism introduced to help Canadian producers during a global economic slump. Practices like dumping become issues in talks on the liberalization of trade.

Web Link

Follow the link at www.internationalbusiness.nelson.com to find out more about the workings of the Canadian International Trade Tribunal.

ICE Activities for 10.2

Ideas	Connections	Extensions
1. (a) List and describe the different categories of stakeholder issues discussed in this section of Chapter 10.	(b) Select a well-known Canadian multinational company and describe how it deals with international environmental issues.	(c) Using the company you selected, create an organizer to show the advantages and disadvantages of the company's policies for the citizens in one host country.
2. (a) Summarize how Johnson & Johnson dealt with the tampering of their Tylenol product.	(b) With a partner, summarize the main ideas in two current news stories about consumer product safety. Identify the companies involved.	(c) Using the Internet, look up the codes of ethics of these two companies from 2. (b). Compare their policies.
3. (a) Explain the different kinds of employee issues that multinational companies face.	(b) Research Canadian workplace and safety standards. Use a concept web or a mind map to organize your findings.	(c) In small groups, brainstorm ways that Canadian multinational companies could use the Canadian standards to improve conditions for workers in one foreign country.

10.3 Taking Action, Ethically

The Multinational Challenge

Multinational companies have an extensive international presence, controlling production, distribution, services, or other facilities outside the country in which they are based. As you learned in previous chapters, Canadian businesses take a number of risks when they expand into other countries. Over distance and time zones, in the face of different cultures and customs, multinational companies face governmental and foreign exchange regulations and restrictions in the host country. They risk the prospect that if contracts are broken, they have no legal recourse.

GLOBAL THOUGHT

The test of progress is not whether we add more to the abundance of those who have much, it is whether we provide enough for those who have little.

– *Franklin Delano Roosevelt*

If they produce in foreign countries, they must work out the logistics of labour, resources, and shipping to market—and earn a return on investment for shareholders.

International businesses can earn large profits for their shareholders and at the same time provide employment for host country workers, improve the economy, and introduce technologies that help develop businesses in their host country.

Nonetheless, multinational corporations have come under attack from a number of stakeholders worldwide. What may have seemed like a "win-win" situation for both the companies and the host countries is perceived by critics to be unbalanced in favour of the corporations. The reputation of multinational corporations in regard to their operations in developing countries is by no means untarnished. They are accused, among other things, of polluting the environment in their host countries, of taking profits out of those countries without significantly investing in their economies, of imposing their values and customs, and of using cheap labour without considering the welfare of their workers.

Coltan, Conflict, and Cell Phones

Clearly, multinational corporations face many challenges if they are to be accountable to all their stakeholders. Sometimes, behaving in an ethical and socially responsible way requires partnerships among the companies and a number of international agencies. Such was the case with the production of coltan in the Democratic Republic of Congo.

As you learned in Chapter 4, coltan (columbite-tantalum) is an ore that produces a metal powder called "tantalum." As a key component of cell phones and computer chips, it is now one of the Western world's most sought-after, and expensive, materials. One of the major sources of coltan is the Democratic Republic of Congo. Congolese tantalum comes from coltan mines whose operators brutally exploit their workers and dominate the Congolese population, displacing farmers from coltan-rich land, destroying vast tracts of rainforest, and endangering local wildlife species, as well as using the profits to finance a long-standing civil war.

Since these abuses have been exposed, many makers of high-tech components are demanding that their suppliers comply with their corporate environmental, ethics, and human rights policies, and guarantee "conflict-free" coltan. But it is difficult for the consumer or the manufacturer to be entirely sure of the ultimate source of any coltan that comes from Africa. Some manufacturers are now buying their coltan from Canada, Australia, or Brazil, to be sure that they do not add to the human rights violations in the Congo. The United Nations has proposed a temporary trade embargo on coltan originating in the rebel-held areas of the Congo.

Figure 10.15 Gorillas native to the Congo are being endangered by coltan mining.

Consumer Activism

Consumer awareness and activism are affecting how multinational companies operate. For example, companies now face rising protest when they use—or when consumers are persuaded that they use—sweatshops. "Vigilante consumers" in North America and elsewhere often resist buying sweatshop-produced products on ethical grounds, and seek to change conditions and even punish unethical manufacturers. Organizations such as Students Against Sweatshops (which originated at the University of Toronto) have proposed a number of strategies to hold international companies accountable and to end the exploitation of workers. According to such organizations, companies should provide full public disclosure of where goods are made and how workers are treated. The organizations also recommend that independent groups monitor the standards to ensure that they are reliable and effective and that violators are punished. Many workers need to become aware of their rights and need international support for improved conditions without fear of retaliation. In addition, even though a factory may be clean, well organized, and monitored, if its workers are not making reasonable and competitive wages, it may still be called a sweatshop.

Excerpts from the United Nations Universal Declaration of Human Rights:

Article 23:

(1) Everyone has the right to work, to free choice of employment, to just and favourable conditions of work, and to protection against unemployment.

(2) Everyone, without any discrimination, has the right to equal pay for equal work.

(3) Everyone who works has the right to just and favourable remuneration ensuring for himself and his family an existence worthy of human dignity, and supplemented, if necessary, by other means of social protection.

(4) Everyone has the right to rest and leisure, including reasonable limitation of working hours and periodic holidays with pay.

However, there is a contrasting viewpoint on this issue. This view says that these so-called sweatshops are actually welcomed by some labourers in developing countries. Sewing jeans in an overheated factory for $0.70 an hour may be unpleasant work, but to a rice farmer in Thailand who makes only $1.00 a day working a small plot of land, moving to the city and working in a factory may actually lead to an improvement in lifestyle and standard of living. Poverty is often worse in rural areas than in towns and cities throughout the developing world.

TRADE TALK

CARE Canada's "Tools for Development" program sends to developing countries used tools and equipment contributed by Canadian companies and individuals. Over the past 15 years, CARE has shipped more than 4000 pieces of equipment to 1600 small businesses in developing countries.

Here are some of the tough issues that multinational companies face as they move their production into foreign countries:

- Should workers be paid the local wages or higher?
- Should better health and safety practices be adopted to improve the host country's standards?
- When is it acceptable to hire a person below school-leaving age, and what constitutes child labour?
- Should the company monitor and enforce workplace standards if local authorities do not?

Figure 10.16 IKEA, in conjunction with local aid organizations, has initiated projects in developing countries that make education for women and children more readily available, a highly effective way of preventing child labour.

Companies are responding to consumer concerns about the plight of workers in foreign countries. Nike, the American sportswear manufacturer, has been the target of anti-sweatshop activists, who want the company held responsible for the conditions of workers in its apparel-assembly operations around the world. Nike has taken such criticism seriously, stating that its mission is "to make responsible sourcing a business reality that enhances workers' lives." Other activist campaigns have influenced large retailers like Home Depot and IKEA to stop buying wood cut from old-growth forests. Large retailers and clothing manufacturers like Wal-Mart and GAP have agreed to corporate codes of conduct that ban clothing produced by child labour or that is assembled under unsafe working conditions. To keep their brand and reputation intact, many multinational corporations are now paying external organizations to monitor the operations of their suppliers in other countries to ensure that those suppliers comply with the codes.

Future Directions for Multinational Corporations

The future for you and many of today's young people may include working for a multinational corporation at home or abroad. It will be important for you to know the ethical stance of the company you choose to ally yourself with. Individual companies establish their own voluntary corporate code of conduct that defines their ethical standards. Although such codes are voluntary and not enforceable, some organizations may require acceptance of their codes as a condition for membership or licensing agreements.

Contributions of NGOs and NPOs

Much creative change has resulted from the cooperation of individuals working together to influence business or government behaviour and policies. Some of these groups, commonly referred to as **non-governmental organizations (NGOs)** or **nonprofit** or **not-for-profit organizations (NPOs)**, work to bring about positive and necessary change through **lobbying**, which generally occurs through meetings and discussions.

Most NGOs or NPOs finance their ventures with contributions from members of the public. They can sometimes access project funds from such organizations as the World Bank, Asian Development Bank, trusts, and philanthropic foundations. They also seek sponsorships from corporations. In policies known as **corporate philanthropy**, many companies today donate significant financial and material resources to support such organizations and social causes.

GLOBAL THOUGHT

For development to be sustainable, it must integrate environmental stewardship, economic development, and the well-being of all people— not just for today but for countless generations to come. This is the challenge facing governments, non-governmental organizations, private enterprises, communities, and individuals.

– *International Institute for Sustainable Development*

Some of the organizations that are working toward ethical business practices for today and for the future include the following:

- The World Business Council for Sustainable Development is a coalition of 160 international companies from 30 countries and 20 major industrial sectors "united by a shared commitment to sustainable development via the three pillars of economic growth, ecological balance, and social progress." The Council focuses on projects that are based on corporate social sustainability, sustainable livelihoods, building capacity through education, and stakeholder dialogues.

- Canadian Business for Social Responsibility (CBSR) works with for-profit businesses to encourage socially responsible and sustainable business practices. CBSR has developed comprehensive guidelines for communities, employees, customers, suppliers, shareholders, the environment, and the international market.

- Ethicscentre.ca (formerly The Canadian Centre for Ethics and Corporate Policy) is an organization made up of volunteers from corporations and the general public. On its Web site, the organization offers articles by prominent Canadians on topics dealing with current issues in business ethics.

- The mission of the Institute for Global Ethics is to use its educational and public policy reports, seminars, and publications to "promote ethical behaviour in individuals, institutions, and nations through research, public discourse, and practical action."

- The International Institute for Sustainable Development makes policy recommendations on international trade and investment, economic policy, climate change, measurement and indicators, and natural resource management to support sustainable development.

- TakingITGlobal (TIG) is a not-for-profit organization with thousands of members from over 190 countries. TakingITGlobal's vision is to "create a community that inspires young people around the world to create positive change on a local and global level." The company creates virtual and physical environments where people are exposed to new thinking, a diversity of voices, and new opportunities.

Figure 10.17 Jennifer Corriero and Michael Furyk are the cofounders of TakingITGlobal.

Follow the link at www.internationalbusiness.nelson.com to find out more about organizations that are working toward ensuring international business ethics.

The International Chamber of Commerce

The first international code of conduct for multinationals was created by the International Chamber of Commerce (ICC) in 1937. The ICC promotes "an open international trade and investment system and the market economy."

As you learned in Chapter 5, the ICC has an International Court of Arbitration and recommends guidelines and rules of conduct in a wide range of business activities: for example, anti-corruption, business law, commercial crime, customs and trade regulations, e-business, environment and energy, and trade and investment policies.

The ICC, in conjunction with the United Nations Environment Programme, gives "World Summit Business Awards for Sustainable Development Partnerships." Among the 2002 recipients was Alcan Inc., which is a Canadian-based aluminum and specialty packaging company. More than ten years ago, Alcan started a program with an elementary school in Quebec to promote recycling and educate students about entrepreneurship. Today, the program, which is called the "Micro-Business Network," has more than 32 000 students participating in Canada, Brazil, Malaysia, and Thailand. In British Columbia, young entrepreneurs at Cormorant Elementary School have set up a business designing, producing, and selling greeting cards made from recycled paper collected at local Alcan facilities. Alcan helps students by providing the necessary equipment and training manuals to guide the new businesses.

Figure 10.18 Alcan Inc. headquarters. The company was a 2002 recipient of the "World Summit Business Awards for Sustainable Development Partnerships."

Web Link

Follow the link at www.internationalbusiness.nelson.com to find out more about the International Chamber of Commerce.

Other recipients of ICC awards include these bodies:

- **Axel Springer Verlag AG** (a newspaper publisher) has partnered with Otto Versand (a mail-order group), 8900 Norwegian forest growers, the World Wildlife Fund, and Greenpeace Russia (among others) to establish the "Newspapers that know their trees" program. Using the Internet, readers can find out which region of the world the newsprint for a newspaper comes from. This enables readers to know whether the publishing company practises sustainable development.

- The **Business Trust of South Africa** is an alliance of 145 corporate partners and the South African Departments of Education, Environmental Affairs and Tourism, Labour, and Safety and Security. The alliance works to create jobs and bolster economic growth in South Africa through education, the eradication of crime, the fight against malaria, and the creation of jobs for young people. The Trust is committed to the sustainable development of South Africa.

- The **Municipality of Calvia** in Spain and hotel and commercial associations, are working together to tackle the issue of municipal waste. Hotel and shop owners and their patrons have agreed to cooperate with this initiative in return for a 15 percent reduction in the annual tax payment. The citizens also preserve their natural environment, which is a tourist attraction and contributes to the economic well being of the area.

Figure 10.19
The Municipality of Calvia decided to tackle the issue of municipal waste by offering local businesses reduced tax payments.

Daniel Abichandani

Junior Achiever

Daniel Abichandani has a good idea of what it means to be an ethical and socially responsible global citizen. Immediately after finishing high school, he attended the first Marmon Group Global Trade Institute, organized by Junior Achievement International. The eight-day conference, attended by 93 young people from 62 countries, had workshops on networking, team-building, entrepreneurship, global trade, and ethics.

During a session on ethics, small groups had five minutes to discuss an ethical situation and decide how to handle it. Then in one-minute speeches, they gave their recommendations to the full assembly. Daniel also took part in two competitions at the conference: the development of a one-page business plan, and a five-minute speech on ethics in global trade. He won both. His speech addressed these concepts:

- Corporate Karma: the idea that businesses that invest in and practise a strong code of ethics will achieve greater financial return, thanks to an "ethical profit."
- Ethical Consumerism: consumers' growing awareness of ethical issues, and their tendency to establish loyalty with "ethical brands."

Daniel moved on to the University of Western Ontario, planning to study advertising and entertainment law at its Ivey School of Business. There, he was a member of the student council and the business case club called DEX, and participated in a production of *West Side Story*. In his three years as a member of Junior Achievement, he won three awards for his success as an "achiever."

In Daniel's view, students from different cultures can bring unique contributions to business ethics. "The logical group to bring about changes in global business codes of ethics is today's youth. At an age when we are trying to find ourselves and define our roles in society, we have an opportunity to work toward defining ethical principles in business practices of today—and tomorrow. As future leaders in our fields, we have this obligation."

Daniel's simple rules of business ethics may be considered somewhat idealistic, he says, but adhering to them may help build a secure future for the world:

- Do not steal from others.
- Do not fabricate or conceal the truth.
- Do not suppress basic human rights for the sake of profit.
- Do not strive to attain above and beyond what one truly needs.
- Give back to communities the resources that you employ and consume.
- Treat other cultures and religions with the respect they deserve.

GLOBAL THOUGHT

Conferences like this one give true insight into the concept of a 'global village' ... Eating, drinking and sleeping next to people from very different places and backgrounds has a magical way of encouraging people to share their perspectives. Canadian Junior Achievement Conference (CANJAC) is a great way to learn about others, the business world, and most importantly, yourself.

– *Daniel Abichandani*

1. What did Daniel Abichandani learn from his participation in Junior Achievement International?

2. Write a paragraph explaining how, in your opinion, Daniel's experiences in school and as a member of Junior Achievement helped him acquire the skills and competencies required for employment in international business.

ICE Activities for 10.3

Ideas	Connections	Extensions
1. (a) List some of the challenges that multinational companies face as they try to use ethical practices in foreign countries.	(b) Research ethical business practices of one Canadian multinational company.	(c) What are some of the consequences of unethical international business practices?
2. (a) Describe three ethical concerns about multinational products that have been expressed by consumers.	(b) With a partner, identify some additional ethical concerns that you think consumers should take action on. Then share your ideas in a larger group.	(c) Develop an action plan that you think could be used to increase awareness of one of the concerns you identified in 2. (b).
3. (a) Explain how three NGOs have helped improve the business conditions in developing countries.	(b) Research one of the NGOs mentioned in this chapter and report on its current activities.	(c) Write an editorial expressing your opinion of how the activity you reported on 3. (b) will affect business in developing countries. Consider both drawbacks and benefits.

Canada's Trading Partners: Focus on Mexico

We cannot escape globalization. It's here to stay. It is not good or bad, but we need to create a more human face to it.

– Vicente Fox

Figure 10.20 Vicente Fox, President of Mexico.

On December 1, 2000, Vicente Fox Quesada was sworn in as president of Mexico. He is seen as a popular leader who wants to improve the country for all Mexicans. A highly successful businessman before he was a politician, he once headed Coca-Cola's Mexican operations.

Mexico is in the midst of an industrial boom. Despite being a country characterized by widespread poverty and endemic corruption, it is benefiting very strongly from the North American Free Trade Agreement (NAFTA). Under NAFTA, exports from Mexico have risen significantly.

President Fox believes Mexico offers tremendous opportunities for investors from around the world and has great potential for future growth. "It is very sad," Fox says, "we don't have a middle class in Mexico. We have the worst distribution of income in the world. We only compare with Africa." In a country of over 100 million, only 1 in 10 Mexicans has a bank account.

Because Mexico's middle class is so small, Mexico has not developed a strong internal (indigenous) market. Its own people cannot afford the consumer goods it manufactures. Therefore, the country's prosperity is almost entirely dependent on exports. Mexican car factories produced 1.6 million vehicles in 2000, and fewer than a quarter of them stayed in Mexico. Many of these exports are made in border manufacturing plants called maquiladoras, foreign-owned factories (American, South Korean, Canadian, for example), which are allowed to operate in duty-free zones within Mexico with special privileges, in return for hiring Mexican labour.

Fox has three strategic objectives that embody his vision for Mexico:

- Grow the economy and distribute income more fairly.
- Establish the rule of law and justice in the battle against corruption and poverty.
- Make significant improvements in education and health care.

He believes that the human resources of the Mexican people and their entrepreneurial ability will provide Mexico with true competitive advantage in world trade.

Now that President Fox is instilling values that will encourage fairness in trade and in dealings both internally and globally, Mexico's future seems brighter. Mexico is Canada's largest trading partner in Latin America. Negotiations are ongoing with the United States to improve the situation for cross-border workers and to normalize the border between the two countries.

Mexico's economy has been transformed from one based largely on mining to one that includes strong agriculture and petroleum sectors. This move to a more diversified economy has also prompted more deregulation and privatization in areas such as telecommunications. Mexico's current challenges include combatting the devaluation of its currency and its ongoing poverty.

Mexico represents tremendous business potential for Canada. Because of its close ties to the United States, most investment risks remain lower in Mexico than in comparable emerging markets.

Mexico's proximity to the United States also means that, like Canada, it is subject to strong American political, economic, and cultural influences and forces. And, like Canada, Mexico looks forward to a more prosperous future as a full member in NAFTA and other trade associations.

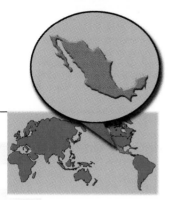

A SNAPSHOT OF MEXICO

Size: 1 958 200 sq. km

World Region: North America (Latin America)

Capital City: Mexico City

Language: Spanish

Currency: New Mexican Peso

Population: 103.4 million

Time: Noon in Ottawa (EST) is 11:00 A.M. in Mexico City.

Climate: Varies from tropical lowlands to dry desert lands and cooler high plateaus

Type of Government: Federal republic

Labour Force by Occupation: 24 percent agriculture, 21 percent industry, 55 percent services.

Membership in World Organizations: NAFTA, WTO

Importing Partners and Products:
Partners: United States (75 percent of the total), Germany, Japan, Canada.
Products: Automobiles, wire and cable, data processing machines. Ontario imports nearly 10 times more from Mexico than it exports to Mexico.

Exporting Partners and Products:
Partners: United States (84 percent of the total), Canada, Germany.
Products: Ontario represents more than 50 percent of all Canadian exports to Mexico, in the form of motor vehicle parts, electronic equipment, plastics, and agricultural products.

Travel Advisory: When visiting Mexico for less than 30 days for business purposes, an entry form is needed. It can be obtained from a port of entry with photo ID and proof of citizenship. For longer than 30 days, or for multiple entries, a visa is required. Serious crime, often involving violence, is high in urban centres.

Business Etiquette: Business titles and courtesy are very important. Prolonged lunch breaks lasting two to three hours are customary, and business takes place into the early evening hours. Family values and relationships are very important.

Country Link

To find out more about Mexico, follow the links at
www.internationalbusiness.nelson.com.

Figure 10.21 Mexico's San Miguel de Allende is a popular winter haven for artists.

Chapter Challenges

Knowledge/Understanding

1. Match each of the following terms to the correct definition or description below:
   (a) business ethics
   (b) stakeholders
   (c) coltan
   (d) ethical dilemmas
   (e) CSR
   (f) ethical imperialism
   (g) legislated code
   (h) cultural relativism
   (i) lobbying

   (i) corporate standards and practices regarding human rights, the environment, human resources, and community relations
   (ii) the belief that certain forms of behaviour are categorically right or wrong
   (iii) laws
   (iv) the belief that behaviour should be governed by what will bring about the greatest good for the greatest number of people
   (v) the behaviour of businesses related to moral duty and obligation
   (vi) meetings and discussions intended to solve problems and resolve issues
   (vii) the community, employees, customers, suppliers, investors, and society in general
   (viii) the ore used in cell phones
   (ix) conflict between "right" courses of action

2. Identify and describe five ways in which a multinational company can cause positive and negative effects in the countries in which it operates.

3. Create an organizer to help you explain how international companies mentioned in this chapter reflect their business ethics in their treatment of employees, society, stockholders, and consumers.

Thinking/Inquiry

1. In small groups, brainstorm possible answers to the question, "Can a country move forward and improve itself without the intervention or investment of multinational corporations?" Then evaluate the suggestions from your session, select the arguments you consider to be most valid, and present your findings to the rest of the class.

2. Working with a partner, visit the Web site of one of the following organizations. Select and summarize the organization's guidelines for one of the following stakeholders: communities, employees, customers, suppliers, or shareholders. Present your findings to the rest of the class. Include in your presentation your view of the guidelines. Do you agree with them? How could they be improved?
   • The International Chamber of Commerce
   • The World Business Council for Sustainable Development
   • The Canadian Business for Social Responsibility
   • Ethicscentre.ca
   • The Institute for Global Ethics
   • The International Institute for Sustainable Development
   • TakingITGlobal (TIG)

3. Research a company either on the Internet or in your community. Find a copy of its code of ethics. Identify the key words in its code. Then compare your code with those collected by other students in your class. How similar or different are the codes?

Communication

1. Prepare written arguments for and against one of the following statements. Then find other students in your class who have chosen the same statement as you have and discuss the two sides of the issue. As a group, negotiate your way through the different viewpoints to come to a consensus on the issue.
   • Canada should not do business with nations that have poor human rights records.
   • There are universal ethical values and absolute truths that all nations and cultures should follow.
   • If trading partners can have a common currency, they should also be able to have a common code of ethics.

2. Research one of the following issues as it relates to ethical behaviour in the multinational business environment: environmental concerns; product safety standards; workplace safety; affirmative action; human rights; stockholders' rights; health and well-being; or treatment of labour. Plan, draft,

and write a one-page report (350–500 words) on the impact of this issue on Canadian companies as they do business internationally in the future.

3. Given all the ethical challenges in international business, it is not uncommon for Canadian entrepreneurs to shy away from international expansion and stay home, where they are familiar with the market and the laws. From what you have learned in this chapter, prepare a multimedia presentation or a brochure for young Canadian entrepreneurs in which you present the pros and cons of dealing with the ethical issues in international business.

Application

1. In the "Canada's Trading Partners" feature in this chapter, President Vicente Fox is quoted as saying that Mexico cannot escape globalization. His goal is to "put a more human face" on it. On Fox's agenda for creating a more just society for Mexican workers, he believes that he needs to
   - expand the Mexican economy and distribute income more fairly among the country's citizens
   - establish the rule of law and justice in the battle against corruption and poverty
   - improve education and health care

Research ethical issues in one of Vicente Fox's goals. Create at least three research questions to guide you in your investigation. Then, plan, draft, and prepare an illustrated report on your findings.

2. Follow the links at **www.internationalbusiness.nelson.com** for CARE Canada. Find the section of the site about the campaign to collect used tools. Draw up a plan that would enable your class to collect tools for CARE and ship them to the organization. What information would you need for such a campaign to be useful and effective? What ethical issues would you need to consider in your plan?

3. North Americans make up approximately one-fifth of the world's population, yet they consume most of the world's resources. Vancouver-based Adbusters Media Foundation recently launched a 24-hour "Buy Nothing Day," designed to challenge the "more is better" mentality. Now shared in more than 30 countries, the day of reflection usually takes place on the Friday after the American Thanksgiving, the biggest shopping day of the year in the United States. Activities range from poster campaigns to full-day carnivals celebrating sustainable alternatives to consumer society. Suggest how you could organize a "Buy Nothing Day" at your school to create awareness of this issue.

International Business Portfolio

Global Business Ethics and Social Responsibility

Some companies and organizations will choose not to conduct business or relations with a country because of its political, economic, social, cultural, ethical, or religious policies or actions. Many North American consumers consider the ethical position of a country when making their purchasing decisions. International boycotts of products from a certain country can have devastating consequences on that nation's economy. An extreme strategy for dealing with an unethical country or organization might be to develop a trade blockade, thereby preventing the transport of their goods and services. For example, many consumers look for coffee bearing the Fair Trade logo to ensure that the workers who grew, harvested, and processed the coffee are treated ethically. What are some of the ethical issues your IBP country grapples with? Canada's Department of Foreign Affairs and International Trade provides country profiles, reports, and links to help with this. The American Government's State Department also provides background notes on most countries that include an assessment of current issues. Follow the links at **www.internationalbusiness.nelson.com**.

Activity

Find out whether any of the following issues are present in your IBP country, and describe them briefly, using the following headings where appropriate:
- environment
- product safety
- workplace safety
- sexual harassment
- misuse of new technology
- human rights
- conflict of interest
- bribes, graft, unauthorized payments and/or copyright infringement, etc. (corruption)
- health and well-being
- advertising content
- privacy and security of company records
- treatment of labour (wages, conditions, etc.)

Chapter 11

International Marketing

Marketing is the sale and distribution of products and services to a particular market. This chapter discusses the different marketing strategies businesses use to sell their goods and services internationally, the changes in the marketing mix that a company needs to consider before trying to sell its products abroad, and some of the unique problems posed by different consumer markets and government regulations.

Chapter Topics

➤ 11.1 – International Marketing Strategies 336

➤ 11.2 – Global Marketing 345

➤ 11.3 – The International Marketing Mix 354

➤ *Canada's Trading Partners: Focus on* Spain 364

➤ Chapter Challenges 366

Prior Knowledge

- How would you define marketing?
- What makes a successful marketing campaign? What factors contribute to its success?
- What kinds of challenges would a Canadian company face if it decided to market its products or services internationally?

Inquiries/Expectations

- What are some of the challenges faced by a business that wants to market a product internationally?
- To market a product internationally, what adaptations need to be made to its marketing mix?
- What kinds of market research are necessary to prepare a business for entering foreign markets?
- What are some of the legal, cultural, and economic factors that must be addressed to market a product internationally?

Important Terms

brand acquisition strategy	glocal
brand development strategy	market segment
brand equity	marketing
centralized marketing strategy	marketing mix
channels of distribution	marketing opportunity analysis
decentralized marketing strategy	
demographics	marketing plan
discretionary buying power	marketing research
disposable income	product differentiation
economies of scale	pull strategy
flagship brand	push strategy

11.1 International Marketing Strategies

"I'd like to buy the world a Coke, and keep it company." Coca-Cola's marketing campaign of the early seventies promoted the idea of global peace and harmony through the universal consumption of Coca-Cola. Coca-Cola did not really want to buy the world a Coke, however. It wanted to *sell* the world a Coke. The company looked at the world as a market for its product, Coca-Cola, and it still does. Coca-Cola is interested in marketing its product to six billion consumers.

Marketing is the sum of all the activities involved in the planning, pricing, promotion, distribution, and sale of goods and services to satisfy consumers' needs and wants. When a company markets a product or service internationally, it must formulate a number of business decisions called **marketing strategies**. Every company that wishes to expand its marketing efforts, either at home or beyond its domestic market, must select the strategy that will be most effective for its purpose. An international business can look at several methods of marketing a product or service internationally, including

- choosing between a centralized and decentralized strategy
- incorporating push marketing or pull marketing
- deciding to focus on international brand acquisition or brand development

Centralized and Decentralized Marketing Strategies

A **centralized marketing strategy** focuses on the production and sale of goods from one central location. A centralized business produces all its products in one country, then exports the finished goods to other countries. The overriding marketing philosophy here is to "think local, act global." For example, a Canadian pottery maker who designs a Web site and sells his or her products internationally is a centralized marketer. The potter is taking advantage of the global marketplace but has no intention of setting up a manufacturing plant in another country.

Figure 11.1 Global expansion of Applesnax products has resulted in export to Japan, Taiwan, Israel, and France.

Centralized companies often have several marketing divisions, each responsible for a specific area of the world that is a market or a potential market. These companies use common marketing themes to create international marketing campaigns. These campaigns are effective within relatively homogeneous regions grouped by common language, culture, or trading area. Rather than have a specific marketing office in each national market, centralized marketers prepare promotion and distribution strategies that cover large geographic areas and still take cultural differences into account.

There are a number of advantages to using a centralized marketing strategy.

- **Brand building (global brands):** According to a report in the August 6, 2001, issue of *Business Week* magazine, Coca-Cola is the number one global brand—that is, it is recognized by more people around the world than any other brand. Nike (number 34), Gap (number 31), and KFC (number 51) are also high-ranking global brands. These companies invest millions of dollars of advertising in international **brand equity**—making a brand recognizable throughout the world and giving that brand a positive image. Global marketers use a centralized strategy to build brand equity through consistent promotion, packaging, and product features. Imagine how Coca-Cola's brand equity would be affected if local marketers could change the colour of the can or the flavour of the product!

Web Link

Follow the link at www.internationalbusiness.nelson.com to find out more about the ratings for different global brands.

Figure 11.2 The Coca-Cola label is recognized worldwide. Here, Coca-Cola uses a large Coca-Cola can to advertise its product on a busy street in Moscow.

Figure 11.3 Individually, a banana and ice cream are both tasty. Together, they're quite delicious—a perfect example of synergy!

- **Synergy:** Synergy occurs when two agents or forces work together to produce an effect that is greater than the sum of their individual effects. Centralized marketing can bring together research and development, creative advertising, and global sales efforts to create an international marketing campaign that is more effective than the marketing efforts of smaller local suppliers or distributors.

- **Cost benefits (economies of scale):** In marketing, bigger is not always better, but it is often less expensive. Duplication of effort is a waste of money, and centralized marketing prevents duplication, especially in areas such as research and development and advertising and promotion. Head-office control of these areas provides more resources for local marketing efforts. A new product, new manufacturing system, or new advertising campaign developed by centralized management provides cost savings that will lower costs and increase sales and profits for local distributors.

A **decentralized marketing strategy** uses the "think global, act local" philosophy. Companies with a decentralized strategy use local production facilities, distribution centres, advertising agencies, market research companies, sales representatives, and/or retail partnerships to target specific international markets. Companies that produce a number of product brands may leave all advertising, sales distribution, and promotional decisions to local marketing representatives in other countries.

Multinational companies that operate on a local basis throughout the world are called **glocal** companies, a term used by business people to describe a company with a decentralized marketing philosophy.

There are many advantages to using a decentralized marketing strategy.

- **Proximity to markets:** A company that manufactures locally can distribute locally as well, targeting smaller communities in an area that centralized companies may find too expensive to target. The savings in transportation and storage costs are also significant. Even if companies choose not to set up manufacturing plants in foreign markets, they can still decentralize somewhat by renting warehouse space and hiring a local sales force to distribute their product to gain better access to the market.

- **Flexibility:** As a brand shows major growth in a specific region, a decentralized company can spot the trend quickly, respond, and, therefore, maximize sales. Advertising and promotional activities matched to specific local events, competitive pricing strategies used to fight a new competitor, and sales efforts targeted at the newest retail distributor in a foreign city are some of the opportunities available to decentralized businesses. Centralized companies do not have the same flexibility because their decision-making is done by head-office managers who are looking at the global picture and not the local one.

- **Cultural sensitivity:** Local people know local customs and can help tailor advertising messages, package designs, and distribution strategies to accommodate the local culture. Centralized companies will be more likely to make cultural errors that could affect sales.

Smaller companies often do not have the budget to use a decentralized marketing strategy. For example, the Newville Candle Company in St. Davids, Ontario sells candles internationally, but is not yet large enough to consider manufacturing candles in other countries. Nor is its access to international markets large enough to warrant establishing distribution centres in foreign countries. For now, the Newville Candle Company will "think local" by making candles to meet the needs of Canadian consumers, but "act global" by registering in the Canadian Exporters Catalogue and maintaining a Web site to make future international distribution possible.

Multinational companies, however, do have a choice of strategies. Very few companies are totally centralized or totally decentralized. Coca-Cola, for example, maintains a centralized strategy for its **flagship brand**, Coca-Cola, the product that carries the corporate name. But Coca-Cola maintains a decentralized strategy for its other products, using a network of local bottlers around the world. Fanta, for example, is a highly successful Coca-Cola brand in Europe, and bottlers in various European countries tailor promotional efforts to their local markets. Coca-Cola develops or acquires local brands that are suited to local tastes, such as Kuat in Brazil, Georgia Coffee in Japan, and Lift in Australia.

Web Link

Follow the link at www.internationalbusiness.nelson.com to find out more about the Canadian Exporters Catalogue.

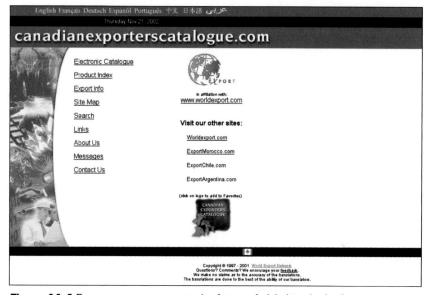

Figure 11.4 E-commerce represents the future of global trade. It allows exporters to quickly transact with clients' overseas and results in reduced costs, increased revenue, expanded markets, efficiency, and enhanced communications between buyers and suppliers.

Push and Pull Strategies

Marketers who use a **push strategy** sell their product to retailers, importers, or wholesalers but not to end-use consumers. These companies try to move products through the **channels of distribution**, that is, through businesses such as importers, wholesalers, and retailers that connect any manufacturer's product to the target market. Marketers adopt a push strategy in the belief that if their product is displayed in stores for consumers to see, consumers will buy it. The store display space is a silent salesperson and is often directly controlled by the retailer, not the manufacturer. Push strategists direct their advertising and promotional efforts towards dealers, to convince them to carry the product. Push strategists may rent space at trade shows, hire effective sales representatives, and create advertising and promotional efforts to convince dealers to carry the product.

Figure 11.5 There are many valuable reasons to exhibit at a trade show. Product introduction is the focus of these new and established authors and publishers at this book fair in Frankfurt, Germany.

Figure 11.6 Sales agents meet and discuss their line of products with potential customers. Agents are paid a commision and are responsible for selling a product in a defined area.

- **International trade shows:** A company with a product to sell internationally can rent space at an international trade show. Dealers from the region attend in search of new products to carry in their stores or to distribute as sales agents. International trade shows allow retailers to examine a variety of products available from around the world and to select those that will fit into their marketing plans. For example, a Canadian manufacturer of children's clothing could display products at trade shows in Lisbon, Frankfurt, Birmingham, Cologne, Hong Kong, Athens, Florence, Singapore, and Beirut, among others. At any of these shows, manufacturers display their lines and try to attract foreign buyers. It is then the responsibility of the retailer to promote the product after the sale is made.

- **Sales agents:** Many companies with a push strategy hire sales agents or sales representatives to sell their line of products in other countries. These agents are paid a commission (a percentage of the dollar sales they make for the company, usually 10 percent) on every order they take. They travel through a region, often using a catalogue and some sample products, to try to place company products in stores. These sales agents are experts in the industry and are efficient and effective players in international marketing.

- **Dealer advertising and promotions:** Instead of advertising to the consumer, businesses using a push strategy spend their promotional budgets on building a distributor or dealer network. Advertising and promotion in companies with a push strategy offer incentives to retailers (for example, a special company jacket if the store sells more than a certain amount of product); contests that only dealers can enter; special display fixtures, signs, and banners; and colourful advertising brochures and catalogues that emphasize the profitability of the product instead of its consumer benefits.

A **pull strategy** targets the consumer directly. Advertising and promotional efforts try to convince consumers that they need a product and, therefore, "pull" these consumers into stores to look for the brand. The retailer is also exposed to the consumer advertising, of course. If the pull strategy has worked and consumers are asking for the product in stores, the retailer will contact the supplier and purchase the product.

Even though many international brands have been successful using pull strategies, such strategies can be challenging. To build demand for their products, international marketers must create advertisements in foreign languages, while being respectful of cultural differences. As you saw in Chapter 8, this is not an easy task. The benefits are significant, however, because after brand awareness is established, very little sales effort is required, as global brands such as Pepsi or Adidas demonstrate. Marketers who favour the pull strategy focus their time and resources on maintaining brand equity.

Combined Push and Pull Strategies

Figure 11.7 This diagram illustrates the combined push-pull strategy, which is the most common marketing strategy used by international marketers. Company A tries to establish brand awareness with consumer advertising and uses sales agents, trade shows, dealer promotions, or a combination to be sure local retailers have the product in the stores when consumers begin to look for it.

Brand Acquisition and Development Strategies

Many successful brands already exist in foreign markets, and international companies trying to enter those markets may fail to sell their own brands because of strong local competition. Under such circumstances, an international company may add local brands to its international line of products by using a **brand acquisition strategy**. In other words, the international company purchases an existing company in the foreign country or acquires the rights to distribute the brand locally.

Buying a foreign company is an expensive but effective way of controlling competition. The advantage of acquiring or merging with a foreign company is that the workforce, management, and company goodwill (the positive reputation a company has in the minds of its customers) come with the company. When two companies merge in the same country, it is often a rationalization effort that results in downsizing or even the elimination of one of the participants entirely. Internationally, acquisitions and mergers are often undertaken to gain a viable asset to assist in the company's marketing strategy.

Contracts for Distribution Rights

A less expensive way to add a product or a line to a company's product mix is to obtain the rights to manufacture or distribute the product, or both. This strategy has two options associated with it:

- **Manufacturing and distribution rights:** One company can license to another company the rights to make a product and sell it in a specific region. Products are often marked "Manufactured Under Licence," which means that the local manufacturer does not own the rights to the product, but only "leases" them from the original owner in another country. For example, Pepsi-Cola manufactures Lipton products (Brisk, Lipton Iced Tea) under licence from Unilever, Lipton's British parent company. Often, the arrangement is more than a simple licensing agreement and becomes a joint venture, which is a business enterprise jointly undertaken by two or more companies that share the initial investment, risks, and profit. If Unilever were to invest capital to help develop the Lipton bottling plant along with Pepsi, then the arrangement would go beyond licensing and become a joint venture.

- **Exclusive distribution rights:** Negotiating for the exclusive distribution rights to a product or product line for a specific country or region is a strategy that has been very effective for smaller companies that cannot afford to build large factories in foreign countries. Canadian giftware distributors, for example, search the trade shows in Atlanta, Los Angeles, Munich, and Manchester to find exceptional products that are not yet sold in Canada. The distributors then ask for the rights to distribute the product in Canada exclusively for a trial period, usually two years. The product manufacturer, which is looking for global distribution, is pleased to have representation in a market of 32 million people, and the distributor has a new and potentially successful product line to offer Canadian customers. Often, the deal is so good for both parties that it is free—that is, there is no licensing fee. The manufacturer provides samples and catalogues; the two parties sign a contract that states that the manufacturer will not sell to any Canadian business unless the distributor has taken the order; and the distributor starts to take orders in Canada. If the product is successful, the distributor might lease warehouse space and buy the product in quantity to save shipping charges and respond more quickly to consumer demand, but it is not required for most deals.

Brand Development Strategy

The **brand development strategy** is often used with a decentralized marketing strategy. Instead of purchasing a competitor, the international marketer may use its own foreign subsidiary to develop a product to compete in the local market. You have already learned about examples of local brands developed by Coca-Cola's international subsidiaries. Many other companies, including McCain Foods, Maple Leaf Foods Incorporated, and Bombardier enlist the support of their foreign branches to develop products for local markets.

The brand development strategy is expensive and complex, and is available only to those multinational companies that market branded consumer goods. Most of Canada's top exporters are involved in primary industries, processed or semi-processed materials, or industrial products, which do not lend themselves to product development abroad. Ideal candidates for the brand development strategy are companies that can afford research facilities in local markets, that can enlist the support of local researchers and marketing consultants, and that can support the risk of developing new products for new markets.

Rene Van Haren

CEO, Innovation Giftware Corporation

In 1970, Canadian Rene Van Haren began his career as a sales clerk in the men's wear department of a major retail chain. At that time, alpaca sweaters from South America were popular, and sales people were paid extra commission for each alpaca sweater they sold. Van Haren sold more alpaca sweaters than anyone else. He could sell only what the manager bought, however, and the store was always running out. Van Haren soon realized he could do better working for himself.

He left to work for his father while waiting for other opportunities. His father had a retail giftware business and had purchased some dolls from Moscow that sold well. Van Haren was interested in carrying more Russian merchandise from the same supplier. The supplier agreed to let Van Haren sell his line of products exclusively in Canada. Van Haren began to work as an independent sales representative, carrying the Russian line as well as lines from other suppliers.

As a sales representative, Van Haren's suppliers paid him 10 percent commission on everything he sold, and he was beginning to make a comfortable living. One of his best lines was from the Weil Company. In 1975, Weil imported Cuisinart food processors from France, and Van Haren made the first Canadian sale.

Van Haren opened his first warehouse to carry Cuisinarts for retailers from Vancouver to Winnipeg. These retailers were having problems getting their orders filled for this increasingly popular kitchen appliance. Van Haren now saw the difference between selling someone else's line and importing his own. In 1978, he started Innovation Giftware Corporation so that he could import his own lines of products.

For five years, he imported linens and kitchenware while continuing to work as a sales representative for Weil. A popular line of Christmas tins inspired Van Haren to travel to the Asia-Pacific region in 1983 to investigate import opportunities for Christmas decorations. He learned that Canadian importers were not developing a Christmas line because of the risk. Van Haren decided to take the risk himself and imported decorations that sold for 99 cents each instead of several dollars. He soon sold all of his Christmas stock.

Sales representatives from the United States now wanted to carry his Christmas line. Van Haren became an exporter. He then hired designers to create his own products, which he had manufactured overseas. He built a warehouse in Great Britain and developed a team of sales representatives to carry his company's lines in Europe. Today more than 40 percent of his company's sales are in Europe. Fifteen percent are in the United States.

With each decision, Van Haren took more control of his own destiny. Van Haren offers this advice for new entrepreneurs: "Don't look for a reward for what you do. Use your skill and talent to do something that will give you excitement, pride, and self-satisfaction while you do it."

• •

1. In what ways has Rene Van Haren been involved in international marketing throughout his career?
2. In your opinion, which of Van Haren's characteristics or attributes has been most important to his business success? Explain your choice.

ICE Activities for 11.1

Ideas	Connections	Extensions
1. (a) Using an organizer, describe each pair of marketing strategies.	(b) Visit the specialty foods section of your local supermarket. List five brands that you have never seen advertised in Canada. How do these products illustrate the "push" marketing strategy? Suggest a way that at least one of these products might use the "pull" strategy as well.	(c) Imagine you are the brand manager of one of your favourite soft drinks. Discuss how you would use either the push strategy or the pull strategy to market your products in three different countries.
2. (a) Describe one advantage and one disadvantage for each of the six marketing strategies mentioned in this section of the chapter.	(b) Go to **www.international business.nelson.com** to find the links to the *National Post* or *Globe and Mail's* list of top Canadian corporations. Select five Canadian corporations that market their products or services internationally. Determine whether each corporation uses a centralized or decentralized marketing strategy.	(c) Compare your list from 2. (b) with the lists of other students to discover whether most major Canadian corporations use a centralized, decentralized, or combination marketing strategy.
3. (a) Explain what a brand acquisition strategy is.	(b) Find an article in a business publication that describes a recent acquisition or merger involving a Canadian corporation. Describe the acquisition or merger and the benefits that at least one of the companies hopes to derive from it.	(c) How might foreign companies acquiring Canadian companies affect Canadian business, the Canadian economy, and Canadian consumers?

11.2 Global Marketing

KFC

Baskin-Robbins

Subway®

Figure 11.8 Three successful franchise operations

Successful global marketers have to be able to deliver products that consumers in different countries will want to buy. Marketing is complex enough in one's own country, but it becomes even more challenging in global markets. Having a brand that is recognized throughout the world is helpful, but so is having a reputation for being a company that is able to respond to consumer needs.

As you learned in Chapter 5, franchising is one strategy that a company can use to gain a global presence. The franchisee pays a fee and a percentage of revenue to the franchisor; the franchisee is also helped by the franchisor's marketing expertise and by the reputation of the brand. International franchise operators run successful businesses in many countries around the world. While these operators have the well-known brand to help them market their product, they also have the advantage of belonging to the society and the culture of their home country. They know the preferences and customs of consumers in their own country. They know first-hand about the economic marketing factors and the demographic factors that influence consumer buying. They are also able to help the international franchisor with marketing research in their home countries.

Three franchise companies that have proven themselves to be very successful global marketers are Baskin-Robbins Inc., Subway®, and KFC. Baskin-Robbins is the world's largest franchise chain of ice cream specialty stores. In 1945, brothers-in-law Burt Baskin and Irv Robbins each opened an ice cream store in southern California. In 1946, they became partners and within two years they had six Baskin-Robbins outlets in the region. In 1948, as their brand name became known, they decided to franchise their operations. By the 1970s they sold their scooped ice cream, sundaes, frozen drinks, and ice cream cakes in international markets. In 2002, Baskin-Robbins had over 4500 locations in 35 countries including Canada, Egypt, and Russia.

Subway restaurants now rival McDonald's Corp. in the United States and internationally. According to Jessica Bujol of Associated Press, by February 2002 there were more Subway restaurants than McDonald's in the United States. Subway started in 1965 when Fred DeLuca and Peter Buck became partners and opened Pete's Super Submarine restaurant in Bridgeport, Connecticut. By 1974, they owned and operated 16 Subway restaurants throughout Connecticut. It was then that they decided to franchise their restaurants. They realized that consumers had become more health-conscious so they designed their marketing campaigns to promote their nutritious sandwiches, salads, breads, and soups. By 2002, Subway had 17 729 stores in 71 countries including Canada, Israel, Iceland, and Uruguay.

The franchising business of KFC, now a subsidiary of Yum! Brands Inc., was started in 1952 by Colonel Harland Sanders. The Colonel had worked as a chef for many years and had perfected his recipe for fried chicken. By 1964, there were 600 KFC restaurants in the United States and Canada. By 2003, there were more than 11 000 KFC restaurants in 80 countries. KFC opened its first restaurant in China in 1987 and has since built a strong market presence in the country. According to ACNielsen, KFC is the most recognized international brand throughout China.

Economic Marketing Factors

To be a viable market for an international company, a nation must have an economy that provides an income to its people. Once that income exists, international companies develop marketing strategies to help people spend their income.

There are a number of ways of measuring the wealth of nations. For marketers, two major factors stand out: wages and prices. Marketers consider these factors to decide whether

- there is a market
- there is a market for essential goods only
- there is a market for non-essential as well as for essential goods

If consumers earn wages, they will have money to spend and will create a market. If they do not earn money, then no market exists. Because the 900 million peasant farmers in China are not considered high-wage earners, they are not yet regarded as a market.

There are certain fixed items that people need, such as food, clothing, and shelter, and the sale of these items creates a market for essential goods. International marketers of essential goods need to use a push strategy and an extremely decentralized marketing strategy to keep distribution, advertising, and product manufacturing costs low. For example, a Canadian bread manufacturer could not manufacture bread in Canada and send it to a country that considers bread an essential product. The price would be too high for a market focused on essential goods.

Figure 11.9 Manoucher Bread Company of Toronto makes breads from all over the world—focacchio, barbarees, baguettes, basil loafs—and now distributes its products to countries in North America, Europe, and the Far East.

If the total cost of the goods that a person needs to buy is less than his or her salary, that person has **disposable income**. Disposable income provides **discretionary buying** or **purchasing power**, which creates other types of markets: non-essential items (to fill wants), or an increased choice among essential items (to fill needs). For example, buying rice for supper or dining in an elaborate restaurant both fulfill the need for food, but a person with high disposable income and more discretionary buying power can choose between the rice and the restaurant.

The marketer who researches the economics of a city, region, or country needs to decide whether to

- consider the new market
- sell only basic, essential goods (such as rice)
- create a marketing campaign that encourages consumers to spend their discretionary income (such as the restaurant)

Each international market requires a different marketing response. A Canadian bread manufacturer could sell bread to a foreign market with high disposable income and discretionary buying power. In fact, Manoucher's Bread in Toronto ships its gourmet bread to Europe, where it sells for more than $20 CAD a loaf.

Cities with the Highest and Lowest Purchasing Power, 2000

	Top Ten Cities (1 is the highest)	Bottom Ten (10 is the lowest)
1	Luxembourg	Mexico City
2	Houston	Caracas
3	Zurich	Warsaw
4	Los Angeles	Manila
5	Geneva	Bombay
6	New York	Budapest
7	Chicago	Shanghai
8	Montreal	Moscow
9	Tokyo	Jakarta
10	Berlin	Nairobi

Figure 11.10 Consumers in cities with high purchasing power are more likely to have disposable income for discretionary buying.

Consumer Profiles

Just as domestic marketers target consumers within their own country, international marketers must also target consumers in the countries where they do business. An international company must develop an image of the ideal local consumer. This image consists of a demographic profile, a motivational profile, and a purchasing profile.

GLOBAL THOUGHT

Demography, the study of human populations, is the most powerful—and most underutilized—tool we have to understand the past and to foretell the future... . Demographics explain about two-thirds of everything. They tell us a great deal about which products will be in demand in five years. They allow us to forecast which drugs will be in fashion ten years down the road, as well as what crimes will be on the increase. They help us to know when houses will go up in value, and when they will go down.

– *David Foot* and *Daniel Stoffman*

Demographic Profiles

Demographics are the characteristics of and statistics about human populations. They are obvious, measurable facts about groups of people. Marketers are interested in the demographic profile of a country because such profiles can help them determine the size of the market, the market's purchasing power, and the population divisions that will influence purchasing decisions. Marketers are interested in their target population's age, gender, family lifestyle, and religious and ethnic background.

Age

People's buying decisions change as they age. Their tastes change, their needs change, and their income level changes. Children, who are consumers of goods and services provided by their parents or guardians, develop into customers themselves as they reach school age. Children buy toys and candy, and their parents buy them furniture and clothing. Teenagers, on the other hand, have different tastes. Often styles, trends, and fads matter to this market segment. Young adults are just finishing school or just starting a career or a family.

Figure 11.11 Personal circumstance, such as age, occupation, income, and lifestyle, influence people's buying decisions.

They need new household furnishings. It is at this point that people start making buying decisions for others (such as a partner or child). Middle-aged adults have established income levels and spending patterns. Often, their needs revolve around their family—for example, education, clothing, food, and vacations. Mature adults retire, their children leave them with an empty nest, and their disposable income reaches its highest level as their major debts are paid and their spending patterns change. Travel and leisure become a major focus for this group.

The international marketer can discover how many mature adults, how many school-aged children, or how many teenagers are in a country or a city, but that demographic statistic will not tell the marketer what a teenager in Brazil finds trendy, what a retired worker in Sweden has planned for his or her future, or what a school child in Japan likes for an after-school snack. The marketer does know, however, that most teenagers like to be trendy; most retired people in developed countries are making plans for the rest of their lives; and most school children like something to eat after school. By profiling a market by age, international marketers can tell, for example, that there are enough school children in the market to make it worthwhile to promote a new after-school snack.

THINK ABOUT IT

How representative are you of your demographic group? How do marketers appeal to people in your group?

Gender

The roles of men and women are culturally based (see Chapter 8). Understanding these roles is important to a business marketing a product in another country. For example, demographics studies will supply marketers with the statistics that measure the number of women in the workforce and their average income compared to men. A company can then use these statistics to make decisions about advertising, product selection, and distribution.

The idea of "women's" products and "men's" products is sometimes universal and sometimes culturally based. It would be a waste of time, money, and possibly the entire marketing effort if a company directs its marketing of a product to the wrong gender. Consider automobiles. Until the 1980s, North American automobile manufacturers did not seem to recognize that women owned cars—their advertising did not portray women as car buyers. Automobile marketing has changed, however, in North America, because the demographics of the North American market have changed. Women formed a significant market for automobiles in the 1980s because of the dramatic increase of women in the workforce and the changing roles of women in society. Marketers may have been slow to perceive this shift, but once they realized the potential of this new market, their advertising changed quickly. In other countries, marketers of automobiles continue to watch the roles of men and women carefully to be sure that they are selling to the right market. For example, in Saudi Arabia, women are not allowed to drive automobiles.

Figure 11.12 In Canada, women currently represent over 50 percent of automobile drivers and purchasers.

Family Lifestyle

Family life and societal expectations concerning families vary greatly from country to country. A 17-year-old British teenager lives a different life from her Indian counterpart, who may be married and expecting a child at this age—the average age for first marriage in India is 17. Marriage in any country or at any age is often followed by the arrival of children and the lifestyle that having a family brings.

How a family lives is of great interest to marketers. A young single female living with her parents has a different life from a young single mother living with her two children. The demands on time, income, and physical and emotional energy are not the same at all. A retired couple who has never had children has different interests from a couple with three children under the age of 10. Marketers consider the products and services that these groups need, provide the product, and distribute it to where the target group shops.

Motivational Profile

Possibly the most difficult thing to do in marketing is to understand why consumers buy. It is especially hard when the marketing company is outside the cultural context of the society it wants to market to. Several theories exist to explain consumer behaviour; among these are Thorndyke's pain versus pleasure theory, Maslow's hierarchy of needs, and the emotional/rational theory.

Thorndyke's Pleasure/Pain Theory

On its simplest level, Thorndyke's theory states that people's behaviour is controlled by a desire to either achieve pleasure or avoid pain. We buy movie tickets, pizzas, and new clothing to gain pleasure. We buy security systems, insurance, and medicine to avoid pain. To understand what gives people pleasure (comfort, fun, excitement) in other cultures and what causes them pain (embarrassment, social rejection, fear, stress, and so on) is very important, because things that cause pain and pleasure in one culture may not do so in another culture. Marketers develop products and services, advertising campaigns, and distribution channels to meet the specific pleasure/pain profile of a specific population.

Maslow's Hierarchy of Needs

Maslow believed that everyone can develop a self-actualized personality—in other words, we can fully develop all of our potential—and that we all strive to reach that goal. But each of the other need levels must be fulfilled before anyone can move up the hierarchy. Biological needs, such as food and shelter, must be satisfied first. If these needs are always present in a person, he or she will never be able to move to a higher level. Security needs follow, because people, especially children, need to feel safe. Adults with income security and a safe place to live and work have these needs satisfied and can move on to the next level. Relationships with friends or partners can only be developed if a person's security needs are met. According to Maslow, we need to feel we belong and are cared for before we move on to care for ourselves. We develop self-respect as the result of respect from others, and we move towards self-actualization only after we feel confident about our worth. The self-actualizing person has the capability of becoming fully human, developing all his or her talents and abilities, and exploring new areas for growth. This is an ongoing process of development and is never completed.

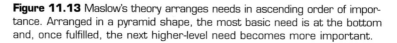

Figure 11.13 Maslow's theory arranges needs in ascending order of importance. Arranged in a pyramid shape, the most basic need is at the bottom and, once fulfilled, the next higher-level need becomes more important.

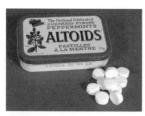

Figure 11.14 Altoids were originally packaged in cardboard cartons. In the 1920s, the distinctive metal tins were introduced.

What is the relationship between Maslow's theory and marketing? If a marketer can determine whether the primary market for a product is at the esteem needs level or the relationship level, the marketing campaign will be designed accordingly. Altoids, the British mint in a tin, is enjoying success in the North American market. The company could have aimed its product at the security needs level, to sell people on the "fresh breath, less stress" angle; the "offer one to a friend" message would have attracted people at the relationship level. But the pricing, packaging, and quirky "this-is-not-for-everyone" advertising message ("the curiously strong mint") that Altoids did use attracted consumers at the esteem level.

Rational/Emotional Theory

The most basic way to explain consumer behaviour is to recognize that purchases are influenced partly by a practical, logical, intellectual side of every human being that asks, "Do I need this?" (rational) and partly by a sentimental, fun-loving, adventurous side that proclaims, "I really want this!" (emotional). Consumers around the world are torn by the same struggle but have different wants and needs. Each culture will dictate the rational and emotional buying motives that are associated with specific products, and it is essential for the international marketer to understand the differences. The Japanese or North American teenager considers a cellular phone an essential item for communicating with friends, and can offer rational reasons for owning one. Teenagers in other countries may want a cell phone but do not have the same motive.

Figure 11.15 CDs, videos, and DVDs fall into the category of "want" (emotional) rather than "need" (rational).

Companies that sell industrial goods, goods for resale, and raw materials reject emotional motives altogether, and focus on the rational. Business-to-business advertising stresses the convenience, profitability, ease of use, ease of display, and other product features that will simplify and add to the success of their target market's enterprise.

Businesses such as foreign banks, investment companies, and other financial institutions that one expects to be rational often include emotional appeals in their marketing, such as confidence, trust, and friendly service. Purely emotional advertising is almost always associated with products that help build relationships, provide status or comfort, or appeal to a consumer's desire for beauty and peace.

Purchasing Profile

To complete the consumer profile for an international marketing campaign, the marketer needs to determine who purchases the product, when, where, and how. Marketers analyze the retail marketplace in their target country to determine the type of store that should carry their product. They study the buying patterns of consumers to discover the most popular buying seasons or busiest shopping days (in the United States, for example, the Thanksgiving weekend in November generates the most retail sales in the year). They examine who does the shopping for various household products and who makes the buying decisions about food, furniture, clothing, and cars. International marketers also look at the methods of payment accepted in various countries. How common are credit cards, debit cards, and consumer loans? Can the consumers in this country obtain credit easily, or is it difficult, even impossible, to get substantial loans for a house, furniture, or an automobile?

Figure 11.16 Retailers, from card manufacturers, florists, and jewelers to some car manufacturers, advertise and promote their products to the consumer as potential Valentine's Day gifts.

International Marketing Research

When demographic statistics, motivational studies, and purchasing information have been collected, a profile of the target consumer emerges, and the international marketer is now ready to organize the marketing mix for the product and to prepare it for market. However, it is important to consider how this information was collected in the first place to assess whether the conclusions are valid.

Marketing research collects, analyzes, and interprets data used to make marketing decisions. Marketers need two types of data: secondary data and primary data.

Secondary Data

Secondary data is the easiest type of data to collect because other organizations or government agencies have already gathered it. Secondary data is not usually specific to the manufacturer's particular needs, but is often used to make broad-based marketing decisions that rely on population statistics, demographics, and economic factors. The sources of secondary data for international markets are plentiful and easy to access.

The Internet

The Canadian government publishes current and relevant statistics and international market data, including country profiles. Many other organizations also provide Web sites to help the international marketer obtain secondary data. The following are some of the most useful sites:

- The Canadian Department of Foreign Affairs and International Trade provides hundreds of country profiles with detailed marketing data.
- Industry Canada maintains a Web site called *Strategis*, which is essential for Canadian businesses wishing to trade. The site contains hundreds of links to other secondary sources of important marketing data.
- The Canadian government's definitive source of secondary data is Statistics Canada, which also provides information for international marketers.
- The Canadian Exporters Catalogue lists numerous Canadian businesses that are already exporting and provides links to hundreds of country profiles.
- The U.S. Census Bureau provides a separate section on trade statistics.
- The International Trade Center offers an index for trade information sources by country and region.
- Global Edge is a site maintained by Michigan State University and is full of information for the global marketer.
- The International Marketing Web site maintained by the University of Minnesota is a rich source of international marketing information.

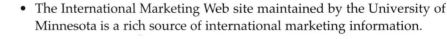

Web Link

Go to
www.internationalbusiness.nelson.com
to find the links to the Web sites
mentioned in this list.

Periodicals and Publications

Canada's daily newspapers, especially *The Globe and Mail* and *National Post*, often have articles that are important to international marketers. *Canadian Business*, *Marketing*, and *Profit* are magazines that provide important marketing data. Outside of Canada, each country has newspapers and periodicals available from their Web sites or international magazine stores that provide helpful marketing information. Many of these periodicals are published in English.

Country Organizations

Local chambers of commerce, boards of trade, and government trade associations are all excellent sources of information for the potential international marketer. Country Web sites usually provide names and addresses of these organizations.

Primary Data

Primary data is information collected directly from the marketplace by a marketing research company or by the company that wishes to use the information. Methods of primary data collection include surveys, test marketing, interviews, data mining, and focus groups. Each of these activities is common to marketers who are selling their products and services within their own country.

For the international marketer, however, it is often difficult to collect primary data. Most, if not all, companies that need primary data from a foreign market use a marketing research firm situated in the target country. These firms are experienced in collecting and analyzing local market data, and they take direction from their clients.

For example, if a marketer wants to know the size of the popcorn market in Japan, a Japanese marketing research firm can use standard data collection methods to determine who eats popcorn and when, how much popcorn is consumed, what kind of popcorn is preferred, where the popcorn is eaten, and how much consumers will spend on popcorn. These questions could not be answered using secondary data, nor could a non-Japanese firm be confident of the accuracy of any research it conducts. A marketing company that expects to be a major participant in any foreign market needs to spend money on good primary marketing research.

Follow the link at www.internationalbusiness.nelson.com to investigate a directory of international marketing research firms.

Figure 11.17 Focus groups are an invaluable tool for companies developing new products.

Ideas	Connections	Extensions
1. (a) What are the two major factors used to measure the wealth of nations? How do marketers use these factors?	(b) Working with a partner, profile a successful international or multinational company and discuss how the firm used the three major marketing factors to achieve its success.	(c) Why should a multinational company assist in the economic development of less developed countries?
2. (a) What are the three parts of an international consumer profile?	(b) Select a product from the Canadian Exporters Catalogue. Pick a country that you feel is an appropriate export market for this product. Develop a consumer profile of the ideal consumer for this product.	(c) Examine an advertisement for a product from another country. Profile the target market in Canada that the marketing focus in the advertisement is showing.
3. (a) Describe briefly the two main types of marketing research data.	(b) Using the directory of International Marketing Research Companies, research one of the companies listed and report on the services it provides.	(c) Explore one of the Internet sites listed as a source of secondary data for marketers. Prepare a report on the site that outlines the type of information available there. Share your report with a small group so that the group can develop a resource list for future marketing research.

11.3 The International Marketing Mix

When a company decides to market its goods or services in another country, it must analyze all the research it has collected and prepare a marketing campaign to introduce the product or service into the new market. The introduction of a new product to a market is called a **product launch**. To be successful, a product launch requires the coordination of all the activities involved in marketing the product or service. A successful launch can lead to high sales volume and profitability.

When the various marketing activities are coordinated into a unified marketing campaign, they are referred to collectively as the **marketing mix**. The parts of the marketing mix are often referred to as the "four Ps" of marketing:

Product: product development

Place: distribution

Price: pricing

Promotion: the combination of advertising, sales promotion, and publicity promotion

Product

Choosing the correct product is the first step in preparing the marketing mix. Without the correct product, the most innovative marketing efforts will fail. Chapter 8 presented the cultural factors that limit the sale of some products in other countries. It may be necessary to develop new products or adapt existing ones to meet the needs of specific international markets.

Consumer research will provide an indication of the potential success of a product, but it will not tell the company about the products that are already in the foreign market. Some companies fail through arrogance, believing that because their product has been successful at home, everyone else on the planet will want it, too. Foreign countries have manufacturers and importers as well, and these firms market their products successfully. It is important that any firm entering a foreign market include competitive research in the marketing plan. What products are in competition with the import, how popular are the local items, and how difficult will it be to compete with them? When the marketer has considered the product in the marketing mix, it can move on to price.

Product Features

What makes one product distinct from another? Food products have different flavours, clothing has different styles, cars have different qualities, and perfumes have different scents. Each product should have **product differentiation**—one thing, at least, that sets it apart from every other product. In a blind taste test, could you tell the difference between Coke and Pepsi? Between Hostess and store-brand potato chips? Between Tropicana and McCain's orange juice? Often these differences are not real, but imagined, and the advertising or pricing become the most important part of the mix. In many cases, however, there are real differences that lead consumers to select one brand instead of a similar competing brand.

Product developers need to consider these real differences when they are creating a new product or adapting an existing one for international markets. For example, Faces, a Toronto-based cosmetics company, markets its line all over the world, offering products for women of all ethnic backgrounds. The line includes 25 different foundations, spanning virtually every skin tone, along with 200 lipstick colours, and 150 eye shadow colours.

Companies that manufacture a number of different brands look for gaps in the international marketplace. This is called a **marketing opportunity analysis** and requires the manufacturer to examine all the competitive products within a particular product category or **market segment**. A market segment is the part of a market defined by a specific characteristic. The sports drink segment, for example, consists of all the products that compete for the active, health-conscious consumer. Products such as Gatorade or Powerade are in this segment.

It is up to the marketing department to find out whether consumers in a selected market segment in a particular country would be interested in a product, and to consider product modifications that would make the product appealing to the foreign consumer. These modifications may involve changing the features of the product, but are often simply a change in branding or packaging.

Cinnaroll Bakeries

Figure 11.18 The first non-Canadian franchise for Cinnaroll was granted to two women who had tasted the rolls while studying in Canada.

The enticing smell of freshly baked cinnamon rolls in your local shopping mall could be coming from CinnZeo. Cinnaroll is the Calgary-based owner/franchiser of CinnZeo, a retail chain that makes fresh cinnamon buns daily in stores across Canada.

Until recently, Cinnaroll held rights to the U.S.-based Cinnabon franchise for Western Canada. This company, in turn, is owned by U.S.-based AFC Enterprises, Inc., with more than 3850 restaurants, bakeries, and cafés in more than 30 countries. Brian Latham, the president of Cinnaroll, felt that AFC Enterprises was too diverse, and that he and his partners could operate a cinnamon roll chain in Canada more effectively for the Canadian market. In 1997, Latham and his partners converted the Western Canadian Cinnabon operations and renamed the company CinnZeo.

Latham and his team have now expanded internationally, and CinnZeo is the second-largest cinnamon roll maker in the world (Cinnabon is still the largest). Cinnaroll has used franchising as a domestic and international expansion strategy.

Franchising is a licensing agreement between the owner of an idea (the franchisor) and the user of the idea (the franchisee). Typically, the franchisee pays the franchiser a one-time fee to buy the rights to use the idea (franchise fee) and to pay for store acquisition costs such as real estate, construction, equipment, and initial training and inventory. After the up-front costs are paid, the franchisee pays the franchisor a percentage of sales revenue each month. The franchisee receives a successful business plan, a concept with mitigated risk with regard to profitability, expert training, and the business secrets that only the franchisor possesses. It is an excellent method for international expansion for retail chains as long as the proper research has been done to ensure the new market will be a welcoming one.

Cinnaroll expanded internationally when the company granted its first non-Canadian franchise to two women from the Philippines. The women had tasted CinnZeo cinnamon rolls while studying in Canada and believed that there was a market for the sweet, fragrant rolls in their home country. Now, international CinnZeo franchise stores are also established in the United States, Southeast Asia, and the Middle East.

Each new country means new opportunities, as well as new markets. A CinnZeo store in Manila is not the same as a CinnZeo store in Calgary. The people of the Philippines do not typically eat cinnamon rolls for breakfast, but rather enjoy them as a late-night treat. CinnZeo's hours of operation, décor, seating arrangements, and menus are different in each new international market. It is never a case of applying a set formula that works in Canada to the international marketplace. Rather, the demographics, user patterns, local preferences, and market structures are studied and a successful business plan developed for each new franchisee. Cinnaroll thinks globally but acts locally in each new international market.

1. Describe what kind of arrangements are involved in a franchise arrangement.

2. What aspects of CinnZeo's international marketing strategies have contributed to the company's success?

THINK ABOUT IT

The appearance of brand name products or company names in movies and television is called product placement. Sometimes the company pays to have its brand appear. Other times, the producers use the product to help set a scene or develop a character. Is this an ethical way of "advertising"?

Figure 11.19 Product photos can overcome language barriers. Staple foods, such as the salt shown here, are often packaged with no accompanying photo, relying on a consumer's familiarity with the product.

Figure 11.20 This label comprises product information in five languages. To help the consumer, the packager included flags to denote each country.

Branding

The most effective marketing tools available to international marketers are the brand recognition and brand equity that already exist for their products in international markets. Even though consumers live in other lands, they are exposed daily, through international magazines, television programs, books, movies, music, newspaper articles, and international travel, to a large variety of product images from other countries. A company that can **leverage** its brand equity (use the brand's solid reputation to expand into other markets) is already ahead of other companies, even local ones that do not have the same well-established image.

Packaging and Labelling

An international package should provide, first and foremost, protection for its product. One of the reasons that Pringles Potato Chips are so popular in other countries is that they are packaged in a can and are, therefore, not crushed when the consumer receives them. Potato chip manufacturers that package their product in bags will find international marketing difficult unless they make a large capital investment in local plants or design a new protective package.

Packages should also be designed for easy display, and they should help sell the product. International retailers appreciate products that take up a minimum of shelf space, because space is expensive in many dense markets. The package should stack easily, to create more display room.

The illustration on the package should explain what the product is or how it could be used. Some pictures on the labels can create confusion in an international market. For example, Canadian consumers are used to seeing a picture on a box of rice that illustrates how the cooked rice might be served with meat or vegetables. In other countries, this picture could create the expectation that meat or vegetables are included in the package.

Most countries have labelling regulations or rules that set out what must be printed on the label and specify the language or languages that must be used. Several countries, like Canada, have more than one official language. Wales, Ireland, Sweden, Switzerland, Paraguay, Singapore, Malaysia, Israel, Belgium, and Finland are some countries that are either officially multilingual or bilingual. Any business interested in selling in Paraguay, for example, should translate its labels into Spanish and Gurani, although only Spanish is required. More than 90 percent of the population in Paraguay speaks Gurani.

Place (Distribution)

Products are distributed to consumers in foreign markets in three main ways, each dependent on the type of product that the company is selling. Industrial products, such as pulp and paper, agricultural products, steel, minerals, and chemicals are sold by an industrial sales representative who deals directly with the end user. Consumer goods can be sold through retailers, and through specialty channels such as vending machines or e-commerce. In Chapter 12, you will learn about the factors affecting physical distribution and the modes of transportation used to carry goods to their markets.

Industrial Sales Representatives

The specialized nature of industrial products requires a face-to-face sales effort. No company can expect to arrange a multimillion-dollar deal for aluminum, for example, without a sales call in which payment terms, product specifications, and shipping information are arranged. Canada is a major supplier of raw materials and semi-processed and processed goods to world industries, and many of Canada's marketing efforts are performed at this level. The average Canadian consumer is rarely aware of the hundreds of deals made each day for Canadian lumber, fish, wheat, chemicals, and minerals. Yet the marketing of these products is just as essential for Canada's success in foreign markets as the more obvious efforts by providers of consumer goods such as the Great Canadian Bagel Company or Clearly Canadian Beverages.

Many industrial goods manufacturers rely on Industry Canada and the various national and provincial trade missions to develop market contacts. After these contacts are made, the company follows up on the leads through sales representatives who are either hired by the company to perform this job regularly or contracted from a pool of industry experts within the target market. The personal contact, however, is essential.

Figure 11.21 Merchants sell their products at a bazaar in Istanbul, Turkey.

Retail Marketing

In the Middle East, open-air markets, called souks or bazaars, sell everything from auto parts to zebra skins. The merchant sets up a small stall or sits under a canopy and tries to persuade passersby that his or her product is the best, most interesting, or most necessary to buy at that moment. This type of market is nothing like an organized department store or a trendy boutique, but it is the way millions of consumers buy their goods, and it is one of the channels of distribution used to reach the Middle Eastern consumer.

When a marketer enters a foreign market, she or he must understand how products are distributed in the new market. Most companies that want to distribute products through retail markets in foreign countries need to use a trade show or foreign sales office. Distributors within the country will then place the product in the most advantageous retail environment.

Figure 11.22 Since chocolate is considered an impulse product, chocolate manufacturers want to break this mould and make chocolate consumption a more regular habit.

An effective but expensive way to ensure good retail distribution is to acquire or partner with an existing company that has already opened successful retail channels. In 1996, Cadbury Schweppes, a British beverages and confectionery company, bought Neilson Cadbury, a Canadian confectionery company. Today, Cadbury Schweppes not only owns successful Neilson products such as Crispy Crunch and Caramilk, but also has access to the network of distribution channels that Neilson had established for its products. Cadbury Schweppes simply adds its brands to the former Neilson line and has instant retail exposure in the thousands of stores that sell Neilson chocolate bars.

To ensure distribution, many businesses build their own retail stores, especially in the service sector. McDonald's, Gap, IKEA, KFC, and Nike are examples of companies that have worldwide retail outlets. The economies of scale, especially volume buying, give these companies a great price advantage in foreign markets.

Specialty Channels

Many companies find it cost-effective to go to where the consumers are rather than set up a retail shop and wait for them to visit. The most important development in this area is the growth of e-commerce, but specialty channels such as vending machines, catalogues, television sales, and telemarketing are still popular.

E-commerce

Figure 11.23 Jones Soda Co. develops, produces, markets, and distributes alternative beverages.

The Internet is truly an international marketing tool. Both large and small companies with something to sell can set up a Web site and be in business instantly. Most major companies provide opportunities for anyone in the world to view their product line and order their goods. For example, Jones Soda, a Canadian beverage manufacturer in Vancouver, does no formal advertising, but depends on the "push" strategy and an effective Web site to promote its soft drinks. Visitors to the Jones Cola site can order custom-labelled beverages in any one of Jones's flavours in cases of 12. The consumer can have the bottles customized with their photo on the front and a personal quotation on the back. Jones Soda ships its product all over the world.

Vending Machines

In places where space is at a premium, vending machines provide an efficient distribution method for a variety of products, from soft drinks to French fries, ice cream to underwear. The manufacturer, such as Pepsi-Cola, often owns the machines. Pepsi contracts with the owner of various locations, such as supermarkets, convenience stores, colleges and universities, high schools, and hundreds of other places, for permission to install a machine. The Pepsi-Cola Company is responsible for machine security, inventory, and repairs, and pays a percentage of the revenue to the property owner. Many student governments and athletic associations in high schools across Canada receive revenue from vending machines.

Web Link

Follow the link at www.internationalbusiness.nelson.com to check out the Jones Cola Web site.

Figure 11.24 Jidohanbaiki (vending machine in Japanese) contain just about anything you need—shooters, sake, cold canned coffee, mobile phones, and fresh coffee.

Figure 11.25 Television shopping is a 24-hour, seven day per week broadcast retailer available on a variety of cable channels.

TRADE TALK

The Home Shopping Network pioneered the electronic retailing industry in 1977. It has since grown into a global multichannel retailer with worldwide consolidated sales of $1.8 billion USD in 2000, and a growing customer base of more than five million. Its 24-hour programming reaches more than 154 million households worldwide. Last year, HSN received more than 75 million sales and customer service calls and shipped more than 41 million packages around the world.

Many vending machines are owned and operated independently. Entrepreneurs contact a vending machine manufacturer and for between $2000 and $10 000 CAD they can own their own vending machine, buy products from a distributor, and stock their machine. To be in business, all they need is a location or two and a popular product to sell. The effort comes from keeping the machine stocked and repaired. A number of specialty machines are operated this way, especially in Japan, the country that has the most vending machines per capita in the world.

Catalogues

Canadians have used catalogues to shop since the days of the Eaton's Catalogue, which first appeared in the late 1800s. Today, catalogues are a major channel for the distribution of products to international markets, although many catalogues appear on company Web sites instead of in print. Canadian companies like The Added Touch in Oakville and Lee Valley Tools in Ottawa have been using catalogue sales as a distribution channel for more than 30 years.

Television Shopping

The Shopping Channel in Canada, The Home Shopping Network (HSN) in the United States, and other international television shopping channels give consumers an opportunity to shop at home, and give international marketers a chance to display their products to millions of potential customers. Numerous other "infomercials" create excitement for products from all over the world. An astute marketer can purchase a container of an inexpensive household gadget made abroad, buy space on local television stations on Sunday morning (the least expensive time), and distribute the gadget to anyone who calls the toll-free number. This is another method for Canadian businesses to sell their products in foreign markets.

Telemarketing

Some marketers use the telephone to introduce new products to potential customers. These phone calls lead to an in-home sales call. Although telemarketing is annoying to many, it is an effective distribution method for international as well as national Canadian marketers. The important thing to remember here, however, is that unsolicited phone calls are unpopular in every culture.

Price

International marketers must be able to price their product to compete in whatever market they enter. This is extremely difficult, given all the impacts on price any trading effort generates. Pricing is a complex task that is crucial for a successful marketing mix that will create sales and, more importantly, profit.

Many factors influence the price of a product in a foreign market, including exchange rates, tariffs and duties, transportation costs, hidden costs (such as insurance), and travel costs. These factors do not influence domestic pricing in the same way. As a result, the foreign price is often higher than the domestic price. Marketers must plan what to charge the new consumers so that they may earn a reasonable profit for their company at the same time as competing with the price of similar products already available in the target market.

A major influence on price are economies of scale, especially as they relate to a foreign market. Economies of scale mean that the more products a company makes, the less expensive they become. A company's fixed costs, such as rent, utilities, and insurance, do not change no matter how many products the factory makes. If fixed costs are $1000 per day and a company makes two products a day, the products will cost $500 each in fixed costs. If the company makes 1000 products a day, each will cost only $1 in fixed costs. Foreign markets can increase production and, therefore, decrease production costs, which may result in a lower price for both foreign and domestic markets.

Promotion

Advertising at home or abroad requires two steps: creating an effective sales message and selecting an advertising medium that will deliver the sales message to a target audience. However, it is much easier to create an effective sales message for a target audience that you know and to select an advertising medium with which you are familiar. Foreign advertising requires foreign expertise.

Most international marketers that have achieved success in foreign markets hire an advertising agency in the foreign country to handle both the creation of the sales message and the selection of the media. It is wise to allow professionals, who understand the market, to create the advertisement that will attract the attention of the target audience, capture their interest, build their desire, and motivate them to buy. Canadian advertisers may be able to create effective messages for the Canadian market, but they would have difficulty creating an appropriate message for the Brazilian market, or the Italian market, or any other unfamiliar international marketplace.

Another advantage of using foreign advertising agencies is that they are also familiar with foreign media. The agency understands who reads which magazines, listens to which radio stations, reads which newspapers, and watches which television programs. For example, the agency will know if advertising on the foreign equivalent of a new show will reach 40-year-old women or 18-year-old males. These foreign agencies will be able to advise a Canadian company in a foreign market whether to advertise their upscale men's cologne in bus and subway ads or in a men's fashion magazine. In a busy Asian city, for example, many men take the bus to work because driving is impossible. As well, they do not have time to read fashion magazines. A Canadian advertiser might have selected the magazine and missed the target market.

Contests, premiums, and coupons are all effective promotional activities in global markets if they are managed correctly. A contest should provide an opportunity to win something that the consumer wants. A sport utility vehicle (SUV) as a prize would be an effective purchase incentive in Australia because Australia has large, open spaces. It would not be an appropriate prize in Italy, where the streets are narrow and the cities are close to one another.

Figure 11.26 Mail-in rebates are popular forms of discounts for computer software and hardware.

THINK ABOUT IT

What would your community look like if all advertising and marketing efforts disappeared overnight?

Premiums are free goods offered with the purchase of a product. A premium might be a plastic toy in a cereal package or a free coffee after the consumer buys ten. Premiums should be something people want, and they should be selected for specific markets. To be effective as a brand reminder item, the premium should carry the company logo or name. Pens, jackets, and glasses are all appropriate as logo-bearing gifts. Collectibility and rarity make a premium desirable and will mean the consumer has a positive reminder of the company for a long time. Premiums should also be tied to the benefits of the product, if possible. For example, a tire company would get a lot of promotional mileage from a road emergency kit.

The cents-off coupon is still an effective promotional tool that is used throughout the world. The higher the face value of the coupon, the higher the **redemption rate** (the percentage of consumers who use the coupon measured against the number of coupons issued). The average redemption rate for coupons distributed by mail is 5 percent, but it approaches 100 percent if the consumer has printed the coupon from a Web site. This is because consumers who take the time to download a coupon from the Internet are most likely going shopping for that product that day. Internet coupons can also cross international boundaries and apply to purchases of international products wherever they are sold. If Colgate toothpaste offers a 20 percent off coupon on the Internet, New Zealand shoppers and Mexican shoppers will be able to receive 20 percent off the price of a tube of Colgate toothpaste with the same coupon.

Promotional companies, like advertising agencies, are located in every major market. Marketers who believe promotional efforts will help their sales but are not familiar with the market should hire a promotional company that will manage contests, premium placement, and coupon distribution, as well as many other promotional activities. Marketing dollars spent on professional market advice or assistance is a wise investment in international marketing.

Developing an International Marketing Plan

Before a company's marketers attempt to market their product outside of their own country, it is essential that they develop a solid international **marketing plan**. This marketing plan determines the marketing mix (product, price, place, promotion) that will be appropriate for the specific foreign market. Each time the company takes its product into a new country, the marketing mix changes, and a new international marketing plan is needed.

The marketing plan is an integral part of the company's international business plan and contributes to the firm's overall international goals. It is always a work in progress, and marketers continually update it to address changes in the market.

- **Product:** The marketing plan begins with an analysis of the product relative to the target market: the product's features, benefits, and value to consumers in the foreign market. Marketing research will give the company information on the demographics of the market, potential sales, and any changes that it needs to make to the product and packaging.

- **Price:** Calculations on the price of the product should ensure that the product is priced competitively for the target market and will include exchange rates; tariffs and duties; transportation, hidden, and travel costs; and economies of scale considerations.

- **Place:** Distribution considerations will include distribution channels and the modes of transportation that will be used to get the goods to the foreign market, as well as any factors that will affect those modes of transportation.

- **Promotion:** Advertising and promotion include the creative strategy, the media plan, and the promotional plan. The promotional plan should have one or more specific goals, such as "establish product awareness among 30 percent of the target market in the first month." In this way, marketers can measure the effectiveness of the campaign against the planned targets and determine whether to alter their promotional strategy.

ICE Activities for 11.3

Ideas	Connections	Extensions
1. (a) Describe briefly the four parts of the marketing mix.	(b) Create an organizer to analyze the marketing mix for a product that has been imported into Canada.	(c) What are Canada's international brands? How are these brands marketed internationally?
2. (a) Discuss how goods are distributed in international markets.	(b) Describe the retail environment for one of the following cities: Tokyo, Tel Aviv, Dar Es Salaam, Le Paz, or Warsaw.	(c) Prepare an illustrated report on the use of any one of the specialty distribution methods in a country outside of North America.
3. (a) Explain the components of an international marketing plan.	(b) Select one of the marketing plan components and report on how one Canadian international company handles the challenges of that component in foreign markets.	(c) Imagine that you are a Canadian entrepreneur who wants to market a specific product internationally. Create research questions—for each category from 3. (a)—that you would need to answer before entering an international market.

Canada's Trading Partners: Focus on Spain

Over the past few years, Spain and Canada have been working to develop a better trade relationship based on common interests in international matters, mutual trade and investment, and academic and cultural exchanges. In 1995, the political and trade relationship between the two countries was damaged when a Canadian Fisheries and Oceans patrol boat seized a Spanish fishing trawler that Canada said was illegally fishing off the coast of Newfoundland. Initially, the European Union threatened to impose trade sanctions against Canada for the action, but the parties in the dispute eventually reached a compromise. Nonetheless, the incident damaged relations between Canada and Spain.

In 1998, Canada and Spain agreed that they should reopen serious trade negotiations, and senior officials began to hold regular political consultations. In October 2000, Canada's International Trade Minister, Pierre Pettigrew, and Canadian business leaders went on a trade mission to Spain where they agreed to intensify scientific and technological relations and work together on joint research projects that would benefit both countries. In May 2001, Spanish Prime Minister José Maria Aznar visited Ottawa to continue developing trade links with Canada. Then, in May 2002, representatives of Canadian companies participated in workshops and seminars held in collaboration with the Canadian Space Agency, the National Research Council, and their Spanish counterparts. Canada also opened a new consulate and trade office in Barcelona, the capital city of the Catalonia region. Catalonia has long been seen as one of the key engines that drive the Spanish economy. Traditionally, the economy of the region has been dominated by the manufacturing sector, led by the chemical and textile industries. Catalonian industry comprises nearly a quarter of total Spanish production.

With the exception of 1996, trade between Canada and Spain has increased steadily as a result of the strong economic growth in both countries in recent years. In 2001, trade between the two countries totalled $1.7 billion CAD. The balance of trade remains in Spain's favour: in 2000, Canadian exports to Spain were $830.4 million, compared with $656.1 million in 2000. Spanish exports to Canada in 2001 were $884.7 million, down from $941.9 million in 2000. The early 2000 sale of 44 Bombardier aircraft to Air Nostrum for a total of $1.2 billion contributed strongly to increasing trade. In addition, Canadian firms are established in Spain in the following sectors: real estate, information technology, telecommunications, the environment, leisure activities, mining, recycling, banking, and petrochemicals. Current Spanish investment in Canada is concentrated in key sectors such as petrochemicals, fashion, building, transport, telecommunications, and construction.

One Canadian industry that has found an appreciative market in Spain is the Canadian film industry. From 1997 to 2002, more than 30 Canadian films have been distributed in commercial movie theatres in Spain, and in November 2000, Canada was the special guest country of the Madrid Experimental Film Week. Spain is especially interested in new trends in Canadian art, visual art, dance, theatre, and literature. Spain now has a large and active network of university professors and researchers interested in studying Canadian society and culture, both as a field of research in its own right and for comparative studies with Spain. The Canadian Studies Foundation together with the Caixa Foundation offers ten scholarships a year for graduate studies or research at a Canadian university.

Canadian Marketing in Spain

The Spanish market is a series of regional markets joined to two major hubs: the cities of Madrid and Barcelona. Most agents, distributors, foreign subsidiaries, and government-controlled entities that make up the economic power of the country operate in these two cities. Dealers, branch offices, or government offices located outside of these two hubs usually obtain their supplies from their Madrid and Barcelona contacts rather than engage in direct importation. The key to a foreign firm's sales success in Spain is to appoint a competent agent or distributor, or to establish an effective subsidiary in either Madrid or Barcelona.

The major competitors of Canadian exporters to Spain are Western European firms. Japanese companies are also becoming formidable competitors. Cost, financing terms, and after-sales servicing play important roles in marketability of a firm in Spain. Since Spain became part of the EU, member states' exports to Spain have benefited from lower tariffs than North American exports. However, Canadian products remain competitive in comparison to EU exporters because of lower production costs and the devaluation of the Canadian dollar compared with the euro.

A SNAPSHOT OF SPAIN

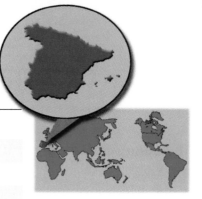

Size: 506 000 sq. km

World Region: Europe

Capital City: Madrid

Languages: Castilian Spanish, Catalan, Galician, Basque

Currency: Euro

Population: 40.0 million

Time: Noon in Ottawa (EST) is 6:00 P.M. in Madrid.

Climate: Temperate

Type of Government: Parliamentary monarchy

Labour Force by Occupation: 68 percent services, 28 percent manufacturing, mining, construction, 4 percent agriculture (2000 est.)

Membership in World Organizations: EU, WTO, OECD

Importing Partners and Products:
Partners: The top 10 EU countries supply Spain with more than 70 percent of its imports. The top three partners are France, Germany, and Italy.
Products: Machinery and equipment, fuels, chemicals, semifinished goods, foodstuffs, and consumer goods (2001 est.).

Exporting Partners and Products:
Partners: Of Spain's total exports, 71 percent goes to the EU. Spain's top export partners are France, Germany, Portugal, Italy, and the UK. Canada imports fruits and pharmaceuticals from Spain.
Products: Agricultural products, machinery, motor vehicles, foodstuffs, consumer goods (2001 est.).

Travel Advisory: The climate in Spain varies from one region to another, depending on whether you are travelling to a coastal region, to the interior lowlands, or into the mountainous region. Canadians should remember when travelling to Spain that Canadian cellular phones cannot be used in the country. It is easy, however, to rent a cell phone upon arrival. Hotels are also well equipped to provide facilities for business travellers who bring their computer and need to connect with their office in Canada.

Business Etiquette: Spanish business people prefer face-to-face meetings, and they expect a personal relationship with suppliers. While the Spanish are more formal in personal relations than North Americans, they are much less rigid than they were ten years ago.

Figure 11.27 A Spanish fishing trawler is seized by a Canadian Fisheries and Ocean's patrol boat for suspected illegal fishing.

Country Link

Follow the link at
www.internationalbusiness.nelson.com.
to find out more about Canada's trade
with Spain.

Chapter Challenges

Knowledge/Understanding

1. Match each of the following terms to the correct definition or description below:
   (a) centralized marketing strategy
   (b) decentralized marketing strategy
   (c) channels of distribution
   (d) disposable income
   (e) discretionary buying power
   (f) brand equity
   (g) brand acquisition strategy
   (h) marketing research
   (i) marketing mix
   (j) economies of scale

   (i) funds left over after filling needs
   (ii) "think global, act local"
   (iii) making a brand recognizable throughout the world and giving it a positive image
   (iv) the collection, analysis, and interpretation of marketing data
   (v) product development, distribution, pricing, and promotion
   (vi) businesses that connect a manufacturer's product to its target market
   (vii) the purchase of an existing company in a foreign country
   (viii) "think local, act global"
   (ix) the capacity to buy non-essential goods
   (x) the more products a company makes, the less expensive they become

2. Why are international consumer profiles important to a company launching a new product in a foreign market?

3. List five products that could be sold in a country whose population has little disposable income. List five other products that you commonly use that would not likely be seen in that country.

Thinking/Inquiry

1. In small groups, brainstorm the meaning of the following statement and the reasons it is or is not valid: "Although the pull marketing strategy is more obvious, the push marketing strategy is more commonly used."

2. Research some of the packaging methods that are popular in other countries but are not used in Canada. Find out why these methods are used in other countries and why they are not used here. Then create cause-and-effect charts to show the consequences of introducing these methods into the Canadian market.

Communication

1. Using Maslow's theory, Thorndyke's theory, and the rational/emotional theory of consumer motivation, account for the popularity of a product of your choice in one region of the world. For ideas about such products, investigate recent stories in local and international newspapers and periodicals. Prepare your argument and then present your conclusions in a brief oral presentation.

2. Create an advertisement (in any medium), a promotional campaign plan, or both, for one Canadian product that you might market internationally. Be sure that your advertisement or campaign plan targets a specific market. Explain your creative strategy.

3. Communicate with a student in another nation outside North America. Ask him or her to describe some trendy products and to explain why they are popular. Report your findings to others in the class.

Application

1. The Canada's Trading Partners feature in this chapter refers to some of the efforts that have been made by the Canadian and Spanish governments to improve relations and to develop a stronger trading partnership. As a Canadian entrepreneur who is interested in exporting Canadian products to Spain, investigate the current situation in one region of Spain. Decide first which product you would want to export to Spain, and then research any recent trade developments that might affect the likelihood of your success. Your main focus questions are

   a) What is the current marketing environment for your product in that region?

   b) What challenges might you face?

   c) How could you accommodate these challenges in your marketing mix and in your marketing plan?

   Present your findings in a written report.

2. Create a marketing plan that a Canadian exporter could use to launch his or her product in a selected country. Include in your plan your suggested marketing strategies and a market profile. Outline the details of the marketing mix that should be used to launch the new product and explain how to deal with any market restrictions or regulations that apply to products entering this market.

3. With students who have moved to Canada recently from other countries acting as your resource people, organize a panel discussion on the topic "Marketing Differences Between My Country and Canada."

International Business Portfolio

International Marketing

In this assignment, you will work with key information that companies need to make appropriate marketing decisions.

Activities

1. Prepare a consumer profile of your IBP country. Look at the number of males and females in a number of age groupings, the per capita income of families, and the literacy level of your country. How big is the market for a simple consumer product priced at less than $5.00 CAD, designed for use in households?

2. Do trade show opportunities exist in your IBP country? Check your province's Canada Business Service Centre for a listing.

3. List the media sources for possible advertising opportunities available in your IBP country, for example, radio stations, television stations, and magazines.

4. Identify a major retailer in your IBP country that might distribute a consumer product. Alternatively, suggest another method of distribution or channel into the country.

5. Research the rules and laws governing advertising messages. Describe ways in which they are different from Canadian regulations.

6. What pricing considerations may be necessary in your IBP country? Why?

7. Identify any labelling or product standards that you must consider in your IBP country. How do they differ from Canada's requirements?

8. If possible, find an advertisement from your country from a print or nonprint source. What advertising techniques are used? Are they different from or similar to Canadian advertisers? How?

Chapter 12

Logistics and Global Distribution

As international business spans the globe, goods are shipped around the world as never before. Companies that learn to manage logistics efficiently will have a competitive advantage in this new global marketplace. Raw materials, semi-manufactured goods, and finished products must travel between companies and their suppliers, distributors, and buyers in many different countries. Satisfying customer delivery requirements is essential to current just-in-time manufacturing and sales practices. Getting the right products to the customer, in the right quantity, at the right price, at the right time, and in the right place is the logistical challenge—and must be carefully planned.

Chapter Topics

➤ 12.1 – Logistics 370

➤ 12.2 – Distribution and Modes of Transport 377

➤ 12.3 – Export Planning 385

➤ *Canada's Trading Partners: Focus on* Japan 392

➤ Chapter Challenges 394

Prior Knowledge

- What process would a Canadian exporter follow to export products to a foreign country?
- What do you think is the most common form of international transportation for delivery of products?
- Why is it important for a business to get the right products to the customer, in the right quantity, at the right price, at the right time, and in the right place?

Inquiries/Expectations

- What are the logistics of delivering a product to a local, a national, and an international market?
- Which key factors influence the ways in which a company may deliver its product to an international market?
- What are the advantages and disadvantages of the different modes of transportation available to distribute a product to different world markets?
- How would having an export plan help a company explore opportunities for doing global business in a new international market?

Important Terms

breakbulk cargo

contract warehouses

customs broker

electronic data interchange (EDI)

freight forwarder

gateway city

information management

intermodal

logistics

physical distribution

private warehouse

public warehouse

sourcing

suboptimization

supply chain

topography

warehousing and storage

12.1 Logistics

The term "logistics" originally referred to the skills used to calculate and plan the movement of military troops and supplies. In military science, logistics is still the aspect of operations that manages the acquisition, maintenance, and transportation of goods, facilities, and personnel. In business terms, **logistics** includes planning for, implementing, and controlling the flow and storage of raw materials, inventory, finished goods, and related information, from the point of origin to the point of consumption.

An effective logistics plan satisfies customer requirements in the most efficient and cost-effective way. Logistics managers ensure that the right products reach the right place in the right quantity at the right time—and at the right price—to satisfy customer demand. Just as poor military logistics has historically led to the defeat of otherwise successful generals such as Napoleon and Rommel, so a lack of logistics planning can have a negative impact on companies, especially companies that do business in international arenas.

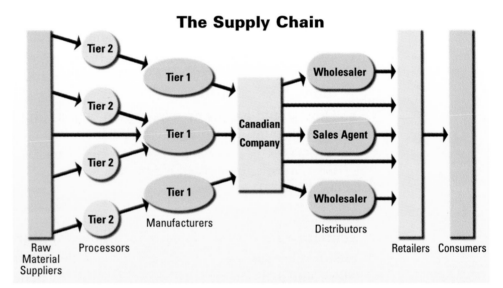

Figure 12.1 In international business, the path is lengthy from the creation of the product through to the distribution to consumers. A good logistics plan will keep the flow going from beginning to end.

The Importance of Logistics

The four basic components of logistics are

- sourcing
- warehousing and storage
- physical distribution
- information management

Consider a small restaurant. The chef/owner prepares meals every day for 40 or 50 people. The restaurant menu might contain 8 appetizers, 12 entrées, and 6 desserts. There is no way that the restaurant will know in advance how many customers will arrive that night for dinner, or how many chicken Dijon entrées customers will order. The owner must find tender chickens, fresh eggs, crisp produce, and all the other ingredients for every item on the menu (**sourcing**) and then arrange the delivery of the ingredients to the restaurant in time for meal preparation (**physical distribution**). The restaurant must have walk-in refrigerators for the food, cupboards for the dishes, and holding areas for the meals that are in various stages of preparation—all kept clean and sanitary at all times (**warehousing and storage**). The owner also needs a system to get the orders from the wait staff to the kitchen and to schedule the delivery of the food to the customers' tables as quickly as possible (**information management**). Like every other business, the restaurant could not operate without logistics. These processes are all interconnected and affect each other.

Now consider a restaurant like Tim Hortons. The components of the logistics involved in managing the supply and distribution chain of this corporation are the same as those for the small local restaurant, only magnified 2065 times (the number of Tim Hortons restaurants in Canada). How much more complex is it for this company now that there are more than 140 Tim Hortons restaurants in the United States? International markets add the complexity of new cultures and different infrastructures, yet still require the management of the four basic components of logistics.

Sourcing

Just as that small restaurant had to find reliable suppliers for the ingredients for its menu items, so other large and small Canadian businesses need to find dependable suppliers for raw materials, machines, technologies, and manufactured components for their products and businesses. At some point in its history, each company has had to decide whether to source certain products or services from outside the company or to make the product or provide the services itself.

A company may decide to have materials supplied by foreign companies for a number of reasons. Sometimes, using international suppliers can reduce production costs, especially where labour costs are lower in another country. However, logistics managers must take into account the additional cost to transport the product from the foreign country to their manufacturing plants. Other times, a company will purchase supplies from another country because

- they are not available locally
- necessary technologies are not developed in the home country
- the best components or products are produced in a foreign country

International companies may get their supplies from their own subsidiaries in another company, from their joint venture partners, or from independent contractors or independent manufacturers. In addition, since the advent of the Internet, electronic sourcing has allowed companies to buy and sell internationally, using regularly updated online catalogues for purchases and electronic procurement sites to log bids with companies that are looking for international suppliers.

While some Canadian companies source materials from other countries, other companies strive to become the supplier of choice for domestic and international businesses. For example, Magna International has built a successful multinational business by becoming the supplier of choice for the automobile industry worldwide. Magna is one of the largest auto parts manufacturers in the world with manufacturing facilities and research and development centres throughout Canada, the United States, and Europe, as well as in Korea, China, Japan, and India. As the source for a wide range of auto parts and complete systems to automobile manufacturers, the company regularly records sales in the billions of dollars—$11 billion USD in sales in 2001.

Magna's first auto parts contract came in 1960, when it supplied brackets for sun visors to General Motors. By 1987, Magna's automotive systems divisions were producing complete interior and exterior systems and had substantially increased their share of content in North American and foreign cars. For example, in 2001, every Mercedes-Benz G-Class automobile contained more than $2000 USD worth of Magna products supplied by the Magna Steyr facility in Austria. Through the years, Magna has acquired European automotive systems suppliers and engineering companies, built research and development facilities, and spun off some of its divisions into separate companies.

Figure 12.2 Magna International has become the supplier of choice for the automobile industry worldwide.

The Canadian federal and provincial governments work with Canadian businesses to increase both sides of the sourcing equation. For example, the International Business Opportunities Centre works with Canada's trade officers to match Canadian sellers with buyers in countries around the world. For Canadian companies seeking international suppliers, many national and regional governments and their agencies also provide trade missions and sources of information.

Warehousing and Storage

Both domestic and international companies need to store inventory. **Warehousing** involves the storage of goods in a company's manufacturing location and the movement of those goods along the stages of transit from source to company and from company to end consumer. For example, a Canadian kitchen appliance manufacturer with a factory in Ontario may need temporary storage for domestic or foreign components used to build its refrigerators. At the end of its manufacturing process, the same company may need warehouse facilities to store the finished refrigerators while they are awaiting distribution to Ontario, Canadian, and international retail outlets. This may mean warehousing at the original plant, at railway terminals, or at ports in Canada and in foreign countries.

The Forum for International Trade Training Inc. (FITT) lists the following four major functions of warehousing:

Web Link

Follow the link at www.internationalbusiness.nelson.com to find out more about Magna's Canadian and international sourcing divisions.

- receiving goods into the warehouse (inbound transportation)
- transferring goods to a location in the warehouse
- selecting a particular combination of goods for customer orders or inputs into manufacturing
- loading goods for shipment to the customer or to the production line

Today's international companies try to warehouse goods at both ends of the chain for as short a time as possible. By shortening storage time, companies minimize the need for space and the charges for using such space. Less storage time also decreases the possibility that products will become obsolete before they are sold. Some business analysts estimate that storage and distribution warehouses represent 25 percent of a company's total physical distribution costs. Supply chain managers must consider the costs of this aspect of logistics planning carefully and look to ways, such as just-in-time delivery, to reduce them.

According to Industry Canada, there are three categories of warehouses:

- **private warehouses**, which are operated as a division of the company whose business is other than warehousing
- **public warehouses**, which offer their services to a broad clientele, usually under 30-day contracts
- **contract warehouses**, which offer services to a more restricted clientele and which have more formalized long-term contracts with their clients

Figure 12.3 Forklifts are small industrial vehicles with power-operated pronged platforms that can be inserted under loads to lift and move them. Such equipment makes organizing a warehouse much simpler and more efficient.

Today's public and contract warehouse companies usually offer their clients a wide range of services as well as storage and distribution of goods, services such as shipping and storage insurance, claims inspection, transport documentation, and the collection and payment of accounts. Warehouses may specialize in particular types of products. For example, they may offer storage facilities in temperature-controlled environments (chilled, frozen, and multi-temperature).

Physical Distribution

Physical distribution refers to the actions required to move and transfer ownership of goods and services from the producer to the consumer. Manufacturers are concerned about both sides of the distribution issue: getting the goods needed for production from their source, and getting the end product out to its business or consumer market. In either case, an international company may need to deal through an intermediary, such as an export trading company.

As you will see in the next section of this chapter, a number of different factors must be considered—and different modes of transport can be used—to distribute a product. These modes can be either used singly or combined into complex **intermodal** operations that link a variety of transport means in different countries, time zones, and climates. For example, refrigerators manufactured by an Ontario appliance company may be trucked to the railway freight terminal; then taken by rail to Halifax, where they will be warehoused until the next available ship arrives; then transferred to a ship for transport to a French port, where they will be transferred to a truck for delivery to a warehouse in France. There, they will await distribution to French retail outlets, where they will be sold to consumers.

Information Management

The management of the movement of information is another aspect of logistics that concerns international companies. More and more suppliers, producers, wholesalers, and retailers are using computerized **electronic data interchange (EDI)**, which allows businesses to use computers to communicate with each other and speeds up transmission of business data, documents, and the transfer of funds. Instead of sending paper documents—purchase orders, bills of lading, invoices, and cheques—companies exchange standard documents by computer and automate the flow of information among their trading partners.

Electronic data interchange can provide benefits to international companies by

- speeding up and reducing costs in the purchase and collection cycles
- streamlining staff and operations at the same time that it improves efficiency and inventory control
- reducing errors associated with double keying and handling paper transactions through various departments
- allowing materials and orders to be tracked during transit
- reducing delivery time and estimates of departure and arrival
- improving marketing by allowing customers to tap into the supplier's host computer 24 hours a day to get updates, place orders, reorder, and back-order

While there are clear advantages to using EDI, there are also some disadvantages:

- Sophisticated electronic interchange systems require compatibility among various systems. While a number of governments and agencies are working towards universal standards, they are not yet in place.
- EDI systems are vulnerable to automated system mistakes, such as transmitting computer viruses, and to breakdowns in the system.
- EDI requires costly initial setup of computer and data systems and frequent updates as technology changes.
- As the systems become more automated, employees are displaced and machines take over.

Supply Chain Management

According to the Institute of Logistics and Transport, UK, the **supply chain** is the total sequence of business processes, within a single or multiple enterprise environment, that enables customer demand for a product or service to be satisfied. Management of the supply chain ensures that all the processes work together to get the products distributed quickly and effectively in both domestic and international environments. The goal of supply chain management is to maintain the links between an organization and its suppliers and customers to achieve strategic advantage.

One important logistical issue in supply chain management within firms is suboptimization. According to the Principia Cybernetica Web of the Free University of Brussels, **suboptimization** refers to using a lower-level decision as a step towards attaining a higher-level objective to which the lower-level decision is to contribute. For example, in spite of increased costs, a decision is made to transport a product by air rather than by ship. Transportation costs will be higher, but just-in-time delivery will be improved and customer demand will be met. In 1996, when the Tickle Me Elmo craze was at its height, the toys were flown by chartered passenger planes to reach North American markets in time for pre-Christmas sales. In such an instance, the decision to increase transportation costs was a suboptimization that produced profits because the product was available sooner to more of the company's customers.

One company that manages its supply chain to satisfy customers' needs well is Wal-Mart Stores Inc., which is the largest retailer in the world, earning $217.7 billion USD in 2001. Wal-Mart is also the largest retailer in Canada. The company has been successful because of its commitment to low prices, and the backbone of that pricing strategy is its supply chain management. Wal-Mart's distribution centres use world-class technology. Kevin Lubin, writing in *Canadian Business*, describes one of the company's distribution facilities as a "labyrinthine maze" where webs of conveyer belts crisscross the massive plant.

Figure 12.4 Wal-Mart is a national discount chain that offers a wide variety of electronics, video games, toys, jewelry, CDs, and home and garden items.

"Of the 100 000 items in the average Wal-Mart Supercenter," Lubin says, "80 percent of them weave their way from unloading dock to loading dock in only a few hours." Back in the Wal-Mart store, the universal product code (UPC) of each purchase is scanned at the cash register and sent electronically to the company's computer data processing centre, from which orders are sent to suppliers. Suppliers quickly send products to the Wal-Mart distribution centre, where trucks are loaded and travel to each store several times a day. In addition, because supplies are replenished so quickly, the stores do not need to waste valuable space for storage.

The Logistics of Just-In-Time Inventory Systems

As you learned in Chapter 4, just-in-time (JIT) is an inventory control system that schedules products to arrive as they are needed for manufacturing or for supply to customers. The JIT principle is governing more and more of the logistics and supply chain management planning of today's industries and retail outlets. Materials are scheduled to arrive at a work station or a facility "just in time" to be used. The economies of JIT make it possible for companies to shorten production times (because everything is on hand when it is needed), reduce inventories, and cut costs (because less storage space is required).

Today, JIT is practised by leading automotive and high-tech corporations—as well as by many smaller businesses—with great success. Analysts estimate that General Motors, for example, saves hundreds of millions of dollars by using JIT. The demands of this type of distribution, however, require sophisticated planning,

GLOBAL THOUGHT

Few products involve as many components as a finished car, hence the hundreds of domestic and global suppliers servicing the automobile industry. As the auto business moves ever closer to a Just-In-Time supply chain, the pressure is on transport providers to satisfy this on-demand service. The range of carriers servicing the auto industry encompasses the entire spectrum, from steamship lines moving finished cars to railroads moving engines and oversized parts to truck firms and small airlines providing emergency lifts. In all cases, speed is of the essence, an objective realized through Internet-based order management, satellite-guided shipment tracing, and computerized documentation and planning systems.

– Russ Banham

as well as cooperation from suppliers and shippers, during all stages of the distribution process. The potential downside of JIT is that any disruptions—strikes or disasters, for example—in the transport network that delay delivery times can cause a work stoppage and a ripple effect of further delays along the supply chain. In the sophisticated and interconnected production lines of today's large factories, a delay in getting just one component from a foreign supplier can cause delays in the production schedule of the whole factory.

ICE Activities for 12.1

Ideas	Connections	Extensions
1. (a) Explain the different components of business logistics.	(b) From newspapers, Internet sources, or trade magazines, collect three ads for jobs related to logistics. What industries require logistics to conduct business effectively?	(c) Which business skills would you need to be a successful logistics manager?
2. (a) What services do warehousers offer their domestic and international customers?	(b) Select an imported product that you use frequently. Draw a flow chart to demonstrate the warehouse facilities that were likely used to store this product on its journey from producer to you.	(c) Describe the ways that a Canadian company exporting goods to a foreign country might use warehouse services.
3. (a) Explain what the term EDI means.	(b) In small groups, brainstorm ways that a Canadian importer and exporter might use EDI in their logistics planning.	(c) In your opinion, do the benefits of EDI technology outweigh the challenges? Support your judgement with at least three pieces of evidence from your brainstorming session in 3. (b).

12.2 Distribution and Modes of Transport

An international business's choice of transportation depends on many factors. Some of the larger considerations are the economic and political situation in the importing or exporting country, and its climatic and topographical conditions. Specific factors for a particular delivery include the time available, distance to travel, weight of goods, budget, and desired delivery location. In general, local, transborder, and overseas shipments have different transportation requirements.

One of the innovations that has most affected the transportation aspect of supply chain systems is containerization. As you learned in Chapter 7, containerization is the stowage of freight in sealed, reusable containers of uniform size and shape. The use of containers has made intermodal freight handling much easier. Intermodal freight handling allows goods to be transferred from one form of transportation to another without the need to handle the goods. Intermodal handling allows the greatest possibility of seamless transport through all the different modes of the transportation network. Containers packed at their source may be loaded directly on to trucks and then transferred to trains, airplanes, or ships the size of apartment blocks. With the greater number of goods travelling greater distances in today's global markets, intermodal freight handling is used to transport much of the world's cargo.

When a company is shipping products internationally, it must also take packaging into account. For example, products shipped by ocean to foreign ports must be able to withstand the rigours of transport, adverse climate conditions, and storage conditions that may differ radically from domestic conditions. When preparing to ship a product overseas, the exporter needs to be aware of packing, labelling, documentation, and insurance requirements, and must follow all shipping regulations to ensure that the goods are shipped properly. Exporters also must consider the risks of breakage resulting from rough handling, moisture in humid climate conditions, exposure to rough weather conditions, temperature control for perishable products, and theft all along the chain.

FRAGILE

DO NOT STACK

Figure 12.5 Universal package symbols communicate important information that can be understood around the world.

Factors that Affect Product Delivery

Topography

Topography refers to the natural features of the Earth's surface. Topographical features of countries and regions affect the transport of goods across distances within and between countries. For example, mountainous land barriers can make transportation difficult in some areas of the world. The building of the transcontinental Canadian railway system through the Rocky Mountains in the late 1800s helped Canada develop economically because it linked producers and manufacturers across Canada and fostered opportunities for trade within Canada and internationally.

In other parts of the world, mountains still create barriers to international trade. For example, travel across the Himalaya Mountains is so difficult that transportation between India and China continues to be primarily by air or sea rather than overland. High altitudes, deserts, and tropical regions can affect the possibility of transporting goods overland. Great distances, such as those across the expanse of large countries like Canada and Australia, may also be barriers to transportation.

The topography of a region also affects where people choose to settle. In many cases, the decision to settle in an area was based on inland and seaport possibilities for trade. For a country to have direct access to ocean shipping, it must have a coast with deep-water harbours, sheltered from the open sea, where ports can be built. In these ports, facilities to load and unload a ship's cargo (wharves, warehouses, technologies to load and unload ships) must be built.

The location of cities and their function as hubs of transportation is also affected by topography. Canadian cities such as Halifax, Montreal, Toronto, and Vancouver grew partly because they could serve as ports for international trade and as centres for the roads, railways, and airports that branch out from them. In Australia, which has one of the highest percentages of urban population in the world, most of the major cities are also seaports. As a consequence, most of the transportation within the country is by coastal shipping rather than rail or road.

Overcoming topographical barriers to transport has led to major changes in the distribution of international trade goods. The building of the Suez Canal in the mid-nineteenth century (which eliminated the need to ship cargo around the south end of the African continent) and the Panama Canal in the early twentieth century (which eliminated the need to ship cargo around the southern tip of South America) cut shipping time to ports around the world.

The building of the St. Lawrence Seaway in 1959 (a joint Canadian-American project) allowed ocean-going ships into and out of the Great Lakes. It is estimated that more than two billion tonnes of cargo, with a value of $300 billion USD, have moved to and from Canada, the United States, and nearly 50 other nations. According to the Seaway Authority, almost 50 percent of its traffic travels to and from overseas ports, especially in Europe, the Middle East, and Africa. In Europe, in 1994, the construction of the Chunnel between England and France allowed for rail transportation of goods in a tunnel under the sea.

Follow the link at www.internationalbusiness.nelson.com to learn more about the St. Lawrence Seaway.

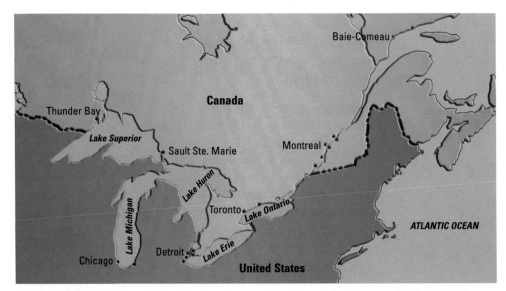

Figure 12.6 The St. Lawrence Seaway is part of the Great Lakes Seaway. Each green dot on the map represents a port. Services offered at the ports include docking, container handling, and warehousing. Railways serve the ports, and highways connect the ports to key cities in Canada and the United States.

Climate

The climate of a region can affect the choice of products to be shipped, the mode of transportation, and how the goods are transported. For example, shipping to very humid countries requires specific and expensive types of packaging to prevent damage from the dampness. In desert areas, dryness and dust can affect both products and means of transportation. Extreme cold can also be a factor for both products and available transportation. For example, the St. Lawrence Seaway is closed from late December until late March or early April depending on when the ice melts. Temperature variation can also severely affect certain types of products or their packaging, travel, or warehouse conditions. For example, potatoes shipped from PEI can be spoiled by temperatures or humidity that is either too high or too low.

Other climatic factors can pose danger to shipments. Hurricanes, floods, earthquakes, and ice storms can slow or even halt distribution. Ships and airplanes can be delayed or endangered by hurricanes and major storms. Land routes can become impassable because of snow, freezing temperatures, or monsoon rains. Even transportation routes designed to help businesses bypass adverse weather conditions can be affected by such conditions. The Confederation Bridge that connects PEI to New Brunswick was built to allow transportation in winter. The bridge, however, is sometimes closed because of high winds.

Cost

As you learned in Chapter 7, there are many costing pitfalls for companies operating internationally. Logistics managers must consider the full landed cost of their imports and exports, calculating all transportation, handling, currency exchange rates, and import or export charges. Tariffs and duties must be added to the calculation. Hidden costs are another factor: travel costs, translation services, phone charges, local taxes, and other government charges, including those that help keep the transportation infrastructure viable in a country.

As you learned in Chapter 11, a company's decision to use a centralized or a decentralized marketing strategy can also affect its transportation costs. For example, a company that manufactures locally can distribute locally as well, marketing to smaller communities that centralized companies would find too expensive to target. The savings in transportation and storage costs are significant in these situations.

National and Transborder Distribution

In terms of volume of goods carried, the greatest proportion of Canada's freight transportation travels within Canada to domestic markets. In 2001, Transport Canada reported that, while most primary products such as grain, forest products, and metallic ores (61 percent of domestic transport in 2000) travel by rail, most manufactured products are transported by truck (70 percent of domestic transport in 2000). Oil and gas travel by pipeline.

According to Transport Canada, between 1997 and 1999, 87 percent of all domestic trade (that is, trade within Canada) was within provinces. The other 13 percent was shipped between provinces and territories. For most products delivered within the smallest of provincial markets—the local market—the owner of the goods usually arranges the transportation directly, rather than using the services of a logistics or forwarding company. The type of transportation is most likely dictated by the nature of the product. Peaches from the Niagara region of Ontario, for example, may be shipped by truck directly to a large retailer in Toronto. A courier parcel delivery arrives by car or van. A shipment of books from a publisher to a local bookstore arrives by truck. None of these items pass through customs, and no cross-border documentation is needed. The same is true of national (domestic) transport.

Canada has an extensive rail and highway system. At over 7800 kilometres in length, the Trans–Canada Highway is the longest national highway in the world. Many producers of consumer products warehouse goods in distribution centres accessible from the Trans–Canada Highway. Canada's whole national road system is made up of more than 900 000 kilometres of road. Trucking is dominant in interprovincial freight transport activities.

There are 51 230 kilometres of railway tracks in Canada. Of these, 85 percent are owned by CN and CP and linked with intermodal terminals.

Interprovincial trade restrictions are sometimes an issue, but they usually apply to services or goods regulated by provincial marketing boards. Because not all provinces have the same sales tax regulations, importers distributing goods from warehousing or distribution centres need to be aware of provincial taxation differences.

Figure 12.7 The Trans-Canada Highway between Victoria, British Columbia and St. John's, Newfoundland is the world's longest national highway with a length of 7821 kilometres. Transport trucks carry their goods across Canada using this highway.

Transportation to the United States

As you learned in Chapter 2, most of Canada's international imports and exports flow from or into the United States. Exports to the United States increased from 66 percent of Canada's total international exports in 1981 to 87 percent in 2001. Percentages of Canada's international imports from the United States varied between 65 percent and 69 percent over the same period.

At one time, most goods were transported to and from the United States by rail, but, in recent years, trucking has become more widely used. From 1991 to 2000, the annual growth rate in Canada–U.S. border crossings by trucks was 7.4 percent. Ontario has the busiest truck border crossings in the country; 61 percent of all truck traffic from Canada to the United States crosses the border in Ontario. In dollar terms, more than 65 percent of trade between the two countries in 2000 was by truck. The Ambassador Bridge in Windsor, Ontario, is the busiest border crossing point in Canada, handling 33.1 percent of all Canada's road trade with the United States: $59.4 billion in exports and $67.3 billion in imports.

In comparison, rail transportation accounted for 16 percent, pipeline for 9 percent, air for 8 percent, and marine for 2 percent of traffic to and from the United States. (All figures are drawn from Transport Canada's 2001 *Annual Report*.)

Comparing International Modes of Transportation

A comprehensive logistics plan manages all aspects of an international supply chain and, therefore, must take many elements into account, including how products are transported. The mode of transportation affects the movement of the product, the timing of delivery, and the cost. The seamless integration of modes of transport is assisted by unimpeded movement of information: planning, clear channels of communication, well-prepared documentation, and even "real-time" tracking. Today's logistics and supply chain managers must be flexible in their use of transportation modes when they respond to individual customers' needs.

Trucks

Trucks have become an important physical distribution link in many countries around the world. They can quickly pick up shipments from one location and deliver them almost anywhere that roads exist. Trucks are used to transport many products, including food, clothing, furniture, lumber, plastic products, and machinery. Automobile products move to and from the United States by truck or by rail, with trucks carrying more volume. Trucks move shipments and containers to and from airports, rail yards, or seaports.

The road and highway network in North America and Mexico makes trucks a convenient choice for transporting manufactured goods or produce. Truck schedules offer importers and exporters more flexibility than rail shipments and often provide for delivery as well as transport.

Truck transport is much less expensive than air freight, and customs clearance is usually faster at highway points than at airports. These factors make highway transport an attractive alternative to air freight for shipments greater than 225 kilograms that need to travel farther than 1600 kilometres.

Trucks offer speed and flexibility in pickup and delivery of products. Goods are usually handled safely, especially when they are packed in a container, trucked, and then delivered directly to their final destination. Trucking firms can adapt to their shippers' pickup and delivery schedules, which means that the shippers can usually count on on-time delivery. Deliveries can also be more frequent than with airline and marine schedules.

However, there are disadvantages to truck transport. Some major highways have load limits (usually approximately 18 000 to 21 000 kilograms per vehicle), and some trucks cannot use older, smaller highways. In some developing countries, the roads cannot bear the weight of large trucks. Even though they can travel quickly, trucks can run into serious border slowdowns of the kind that occurred at the Ambassador Bridge between Windsor and Detroit following the September 11, 2001 attack on the United States. Trucking costs are high compared to rail and ship. For some cargo, such as crude oil from northern Alberta, trucks are impractical because of the distances and volume of product.

Figure 12.8 Trucks are backed up some 10 kilometres away from the Ambassador Bridge linking Windsor, Ontario and Detroit, Michigan, September 13, 2001. Thousands of Canadians felt the effects of a security crackdown at the border, with rigorous searches and long delays.

Rail

Figure 12.9 Train transport remains a cost-effective mode of transporting goods over long distances.

All over the world, especially within the United States and Canada, trains are still a major mode for transporting goods, especially bulk materials and large quantities of freight over long distances over land. The products most often shipped by rail are automobiles, grain, chemicals, coal, lumber, iron, and steel. The use of trains has become more flexible since the introduction of piggyback services, which allow for standard-sized containers to be loaded directly from trucks onto flatcars. From there, the containers can again be loaded on to trucks at the destination, or delivered directly to dockside for ocean transport. As a result, trains have become major participants in the rising use of intermodal transport. Not only are rail carrying rates lower than those for trucks, but trains remain strong performers over long distances. On the downside, trains are slower and have less flexible range and schedules than trucks.

Transportation Used for Trade between Canada and Countries Other than the United States, 1997–2001

Year	Billions of Dollars	Share (percentage)				
		Road	Rail	Marine	Air	Other
Exports						
1997	54.2	9.1	1.7	72.8	16.4	0.0
1998	48.5	7.8	1.3	71.3	19.6	0.0
1999	46.8	6.6	1.7	70.9	20.8	0.0
2000	53.6	6.3	1.3	69.6	22.8	0.0
2001	51.0	6.1	1.7	67.9	24.4	0.0
Imports						
1997	88.5	31.3	4.5	40.1	22.0	2.1
1998	95.0	35.9	3.6	37.5	21.8	1.1
1999	104.7	34.7	3.3	38.2	23.3	0.5
2000	127.2	30.9	3.5	41.3	23.8	0.6
2001	124.6	32.2	3.9	40.3	22.0	1.6

Figure 12.10 Which form of transportation was used the most during this period? Explain why this would be the case.

Marine

Transportation by ship remains the most frequently used mode for Canadian exporting or importing companies operating beyond North America. Major ports on the Pacific and Atlantic coasts, as well as Great Lakes ports, send and receive natural resources and manufactured products to and from countries around the world. Ships are the transportation mode of choice for large volumes of cargo and great weights such as coal, steel, lumber, grain, and oil.

While ocean transport is almost always the least expensive form of international transport, it is also the slowest. Because ocean and water conditions are so variable, ships are the least dependable transportation mode for on-time delivery. Ships must dock at ocean ports and, therefore, have a low reach into a country. Shippers using ocean transport must fit their delivery schedules into the schedules of the marine companies. In addition, a major oil spill such as occurred in 2002 when

Figure 12.11 Breakbulk cargo is a high-risk method of shipping.

the 26-year-old tanker "Prestige" sank off the north-west coast of Spain, an ecologically sensitive area, can have disastrous effects on the environment. The effects of the "Prestige" spill are being compared to that of the Exxon Valdez, which sank off the coast of Alaska in 1989. The Exxon Valdez disaster damaged the wildlife in the area—seabirds, otters, seals, eagles, orcas, salmon, and herring—and cost the company, Exxon, billions of dollars in fines and cleanup costs.

There are two primary forms of ocean transport: bulk liner shipping (breakbulk cargo) and container vessels (intermodal). **Breakbulk cargo** refers to shipping goods by sea without containerization. The goods are usually loaded directly aboard vessels on pallets, in a net, or by a sling, conveyor, or chute. This method of shipping has a high degree of risk. Goods may be exposed to the weather during loading and unloading; damage can occur when goods shift in transit; and theft is easier. Breakbulk cargo shipping has declined rapidly in recent years while containerization has grown. Typical examples of the bulk commodity trade are liquid cargoes such as petroleum, oil, or molasses; grains, soybeans, and salt; and items related to manufacturing, such as scrap metal, woodchips, or steel. Bulk commodities such as grain, coal, potash, and sulphur remain important Canadian exports.

Throughout the world, inland waterways and coastal waters are also important components of marine trade. For example, Northern Transportation Company Ltd. has been a pan-Arctic marine operator since 1934, using its fleet of tug boats and barges to deliver oil and cargo to communities in the far north during the summer and early fall months. The company contracts with international tanker owners and can handle containers at its terminals in the Northwest Territories, Nunavut, and Churchill (Manitoba). In recent years, Northern Transportation has developed links with the northern Hudson Bay Railway, which services northern Manitoba's resource-based industries and has offered its customers logistic support services.

Air

The use of air transport for international trade has been expanding over the past ten years, even though it is almost always the most expensive form of transport. Air is the fastest transportation mode. Shipments that once took 30 days can now be transported in a single day. In some regions of the world—such as Canada's far north—it may be the only available mode of transportation during some periods of the year. Goods shipped by air now include not only equipment parts, specialty products, and perishable goods such as lobsters or flowers, but also large items of machinery and even automobiles. Usually, the size of a shipment may be the greatest limiting factor to the possibility of using air transport.

Figure 12.12 Air carriers offer reduced shipping costs for cargo that is containerized.

It is often necessary to transport large shipments to their destination by truck or rail after they arrive at the **gateway city** of their destination country. In New Zealand, for example, most international flights arrive at the gateway Auckland airport (AKL), with a few arriving in Wellington (WLG). All other flights operating within the country use relatively small aircraft like the DC 9 or Boeing 737. Any freight over 225 kilograms must be trucked unless a charter aircraft is used—at great cost. Central and Eastern Africa have limited infrastructure for air freight beyond the major gateway points. Destinations in smaller countries or some of the developing countries may offer limited international airline services.

Shippers can save money and minimize cargo loss by containerizing their air cargo shipments. Airlines encourage the use of containers by providing special tariffs for containerized freight-all-kinds (FAK) shipments on many routes. Air carriers prefer containerized shipments for a number of reasons:

- They reduce the number of individual pieces of cargo that must be handled in terminals.
- They provide for cost-efficient use of cube capacity of aircraft.
- They permit the most advantageous use of mechanical handling systems and equipment.
- They speed loading and unloading of aircraft.
- They minimize exposure of cargo to weather, theft, and handling damage while in the custody of the carrier.

Pipelines

Pipelines are a dependable, efficient low-cost means of transporting substances such as natural gas and crude oil. Pipelines are the primary means of transporting oil and natural gas relatively inexpensively across great distances from remote northern regions of Canada (for example, northern British Columbia and Alberta, Northwest Territories, and Ontario) to markets in Canada and the United States. In 2000, pipeline transportation accounted for 44 percent of exports to the United States.

Oil is transported by pipeline to Canadian ports, where it is transferred to large tankers that deliver this Canadian export to countries around the world. Natural gas is carried entirely by pipeline, so its export potential is limited by land connections. One advantage that pipelines have over other transportation modes is that once the steel and plastic pipes have been laid, they require little maintenance. In terms of scheduling, oil and gas can be transported uninterrupted 24 hours a day, 7 days a week. In addition, the number of accidents compared to other modes of transportation is low.

While pipelines may be low-cost to run, they are expensive to build. When they rupture because of metal fatigue or faults in the line, they can be hazardous to the environments through which they pass. They are limited in the type of products that they can carry, and liquids travel slowly in them (only a few kilometres per hour).

Figure 12.13 While a dependable means of transportation, pipelines are limited in the type of products they can carry.

ICE Activities for 12.2

Ideas	Connections	Extensions
1. (a) Describe three factors a logistics manager must consider when deciding on international transport of a product.	(b) Research the distribution methods used by one Canadian exporting company, and write a brief profile demonstrating how that company takes the three factors described in 1. (a) into consideration.	(c) Select a product that you would like to export to a specific foreign country and describe the topographic and climatic factors that you would have to consider.
2. (a) Describe the main transportation modes for transport within Canada, to the United States, and overseas.	(b) Working with a partner, create a comparison chart to show the advantages and disadvantages of the different modes of transportation.	(c) Each mode of transportation has some disadvantages. In your opinion, which of these poses the greatest threat to the global environment?
3. (a) Describe the advantages of intermodal transport in international trade.	(b) Create a flow chart to show how intermodal transport is used to ship a product from one Canadian region to international markets.	(c) Using your flow chart, discuss what would happen if one of the links in the transport chain were to break down. How might this problem be solved?

12.3 Export Planning

An export plan is a type of business plan that focuses on the target market, export goals, activities and objectives, necessary resources, and anticipated results. It will guide a company to its goal of successfully exporting a product or service to a foreign country.

Preparing an Export Plan

GLOBAL THOUGHT

Planning and preparation are essential for any business, domestic or international. They set a course and define a purpose. A sound plan tells you where your business is going and how it will get there. It forces you to look at your company's operations and re-evaluate the assumptions upon which it is founded, and it helps you identify weaknesses and strengths in your operations.

– Team Canada Inc

An export plan is a realistic step-by-step outline of the goals that a company hopes to achieve in a particular country and the resources that the company will need to attain its goals. According to Team Canada Inc's publication, *A Step-by-Step Guide to Exporting*, an export plan should contain the following elements:

- **Introduction**, which includes the background to the export plan, a brief summary of the history of the product or service, the reasons the company has decided to introduce it into a foreign market, and pertinent financing and investment details.

- **Description of the company and the export product**, including the structure of the company; its domestic marketing strategies; the human and financial resources that are on hand; and the history of the performance of the product in the domestic market.

- **Short- and long-term export objectives and goals**, perhaps one-year and five-year outlooks. For example, export sales forecasts could be monthly for the next year and yearly over the next five years.

- **Description of the target market and the structure of industry in that market**, including consumer characteristics and projected demand; the competitors in the market and their market share; distribution channels and types of promotion; government regulations; challenges and opportunities in the markets; and cultural factors.

- **Modes of transportation required for delivery.**

- **Climatic or topographical factors** that need to be taken into account.

- **International marketing plan.** (For more information on marketing plans, see Chapter 11.)

- **Production plan**, which includes the physical plant requirements, machinery and equipment, raw materials, inventory requirements, suppliers, required personnel, and an estimate of production costs.

- **Risk assessment analysis**, which includes the political and economic situation in the country; the expected reaction of competitors when the company's products enter the market; contingency plans to handle potential problems; and other internal or external factors in the market that could affect the company's export goals.

- **Plan for implementation and documentation**, which should include the steps that will be taken to achieve export goals, and a description of the personnel and the timeframe for completing the required tasks.

- **Plan for market performance evaluation** to help track and measure progress in the new market and to show how evaluations will affect the current export plan.

  - **Financial statements** (balance sheets and income statements) and forecasts for income and cash flow.

  - **Descriptions of financing arrangements** explaining how the venture will be financed and the financing services that will be used (for example, government or bank).

TRADE TALK

Exporters use the SMART formula to help them set and aim for specific, realistic goals:
- **S**pecific: What exactly is our goal?
- **M**easurable: How much will we accomplish, and how do we determine whether we have been successful?
- **A**chievable: Is our measurable goal achievable?
- **R**ealistic: Are we being realistic in setting this goal?
- **T**ime-focused: When do we want to accomplish our goal? Is this time frame realistic and achievable?

Web Link

Follow the link at www.internationalbusiness.nelson.com to find out more about export planning.

Intermediaries

Both small and large Canadian international trading companies use intermediaries to help them expedite the importing and exporting process. The main types of intermediaries used are freight forwarders, customs brokers, and, increasingly often, logistics companies that perform a number of different functions for their client companies.

Freight Forwarders

When launching a product into an international market or arranging delivery to an overseas destination, a company often uses a **freight forwarder** to look after documentation and transport arrangements. A freight forwarder's services may include negotiating rates with the shipping lines, airlines, and trucking companies that will be used to transport products. They may provide additional logistics services, such as crating, marketing, and storing. For small companies with limited time, volume, or in-house resources, freight forwarders often gather together several small shipments, resulting in lower freight rates. Because freight forwarders generally have knowledge about distributing products to many countries, larger companies may also want to use their services when exporting to new or unfamiliar markets.

Customs Brokers

Customs brokers are intermediaries that specialize in clearing goods through customs in a country. They are licensed in the countries in which they work. They assist with tariff classification, valuation of goods, and duty assessment, and they make sure that goods conform to regulations and statutes. Some companies provide both freight forwarding and customs brokerage services. They may also arrange for warehousing and transportation of goods after they have cleared customs.

Web Link

Demand for certified professional logistics practitioners (logisticians) is growing. Follow the link at www.internationalbusiness.nelson.com to learn more about the Logistics Institute, which is a Canadian not-for-profit association that was created in 1990.

Figure 12.14 Tibbett & Britten is the largest third-party logistics provider in its chosen sector in North America, and the largest in any sector in Canada.

Logistics Companies

Some exporters and importers hire logistics companies to provide complete services from the door of the exporter to the door of the importer, including managing the transport quoting process, surveying the route, expediting purchase orders, providing or sourcing warehousing, arranging insurance, packing for export, smoothing customs clearance, and preparing trade documentation. Specialist logistics companies are now available to manage the complete supply chain on behalf of businesses. Logistics companies often have systems in place to manage conditions such as extreme temperatures, possible natural disasters, and situations of political unrest in regions through which a shipment may be transported. Logistics companies must be flexible, innovative, and able to respond to unexpected circumstances.

For example, the British-based Tibbett & Britten Group offers its clients an array of services ranging from collection and freight forwarding, through storage, product completion/inspection, tracking, documentation, and import handling, to onward delivery. As specialists in supply chain management, the company tailors the mode of transport, routes, timing, and delivery to meet customer needs primarily in the following industries: food and grocery supplies, computers and electronic equipment, clothing, textiles, general merchandise, and raw materials and components.

David Dick

Logistics Practitioner, Canada WorldWide Services

After Dave Dick left high school, he worked on the production line at Facelle, a paper company that manufactures consumer items such as facial tissues and paper towels. A serious accident took him off the line, and he ended up in the traffic department. When Dick first arrived, his only background in traffic was driving in it, but he soon learned the importance of this department and began to enjoy his new duties: arranging for the delivery of products to customers and scheduling the shipment of raw materials and processed goods from Facelle's many suppliers.

Dick wanted to learn more about this field. While working at Facelle, he enrolled in the Canadian Institute of Traffic and Transportation (CITT) and completed the courses through correspondence and weekend study groups. CITT provides graduates with the professional designation that identifies people with core knowledge and heightened professionalism in distribution logistics management. Currently, the full program required to earn the designation consists of courses in physical distribution, logistics, logistics decision modelling, transportation economics, and transportation law. Today, CITT courses are offered in partnership with many community colleges in Ontario, as well as through correspondence.

After Dick completed his CITT courses, he moved from Facelle and worked for a number of transportation and logistics firms. He became assistant manager in Air Export for Murray and Robinson Freight Services,

a logistics planner for Swift Sure Group, and an export consultant to Schenker International. Schenker was the largest company Dave worked for. This company has expertise in land transport, worldwide air and sea freight, and all associated logistics services. It has approximately 32 000 employees at 1000 locations throughout the world.

Dick's last stop was Canada WorldWide Services (CWS), a wholesale courier providing customs clearance and delivery services within Canada for freight imported from all over the world. The movie industry, trade shows, publishing houses, and the airline industry are the biggest clients of CWS, which is open 24 hours a day, 7 days a week to serve the customer's needs at any time. It provides pickups anywhere in Canada and ships to any destination in Canada, providing customs clearance and delivery to the door.

Dick said, "I've seen all sides of the logistics business, from ocean and air export to import handling with intermodal terminals, rail, and every size truck you can think of. It's all still traffic to me." Dick's love of the business was strong: he was in the business for 30 years.

• •

1. What services does Canada WorldWide Services provide?

2. What courses are currently required for the CITT designation?

Export and Import Documentation

According to Team Canada Inc, "export documentation identifies the goods and the terms of sale, provides title to the goods and evidence of insurance coverage, and certifies that the goods are of a certain quality or standard." Export documents include shipping documents and collection documents. The documents include

- a **commercial invoice**, which is an itemized list of the goods being shipped. It should also include basic information about the transaction: the date of issue, the address of the shipper and seller, the invoice or contract number, a description of the goods, the unit price, the total weight and number of packages, shipping marks and numbers, and the delivery and payment terms. The commercial invoice is used as either a shipping or a collection document. It is also required for customs clearance.

- the **export packing list**, which itemizes the material in each package and indicates the type of package (box, crate, drum, or carton, for example). It shows the net, legal, and gross weights and measurements for each package.

- the **export declaration (B13A)**, which is a Canada Customs and Revenue Agency form that must be prepared by exporters for all non-U.S. destinations. Exporters must make a declaration when the value of the goods being exported is $2000 CAD or more. The form is required for goods travelling through the United States to a foreign destination or directly to a destination beyond the United States.

- the **certificate of origin**, which states the origin of imported goods. It is used for customs or foreign exchange purposes, or both. Certificates of origin are sometimes certified by a chamber of commerce in the exporting country, and information about origin may need to be verified by a consul of the foreign country involved. The certificate of origin helps countries determine the tariff rate at which the goods enter a country. For example, a NAFTA certificate of origin is used to secure duty-free, or lower duty rate, entry into the United States and Mexico for Canadian exports.

- a **bill of lading** or **waybill**, which is the shipping document issued by the carrier that states the contract between the owner of the goods and the carrier. The bill of lading serves as a receipt issued to a shipper by a carrier, listing the goods received for shipment in apparent good condition. It defines the contract of carriage of the goods from the port of shipment to the port of destination, and the consignee listed. Depending on the terms agreed upon, when dealing with an ocean carrier, the shipper is most often responsible from dock to dock.

- a **Canada Customs Invoice**, which is required on all shipments passing through customs en route to Canada.

- the **certificate of inspection**, which ensures that the goods being imported are free from any defects. This is particularly important in the import and export of animals, plants, and food products.

- a **certificate of insurance**, which describes the type of insurance that covers the shipment.

On January 31, 1998, Statistics Canada and the Canada Customs and Revenue Agency launched the national implementation of the Canadian Automated Export Declaration (CAED), which is a program that gives registered exporters and agents the opportunity to report goods electronically to the federal government of Canada.

International Company Profile

PBB Global Logistics

Figure 12.15 PBB's Project Cargo helps shippers to overcome logistics challenges.

In 1946, Edward J. Freeland launched Peace Bridge Brokerage Limited (PBB), a one-person, one-office customs brokerage located at the foot of the Fort Erie Peace Bridge. This bridge is one of the busiest gateways linking the United States and Canada. As the brokerage matured, demand grew, and in 1957 PBB opened its first branch office in Welland, Ontario.

In the 1960s, PBB implemented a training program for key staff members to become qualified in the movement of air freight, and to become licensed International Air Transport Association (IATA) Freight Forwarders. The company also opened the Magic Carpet Delivery Service to offer fast and reliable local and medium-haul truck services. In the 1970s, PBB grew to a national organization with offices from coast to coast.

The 1980s brought emerging overseas markets and free trade. In 1981, the company was appointed as the sole Canadian member of the World Air Cargo Organization (WACO), joining a global effort to make international freight forwarding less complex. With the creation of NAFTA, PBB recognized the need for North America-wide services, and it became the first Canadian-owned brokerage to venture into the United States. Its first U.S. office opened in December 1985. It now has 30 offices in the United States.

During this era, PBB introduced customs consulting to help clients with the ever-changing regulations of world trade. It also launched a travel agency to offer customized travel plans for companies around the world.

The 1990s presented new opportunities for PBB when it became a completely integrated global logistics firm, developing new technologies and new partnerships. The company now employs more than 1000 people in 70 locations across North America and has a worldwide network of automated facilities.

In Spring 2000, PBB helped facilitate trade with emerging markets by organizing "China: Trade Mission 2000," the first privately led mission of its kind. The mission is now an annual event, giving North American firms a unique opportunity to explore new business opportunities in China.

In the first couple of years of the new millennium, PBB continued to expand its services, integrating its innovative "Project Cargo" into its range of supply chain solutions. The company also introduced its e-globallogistics.com suite of Internet-based supply management tools.

1. Use a graphic organizer to trace the development of PBB Global Logistics from its beginnings as Peace Bridge Brokerage Limited in 1946 to its current business functions.

2. Go to **www.internationalbusiness.nelson.com** to find the links to the "Services" section of the PBB Global Logistics Web site. In teams, research one of the nine services offered by the company. Summarize the advantages of each and present your findings to the rest of the class in a brief oral report.

Ideas	Connections	Extensions
1. (a) Create a chart listing and explaining the different components of an export plan.	(b) Select one of the components from 1. (a) and research ways that a company might fulfill the requirements of that component.	(c) In the role of a Canadian exporter, use your findings in 1. (b) to prepare a 3-minute oral presentation about how you would deal with the challenges of this part of export planning.
2. (a) Describe the functions of freight forwarders and customs brokers.	(b) Working with a partner, investigate a freight forwarder and a customs broker that operate in your region of Canada. What products do they handle most often? Where are the most common international locations to which and from which products are shipped?	(c) In your opinion, what might be some benefits for a small Canadian company using a logistics company?
3. (a) Explain the purpose of a certificate of origin.	(b) Research one of the Canadian customs documents and explain why the document is required under Canadian law.	(c) Interview (perhaps by e-mail) an international shipper in or near your community who has to complete Canada Customs documents. Ask the shipper to describe some things that the company needs to watch for.

Canada's Trading Partners: Focus on Japan

Japan is Canada's second-largest national trading partner and accounts for 2.2 percent of Canada's total exports. Canada is a leading supplier to Japan of lumber, pulp and paper, minerals, meat, fish, grains and oilseeds, and prefabricated housing. Canada's imports from Japan include vehicles, machinery, electronic equipment, medical equipment, aircraft, and spacecraft. Japan is also the fifth-largest source of direct foreign investment in Canada.

Even though the two countries have enjoyed a strong economic relationship over the years, Canadian governments and businesses believe that our current exports to Japan do not reflect the sophistication of products and services that Canada has to offer. The Department of Foreign Affairs and International Trade is asking Canadian businesses to help research and analyze current business trends to suggest how to revitalize and expand Canada's trade with Japan.

Beginning in the late 1990s, the Canadian government worked with Canadian businesses to strengthen trading ties with Japan. Team Canada, consisting of Prime Minister Chrétien, provincial premiers, territorial leaders, and Canadian business leaders, visited Japan to discuss expanding trade links between the two countries, especially in the high technology sector, which includes aircraft, software, telecommunications equipment, and resource and environmental products and services. At the conclusion of the meetings, Japanese and Canadian government and business leaders agreed to
- undertake studies of bilateral trade and investment opportunities
- facilitate trade wherever possible
- work towards expanding global markets
- exchange knowledge and personnel in the areas of space research and development, Arctic science, social security, and culture

The Canadian government continues to build awareness in Japan that Canada is a sophisticated and technologically advanced country with a variety of high-tech products and services to export. From March to July 2001, the Canadian government sponsored the "Think Canada 2001 Festival" in Japan. Throughout the country, 200 events took place featuring arts and culture, business, science and technology, politics and society, education, and food and living. Back in 1995, Toronto's Harbourfront Centre had hosted a similar event called "Today's Japan," which was the largest contemporary exposition of Japanese culture that had ever been assembled in North America.

TRADE TALK

At the January 2002 World Road Association 11th International Winter Road Congress in Sapporo, Japan, Canadian business people presented some of their new technologies for handling difficult road conditions. The theme of the Congress was "New Challenges for Winter Road Service." Experts from all over the world discussed topics related to road safety: snow and ice control measures, traffic safety, the environment, and Intelligent Transportation Systems (ITS). Sapporo, the largest city north of Tokyo, was an ideal venue for the conference; its 1.8 million inhabitants know all about severe winter conditions, including how to cope with heavy annual snowfalls.

— Sapporo Congress, Government of Canada

Canada's Merchandise Trade with Japan ($billions CAD)

	1995	1996	1997	1998	1999	2000	2001
Exports to Japan (includes re-exports)	12.054	11.160	11.167	8.648	8.354	9.008	8.136
Imports from Japan	12.096	10.444	12.553	13.999	15.031	16.600	14.647
Balance	-0.042	0.716	-1.386	-5.351	-6.615	-7.592	-6.511

— Statistics Canada

Figure 12.16 Describe the trends that you see in imports and exports between Japan and Canada.

A SNAPSHOT OF JAPAN

Size: 377 864 sq. km

World Region: Asia-Pacific

Capital City: Tokyo

Language: Japanese

Currency: Yen

Population: 127 million

Climate: Varies from tropical in the south to cool temperate in the north to cold in mountainous regions

Time: Noon in Ottawa (EST) is 2:00 A.M. the next day in Tokyo.

Labour Force by Occupation: 2 percent agriculture, 36 percent industry, 62 percent services, total labour force 67.7 million (2000 estimates)

Type of Government: Constitutional monarchy

Membership in World Organizations: WTO, G8, APEC, ASEAN

Importing Partners and Products: Total import value $540.58 billion CAD (2001 Japan Tariff Association data). **Partners:** United States 18 percent, China 17 percent, South Korea 5 percent, Indonesia 4 percent, Australia 4 percent. Canada's ranking is 12th at 2 percent. **Products:** fuels, foodstuffs, chemicals, textiles, office machinery.

Exporting Partners and Products: Total export value $625.06 billion CAD (Sources 2001 Japan Tariff Association data). **Partners:** United States 30 percent, China 8 percent, South Korea 6 percent, Taiwan 6 percent, Hong Kong 6 percent. Canada's ranking is 14th at 2 percent. **Products:** motor vehicles, electronic equipment, office machinery, chemicals, textiles, processed foods.

Business Etiquette: Address a Japanese business person with a title and surname, rather than a first name. Punctuality is essential, and meetings are usually structured. It is customary to exchange business cards (in Japanese and English) at first meetings.

Travel Advisory: Japan is a country of islands, and its relative geographic isolation has meant that, in the past, it experienced less cultural interaction than many other countries. Japanese business people combine sophisticated and high-tech business skills with long-standing traditions.

Figure 12.17 Activities on the Tokyo Stock Exchange set the trends for daily trading around the world.

THINK ABOUT IT

What type of product does Canada export to Japan? What type of product does Canada import from Japan? Do the differences between these types of products affect the Canadian economy? Explain.

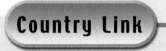

Country Link

Follow the link at www.internationalbusiness.nelson.com to find out more about Canadian trade with Japan.

Chapter Challenges

Knowledge/Understanding

1. Match each of the following terms to the correct definition or description below:
   (a) logistics
   (b) warehousing
   (c) electronic data interchange (EDI)
   (d) topography
   (e) freight forwarder
   (f) intermodal
   (g) physical distribution
   (h) supply chain
   (i) customs broker

   (i) links among a variety of means of transportation
   (ii) the natural and human features of the Earth's surface
   (iii) the total sequence of business processes that enable customer demand for a product or service to be satisfied
   (iv) planning for, implementing, and controlling the flow and storage of raw materials, inventory, finished goods, and related information
   (v) the means by which companies use computers to communicate with each other
   (vi) an individual or company that specializes in moving goods through the customs process
   (vii) an individual or company that arranges to ship goods to customers in foreign countries
   (viii) the storage and movement of goods in a company's manufacturing location, and along the stages of transit from source to company and from company to consumer
   (ix) the activities needed to move and transfer ownership of goods from producer to consumer

2. Compare the advantages and disadvantages of the different modes of transportation for a Canadian company that is a just-in-time supplier for an American company.

3. Explain why effective logistics management is important to the success of Canadian international companies.

Thinking/Inquiry

1. Create a fishbone diagram showing how the trend towards greater use of EDI is likely to affect logistics planning, modes of transportation, or export planning in one Canadian industry over the next ten years.

2. Using an example, explain how the topography of a specific country affects the modes of transportation chosen to transport goods into or out of that country.

3. Create a mind map or a concept web to illustrate some of the concerns that a Canadian exporting company might need to address when it is warehousing its product in different places around the world.

Communication

1. Create an annotated bibliography of ten reliable resources (print or online) related to logistics, physical distribution, and/or export planning that could be used by a Canadian entrepreneur who wants to export products internationally. For each resource, include a description of the organization that publishes it and a brief explanation of why the resource would be helpful to Canadian international businesses.

2. Select a current article from a business publication (Canadian or international, in print or online) that deals with an export planning issue. In a brief oral presentation, summarize the main points in the article.

3. Create a flowchart to demonstrate a possible chain of physical distribution for one of the following:
   - a specialty soft-drinks producer in Vancouver, British Columbia that exports its product to Capetown, South Africa
   - a software developer in Cape Dorset, Nunavut who exports her product to Moscow, Russia
   - a restaurant owner in Charlottetown, PEI who imports avocados from California
   - a retailer in Medicine Hat, Alberta who imports Christmas ornaments from China
   - an artist in Thunder Bay, Ontario who exports his paintings to a gallery in London, England

Application

1. Working in a small group, review the components of an export plan. Find Industry Canada and Canadian Department of Foreign Affairs and International Trade (DFAIT) documents (in print or online) regarding export. Using these documents, prepare a list of questions that a company should ask itself when developing a realistic export plan. When your group has completed its list of questions, post them on an Exporters Bulletin Board that could be used as a resource for your whole class.

2. Research the possible sourcing, warehousing and storage, physical distribution, and information management procedures used by a large Canadian international company. Prepare an illustrated report of your findings using maps, flowcharts, photos, and/or graphs.

3. Investigate Canada's current export and import statistics for trade with Japan. Find one Canadian industry where Canadian exports have increased in the last year. Then do further research on that industry to find out which modes of transport are used to get the product from its Canadian source to its destination in Japan. Create an illustrated flowchart to demonstrate the physical distribution path used by one Canadian company in this industry segment to export its product to Japan.

International Business Portfolio

International Logistics

One of the most complicated parts of logistics is the physical movement of goods from one place to another. This is a special challenge in international business. Shippers must take into account weight, distance, content, tariffs, cost, time, and so on.

Activities

1. Investigate the costs and complications of shipping a 1-kilogram package of promotional materials directed at potential investors or advertisers in the following locations:
   • within the same city
   • a city in a different province or territory
   • the capital of your IBP country
   • a small village or town in your IBP country

   Investigate three shipping methods, which could include Canada Post, a local courier, and an international courier. You could also research (with a bit more difficulty) rail, truck, or air- or ocean-freight rates, where appropriate.

2. How would a freight forwarder help you with the international shipment?

3. Identify the logistics companies that exist in your IBP country.

CONCLUSION:
The International Business Plan

Going Global

Companies entering the international marketplace should do so only after careful consideration and planning. Companies begin by assessing their current situation, setting goals, and then developing plans and strategies to reach those goals. A **strategic plan** takes a long, comprehensive view of what the company hopes to achieve either by exporting to or importing from foreign markets. This might involve researching the political or legal environment of the country. Short-term action plans are referred to as **tactical plans**. These plans use careful and deliberate techniques designed to launch the business plan. An international business plan combines both strategic and tactical plans. It is like a map or navigational system that allows a company to reach its global destinations or markets. While a business plan is important for a domestic company, it is even more essential when a company decides to go global. The plan allows businesses to communicate their vision and business objectives. For example, it might be a starting point for developing finances.

The international business plan serves to

- identify the goals of the company
- demonstrate understanding of different international markets and their customers and preferences
- describe the strategies required to enter new markets and the risks associated with those market entries
- describe the human and material resources, such as logistics, required to reach international markets
- forecast, in a realistic fashion, the costs and sales of the venture
- attract and interest investors at home and abroad

GLOBAL THOUGHT

Regardless of its size, every business should have some kind of plan that outlines its current position in the marketplace, strategic directions, expectations, and objectives. Such plans are useful in getting a consensus within senior management. They can help employees understand how they can best contribute to a company's success. They can inform partners and investors about where a company is headed. And they are usually required by banks and other lenders before they provide financing.

– *Forum for International Trade Training*

Preparing an international business plan is time-consuming, but it is important to take the time upfront to achieve success later on. For most companies, the market entry timeline is anywhere from two to five years. It takes this long to establish a presence in the selected foreign market. For each product in each international market, managers must develop plans that take into consideration the unique cultural, business, political, and social conditions of each market.

Parts of the International Business Plan

Useful business plans contain similar elements. The following table gives a brief description of each necessary component of the international business plan.

Executive Summary or Overview	The executive summary, placed at the beginning of the international business plan, is usually the last part that is written. Often only a page in length, it • provides an overview of the plan • states what makes the business unique and superior to the competition • lists the company's competitive advantages over both domestic and international competition.
Description of the Business	In its description of the company, the international business plan • defines the company's long-term (strategic) and short-term (tactical) goals • provides the company's mission statement • explains the company's organizational structure • outlines the management team's qualifications, usually from the perspective of the five business functions: marketing, finance, production, human resources, and information systems • describes in detail the company's business relationships in target foreign markets
Present Situation	The international business plan describes the product or service and its trade environment: • the product or service to be exported, with the reasons for choosing that product for export • the product being imported, with the reasons for importing that particular product from that particular country, and the targeted industry and customers • the business climate of the target market • a proposed export or import plan
Risk Assessment	The international business plan includes a risk assessment of all types of risk: • political risk • economic and financial risk (focusing on the currency of the country) • social and cultural risk • technical and commercial risk • natural and physical risk
Marketing Activities	The detailed marketing plan in the international business plan includes this information: • details of the opportunities and competition in the existing market • marketing strategy • cultural factors and customs • target customers • international promotion and pricing strategies • advertising and public relations, and a plan for after-sales service in the foreign market • 4-Ps Marketing—Product, Place, Price, and Promotion • marketing logistics • how the good or service will be positioned in the market

Financial Projections	The financial analysis in the international business plan has these elements:
	• sales forecast that includes the facts it is based upon (for example, consumer profile, population statistics, report on competition, and so on)
	• manufacturing plan that specifies manufacturing location, the required volume of production, suppliers, and source of materials. Under capacity, the manufacturing plan projects how much of the item can be produced under current circumstances and how that capacity relates to anticipated product demand. Will expansion be required? (Remember that many companies hire or contract manufacturing and production requirements in foreign markets.)
	• realistic and conservative detailed cost, sales, and profit estimates. Profit equals sales minus costs. (**A tip**: Divide forecast sales by two, and multiply forecasted expenses by two!)
	• break-even analysis. How many units must be sold before costs equal revenue?
	• financing strategy that describes the company plans to obtain the finances required to launch the international operation

Ready, Set, Go!

Chapter by chapter, you have studied factors and issues in international trade and built an International Business Portfolio. You're ready now to develop your own international business plan. Using the descriptions in the table above, gather the information you need to successfully launch your company into the global marketplace. Your teacher can provide you with additional resources and sources.

As an appendix to your plan, prepare a report on careers in international business that appeal to you, and find out the educational requirements required to obtain those types of jobs. Map out a possible route, outlining the education and experience you need, and how you might obtain them, to help you achieve your career goals. Good luck on your journey!

GLOSSARY

A

absolute advantage Full advantage over competitors, or the lack of competitors, so as to enable a company or country to set prices and policies without fear of competition

advising bank Bank that advises a customer regarding revenue due to the customer; in international trade, usually the exporter's bank

aggregate marketing Marketing with no specific target segment; attempting to sell a product to everyone

Agreement on Internal Trade (AIT) An arrangement among Canadian governments intended to harmonize relations and standards among provinces

Asia Pacific Economic Cooperation (APEC) A forum for officials of countries bordering on the Pacific Ocean to promote trade among their countries

asset The value of something owned by a person, business, or organization, including buildings, land, factories, equipment, and accounts receivable

Auto Pact The common term used for the Canada-U.S. Automotive Products Agreement, a trade agreement between the two countries to promote freer trade in automobile components and completed vehicles

B

bank draft An order for payment drawn by one bank on another

benefits In business, usually refers to an employer's benefits plan, which may pay all or part of expenses for full-time employees' medical care and prescription drugs

big box retailers (also called "category killers") Retailers that specialize in providing a wide variety of products in one category

bilateral trade Trade between two countries

bill of lading (waybill) The shipping document issued by a carrier which states the contract between the owner of the goods and the carrier

biotechnology Scientific use and genetic manipulation of living organisms or other biological processes in commercial applications

board of directors Formal group of directors who govern the affairs of an organization or company

BOOT Build-own-operate-transfer, as a planned sequence of events

boycott An organized refusal to buy (a company's or country's) products or services

brand A product line or group that has a distinctive name and logo that is registered and protected by its owner, and that is usually promoted with a certain style, slogan, image, and target market appeal

brand acquisition strategy Purchasing an existing company in the foreign country or acquiring the rights to distribute the brand locally

brand building Increasing the positive image and recognition of a brand (as well as its availability to customers)

brand development strategy The use of a foreign subsidiary to develop a product to compete in a local market

brand equity Making a brand recognizable and giving it a positive image

breakbulk cargo Goods or raw materials shipped by marine vessel without containerization. The goods are usually loaded directly aboard vessels on pallets, in a net or by a sling, conveyor, or chute

bricks and mortar An organization, institution, company, or operation that is not knowledge based (e.g., a factory, a plant, or an office)

broker A person or company that negotiates and acts for others, using knowledge and experience of a particular business

business The manufacture and/or sale of goods and/or services to meet the needs of a marketplace and to produce a profit

business climate The state of the business environment, the economy, and the stock market

business cycle Recurring cycles of increased, then decreased, and then back to increased business or economic activity

business environment The current state of and trends in business and in international business, including government attitudes and regulations applied to foreign companies

business ethics Ethics as applied to business, with regard to the treatment of employees, society, stock-holders, and consumers

business opportunity An occasion or circumstance to increase, expand, or set up a new business

business-to-business (B2B) An activity or relationship between or among businesses

business unit A group with a special function or purpose within a company or organization

buy forward Purchase foreign currency when an order is placed to secure the price of a product

C

Canada Customs Invoice A document that is required on all export shipments passing through customs en route to Canada

Canadian International Development Agency (CIDA) A federal government agency that funds Canadian consultant trust funds at the World Bank and regional development banks

Canadian mosaic A term used to describe Canada's cultural heritage, which is made up of cultures from all over the world

capital Money or other assets that are available for investment purposes

capital intensive industry An industry that requires a substantial amount of money (capital) to start or operate

capital investment Investment in new capital assets such as factories, machinery, and equipment

cash flow The flow of incoming revenues and outgoing use of money, usually expressed in a defined period of time

cellular Electronic wireless communication by means of a network of transmitting and receiving short-wave radio "cells," which are capable of transferring a signal from one cell to the next over an area

centralized marketing strategy The production and sale of goods from one central location

centrally planned economy An economy in which the government regulates the amount, distribution, and price of goods and services

certificate of inspection A document that is used to ensure that the goods being imported are free from any defects

certificate of insurance A document that describes the type of insurance that covers a shipment

certificate of origin A document that contains an affidavit to prove the origin of imported goods

channels of distribution Those businesses—such as importers, wholesalers, and retailers—that connect any manufacturer's product to the target market

chief executive officer (CEO) The most senior manager in a company who is responsible for the company's attainment of its business goals, performance, financial results, general conduct, and financial return to shareholders

code of ethics The principles on which members of an organization base their behaviour

commercial invoice An itemized list of the goods being shipped, usually included among an exporter's collection papers

commercialize To convert a nonprofit activity or research development into a profitable activity

commodities Basic goods, such as raw materials or goods that are partially processed

commune Self-sufficient community based on principles of communal property and shared responsibilities

comparative advantage An advantage usually created when a company or country becomes more efficient, has better technology, and has easier access to resources than its competitors

competitive advantage An advantage in which a country or company outperforms others in terms of productivity, quality and price of products, superior service, better technology, higher profit

conflict of interest A conflict between private interests and the public obligations of a person in an official position

consignee The individual or company to whom a seller or shipper sends merchandise and who, upon presentation of the necessary documents, is recognized as the merchandise owner for the purpose of declaring it and paying any customs duty

consortium A group of independent companies that have joined together to undertake a specific project or business purpose, especially for export sales and related activities, and for major projects

containerization The stowage of freight in sealed, reusable containers of uniform size and shape that makes transportation more effective because it allows goods to be transported without the need to handle the goods

container ship A ship made for the transportation of containers, and requiring port facilities for their efficient handling

controlling share (interest) Ownership of sufficient shares in a company to enable the shareholder to assert control over policy and management

copyright A form of legal protection provided to the authors of original works, including literary, dramatic, musical, artistic, and intellectual works and software programs

corporate philanthropy Policies by which companies donate financial and material resources to support social causes

corporate social responsibility (CSR) Corporate standards and practices regarding human rights, the environment, human resources, and community relations

Corruption Perceptions Index A publication of Transparency International in which 102 countries are ranked according to their degree of corruption as seen by business people, academics, and risk analysts

cost analysis Analysis of all costs of a product, service, or process; can be used for assessing or comparing prices

credit The borrowing capacity of an individual or company; also, a situation in which someone receives something of value now and agrees to pay for it later

credit reference A person or company who can vouch for the trustworthiness and honesty of an applicant for a loan or credit

credit risk Risk of non-payment for goods or services provided; a person, business, organization, or service that has a record of non-payment, slow payment, or is in financial difficulty

cross-invest To have two or more parties invest in each other's business

cultural determinants Factors that shape a country's culture, including its geography, history, intellectual property, and main religion

cultural imperialism The imposition of one group's cultural values and customs on another group

cultural marketing The use of marketing resources to create effective international marketing campaigns that will appeal to consumers in specific countries

cultural norms Cultural expectations, appearance, observances, and behaviour that are normal (standard) in a region or country

cultural relativism The belief that behaviour should be governed by what will bring about the greatest good for the greatest number of people

cultural sovereignty A country's ability and power to retain independence and control over its culture and cultural institutions and not yield to or be dominated by another more powerful country

culture The values, laws, language, technology, art, music, religion, and literature of a community or nation

currency The official medium of exchange of a country; for example, dollar, yen, pound, peso

currency conversion The act of changing units of one currency to the equivalent value in another currency

currency devaluation The reduction by a government of the value of its currency relative to currencies of other nations

currency exchange rate The rate at which one currency can be exchanged for another or for gold

currency fluctuation Change in the value of a currency as compared with other currencies, as a result of activities on the currency market

currency market The trading of national currencies

currency revaluation The adjusting of a country's currency value upwards

custom manufacturing Manufacturing to the specific requirements of a customer

customs The official government department that administers regulations governing imports and collecting duties; also, the social habits and traditional behaviour of a people that reflect their cultural values

customs broker An intermediary who specializes in moving goods through the customs process in a country

D

data mining A marketing research method that determines relationships between the personal information and purchasing behaviour of specific consumers

decentralized marketing strategy The use of local production facilities, distribution centres, advertising agencies, marketing research companies, sales representatives, and/or retail partnerships to target specific international markets

deficit Money paid out, or owed, that is greater than revenue

deliverables The solutions, services, or end-products that are developed to fulfill a request for proposal

democracy Government for and by the people

demographics The statistics about a human population including such details as age, marital status, income, birthplace, and number of certain items in the household

depression A severe form of recession, in which unemployment is high and the sales of goods and services are weak even though prices are declining

deregulate To reduce or eliminate government regulations and controls on business activities; also, to remove government regulations and restrictions from an industry or business area

developed nation An industrialized country that has a high standard of living and produces a sophisticated range of products

developing nation A country that is evolving from being less developed to being more industrialized

direct sales Sales direct to the ultimate customer, rather than through a wholesaler, distributor, agent, or trading house

discretionary income The amount of income that is not committed to paying for necessities

disposable income The amount of income that is left after taxes have been paid

distribution network A system for the distribution of goods through a network of suppliers, forwarders, distributors, dealers, and wholesalers, to business, industrial, or consumer customers

domestic market Relating to one's own country's market

downsizing Reducing the number of employees and business activities

dumping The practice of selling goods at a price that is unfairly lower than market value

duty A tax or tariff levied on goods when they are imported

E

e-commerce Business transacted over the Internet

economic freedom rating A measure of prosperity that correlates to economic growth, per capita income, and material wealth of a country

economic imperialism The policy or act of extending the rule or authority of one country over other countries by dominating those countries' economic structures

economic policy Policy (usually by government) to influence or direct the economic activities and financial well-being of a country

economic sanction To enforce (by penalties or restrictions) a trade agreement or code of ethical behaviour or moral conduct

economic system The factors of production and the rules and regulations involving production and consumption of goods and services

economic union An interdependent unit made up of nations that act together or in like manner in economic matters and policies

economies of scale The tendency of the cost per item to go down when items are bought or produced in large quantities

economy The wealth and resources of a country, region, or community, measuring its production and volume of business activity

electronic data interchange (EDI) The use of computers to speed up transmission of business data, documents, and funds and to automate the flow of information among their trading partners

embryo stage A company, business unit, or business trend in its formative stage

end-product imports/exports Imports/exports of finished manufactured products, ready for use by a consumer or by a producer of goods or services

entrepreneur A person who organizes, manages, and assumes the risk of starting and running a business

environmental controls Controls to minimize or remove pollutants and other negative effects on the environment

equilibrium The point at which a business can sell its product at a profit and where the consumers agree to pay the asking price

ethical dilemma A difficult decision between two or more "right" options

ethical imperialism The belief that certain forms of behaviour are categorically (absolutely) right or wrong

ethical issue An issue involving an ethical dilemma

ethnocentric Evaluation or view of others compared only to one's own criteria or values

European Union (EU) Political and economic alliance of 15 European countries that have eliminated trade barriers among them

exchange controls Political and economic measures used by a government to try to regulate the amount and value of its currency

expatriate One who has left his/her native country in order to live and work in another country

export A good or service that is produced in one country and sold in another country

Export and Import Permits Act A Canadian law that is used to impose trade sanctions on goods by means of the Area Control List, the Export Control List, and the Import Control List

export declaration (B13A) A Canada Customs and Revenue Agency form that must be prepared by exporters for all non-U.S. destinations

export-driven A company, region, or country that has an output or performance priority in producing goods or services for exports, rather than for the domestic market

export packing list An itemized list of the material in each package being exported; also indicates the type of package

export plan A step-by-step outline of the projected goals that a company hopes to achieve in exporting to a particular country and the resources that the company will need to attain its goals

expropriate To take control and ownership (usually by governments) of land, property, assets, or a private enterprise, whether domestic or foreign

F

fabrication Construction or manufacture, especially from prepared components; conversion of materials into units, parts, or manufactured goods

feasibility determination (study) Analyzing whether a proposed business action is feasible from a financial viewpoint

finance Provide money to build, invest in, or make a significant purchase for a company or organization

flagship brand The leading brand of a company; the brand for which the company is best known

floating rate A rate of currency exchange that is not fixed and tends to fluctuate over time through buying and selling on the currency exchange market

foreign direct investment Establishment of a subsidiary operation or a joint venture in a foreign country, used when a company in one country wishes to expand into another country

foreign investment The purchase by non-residents of business enterprises, land, shares, and any other assets with the potential for financial return

franchise A type of business in which a company authorizes a group or an individual to sell its goods and services for a period of time in a particular territory or location, and under contractual arrangements, usually involving a fee and a percentage of revenue or profits

franchisee A person, organization, or company that obtains rights to sell another company's goods or services

franchisor A person, organization, or company that owns exclusive rights and grants them to others (franchisees) on the basis of a legal agreement that stipulates the terms and the remuneration to the franchisee

free market (economy) Market or economy without regulations and controls and that leaves the activities and movement of the market or economy to market forces

free trade International trade without the imposition of tariffs or other trade barriers to the movement of goods and services

Free Trade Area of the Americas (FTAA) Proposed integration of economies of the Western hemisphere into a single free trade zone

freight forwarder A transportation company that carries freight forward from one location and arranges for taking it to its destination

futurist One who observes actions, trends, and developments, and who projects the future

G

G-20 An international forum of finance ministers and central bank governors from 19 countries, the European Union, the International Monetary Fund, and the World Bank

gateway city An official port (or airport) of entry into or departure from a country

general political instability risk Possibility of uncertainty of political or economic change

geocentric Viewed from the perspective of a particular geographic location or area

global Affecting or involving many regions and countries around the world

global brand A brand that is promoted, sold, and recognized around the world

global economy The combined, interdependent economies of all countries

global equity market An international stock market that electronically links stock exchanges in key cities of the world

globalization The growth and spread of interactive international economies and businesses around the world

global mindset A method of approaching business in which one is open to ideas and influences from other countries and cultures

global positioning system (GPS) A 24-satellite navigational system funded and controlled by the U.S. Department of Defense

global presence The maintaining by a country, company, or organization of political and/or corporate interests and influence in many other regions and countries

glocal company A multinational company that operates on a local basis throughout the world; a company with a very decentralized marketing philosophy

goods Raw materials, semi-manufactured goods, or manufactured goods

gross domestic product (GDP) The total value of all goods and services produced in a country during a specific time

gross domestic product (GDP) per capita The GDP divided by the population of a country

growth market A segment of a market that identifies the direction of the market and where people are spending their time and money

growth stage A stage in the product life cycle in which sales increase

guided individualism Taking an individual perspective based on one's own interpretations, experiences, and intuitions

guild Associations of merchants and craftspeople, started in the Middle Ages and organized within a town for mutual aid or business benefit

H

hard currency Currency that is widely accepted on the foreign currency exchange market and can easily be converted to another currency

hidden costs Costs that are not immediately obvious, but are part of the overall costs of some activity

human capital The sum of human knowledge, skills, experience, and capacity of employees, or of an industry or a community

human resources (HR) The employees of a company, organization, or government; also, the department that deals with hiring, training, developing, and management of employees

hyper-competition Intense competition

I

incentive Something given or done to motivate or reward (e.g., a bonus, tax credit, or free service such as delivery)

imperialism Dominating or attempting to dominate another, mainly through competition, acquisition, or takeover

import A good or service brought into a country for sale

import taxes Import duties or tariffs designed to reduce imports (by forcing increases in their prices to customers or consumers), and to reduce foreign competition with domestic goods, as well as to bring the government more revenue

industrialize Produce more through manufacturing, using technology and modern machinery and production methods

industry Everything that produces salable goods and services; can refer to a single company, but usually refers collectively to all producers or to all producers of a particular product or service (e.g., trucking industry, chemical industry)

inflation A persistent rise in the prices of goods and services over a period of time, as measured by the consumer price index (a measure of the changing costs of a "basket" of the same common items)

information technology (IT) Computer systems for storing, retrieving, processing, and sending information

infrastructure The large-scale public systems, services, and facilities of a country or region that are necessary for economic activity

innovation A modification or adaptation of an invention that takes the inventor's initial concept further

intangible assets A salable asset (e.g., patent, trademark, or copyright) that has no value in itself but permits the owner to do, create, or sell, or to grant these rights to others

intellectual capital The sum of knowledge, information, intellectual property, talent, and experience within a country or an organization

intellectual property A collective term referring to new ideas, inventions, designs, writings, and films that are protected by patents, trademarks, or copyright

intentional communities Communities that are or are attempting to become somewhat self-sufficient

interdependence Reliance of two or more groups on the actions of one another to fulfill certain wants or needs

intermediaries Persons, organizations, or companies who act on behalf of more than one party, such as agents, distributors, and trading houses

intermodal operations The use of a variety of linked transport means in different countries, time zones and climates

internal trade Trade among regions, provinces, states, and parts of a country

international business Business activities needed to create, ship, and sell goods and services internationally from producer to consumer; includes international trade, importing and exporting goods and services, licensing the use of assets in other countries, and foreign investment

International Chamber of Commerce (ICC) A world business organization that promotes an open international trade and investment system and market economy

International Monetary Fund (IMF) A multigovernment organization that focuses on international monetary cooperation and stability in foreign exchange

International Organization for Standardization (ISO) A non-governmental organization devoted to developing voluntary standards of quality management and quality assurance

invention A new device, method, or process developed through study and experimentation

inventory Products or materials being stored for later use or distribution

Investment Canada Act (ICA) A Canadian federal act to provide for the review of significant investments in Canada by non-Canadians

issuing bank Bank that issues a document or record; in international trade, usually the importer's bank

J

joint venture An agreement between two or more companies or organizations to share assets and control of a new business for mutual gain

just-in-time system An inventory control system that schedules products to arrive as they are needed for manufacturing or for supplying to customers

K

kanban A Japanese philosophy that has as a major principle the elimination of wasted time, labour, and resources

knowledge-based business A business that is based on providing informational goods and services (e.g., telecommunications, research and development, financial services, education, and software development)

knowledge economy The increased reliance of business, labour, and government on knowledge, information, and ideas

knowledge-intensive Activities and businesses that require workers who have information and knowledge necessary for the business or industry

Kyoto Protocol An agreement by which industrialized countries would voluntarily reduce carbon dioxide emissions levels between 2008 and 2012

L

labour costs All costs associated with the work of people in a company, business, organization, or industry, including wages, vacation pay, company-paid benefits, workers' insurance, and payroll administration

labour-intensive industry An industry that requires a large number of skilled or unskilled workers

labour standards Standards for workers in an industry or company, regarding health and safety, benefits, standards of performance, and workplace conditions

landed cost Total cost of a product including all transportation, handling, tariff, brokerage, and currency exchange rates, as well as import charges

land management Management of land for a specific purpose, such as reforestation, or preservation of wildlife

legislated code of conduct Laws of a country, compliance with which is mandatory

less-developed nation A country with little economic wealth and an emphasis on primary resource production

letter of credit A financial document issued by a bank for an importer in which the bank guarantees payment

leverage To take advantage of the positive reputation of a brand when marketing

licensing Permission from patent or copyright owners that allows others to use their idea or invention for a fee or royalty

life cycle In business, the expected period of time for the life of productive or sales activity of a machine, building, product, brand, or type of business

lobbying The attempt to influence business or government decisions toward an organization's desired goals

logistics Includes planning for, implementing, and controlling the flow and storage of raw materials, inventory, finished goods, and related information, from the point of origin to the point of consumption

logistics company A company that provides complete services from the door of the exporter to the door of the importer including managing the quoting process, surveying the route, expediting purchase orders, warehousing where needed, arranging insurance, packing for export, smoothing customs clearance, and preparing trade documentation

M

manufactured goods Goods made directly from raw materials or from semi-manufactured goods

manufacturing industry (sector) An industry that makes or processes large quantities of raw materials into finished products, usually with machines

market The place where there are potential customers to whom a good or service can be sold; also, to promote the sale of and make available a good or service through advertising, announcing, and point-of-sale material

market-driven Driven by the competitive forces of supply and demand, which determine prices, output, and production methods

market-driven organizations Organizations that respond to market needs by providing customers with high-quality, low-cost goods and services

market economy A system where individual companies and consumers make decisions about what, how, and for whom goods and services are produced

market entry The act of bringing a product or service into a market, including all aspects of preparation and initial activity

marketing All the activities involved in the planning, pricing, promoting, distributing, and selling of goods and services to satisfy consumers' needs and wants

marketing costs All costs related to marketing, including prototypes, models, samples, advertising, brochures, Web marketing, trade show exhibits and fees, sales materials, point-of-sale display materials, product placement costs, communications, entertainment, and staff costs

marketing mix Product development (product), distribution (place), pricing (price), and the combination of advertising, sales promotion, and publicity (promotion)

marketing opportunity analysis An examination of all the competitive products within a particular product category or market segment

marketing plan Plan determining the marketing mix (product, price, place, and promotion) that will be appropriate for the specific market

marketing research The collection, analysis, and interpretation of data used in making marketing decisions

market opportunity An opportunity for sales presented by needs or wants, lack of previous exposure to a product, or changing demographics

market segment A part of a market that is defined by a specific characteristic

market signals Signals or indications from a market, market segment, or customers in reaction to marketing or to a product, service, or business; may indicate a trend

matrix An organizational structure with different communication and responsibilities going through the same person, organization, company, industry, or government

mature A level of activity or development indicating that the maximum level has been reached, after which there will be decline

merchandise Finished products/goods ready for sale

mission statement A presentation of a company's goals and vision, an answer to the question, "Where are we going?"

mixed economy An economy that combines government involvement and private ownership of businesses, has aspects of both market and centrally planned economic systems

mixed system of government A form of government that has characteristics of both democratic and totalitarian systems

monoculture A single culture; a society that lacks diversity in values and beliefs

monopoly Dominance of a business, industry, market, or trade by a single company or country, which enables it to exercise considerable control over supply, prices, quantities, and quality

most-favoured nation (MFN) status A category denoting that a nation will not levy tariffs on imports from or exports to nations with this status

multilateral trade Trade among more than two nations

multinational company (MNC) (transnational company) A business enterprise that conducts business in several countries

N

nationalize To take over an asset, industry, company, land, or service from private ownership on behalf of the state (country)

natural hazards Climatic or geological conditions that endanger human life and property

negotiation style The way in which businesspeople negotiate business relationships, particularly important in international business

network Individuals, organizations, companies, suppliers, customers, or computer and communications that are helpful, informative, useful, or with whom business is transacted; also, to make purposeful contact with those in a network; to connect computers and communications together for a collective function

non-governmental organizations (NGOs) Groups that are not associated with government and that work to bring about change

nonprofit (not-for-profit) organization (NPO) An organization not created for or involved in making a profit

North American Free Trade Agreement (NAFTA) An arrangement among Canada, the United States, and Mexico that has the goal of creating a free-trade zone among the three countries

O

open-market economy Economy that is not regulated or controlled and reacts to market forces (supply and demand)

operating environment The business and competitive environment and conditions in which a company or industry does business

operation(s) System of mechanical, manufacturing, human resources, materials, and work flow in a company or organization; the running of a company or organization

operations risk Possibility that host government policies and acts may impede business operations in another country

opportunity cost Cost and potential benefit of an opportunity that is deferred or sacrificed in order to act on another opportunity

Organization for Economic Cooperation and Development (OECD) A monitoring agency that offers governments a setting in which to discuss and develop economic and social policy

outsource To obtain goods, parts, materials, or services from an outside source

ownership risk Risk of losing ownership of property (plants, factories, offices), business, and assets when threatened by government takeover (nationalization) or by expropriation

P

Pacific Rim Usually refers to the countries or regions bordering the Pacific Ocean

packaging Packing goods for display and sale; the "package" includes the product and sometimes parts and instructional material, plus outer material (of plastic, paper, cardboard), which is designed with brand name, logo, labelling required, and sometimes instructions

parent company A company that wholly owns subsidiary (other) companies

partner A defined, contractual relationship based on a business or professional activity and that shares costs and profits

patent A grant of property right by law to give exclusive rights to the inventor, to protect the rights of the inventor, and to prevent others from making, using, or selling the invention

performance efficiency A measure of capabilities or output, usually expressed as units produced or completed per time period or per worker, machine, department, or industry

performance standards Standards expected or required for output from a machine, performance, department, or company

physical distribution The activities needed to actually move and transfer ownership of goods and services from the producer to the consumer

political risk Risk of negative political change or instability, assessed by looking at the host country's current or future political system and examining how changes to its stability might cause a loss to investors

portfolio investment Purchase of shares and bonds for the income they yield or the capital gains they may bring, and not for exercising of ownership or control

premium In marketing, a free good offered with the purchase of a product

pricing formula A company's standard method for calculating the price to customers of their goods or services; consists of costs, taxes, and profit requirement per unit

primary data Information collected directly from the marketplace by a researcher for a specific purpose

primary industries Industries that are based on raw materials from nature—such as in agriculture, fishing and trapping, forestry and logging, and energy and mining

primary resources Raw materials stemming from a country's primary resources

private sector The part of the economy that is free of government control at any level (except for applicable regulations)

private sector investments The private sector's commitment of money or capital to projects

privatize To sell publicly owned assets or enterprises to the private sector

product A good or service

product differentiation Making a product distinct from its competitors

productivity The amount of work accomplished in a unit of time using the factors of production

product launch Introduction of a new product to a market

product life cycle The four stages of a product's growth: embryo, growth, maturity, and death

product modification Changing a product or package to meet consumers' needs and preferences or to update, change, or modernize a product or its appearance

product placement Placing of a product for greater sales advantage within a retail environment, in films, television shows, and public events

professional development The work- or profession-related developing of a person through educational programs, training, and experience

profit margin The difference between revenue and all costs (of a product, division, or company)

profit sharing Sharing the profits of a company, usually between employer and employees, usually based on a percentage of after-tax profits set aside for the employees

protectionism The practice of protecting domestic industries and economies

protocol Customary and expected behaviour, including rules and etiquette

public sector The part of the economy that is under direct control of the government at any level

public sector investments The public sector's commitment of money or capital to projects in order to gain financial return

pull strategy A marketing strategy that targets consumers directly, attempting to convince people that they must have a certain product

purchasing power A measure of the capacity to purchase basic goods and services

push strategy A marketing strategy that sells a product to retailers, importers, or wholesalers, but not to end-use consumers

Q

quality of life Comparative standards of the life of persons, countries, or regions, measuring services and basic needs available, with quality of health, access to education and employment, and the state of the environment

R

ratify Confirm by formal consent and signature after full consideration

rationalization The process used by an organization or company to change its structure, product line, or production process to make it more efficient, productive, and competitive

raw materials Materials in their natural state, such as cotton, coal, fish, minerals, and wood

recession The phase of the business cycle when demand begins to decrease, businesses lower production of goods and services, and employment rates increase

reciprocity An arrangement of equal actions toward each other

redemption rate Percentage of consumers using a coupon measured against the number of coupons issued

repatriation of earnings Either retaining a portion of profit by a foreign host government, or paying profit to the parent company

request for a proposal (RFP) A detailed proposal in response to a request, showing the costs, time, requirements, quality, specifications, and methods of performing and achieving the requested outcome

research and development (R&D) Scientific, engineering, and design activities that result in inventions, innovations, or improved products or production processes

resource-based imports/exports Imports and exports of primary resources

resources Natural materials or conditions, especially minerals, natural gas, and oil, usually for commercial exploitation

resource utilization The application of resources to the productive uses of a business or industry, often used as a measure

responsible global corporate citizenship Being responsible (ethically, morally, socially, environmentally) in all countries in which a company operates

royalty Payment made to an author/owner for the use of copyright, for the use of a patent, or for each public performance of a work. Also, payment made by a producer of minerals, oil, or natural gas to the owner of the site or of those mineral rights

rule of law Written laws that set standards that citizens are expected to follow

S

secondary data Data collected from others, not usually specific to the manufacturer's particular needs, but often used to make broad-based marketing decisions that rely on population statistics, demographics, and economic factors

self-sufficiency The ability to provide for all of one's basic needs without relying on anyone else

semi-manufactured items (products) Partially manufactured to the specifications of manufacturers, to be finished and used in the final manufacture or assembly of products

services Activities that individuals, groups, organizations, or companies perform to advise or assist other individuals, organizations, or companies

share A unit of ownership in a corporation; also called stock

shareholder A person who owns shares in a corporation; also called stockholder

shipping agent Person or company that advises on and arranges for transporting goods by any means

silent language Nonverbal communication such as body language, gestures, personal distances between people, and appearance

small- and medium-sized enterprises (SMEs) Companies, enterprises, or organizations that are small or medium in size, measured in terms of their human resources and revenue, as compared with others generally or others in their sector

social marketing Promotion of a company so that it is recognized as being socially responsible

social policy Policy regarding the well-being, access to needs and services, and improved quality of life of a population

soft currency Currency that fluctuates and is not considered stable; not easily converted into Canadian dollars

source A place or company from which a manufacturer or company may obtain a product, part, materials, or services; also to obtain or learn where to obtain something from outside sources

Special Economic Measures Act A law that authorizes the Canadian government to apply economic sanctions in response to a serious threat to international peace and security

speculator Person or firm that buys and sells currency on the currency exchange market to profit from changes in currency values

stakeholders The persons or groups affected by the performance of an organization, including employees, customers, suppliers, investors, and society in general

standard of living The way people live as measured by the kinds and quality of goods and services they can afford

startup A company or organization just created and beginning to operate

state-of-the-art Utilizing the most current technology, equipment, techniques, and machinery

stewardship Responsibility for managing policies, activities, and observance of certain codes

strategic alliance Two or more businesses cooperating to co-develop, co-produce, and/or co-market their products

subcontract To hire a person or company to do work as part of a larger contract or project; also, an agreement between the contractor and the subcontractor

suboptimization Using a lower-level decision as a step toward attaining a higher-level objective to which the lower-level decision is to contribute

subsidiary A company wholly owned by another

sunrise opportunities Business opportunities to others in the creation or early development of a company or organization

sunset opportunities Business opportunities to others in the decline or demise of a company or organization

supply and demand The relationship between the demand for something and the supply or availability of it that usually affects prices and production

supply chain The total sequence of business processes, within a single or multiple enterprise environment, that enable customer demand for a product or service to be satisfied

surplus A quantity in excess of what is needed

sustainable Able to be maintained without depletion or loss

system capability The capabilities of a machine or network

T

tariff Customs duty on merchandise imports, the purpose of which is to give a price advantage to similar locally produced goods or to raise revenues for the country

tariff barriers Restrictions or economic barriers created by countries on imports, where prices are forced higher on imports so as to protect domestic industries and businesses and their prices and profits

tax incentive Usually a tax credit, reduced tax, tax deferral, or tax waived in order to stimulate or encourage certain conditions or actions

tax structure The manner in which taxes are calculated; the setting or calculation of taxes for different types of persons, companies, or businesses and industry

technological convergence The linking up of companies in the telecommunications, consumer electronics, software, computer, and entertainment industries

telecommunications Communication over a distance (e.g., by telephone, Internet, radio, or television)

think tank An organization, institution or group that studies and researches specific topics and issues often of an economic and political nature

topography The natural and human features of the Earth's surface

totalitarian rule Government with centralized power that often uses the military to control the country

total quality management (TQM) A system for managing business with a commitment to continuously improving products, processes, and work habits

trade agreement Agreement governing aspects of trade among countries

trade association Association representing the interests of companies in a certain industry business, or type of product or service or business-related activity, usually with bylaws, standards, and a business code of ethics

trade barriers Barriers by a country to limit imports or to force customer prices of imported goods to be less competitive with local goods; includes tariffs, quotas, foreign exchange restrictions, and other regulatory matters

trade commissioner A Canadian government official located in another country to promote trade with and business investments in Canada

trade dispute A dispute, usually between countries, on aspects of trade, often regarding quotas, restrictions, or tariffs

trademark A registered special design, name, or symbol that identifies a good, brand, service, or company

trade mission Group of politicians, and/or an assortment of business people, or industry representatives, usually assisted by government and/or a trade or industry association, who visit a target region or country to learn, make contacts, and promote trade and investments

trade war Situation in which governments act aggressively in international markets and trade negotiations to promote their own countries' trading interests

trading bloc A group of countries that agree to open their markets to cross-border trade and business development

transfer risk The possibility that government policy may adversely affect currency exchange rates

trend A general direction of the marketplace that is occurring or is expected to occur in the immediate future

turnkey operation A standardized process, or a franchised business based on success and market position, in which all supplies, operation, training, layout, and use of recognized name and logo are standardized by the franchisor

turnover Rate of change or replacement, or of sale for a specified time period

U

United Nations Act Canadian Act that incorporates into Canadian law decisions passed by the UN Security Council

utility Value in terms of benefit (financial, quality of life) or usefulness; service providing electricity, water, water treatment, natural gas, or sewage disposal for a certain community, region, or country

V

value added Amount by which value of a good, process, or unfinished good or service is increased at each stage of its manufacturing or building, not including the initial cost

vision A statement of where an organization or business is headed in terms of goals, future activities, results, and attainments

voluntary codes of conduct Initiatives, guidelines, and agreements that are not regulatory

W

warehousing The storage and movement of goods both in a company's manufacturing location, and all along the stages of transit from source to company and from company to end consumer

work culture Atmosphere, behaviour, manner of communicating, and expectations in the work and among the employees in an organization

workplace Place where people work; often infers other considerations, such as working environment, atmosphere, and conditions

World Bank Group One of the world's largest sources of financial and consulting assistance for developing economies, owned by more than 184 member countries

World Economic Forum (WEF) An independent, not-for-profit organization committed to raising the level of corporate citizenship in member countries

World Trade Organization (WTO) The principal international organization that deals with the rules of trade between and among nations

INDEX

A

Abichandani, Daniel, 328
Aboriginal peoples, 8
Aboriginal peoples (Canada)
  self-sufficiency, 4, 12
  trade networks, 4
Absolute advantage, 85
Accommodation, in other
  countries, 237
Accounting, new processes in, 112
Advertising, in international
  marketing, 340, 361
Advertising agencies, 361
Advising banks, 219
Affirmative action, 316
Age, of consumers, 204, 347–48
Agrarian society, 128
Agreement on Internal Trade
  (AIT), 167
Airbus, 150
Air Canada, 196
Airports, 236
Air transportation, 56, 380, 383–84
Alcan Inc., 326
Algonquin people, 10
Amakudari, 152
Ambassador Bridge, 380, 381
American Fur Company, 13
American Revolution, 13
Americas, 8
Americas, exploration of, 7–8
Amish people, 4
Apartheid, 276
APEC. *See* Asia-Pacific Economic
  Cooperation
Apple (computer company), 93
Apples, 255
Arabia, early trade with, 6
Arable land, 248
Arcosanti, 5
Area Control List (ACL), 31
Argentina, Central Bank of, 127
Around-the-clock markets, 290–91
Arthur Andersen, 318, 319
Asia. *See also* China; Japan; Korea;
  Singapore; Thailand
  demographics, 204, 205
  global impact of, 199–200
Asia Minor, 6
Asia-Pacific Economic Cooperation
  (APEC), 34, 163, 165–66
Asia–Pacific Foundation, 165

Assembly line, 87–88
Assiniboine people, 12
Asuransi Jiwa ManuLife Indonesia,
  149
Asylum, 33
Atlantic Canada Opportunities
  Agency, 66
Attitudes, new, 113–14
Automated banking machines
  (ABMs), 126
Automated Teller Machines
  (ATMs), 110
Automobiles
  industry, 115–16
  manufacturing, 87–88
  marketing of, 348
Auto Pact, 115–16
Axel Springer Verlag AG, 327
Aznar, José Maria, 364

B

Baby boomers, 203
Banking
  deregulation of, 126
  international, 125–27
  technology in, 110
Banks
  advising, 219
  chartered, 125
  currency exchange rate and, 28–29
  foreign, in Canada, 126
  issuing, 219
  Schedule I, 125–26
  Schedule II, 126
Bayer AG, 314
Baylis, Trevor, 119
Beaver fur, 10, 14
Beck, Nuala, 92
Belgium, trade with Canada, 174–75
Benelux, 174
Bhopal (India), 312
Big box retailers, 113
Bilateral trade, 157
Biotechnology, 24, 92
Black Sea, 5
Blockbuster Video, 52
Borders, freer, 56–57
Boston Pizza, 145–46
Boycotts, 227
Brain drain, 132
Brand acquisition strategy, 341–42
Brand building, 337

Brand development strategy, 342
Brand equity, 337
Branding, 233, 357
Brands, global, 205
Braun's Bicycle and Fitness, 208
Brazil
  trade with, 276–77
  trade with Canada, 138–39
Breakbulk cargo, 382
Brennan-Peeters, Sarah, 91
Bribery, 281
Britain, early trade of, 6
British East India Company, 287
Broadcast facilities, 236
Broadcast standards, 225
Brooks Pharmacy, 196
Burrowes, Sean, 278
Business climate, 61
Business costs, 59–60
Business cycles, 288
Business(es)
  defined, 110
  domestic *vs.* international, 135–36
  purpose *vs.* goals, 86–87
  smaller. *See* Smaller businesses
  support services, in other
    countries, 237
Business ethics, 61, 304
Business etiquette, 237
Business Information Service for
  Newly Independent States
  (BISNIS), 268
Business opportunities, 186–88
  defined, 180
Business protocol, 261
Business-to-business (B2B)
  relationships, 229
Business Trust of South Africa, 327
Bus transportation, 56
Buying forward, 218

C

Cabot, John, 9
Cabot, Sebastian, 9
Cadbury Schweppes, 359
Calvia (Spain), municipality of, 327
Canada
  border with U.S., 63–64
  climate, 248
  credit rating, 217
  doing business in, 59–65
  domestic market, 90

FTAA and, 16
geography of, 246–47
global challenges, 90–98
location, 249
natural hazards, 249
trade with Asia, 15
trade with Belgium, 174–75
trade with Brazil, 138–39, 276–77
trade with Central/South America, 16
trade with Chile, 16
trade with China, 240–41
trade with Cuba, 36–37, 276
trade with Europe, 12
trade with European Union, 163
trade with Ireland, 210–11
trade with Japan, 15, 392–93
trade with Korea, 298–99
trade with Mexico, 15–16, 330
trade with Russia, 268–69
trade with Spain, 364–65
trade with United Kingdom, 16, 72–73
trade with U.S., 13–14, 16, 63–64
trade with Vietnam, 104–105
transportation, 248
under-population in, 204
Canada/Atlantic Provinces Cooperation Agreement on International Business Development, 66–67
Canadarm, 80
Canada–United States Free Trade Agreement (FTA), 160, 167
Canadian Business for Social Responsibility (CBSR), 325
Canadian Copyright Licensing Agency, 122
Canadian Institute of Traffic and Transportation (CITT), 388
Canadian International Development Agency (CIDA), 69, 125
Canadian Junior Achievement Conference (CANJAC), 328
Canadian mosaic, 249
Canadian official presence, in other countries, 237
Canadian Pacific Railway (CPR), 14
Canadian Tourism Commission, 144–46
Canadian Urban Institute, 134
Canoe travel, 248
Capital
defined, 78
intellectual, 92–93
Capital-intensive industries, 17
CARE Canada, 323
Careers, international, 194–95

Caribbean islands, 8
banks in, 126
Carthage, 5
Catalogues, 360
Cause marketing, 310
CCL Industries Inc., 62–63
C.D. Howe Institute, 172
Cellular communication, 117–19
Cellular phones, 117–19, 236
Central Asia, 5
Centralized marketing strategies, 336–37
Centrally planned economy, 285
Chaebol, 146
Champlain, Samuel de, 10
Change, 110
Channels of distribution, 340
Charles II, King, 10
Charlottetown Metal Products, 67
Chartered banks, 125
Chiang Kai-shek, 279
Chief executive officers (CEOs), 184
Children, employment of, 306, 324
Chile, trade with Canada, 16
China, 276
early trade, 5, 6
IKEA in, 202
Robertson Screws in, 147
selling consumer products in, 228–30
Taiwan and, 279
toothbrushes in, 192
trade with Canada, 240–41
Chopsticks, 203
Chrétien, Jean, 181
Christmas, 252
Chunnel, 378
Churchill (Man.), 383
Cinnaroll Bakeries, 356
Cirque du Soleil, 48, 49
Citizenship, Canadian, 33
Citrus fruit, 253
Cléroux, Dolorès, 264
Climate
culture and, 248
in logistics, 379
Clockwork radio, 119
Clothing size standards, 226
Clusters, 287
Coastal waters, 383
Coca-Cola, 122, 205
Coca-colonization, 277
Cod, 10
Code of ethics, 304, 309
Coffee trade, 26
Coltan, 119, 322
Columbus, Christopher, 8
Communes, 4–5

Communication. See also Telephones; Wireless technology
cellular, 117–19
convergence and, 197
international trade and, 129
nonverbal, 260
satellites, 118, 144
Communication systems, 236
Communication technology, 54
Communities, intentional, 5
Comparative advantage, 85
Competition, global, 24, 57, 195–96
Competitive advantage, 79–85
knowledge and, 93
quality and, 99
Competitiveness, 52
Confederation, 14
Confederation Bridge, 379
Congo, 119
Congo (Democratic Republic of), 322
Constantinople, 7
Consulates, 274
Consulting services, international, 125
Consumers, 128
activism, 323–24
age, 347–48
demographic profiles, 347
family lifestyle, 349
gender, 348
issues regarding, 313–14
Maslow's hierarchy of needs, 350
motivational profiles, 349–51
profiles, 347–54
purchasing profiles, 351
rational/emotional theory, 351
Thorndyke's pleasure/pain theory, 349
Containerization, 221–22, 377, 382, 384
Container ships, 236
Contracting, international, 187
Contract law, 283
Convention on International Trade in Endangered Species of Wild Fauna and Flora (CITES), 30
Copyright, 121
Cormorant Elementary School, 326
Corporate philanthropy, 324
Corporate social responsibility (CSR), 309–10
Corruption, 281, 319–20
Corruption Perceptions Index, 319
Cost benefits, 337
Costing, errors in, 216–24
Costs
hidden, 222, 379
in logistics, 379
transportation, 221–22

Cowichan sweaters, 256
Cows (company), 362
Creativity, 183
Credit control, 295
Credit rating, 217
Cree, 11, 12
Cuba, trade with Canada, 36–37, 276
Cultural determinants, 246
Cultural differences, 254
Cultural identity, and international
    trade, 26
Cultural imperialism, 250
Cultural IQ, 66
Cultural relativism, 306
Cultural sensitivity, 338
Culture
    arable land and, 248
    buying habits and, 234
    climate and, 248
    consumer purchasing and,
        252–55
    defined, 246
    geography and, 246–47
    global, 265–66
    history and, 250
    international business practices
        and, 258–64
    laws and, 259
    location and, 249
    natural hazards and, 249
    religion and, 250–51
    transportation and, 248
Currency. *See also* Euro; Hard
    currency; Soft currency
    common, 291–92
    exchange market, 218
    fluctuations, 28–29, 34, 218–19
    risk factors, 293–94
    strength of, 83
Currency devaluation, 293–94
Currency exchange rate, 28–29, 83,
    217–18, 293
Currency revaluation, 293
Custom House Currency Exchange,
    293
Customs
    buying habits and, 234
    defined, 246
Customs brokers, 387

D

Daewoo Motor Company, 317
Daimler Chrysler, 96
Dalhousie University Centre for
    International Business Studies,
    66–67
Data mining, 113
Decentralized marketing strategies,
    338–39

Defense Advanced Research
    Projects Agency (DARPA), 110
Deliverables, 187
Demand, law of, 284
Deming, W. Edwards, 99, 101
Democracy, 275
Demographic profiles, of consumers,
    203–204, 347
Demographics, defined, 347
Depression, 288
Dept. of Foreign Affairs and
    International Trade (DFAIT), 238
    Web site, 120
des Groseillers, Sieur, 10
Developed nations, 277
    defined, 97
Developing nations, 97–98, 277
    defined, 97
    dumping and, 320
    innovation and, 98
    international trade and, 131
    poverty in, 323
    technology and, 98
Development, sustainable, 324
Diamond trade, 174
Dias, Bartolomeu, 8
Dick, Dave, 388
Discretionary buying, 346
Disney, 122
Disneyland Paris, 49, 57
Disposable income, 346
Distribution
    channels of, 340
    new processes, 111
    physical, 371, 373
Distribution rights
    contracts for, 341–42
    exclusive, 342
    manufacturing and, 342
Diversification, 52
Dog sleds, 248
Dollarization, 291
Domestic transportation, 379–80
Downsizing, 96
Dress, style of
    cultural issues, 261
Dumping, 320
Durabelt, Inc., 67
Duties, 220
Duty-free zones, 167

E

EarthLink, 310
E-commerce, 359
Economic imperialism, 277
Economic systems, 284–86
    defined, 284
    global, 286–87
Economies of scale, 96, 337, 361

The Economist, 61, 64
Economist Intelligence Unit, 64–65
Ecotourism, 308
E.D. Smith & Sons Ltd., 220, 223
Education, in other countries, 237
Egypt, early trade, 6
Electrical standards, 225
Electric Arc Furnace, 122
Electronic data interchange
    (EDI), 374
Embassies, 274
Emerge2 Digital, 208
Employees
    culture of, 263–64
    expatriate, 194
    management, 263–64
    obligations toward, 317
Employment
    of children, 306, 324
    laws, 282
    lifetime, 194
    reductions in, 317
The End of Globalization (Rugman),
    152–53
End-product exports, 17
Engineers Without Borders (EWB),
    188
England, 8
England, treaty with Dutch, 12
English language, 203, 259
Enron, 318–19
Entertaining, business
    cultural issues, 263
Entertainment industry, 195
Entrepreneurs
    defined, 189
    global, 189–90
Entrepreneurship, 84
    models for, 190–91
Environmental issues, 27, 312–13
Environmental protection, 307
Environmental restrictions, 30, 35
Equality issues, 316
Equilibrium, 284
Estée Lauder Companies Inc.,
    50–51, 54
Ethical dilemmas, 305
Ethical imperialism, 306
Ethical standards, 227
Ethics
    business. *See* Business ethics
    code of. *See* Code of ethics
    defined, 304
    legality *vs.*, 305
    values and, 304–305
Ethicscentre.ca, 325
Ethnocentric MNCs, 151
Euro, 162, 217, 291
EuroDisney, 49
European Common Market, 174

European Economic Community (EEC), 174
European Union (EU), 60, 162–63, 174
Evans, Dierdre, 67
Exchange controls, 294
Exchange rate, 293
Expatriate employees, 194
ExpertSource, 172
Exploration, and trade, 7–8
Export and Import Permits Act, 30, 31
Export Control List (ECL), 31
Export Development Canada (EDC), 45
Exporting, 44, 145
  defined, 42
  starting a business in, 44–45
Export plans, 385–86
Exports, 23
  devaluation and, 294
  documentation, 389–90
  end-product, 17
  resource-based, 17
  semi-manufactured, 17
Extractive industries, 18
Extremist groups, 281
Exxon Valdez oil spill, 312, 383

F

Family lifestyle, of consumers, 349
Fanta, 339
Far East, trade with, 7, 8
Feather, Frank, 204
Feudal towns, 6
Financial risk, managing, 295
Financial services, in other countries, 237
Fish, 9
Fisher, Matthew, 297
Flagship brands, 338
Flexibility, in decentralized marketing, 338
Floating rate, 293
Food, in other countries, 237
Ford Motor Company, 96, 150, 313
Foreign direct investments (FDI), 48
Foreign exchange management, 295
Foreign Investment Review Act, 34
Foreign investments, 48–49
  defined, 296
  taxation and, 95
Foreign relations, and international trade, 30–31
Forrec Ltd., 57
Forum for International Trade Training (FITT), 172, 372
Fox, Vincente, 330
France, 8, 35
  fur trade and, 10

Franchises, 145–46, 345
Franchising, 356
Freedoms, withdrawal of, 281
Freeland, Edward J., 390
Free Market Model, of entrepreneurship, 191
Freer trade policies, 34
Free trade, 158, 167
  banking and, 126
Free Trade Agreement (FTA), 160
Free trade agreements, 28, 84
Free Trade Area of the Americas (FTAA), 16, 34, 159, 161–62
Freight-all-kinds (FAK) shipments, 384
Freight forwarders, 221, 387
Freight handling, intermodal, 377
Friedman, Thomas L., 185
Fur trade, 10–11, 13–14, 25

G

G8, 60, 84
G20, 168
Gaku batsu, 152
GAP, 324
G.A.P. Adventures, 308
Gateway cities, 384
Gatorade, 229
GATS (General Agreementon Trade in Services), 46, 159
Gaul, 6
Gender, of consumers, 348
Gender roles, 316, 348
General Agreement on Tariffs and Trade (GATT), 169
General instability risk, 280
Genetically modified foods, 314
Geocentric MNC, 151
Geography, 246–47
  culture and, 246–47
Georgia Coffee, 339
Germany, 6
Gestures (in culture), 260
Gift giving, 262
Gilchrist, Brady, 201
Glass border, 204
Glass ceiling effect, 316
Global brands, 205
Global companies, 148. *See also* International companies; Multinational companies
  governments *vs.*, 206–208
Global competition, 24, 57, 195–96
Global Competitiveness Report, 79
Global culture, 265–66
Global economy, 286–87
Global entrepreneurs, 189–90
Global Entrepreneurship Monitor (GEM), 290

Global equity market, 290–91
Globalization, 78, 287
  defined, 150
  importing and, 129
  labour costs and, 129–31
  of marketing, 129–31
  and the new office, 132–34
  values and, 307
  workplace and, 194–95
Global mindset, 190
Global positioning, 144–46
Global positioning system (GPS), 144
Global presence, 78–82
Global Trends 2015, 196
Global trends, identification of, 191
Global Vision, 278
Global warming, 313
Glocal companies, 338
Goods
  defined, 42
  exporting, 46
Governments
  involvement of, 84
  military role in, 281
  role in international trade, 274–79
  role of, 206
Government services, 236–37
Grant MacEwan College, 70
Greece, early trade, 5, 6
Greetings, forms of, 260–61
Gross domestic product (GDP), 80, 130, 163
Group of Eight, 172
Growth markets, 191
Gruetzner, John, 232
Guided Individualism Model, of entrepreneurship, 191
Guilds, 6
Guy, Ray, 47

H

Hackers, 206
Hakuto, Ken, 187–88
Handshakes, 260
Hard currency, 217–18
Harlequin Books, 185–86
Hazardous materials, storage of, 313
Health, in other countries, 237
Hewlett-Packard, 184
Hidden costs, 222, 379
High-tech industries, 287
Highway system, 380
History, and culture, 250
Hockey pucks, manufacture of, 101
Home office, 132–33
Home Shopping Network (HSN), 360
Honda of Canada, 153
Hong Kong, 240
Hong Kong Bank of Canada, 126
Horibe, Frances, 93

Howe, Clarence Decatur, 172
Hudson Bay Railway, 383
Hudson's Bay Company (HBC), 10–11, 13–14
Hula hoops, 187
Human rights issues, 316–17
Humber College, 70
Huron people, 4
Hutcheson Sand and Mixes, 86
Hydro One, 286

I

ICC. *See* International Chamber of Commerce
Ideas. *See* Creativity; Innovation
IKEA, 202
IMF. *See* International Monetary Fund
Immigrants, 33
Immigration, 266
   changing patterns, 132
   policies, 32–33, 34
Import Control List (ICL), 31
Importing, 42–43, 145
   defined, 42
   globalization and, 129
   starting a business in, 44–45
Incan empire, 8
Income, disposable, 346
India, early trade from, 5
Industrial Revolution, 128
Industrial sales representatives, 358
Industries
   biotechnology, 24
   capital intensive, 17
   extractive, 18
   high-tech, 287
   knowledge, 92
   labour intensive, 17
   primary, 18
   service, 20–21
   tourism, 32
Industry Canada
   Strategis, 120
Information, 119–21
   as commodity, 120–21
   decision making and, 119–20
   value of, 131–32
Information management, 371, 374
Information technology (IT), 92–93, 131
Infrastructure, 64, 83
   defined, 235
   research into, 237–38
Infrastructure Canada, 64
ING, 78
Inland waterways, 383

Innovation(s), 183. *See also* Technology
   defined, 110
   developing nations and, 98
   quality and, 94
   taxation and, 95
Innovativeness, in international business, 184–86
Inputs *vs.* outputs, 87
Institute for Global Ethics, 325
Insurance, 295
Intangibles, 20
Intellectual capital, 92–93
Intentional communities, 5
Intercultural communications, 69
Interdependence, 12
   political, 276–77
Intermediaries, in logistics, 386–88
Intermodal freight handling, 377
Intermodal operations, 373
International business consultancy, 232
International business(es)
   communication technology and, 54
   competitiveness, 52
   confidence in, 57
   defined, 42
   diversification, 52
   English as language of, 259
   expense control in, 51
   innovative, 184–86
   knowledge for, 69–70
   political risk and, 279
   reasons for, 50–53
   skills for, 69–70
   transportation and, 56
International Business Opportunities Centre, 186, 372
International careers, research regarding, 68
International Chamber of Commerce (ICC), 171, 326–27
International companies, 148. *See also* Global companies; Multinational companies
   organizational structure, 154–56
International date line, 55
International Electrotechnical Commission (IEC), 102
International Institute for Sustainable Development, 325
International Labour Organization (ILO), 326
International markets. *See also* Markets
   business opportunities in, 180–81
International Monetary Fund (IMF), 171

International Organization for Standardization (ISO), 102, 226
International Space Station, 144
International trade. *See also names of specific agreements*
   advantages, 22–24
   agreements, 157
   barriers to, 28–35
   communications and, 129
   cultural identity and, 26
   currency fluctuations and, 28–29, 34
   disadvantages, 26–27
   environment and, 27, 30, 34
   foreign relations and, 30–31
   government role, 274–79
   growth of, 129–31
   immigration policies and, 32–33, 34
   investment and, 24
   job creation and, 23–24
   needs and, 23
   non-democratic systems and, 26
   political issues and, 27
   political risk in, 274–75
   safety regulations and, 31
   social welfare and, 26
   trade sanctions and, 30–31
   transportation and, 129
   wars and, 27
International Youth Internship Program (IYIP), 68
Internet, 186
   cafés, 199
   global business and, 207–208
   marketing research and, 352
   per-capita usage, 198–99
   research, using, 237–38
Internet Protocol (IP), 110
Inventions, 110–11, 120–21
Inventory control, new processes in, 112
Investment
   international trade and, 24
   regulations, 29
Investment Canada Act (ICA), 29, 34
Ireland, trade with Canada, 210–11
Iroquois people, 10
Issuing banks, 219
Istanbul, 7
IT. *See* Information technology

J

Jaffa Citrus Fruit, 253
Jaffa Sweeties, 253
Jagros, Tina, 25
Japan
   climate, 247, 248
   economy of, 99, 101

geography of, 247
international trade, 15
location, 249
manufacturing, 15
natural hazards, 249
trade with Canada, 392–93
transportation, 248
Jean Coutu Group Inc., 196
Job creation, and international
trade, 23–24
Joint ventures, 123, 146, 229, 342
Jones Soda, 359
Journalists, 297
Junior Team Canada (JTC), 278
Just-in-time (JIT), 375–76
defined, 112
terrorism and, 282

K

Kaizen, 99
Kaminsky, Laraine, 164
Kanban, 112
Kei batsu, 152
Keiretsu, 146
Kenya, infrastructure, 238
Kentucky Fried Chicken, 345
Kerr, Richard, 187
Kibbutzim, 5
Knowledge economy, 90, 92, 93–94
Knowledge workers, 129
Korea. *See also* South Korea
trade with Canada, 298–99
Krispy Kreme Doughnuts Inc., 196
Kuat, 339
Kyoto Protocol, 313

L

Labelling, 357
Canadian requirements, 233–34
Labour
issues in, 317
skilled, 132
Labour costs, 59
globalization and, 129–31
taxation and, 95
Labour-intensive industries, 17
Landed cost, 216
Landline infrastructure, 118
Language
English, 203, 259
international business practices
and, 203, 259–60
silent, 260
Latham, Brian, 356
Lauder, Estée, 54
Laws
contract, 283
employment, 282
ethics and, 304–305

international business practices
and, 259
liability, 283
political risk and, 282–83
property, 283
taxation, 282
Legislated codes, 311
Legoland Deutschland, 57
Less developed nations
defined, 98
Letters of credit, 219
Leverage, 357
Liability laws, 283
Licensing, 122
Lift (drink), 339
Linkletter, Scott, 362
Lobbying, 324
Location, and culture, 249
Logistics
companies, 387–88
defined, 370
practitioners, 388
Los Horcones, 5
Loyalists, 13
Lubin, Kevin, 375

M

Maastricht Treaty, 174
M.A.C. Cosmetics, 50–51
Macao, 240
Mad cow disease virus, 276–77
Magic Carpet Delivery Service, 390
Magna International, 181–182,
371–72
MALKAM Cross-Cultural
Training, 164
Manoucher's Bread, 346
Manual labour, 128
Manufacturing, 19–20
distribution rights and, 342
new processes, 111
Manufacturing and mercantile
society, 128
Maquiladoras, 330
Marine transportation, 380, 382–83
Market differentiation, 265–66
Market-driven organizations
defined, 101
Market economies, 284
Marketing
defined, 334, 336
failures, 228
four Ps of, 354
globalization of, 129–31
new processes, 113
Marketing mix, 354–63
Marketing opportunity analysis, 355
Marketing plans, 362–63
Marketing research
companies, 230

country organizations and, 353
defined, 352
periodicals in, 353
primary data, 353
publications in, 353
secondary data, 352
Marketing strategies, 336–44
centralized, 336–37
decentralized, 338–39
Markets. *See also* International
markets
composition of, 230–31
growth, 191
proximity to, 338
size of, 230
Market segments, 355
Marmon Group, 147
Martin, Ricky, 150
Marx, Karl, 285
Maslow's hierarchy of needs, 350
Mayan empire, 8
McSweeney, Eric, 134
MD Robotics, 80
Media, 236
Medications, safety of, 314
Mediterranean Sea, 5
Meetings, scheduling of, 262
Megatrends Asia (Naisbitt), 199
Melin, Arthur, 187
Mennonite groups, 4
Mexico
trade with Canada, 15–16, 330
trade with U.S., 161
Micro-Business Network, 326
Middle Ages, 6
Military
role in government, 281
Mission statement, 184
Mitchell, Parker, 188
Mixed economies, 285–86
Mixed economy, 275
Molasses, 13
Monoculture, 202, 206
Monopolies, 206
Monsanto Canada Inc., 314
Montagnais people, 10
Most-Favoured-Nation (MFN)
tariff, 220
Motorola Inc., 118
Mountain Equipment Co-op
(MEC), 310–11, 316–17
Mounted Police Foundation, 122
Mozal Aluminum Smelter, 124
Multinational companies (MNCs),
150–52, 202, 277, 315, 321–22.
See also Global companies;
International companies
defined, 150
Municipal government consultants,
134

N

Naisbitt, John, 199
NASA space shuttle program, 80
National distribution, 379–80
National Research Council, 80
Natural gas, transportation of, 384
Natural hazards, 249
  culture and, 249
Natural resources, 83
  technology in extraction of, 17
Negotiation styles, 258–59
Neilson Cadbury, 359
Netherlands, 8
  traders from, 12
Netscape, 92–93
Newfoundland, 9–10
Newly industrialized economies
  (NIEs), 97–98
New Ventures, 48
New York City, 12
New Zealand, 384
Nike, 324
Non-democratic systems
  international trade and, 26
Non-governmental organizations
  (NGOs), 324
Nonverbal communication, 260
Nortel Networks, 230
North Africa, early trade, 6
North America, location of, 249
North American Free Trade
  Agreement (NAFTA), 15,
  160–61, 163, 167, 220, 330
North American Fur Association
  (NAFA), 25
Northern Transportation Company,
  383
North West Company, 13–14
Not-for-profit organizations
  (NPOs), 324
Nunavut, 383

O

OECD. See Organization for
  Economic Co-operation and
  Development (OECD)
Offices. See also Workplaces
  in foreign countries, 133–34
  globalization and, 132–34
  home, 132–33
  hotel, 133
  travelling, 133
Oil, transportation of, 384
Ontario Hydro, 286
Open accounts, 295
Operations risk, 280
Opportunity cost, 84

Organizational structure, of inter-
  national companies, 154–56
Organization for Economic
  Cooperation and Development
  (OECD), 60, 65, 158, 170
Organization of Petroleum Exporting
  Countries (OPEC), 115
Outputs vs. inputs, 87
Outsourcing, 51
Ownership risk, 280

P

Pacific Rim, 15, 165
Packaging, 233, 357, 377
Pangaia, 5
Patent Cooperation Treaty, 121
Patents, 120–21
Peace Bridge Brokerage Limited
  (PBB), 390
Periodicals, in marketing research,
  353
Pettigrew, Pierre, 59, 364
Pharmaceutical companies, 96–97
Philip Morris, 150
Philippine Islands, 7–8
Phoenicians, 5
Physical distribution, 371, 373
  defined, 373
Pipeline transportation, 56, 379,
  380, 384
Place
  in marketing mix, 358–60
  in marketing plan, 363
Pohang Steel, 183
Political instability, 84, 280
Political interdependence, 276–77
Political issues, and international
  trade, 27
Political risk, 274–75
  defined, 274
  ethnic pressure, 281
  evaluating, 281
  extremist groups, 281
  laws and, 282–83
  military and, 281
  operations, 280
  ownership, 280
  political instability, 280
  religious pressure, 281
  terrorism, 280
  transfer, 280
  types of, 280–81
  withdrawal of freedoms and, 281
Political systems, types of, 275–76
Polycentric MNCs, 151
Poon Tip, Bruce, 308
Population growth, 204
Portfolio investments, 48

Ports, 236, 378, 382
Post-it notes, 93
Poverty, in developing countries, 323
Power centres, 113
Premiums, 362
Prestige oil spill, 382–383
Price(s), 360–61
  in marketing mix, 360–61
  in marketing plan, 363
Primary industries, 17, 18
Primary resources, 17
Private-sector investments, 48
Privatization, 97, 286
Processes, new, 111–13
Product
  in marketing mix, 355–57
  in marketing plan, 362
Product differentiation, 355
Production, and terrorism, 282
Production input costs, 60
Production standards, 225–26
Productivity, 86–89
  of countries, 87–89
  defined, 86
  technology and, 87–88
Product launch, 354
Product life cycle, 191–92
Product quality. See also Quality
  mass production and, 135–36
Promotion, 361–62
  in international marketing, 340
  in marketing mix, 361–62
  in marketing plan, 363
Property law, 283
Prosperity, 288
Protectionism, 13
Protocol, defined, 261
Proximity to markets, 338
Public-sector investments, 48
Pull strategies, 340–41
Punctuality, 262, 263
Purchasing power, 346–47
Purchasing profiles, 351
Push strategies, 339–40

Q

Quality
  competitive advantage and, 99
  innovation and, 94
  mass production and, 135–36
Quality control, 99, 101
Quality Management System
  (QMS), 102
Quality of life, 65
  small business and, 136
Quanxi, 230

R

Rail transportation, 14, 56, 236, 379, 380, 382
Rationalization, 95–97
RCMP (Royal Canadian Mounted Police), 122
Recession, 288
Recovery, of economy, 288
Redemption rate, 362
Refugees, 33
Religion, and culture, 250–51
Repatriation of earnings, 280
Request for proposal (RFP), 187
Research and development (R&D), 80, 83, 97
Resource-based exports, 17
Retail marketing, 358–59
Richard Ivey School of Business, 70
Road system, 236
Robertson, Peter Lymburner, 147
Robertson Screws, 147
Robotic technology, 88
Rocky Mountain Bicycles, 100
Roman empire, 6
Roter, George, 188
Rugman, Alan, 152–53
Rule of law, 304
Rum, 13
Russell car, 116
Russia, 276
    corruption in, 319
    trade with Canada, 268–69

S

Sa-Cinn Native Enterprises Limited, 256
Safety, in other countries, 237
Safety regulations, for products, 31
Sales agents, 340
Satellites, 118, 144
Schermerhorn, John R., 183
Scotiabank, 127
Second Cup, 254
Sei-kan-zai ittaikiko, 152
Self-sufficiency, 4–5, 6, 12, 248
    defined, 4
Semi-manufactured exports, 17
September 2001 terrorism attacks, 282
Service industries, 20–21, 136, 194
Services
    defined, 42
    exporting, 46, 48
    trade in, 17
Settlement, 12
Shareholders. See Stockholders
Shipping, 56
Shipping companies, 221

Ships, 382
Shoppers Drug Mart, 196
Silent language, 260
Silk, 14
Silver, 8
Singapore, Taco Bell in, 345
Skilled labour, 132
Slessor, Lindsay, 67
Small and medium-sized enterprises (SMEs), 207
Smaller businesses
    global opportunities, 207–208
    quality of life and, 136
SMART formula, 386
Smoking policies, 306
SNC-Lavalin Group Inc., 123–24
Social Democratic Model, of entrepreneurship, 191
Social marketing, 310
Social welfare, and international trade, 26
Societal characteristics, 84
Soft currency, 217–18
Sony, 15
Sourcing, 371–72
South Africa, 276
South Korea, 183
Spaak, Paul-Henri, 174
Spain
    early trade, 6
    trade with Americas, 7–8
    trade with Canada, 364–65
Spanish empire, 7–8
Special Economic Measures Act (SEMA), 30, 31
Speculators, 294
Spice trade, 7
Spin Master Toys, 91
St. Lawrence Seaway, 378
Standard of living, 90
Standards, 224–28
    broadcast, 225
    clothing size, 226
    electrical, 225
    ethical, 227
    production, 225–26
Standards Council of Canada, 102
Standard Time, 55
Stock exchanges, 290–91
Stockholders, 318–19
Stock markets, and terrorism, 282
Storage, 372–73
Strategic alliance, 146
Stronach, Belinda, 182
Stronach, Frank, 181–182
Students Against Sweatshops, 323
Suboptimization, defined, 374–75
Subsidiaries, 146
Suez Canal, 378
Sugar trade, 8, 13

Summit of the Americas, 15–16
Sunrise/sunset opportunities, 191
Suppliers, 371
Supply, law of, 284
Supply chain, 374–75
Sustainable development, 324
Sweatshirts, 254
Sweatshops, 323–24
Swedish Centre for Business and Policy Studies, 287
Synergy, 337

T

"Taco", 187–88
Taiwan, 279
TakingITGlobal (TIG), 325
Tangible items, 20
Tariffs, 28, 220
    defined, 28
Taxation
    corporate, 95
    foreign investment and, 95
    innovation and, 95
    labour costs and, 95
    laws, 282
Tax environment, 84
Tea, 230, 231
Team Canada Inc, 45–46, 172, 268, 392. See also Junior Team Canada (JTC)
Technological convergence, 197–99
Technology. See also Innovation
    communication. See Communication technology
    consulting services, 125
    developing nations and, 98
    development of, 24
    information (IT), 92–93
    monoculture and, 206
    in natural resources extraction, 17
    new, 110–11
    productivity and, 87–88
    wireless, 117–18
Teenagers, 206
Telecommunication, 117
Telemarketing, 360
Telephones
    cellular, 117–19
    innovations to, 110
Television
    advertising and, 205
    shopping, 360
Terrorism, 280, 282
    business travel and, 282
    IRA, 282
    just-in-time inventory and, 282
    Palestinian, 282
    production and, 282
    stock markets and, 282

Thailand, 204
Think Canada 2001 Festival, 392
Think tanks, 289
Thorndyke's pleasure/pain theory, 349
3M Corporation, 93
Tibbett & Britten Group, 387–88
Tickle Me Elmo toys, 375
Tigris-Euphrates region, 5
Tilley Endurables, 203
Time zones, 54, 55
Tires, recall of, 313
Tools for Development program, 323
Toothbrushes, 192
Topography, in logistics, 377–78
Totalitarian nations, 275
Total Quality Management (TQM), 101
Totsuko Company, 15
Tourism industry, 32, 34
Towns, feudal, 6
Toy market, 252
Tractor-trailer transportation, 56
Trade
    bilateral, 157
    early, 5–6
    exploration and, 7–8
    international. *See* International trade
    multilateral, 157
    regulations, 6
    in services, 17
Trade Commissioners, 34, 47
Trade consulates, 274
Trade missions, 45–46
Trade sanctions, 30–31
Trade shows, 46, 340
Trade war, 276
Trading blocs, 157
Trains, 236
Transfer risk, 280
Transistor radios, 15
Translators, 264
Transmission Control Protocol (TCP), 110
Transportation
    air. *See* Air transportation
    bus, 56
    choice of, 377
    costs, 221–22
    culture and, 248
    developments in, 56
    to the Far East, 7
    international trade and, 129
    marine, 380, 382–83
    modes of, 381–84
    pipeline, 56, 379, 384
    rail. *See* Rail transportation
    systems, 235–36

tractor-trailer, 56
truck, 56, 379–381, 392
Trans Union, 149
Travel
    cultural understanding and, 266
    terrorism and, 282
Treaty of Rome, 174
Treaty on European Union, 174
Trends
    defined, 191
    global, 191
    stages of, 191–92
Triad, 152–53
Truck transportation, 56, 236, 379, 380, 381, 392
Trudeau, Pierre, 180
Tundra Semiconductor Corporation, 118
Turkish empire, 7
Turkmenistan, 246
Tylenol, 314

U

Under-population, in Canada, 204
Union Carbide, 312
United Kingdom, trade with Canada, 16
United Nations Act, 30
United Nations Charter, 30
United Nations Security Council (UNSC), 30, 31
United States
    companies in Canada, 196
    expansion into, 196
    exploration of, 12
    FTAA and, 16
    protectionism of, 13
    trade with Canada, 13–14, 16, 63–64, 72–73
    trade with Mexico, 161
    trade with West Indies, 12–13
    transportation to, 380
Universal product code (UPC), 375
University of Victoria, Faculty of Business, 70
Utility, economic, 82

V

Values, societal, 304–305, 307
Van Haren, Rene, 343
Vending machines, 359
Vietnam
    skilled worker shortage in, 327
    trade with Canada, 104–105
Visitors, to Canada, 32
Volkswagen "Bug", 192
Voluntary codes of conduct, 310–11

W

Wacky Wallwalker, 188
Wages, and purchasing power, 346
Wal-Mart, 196, 324, 375
Warehousing, 371, 372–73
    defined, 372
War of 1812, 13
Wars, and international trade, 27
Warson, Albert, 57
Water
    export of, 313
    from icebergs, 182
Wealth, of nations, 346
Wee, Heesum, 314
West India Company, 12
West Indies, 8
    trade with United States, 12–13
Weston, Galen, 183
Wheat farming, 18
Wildlife Conservation Society, 119
Wilfrid Laurier University School of Business and Economics, 320
Wines, 203
Wireless technology, 117–18, 198
Wolfensohn, James D., 171
Women, travel in employment, 204
Work, changing nature of, 128–29
Workers. *See* Employees
Worker safety, 307
Work ethic, and culture, 263–64
Work experience
    exchanges, 67
    international, 66–67
Workforce, characteristics of, 83
Workplace health/safety, 315
Workplaces. *See also* Offices
    global, 194–95
World Air Cargo Organization (WACO), 390
World Bank Group, 125, 170–71
World Business Council for Sustainable Development, 325
World Economic Forum (WEF), 79, 170
World Economic Freedom Index, 289
World Intellectual Property Organization (WIPO), 283
World Summit Business Awards for Sustainable Development Partnerships, 326
World Trade Center, 282
    attacks on, 63
World Trade Organization (WTO), 29, 34, 169, 220
    banking and, 126
    China in, 240

X

Xerox, 93

CREDITS

Photo Credits

Unit Opening Photos: Unit 1: firstlight.ca; Unit 2: HPM/firstlight.ca; Unit 4: Adastra/Getty Images; Unit 5: CP PHOTO/Ryan Remiorz; Unit 7: Gandee Vasan/Getty Images; Unit 8: Mark Scott/Getty Images; Unit 9: © SERRA ANTOINE/CORBIS SYGMA/MAGMA; Unit 10 ©Alison Wright/CORBIS/MAGMA; Unit 11: © Liu Liqun/CORBIS/MAGMA; Unit 12: Shepard Sherbell/CORBIS SABA/MAGMA.

Chapter 1: p 4 (fig 1.1) www.canadianheritage.org ID #10046, National Archives of Canada PA-29120; p 5 (fig 1.2) City of Vancouver Archives; p 6 (fig 1.4) Greg Locke/Stray Light Pictures; p 7 (fig 1.5) © Wolfgang Kaehler/CORBIS; p 10 (fig 1.7) HBC Archives Documentary Art, P-210, (fig 1.8) HBC Archives Photographs 1987/363-T-32/27 (N3912); p 11 (fig 1.9) reprinted by permission of Hudson's Bay Company. Hudson's Bay Company is a registered trade-mark of and is used with the permission of the Hudson's Bay Company; p 12 (fig 1.11) ©#421585 Index Stock Imagery, Inc.; p 14 (fig 1.13) Source: Canadian Pacific Archives N.A. 13561-2; p 15 (fig 1.14) courtesy of SONY products; p 17 (fig 1.15) left R. Maisonneuve/firstlight.ca , right ©Willliam Taufic/CORBIS/MAGMA; p 19 top courtesy of Clover Leaf Foods; 2nd from top courtesy of Roots, Canada; 3rd from top courtesy of Kraus Carpets; 3rd from bottom ©Michael Prince/CORBIS; 2nd from bottom ©2001 by Irwin Publishing Ltd.; bottom courtesy of Alcan Products, Canada; p 20 top 3 Photodisc/Getty Images; 2nd from bottom courtesy of Petro Canada; bottom courtesy of Bauer Products; p 25 reprinted by permission of Tina Jagros; p 26 (fig 1.21) reprinted by permission of Transfair Canada; p 32 (fig 1.23) courtesy of Communications Branch, Citizenship and Immigration Canada; p 34 (fig 1.24) © Reuters NewMedia Inc./ CORBIS; p 36 (fig 1.25) courtesy of Tim Johnston; p 37 (fig 1.26) Robert Van Der Hilst/Getty Images.

Chapter 2: p 44 (fig 2.2) masterfile; p 45 (fig 2.3) CP PHOTO/Fred Chartrand; p 48 (fig 2.4) ©Pierre-Paul Poulin/Magma; p 50 (fig 2.5) AP Photo/PA, Ian West; p 52 (fig 2.6) © James Leynse/Corbis Saba; p 54 (fig 2.7) AP Photo/Susan Ragan; p 56 (fig 2.9) top ©Reuters NewMedia Inc./CORBIS clockwise ©Bettmann/CORBIS; © The Mariners' Museum/CORBIS/MAGMA ©Bettmann/ CORBIS; p 63 (fig 2.14) reprinted by permission of CCL Industries; p 69 (fig 2.16) photo courtesy of Vineet Saxena.

Chapter 3: p 80 (fig 3.3) courtesy of Macdonald Dettwiler Space and Advanced Robotics Ltd.; p 83 (fig 3.4) Pierre-Paul Poulin/Magma Photos; p 83 (fig 3.5) Mike Ridewood/Magma; p 85 (fig 3.6) Oliver Mackay/firstlight.ca; p 86 (fig 3.7) courtesy of Hutcheson Sand and Mixes; p 91 reprinted by permission of Sarah Brennan-Peeters; p 92 (fig 3.11) © John A Rizza/firstlight.ca; p 93 (fig 3.12) © Javier Larrea/firstlight.ca; p 95 (fig 3.13) © Paul A.

Souders/Magma/Corbis; p 99 (fig 3.14) © Catherine Karnow/CORBIS/MAGMA; p 100 (fig 3.15) reprinted by permission of Blake Jorgenson; p 102 (fig 3.16) courtesy of Martin Tooke; p 104 (fig 3.17) © Bleibtreu Jason/CORBIS/MAGMA; p 105 (fig 3.18) © Lorne Reswick/firstlight.ca.

Chapter 4: p 111 (fig 4.1) top Eyewire/Getty Images; middle Fox Photos/Hulton Archivep; bottom © David Arky/CORBIS; p 112 (fig 4.2) CP PHOTO 1997, Kevin Frayer; p 114 (fig 4.4) Ron Sangha/Maxx Images; p 116 (fig 4.5) © Reuters NewMedia Inc./CORBIS; p 117 (fig 4.6) Ghislain and Marie David de Lossy/Getty Images; p 119 (fig 4.8) bottom © James Leynse/CORBIS SABA; p 122 (fig 4.10) Ron Sangha/Maxx Images; p 124 (fig 4.11) reprinted by permission of SNC-Lavalin, photo: Charles Corbett; p 126 (fig 4.12) J.A. Kraulis/Masterfile; www.masterfile.com; p 127 (fig 4.13) AP Photo/Eduardo Di Baia; p 128 (fig 4.14) © Hulton-Deutsch Collection/CORBIS, (fig 4.15) Jeff Greenberg/firstlight.ca, (fig 4.16) Lester Lefkowitz/Getty Images; p 130 (fig 4.17) ©256934 Index Stock Imagery Inc.; p 132 (fig 4.18) Mark Richards/PhotoEdit, Inc.; p 133 (fig 4.19) AJA Productions/Getty Images; (fig 4.20) Rob Melnuchuck/Getty Images; p 135 (fig 4.21) © Mug Shots/CORBIS/ MAGMA; p 139 (fig 4.22) AP Photo/Amy Sancetta.

Chapter 5: p 144 (fig 5.1) © Crackshots/CORBIS; p 145 (fig 5.2) reprinted by permission of the Canadian Tourism Commission; p 146 (fig 5.3) BPI International Rights Holding, Inc.; p 147 (fig 5.4) reprinted by permission of Robertson Inc.; p 148 (fig 5.5) © Jose Luis Pelaez, Inc./CORBIS; p 153 (fig 5.6) CP PHOTO/Globe and Mail-Fred Lum; p 161 (fig 5.10) © Reuters NewMedia Inc./CORBIS; p 164 reprinted by permission of Laraine Kaminsky; p 174 (fig 5.15) © Bettmann/CORBIS; (fig 5.16) © Royalty-Free/CORBIS; (fig 5.17) © VAN PARYS/CORBIS SYGMA; p 175 © Gail Mooney/CORBIS/Magma.

Chapter 6: p 178 Greg Locke/Stray Light Pictures; p 180 (fig 6.1) © Reuters NewMedia Inc./CORBIS; p 181 (fig 6.2) © AFP/CORBIS; p 182 (fig 6.3) CP PHOTO/Kevin Frayer; p 183 (fig 6.4) reprinted by permission of Pohang Iron & Steel Co., Ltd.; p 185 (fig 6.6) CP PHOTO/ Globe and Mail-Patti Gower; p 187 (fig 6.8) © Ariel Skelley/CORBIS; p 186 (fig 6.7) courtesy of IBOC Industries; p 188 (fig 6.9) reprinted by permission of the *National Post*; p 192 (fig 6.10) top VW Canada Inc.; bottom © Alan Schein Photography/CORBIS; p 196 (fig 6.12) CP PHOTO/Toronto Star/Tony Bock; p 198 (fig 6.15) courtesy of Rapid Transit Project 2000 Ltd.; p 202 (fig 6.18) © Macduff Everton/CORBIS; p 205 (fig 6.19) © Robert Holmes/CORBIS; p 208 (fig 6.21) reprinted by permission of Fred Lum, *Globe and Mail*; p 210 (fig 6.22) © Reuters NewMedia Inc./CORBIS; p 211 (fig 6.23) top courtesy of Kaari Turk, bottom © Milepost 92_/ CORBIS.

Chapter 7: p 216 (fig 7.1) Ed Honowitz/Getty Images; p 217 (fig 7.2) Franz-Marc Frei/CORBIS/Magma; p 218 (fig 7.3) Janet Wishnetsky/CORBIS/Magma; p 220 (fig 7.4) Photodisc/Getty Images; p 222 (fig 7.7) Andrew Vaughan/Canadian Press; p 223 (fig 7.8) © Lois Ellen Frank/CORBIS/MAGMA; p 226 (fig 7.11) AFP/CORBIS/MAGMA; p 227 (fig 7.12) Jacques M. Chenet/CORBIS/MAGMA; p 229 (fig 7.13 © Reuters NewMedia Inc./CORBIS; p 231 (fig 7.14) CORBIS/MAGMA; (fig. 7.15) Reuters NewMedia Inc./CORBIS/MAGMA; p 238 (fig 7.17) Richard T. Nowitz/CORBIS/MAGMA; p 240 (fig 7.18) AFP Photo/Rabih Moghrabi © AFP/CORBIS; p 24 (fig 7.19) 1 Hulton Archive/Getty Images.

Chapter 8: p 248 (fig 8.1) Michael Melford/Getty Images; p 249 (fig 8.2) AP Photo/Kyodo; p 250 (fig 8.3) Hugh Sitton/Getty Images; p 251 (fig 8.4) Will & Deni McIntyre/Getty Images; p 252 (fig 8.5) ©Lynn/CORBIS/MAGMA; p 253 (fig 8.6) Dick Hemingway Photographs; p 254 (fig 8.7) Photodisc/Getty Images; p 255 (fig 8.8) Jason Homa/Getty Images; p 255 (fig 8.9) Leigh Beisch/Getty Images; p 260 (fig 8.11) AP Photo/Jose Goitia; p 261 (fig 8.12) Photodisc/Getty Images; (fig 8.13) Jon Gray/Getty Images; (fig 8.13) Photodisc/Getty Images; p 263 (fig 8.14) Wayne Eastep/Getty Images; p 264 Photo by David Bell; p 265 (fig 8.15) Dick Hemingway Photographs; p 268 (fig 8.16) AP Photo/Maxim Marmur; p 269 (fig 8.17) Harald Sund/Getty Images.

Chapter 9: p 275 (fig 9.1) CP PHOTO/Ryan Remiorz; p 277 (fig 9.3) AP Photo/Dado Galdieri; p 283 (fig 9.5) AP Photo/Apichart Weerawong; p 285 (fig 9.7) ©Bettmann/CORBIS; p 286 (fig 9.8) Rathavary Duong/Reuters; p 287 (fig 9.9) Crowther and Carter/Getty Images; p 290 (fig 9.12) Michael Simson/Getty Images; p 291 (fig 9.13) AP Photo/Frank Rumpenhorst; p 297 (fig 9.14) AP Photo/str; p 298 (fig 9.15) AP PHOTO/Yonhap/POOL.

Chapter 10: p 306 (fig 10.2) © Ted Spiegel/CORBIS; p 307 (fig 10.4) left AP Photo/Dario Lopez-Mills, right James L. Amos/CORBIS/MAGMA; p 308 Chris Bolin/*National Post*; p 312 (fig 10.6) AP Photo/John Gaps III, File; p 313 (fig 10.7) CP PHOTO/Andrew Vaughan; p 314 (fig 10.8) AP Photo/John Swart; p 315 (fig 10.9) © Michael S. Yamashita/CORBIS/MAGMA; p 316 (fig 10.10) reprinted by permission of Mountain Equipment Co-op; p 317 (fig 10.11) AP Photo/Ahn Young-joon; p 318 (fig 10.12) AP Photo/Pat Sullivan; p 322 (fig 10.15) Kennan Ward/Corbis/Magma; p 324 (fig 10.16) James Leynse/CORBIS SABA; p 325 (fig 10.17) reprinted by permission of TakingITGlobal/Michael Furyk; p 326 (fig 10.18) reprinted by permission of Alcan Aluminum Corporation; p 327 (fig 10.19) reprinted by permission of Municipality of Calvia; p 330 (fig 10.20) AP Photo/Marco